Teach Yourself®
America Online®

Teach Yourself®
America Online®

Charles Bowen with Jennifer Watson

IDG Books Worldwide, Inc.

An International Data Group Company

Foster City, CA • Chicago, IL • Indianapolis, IN • New York, NY

Teach Yourself® America Online®

Published by
IDG Books Worldwide, Inc.
An International Data Group Company
919 E. Hillsdale Blvd., Suite 400
Foster City, CA 94404
`www.idgbooks.com` (IDG Books Worldwide Web site)

Library of Congress Catalog Card Number: 98-88387

ISBN: 0-7645-7500-7

Printed in the United States of America

10 9 8 7 6 5 4 3

1P/RV/QW/ZZ/IN

Distributed in the United States by IDG Books Worldwide, Inc.

Distributed by CDG Books Canada Inc. for Canada; by Transworld Publishers Limited in the United Kingdom; by IDG Norge Books for Norway; by IDG Sweden Books for Sweden; by IDG Books Australia Publishing Corporation Pty. Ltd. for Australia and New Zealand; by TransQuest Publishers Pte Ltd. for Singapore, Malaysia, Thailand, Indonesia, and Hong Kong; by Gotop Information Inc. for Taiwan; by ICG Muse, Inc. for Japan; by Norma Comunicaciones S.A. for Colombia; by Intersoft for South Africa; by Eyrolles for France; by International Thomson Publishing for Germany, Austria and Switzerland; by Distribuidora Cuspide for Argentina; by Livraria Cultura for Brazil; by Ediciones ZETA S.C.R. Ltda. for Peru; by WS Computer Publishing Corporation, Inc., for the Philippines; by Contemporanea de Ediciones for Venezuela; by Express Computer Distributors for the Caribbean and West Indies; by Micronesia Media Distributor, Inc. for Micronesia; by Grupo Editorial Norma S.A. for Guatemala; by Chips Computadoras S.A. de C.V. for Mexico; by Editorial Norma de Panama S.A. for Panama; by American Bookshops for Finland. Authorized Sales Agent: Anthony Rudkin Associates for the Middle East and North Africa.

For general information on IDG Books Worldwide's books in the U.S., please call our Consumer Customer Service department at 800-762-2974. For reseller information, including discounts and premium sales, please call our Reseller Customer Service department at 800-434-3422.

For information on where to purchase IDG Books Worldwide's books outside the U.S., please contact our International Sales department at 317-596-5530 or fax 317-596-5692.

For consumer information on foreign language translations, please contact our Customer Service department at 1-800-434-3422, fax 317-596-5692, or e-mail rights@idgbooks.com.

For information on licensing foreign or domestic rights, please phone +1-650-655-3109.

For sales inquiries and special prices for bulk quantities, please contact our Sales department at 650-655-3200 or write to the address above.

For information on using IDG Books Worldwide's books in the classroom or for ordering examination copies, please contact our Educational Sales department at 800-434-2086 or fax 317-596-5499.

For press review copies, author interviews, or other publicity information, please contact our Public Relations department at 650-655-3000 or fax 650-655-3299.

For authorization to photocopy items for corporate, personal, or educational use, please contact Copyright Clearance Center, 222 Rosewood Drive, Danvers, MA 01923, or fax 978-750-4470.

ABOUT IDG BOOKS WORLDWIDE

Welcome to the world of IDG Books Worldwide.

IDG Books Worldwide, Inc., is a subsidiary of International Data Group, the world's largest publisher of computer-related information and the leading global provider of information services on information technology. IDG was founded more than 30 years ago by Patrick J. McGovern and now employs more than 9,000 people worldwide. IDG publishes more than 290 computer publications in over 75 countries. More than 90 million people read one or more IDG publications each month.

Launched in 1990, IDG Books Worldwide is today the #1 publisher of best-selling computer books in the United States. We are proud to have received eight awards from the Computer Press Association in recognition of editorial excellence and three from Computer Currents' First Annual Readers' Choice Awards. Our best-selling *...For Dummies®* series has more than 50 million copies in print with translations in 31 languages. IDG Books Worldwide, through a joint venture with IDG's Hi-Tech Beijing, became the first U.S. publisher to publish a computer book in the People's Republic of China. In record time, IDG Books Worldwide has become the first choice for millions of readers around the world who want to learn how to better manage their businesses.

Our mission is simple: Every one of our books is designed to bring extra value and skill-building instructions to the reader. Our books are written by experts who understand and care about our readers. The knowledge base of our editorial staff comes from years of experience in publishing, education, and journalism — experience we use to produce books to carry us into the new millennium. In short, we care about books, so we attract the best people. We devote special attention to details such as audience, interior design, use of icons, and illustrations. And because we use an efficient process of authoring, editing, and desktop publishing our books electronically, we can spend more time ensuring superior content and less time on the technicalities of making books.

You can count on our commitment to deliver high-quality books at competitive prices on topics you want to read about. At IDG Books Worldwide, we continue in the IDG tradition of delivering quality for more than 30 years. You'll find no better book on a subject than one from IDG Books Worldwide.

John Kilcullen
Chairman and CEO
IDG Books Worldwide, Inc.

Steven Berkowitz
President and Publisher
IDG Books Worldwide, Inc.

*Eighth Annual
Computer Press
Awards ≥1992*

*Ninth Annual
Computer Press
Awards ≥1993*

*Tenth Annual
Computer Press
Awards ≥ 1994*

*Eleventh Annual
Computer Press
Awards ≥1995*

IDG is the world's leading IT media, research and exposition company. Founded in 1964, IDG had 1997 revenues of $2.05 billion and has more than 9,000 employees worldwide. IDG offers the widest range of media options that reach IT buyers in 75 countries representing 95% of worldwide IT spending. IDG's diverse product and services portfolio spans six key areas including print publishing, online publishing, expositions and conferences, market research, education and training, and global marketing services. More than 90 million people read one or more of IDG's 290 magazines and newspapers, including IDG's leading global brands — Computerworld, PC World, Network World, Macworld and the Channel World family of publications. IDG Books Worldwide is one of the fastest-growing computer book publishers in the world, with more than 700 titles in 36 languages. The "...For Dummies®" series alone has more than 50 million copies in print. IDG offers online users the largest network of technology-specific Web sites around the world through IDG.net (http://www.idg.net), which comprises more than 225 targeted Web sites in 55 countries worldwide. International Data Corporation (IDC) is the world's largest provider of information technology data, analysis and consulting, with research centers in over 41 countries and more than 400 research analysts worldwide. IDG World Expo is a leading producer of more than 168 globally branded conferences and expositions in 35 countries including E3 (Electronic Entertainment Expo), Macworld Expo, ComNet, Windows World Expo, ICE (Internet Commerce Expo), Agenda, DEMO, and Spotlight. IDG's training subsidiary, ExecuTrain, is the world's largest computer training company, with more than 230 locations worldwide and 785 training courses. IDG Marketing Services helps industry-leading IT companies build international brand recognition by developing global integrated marketing programs via IDG's print, online and exposition products worldwide. Further information about the company can be found at www.idg.com.
1/24/99

Credits

Acquisitions Editor
Andy Cummings

Development Editor
Chip Wescott

Technical Editor
Susan Glinert

Copy Editor
Timothy J. Borek

Production Coordinator
Valery Bourke

Cover Coordinator
Cyndra Robbins

Book Designers
Daniel Ziegler Design,
Câtâlin Dulfu, Kurt Krames

Layout and Graphics
Lou Boudreau, Linda M. Boyer,
Angela F. Hunckler, Jane E. Martin,
Brent Savage, Kate Snell

Proofreaders
Kelli Botta, Vickie Broyles,
Michelle Croninger, Rachel Garvey,
Nancy Price, Rebecca Senninger,
Robert Springer, Janet M. Withers

Indexer
Joan Griffitts

About the Authors

Charles Bowen has been writing about online services since 1982. This is his 15th book about life in cyberspace. He also has been a contributing editor and columnist for assorted magazines, including *Home PC, Editor & Publisher,* and *America West.* In addition, he is the host of a daily syndicated radio show called *The Internet News,* carried in the U.S. and, via Voice of America, on more than 600 stations worldwide. He is 49 years old and lives in Huntington, West Virginia, with his wife, Pamela.

Jennifer Watson is one of AOL's foremost teachers. As founder of the VirtualLeader Academy — an online training center for AOL's volunteers, partners, and employees — she teaches AOL leaders how to make the AOL community come alive. Her compilation of tips and tricks, prepared and shared with AOL's membership, became the best-selling *AOL Companion* (now in its 2nd Edition). Jennifer is also the AOL keywords collector and author of *AOL Keywords, 3rd Edition.*

To Peggy Caldwell, one of America Online's newest and most enthusiastic electronic citizens. This one's for you, Mom!

Welcome to Teach Yourself

Welcome to Teach Yourself, a series read and trusted by millions for nearly a decade. Although you may have seen the Teach Yourself name on other books, ours is the original. In addition, no Teach Yourself series has ever delivered more on the promise of its name than this series. That's because IDG Books Worldwide recently transformed Teach Yourself into a new cutting-edge format that gives you all the information you need to learn quickly and easily.

Readers told us that they want to learn by doing and that they want to learn as much as they can in as short a time as possible. We listened to you and believe that our new task-by-task format and suite of learning tools deliver the book you need to successfully teach yourself any technology topic. Features such as our Personal Workbook, which helps you practice and reinforce the skills you've just learned, help ensure that you get full value out of the time you invest in your learning. Handy cross-references to related topics and online sites broaden your knowledge and give you control over the kind of information you want, when you want it.

More Answers . . .

In designing the latest incarnation of this series, we started with the premise that people like you, who are beginning to intermediate computer users, want to take control of their own learning. To do this, you need the proper tools to find answers to questions so you can solve problems now.

In designing a series of books that provide such tools, we created a unique and concise visual format. The added bonus: Teach Yourself books actually pack more information into their pages than other books written on the same subjects. Skill for skill, you typically get much more information in a Teach Yourself book. In fact, Teach Yourself books, on average, cover twice the skills covered by other computer books — as many as 125 skills per book — so they're more likely to address your specific needs.

...In Less Time

We know you don't want to spend twice the time to get all this great information, so we provide lots of time-saving features:

▶ A modular task-by-task organization of information: any task you want to perform is easy to find and includes simple-to-follow steps

▶ A larger size than standard makes the book easy to read and convenient to use at a computer workstation. The large format also enables us to include many more illustrations — 500 screen shots show you how to get everything done!

▶ A Personal Workbook at the end of each chapter reinforces learning with extra practice, real-world applications for your learning, and questions and answers to test your knowledge

▶ Cross-references appearing at the bottom of each task page refer you to related information, providing a path through the book for learning particular aspects of the software thoroughly

▶ A Find It Online feature offers valuable ideas on where to go on the Internet to get more information or to download useful files

▶ Take Note sidebars provide added-value information from our expert authors for more in-depth learning

▶ An attractive, consistent organization of information helps you quickly find and learn the skills you need

These Teach Yourself features are designed to help you learn the essential skills about a technology in the least amount of time, with the most benefit. We've placed these features consistently throughout the book, so you quickly learn where to go to find just the information you need — whether you work through the book from cover to cover or use it later to solve a new problem.

You will find a Teach Yourself book on almost any technology subject — from the Internet to Windows to Microsoft Office. Take control of your learning today, with IDG Books Worldwide's Teach Yourself series.

Teach Yourself
More Answers in Less Time

Go to this area if you want special tips, cautions, and notes that provide added insight into the current task.

Search through the task headings to find the topic you want right away. To learn a new skill, search the Contents, Chapter Opener, or the extensive index to find what you need. Then find — at a glance — the clear Task Heading that matches it.

Using Keywords

Options in the previous section enable you to quickly retrace your steps online. What if you want to move ahead to a new window you haven't yet visited or just go back to one you have visited quicker? A navigational tool even bigger and better is ahead, completely independent of such buttons and History Trails.

Keywords are the transportation tool of choice for all savvy AOL members. Many pages throughout the massive America Online network have their own keywords — often more than one keyword, actually — operating like street addresses in a city. Only keywords are faster and easier. By knowing a page's keyword, you can jump right to it, bypassing scores of introductory pages and saving lots of time.

How to Use the Keyword Button

Keywords are such an important part of America Online that the new AOL version 4.0 software puts a Keyword option right on the toolbar at the top of screen. To use it, click the Keyword button on the toolbar to open a keyword window. In the "Enter word(s)" field, type the name of the AOL area you want to visit, such as AOL TODAY (for the AOL Today channel) or NEWS (for the News channel). Click the Go button to get under way.

To give this new concept a try, use the Keyword option to reach the next few stops on the Channels tour. For instance, the next stop is the Sports channel

and its keyword is SPORTS. So, click the Keyword button, type SPORTS in the resulting window, and click Go (or just press Enter).

TAKE NOTE

HOW THIS BOOK LISTS KEYWORDS
Throughout this book, keywords are listed in parentheses as in (KEYWORDS). While the book uses all capital letters to set keywords apart from the rest of the text, you don't have to enter them in all caps. America Online's keywords are not case sensitive. Nor are they space sensitive, which means KEY WORDS would work fine too.

MULTIPLE DESTINATIONS
In a few cases, the same keyword applies to more than one area of the system. If this happens, you are presented with a window displaying possible destinations. Click the icon or link to go to the site you want to visit.

CONTINUING THE TOUR WITH THE SPORTS CHANNEL
This is the AOL Sports desk, for news, scores, statistics, discussion groups, and upcoming events. Standing departments are devoted to all major competitions, including basketball, baseball, football, golf, auto racing, tennis, with separate sections for professional and college sports and breaking news from the sports world. Also, don't miss the Grandstand, where fans talk, write, and at times, yell about the latest happenings on and off the field, court, rink, ring, and track.

Learn the concepts behind the task at hand and, more important, learn why the task is important in the real world. Time-saving suggestions and advice show you how to make the most of each skill.

After you learn the task at hand, you may have more questions, or you may want to read about other tasks related to that topic. Use the Cross References to find different to make your learning more efficient.

CROSS-REFERENCE
For more information about AOL's Sports channel, see Chapter 8.

FIND IT ONLINE
You can get more background on the use of keywords from the system itself. From the menu bar, click Help ⇨ Help with Keywords.

56

Use the Find It Online element to locate Internet resources that provide more background, take you on interesting side trips, and offer additional tools for mastering and using the skills you need. (Occasionally you'll find a handy shortcut here).

The current chapter name and number are always in the top right hand corner of every task page spread, so you always know exactly where you are in the book.

Who This Book Is For

This book is written for you, a beginning to intermediate PC user who isn't afraid to take charge of his or her own learning experience. You don't want a lot of technical jargon; you *do* want to learn as much about PC technology as you can in a limited amount of time. You need a book that is straightforward, easy to follow, and logically organized, so you can find answers to your questions easily. And, you appreciate simple-to-use tools such as handy cross-references and visual step-by-step procedures that help you make the most of your learning. We have created the unique Teach Yourself format specifically to meet your needs.

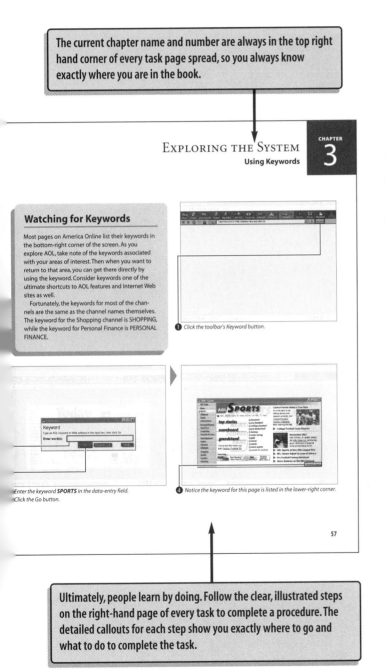

EXPLORING THE SYSTEM
Using Keywords

CHAPTER 3

Watching for Keywords

Most pages on America Online list their keywords in the bottom-right corner of the screen. As you explore AOL, take note of the keywords associated with your areas of interest. Then when you want to return to that area, you can get there directly by using the keyword. Consider keywords one of the ultimate shortcuts to AOL features and Internet Web sites as well.

Fortunately, the keywords for most of the channels are the same as the channel names themselves. The keyword for the Shopping channel is SHOPPING, while the keyword for Personal Finance is PERSONAL FINANCE.

➊ Click the toolbar's Keyword button.

Enter the keyword *SPORTS* in the data-entry field.
Click the Go button.

➍ Notice the keyword for this page is listed in the lower-right corner.

57

Ultimately, people learn by doing. Follow the clear, illustrated steps on the right-hand page of every task to complete a procedure. The detailed callouts for each step show you exactly where to go and what to do to complete the task.

Personal Workbook

It's a well-known fact that much of what we learn is lost soon after we learn it if we don't reinforce our newly acquired skills with practice and repetition. That's why each Teach Yourself chapter ends with your own Personal Workbook. Here's where you can get extra practice, test your knowledge, and discover ideas for using what you've learned in the real world. There's even a visual quiz to help you remember your way around the topic's software environment.

Feedback

Please let us know what you think about this book, and whether you have any suggestions for improvements. You can send questions and comments to the Teach Yourself team on the IDG Books Worldwide Web site at **www.idgbooks.com**.

Personal Workbook

Q&A

1 What are at least two ways to enter a keyword?

_____

_____

_____

2 What does the History Trail feature do?

_____

_____

_____

3 Which channel would you visit if you were interested learning how to cook dishes from other countries?

_____

_____

_____

4 How do you save a page as a Favorite Place?

_____

_____

_____

5 What do you do to return to one of your Favorite Places?

_____

_____

6 What is the fastest way to go back to the page you were viewing just before the current one?

_____

_____

_____

7 What are at least two ways to get to the AOL's Find Central to search for keywords?

_____

_____

_____

8 Bonus Question: What is the keyword for the AOL's list of keywords?

_____

_____

ANSWERS: PAGE 336

70

After working through the tasks in each chapter, you can test your progress and reinforce your learning by answering the questions in the Q&A. Then check your answers in the Q&A appendix at the back of the book.

Another practical way to reinforce your skills is to do additional exercises on the same skills you just learned without the benefit of the chapter's visual steps. If you struggle with any of these exercises, it's a good idea to refer to the chapter's tasks to be sure you've mastered them.

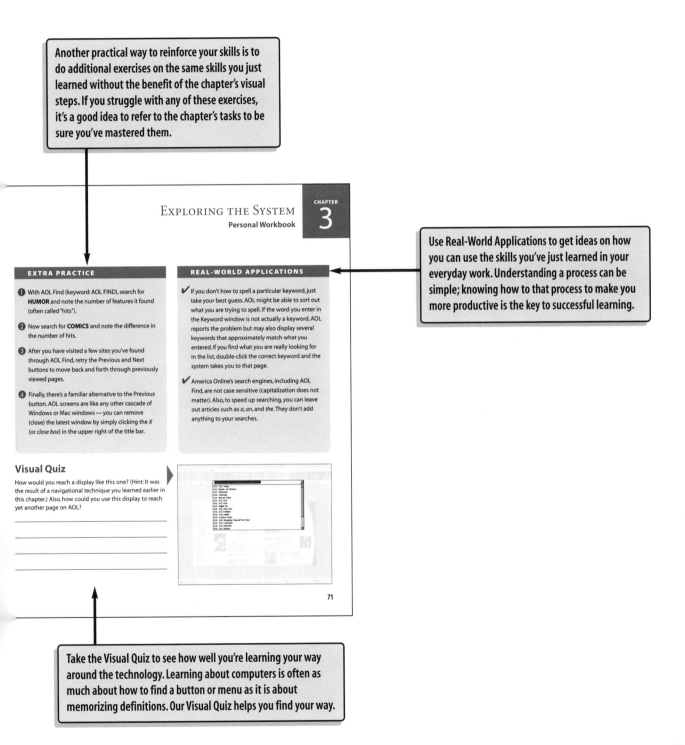

Exploring the System
Personal Workbook

CHAPTER 3

Use Real-World Applications to get ideas on how you can use the skills you've just learned in your everyday work. Understanding a process can be simple; knowing how to that process to make you more productive is the key to successful learning.

EXTRA PRACTICE

1. With AOL Find (keyword: AOL FIND), search for **HUMOR** and note the number of features it found (often called "hits").

2. Now search for **COMICS** and note the difference in the number of hits.

3. After you have visited a few sites you've found through AOL Find, retry the Previous and Next buttons to move back and forth through previously viewed pages.

4. Finally, there's a familiar alternative to the Previous button. AOL screens are like any other cascade of Windows or Mac windows — you can remove (close) the latest window by simply clicking the *X* (or *close box*) in the upper right of the title bar.

REAL-WORLD APPLICATIONS

✔ If you don't how to spell a particular keyword, just take your best guess. AOL might be able to sort out what you are trying to spell. If the word you enter in the Keyword window is not actually a keyword, AOL reports the problem but may also display several keywords that approximately match what you entered. If you find what you are really looking for in the list, double-click the correct keyword and the system takes you to that page.

✔ America Online's search engines, including AOL Find, are not case sensitive (capitalization does not matter). Also, to speed up searching, you can leave out articles such as *a, an,* and *the.* They don't add anything to your searches.

Visual Quiz

How would you reach a display like this one? (Hint: It was the result of a navigational technique you learned earlier in this chapter.) Also, how could you use this display to reach yet another page on AOL?

_____

_____

_____

_____

Take the Visual Quiz to see how well you're learning your way around the technology. Learning about computers is often as much about how to find a button or menu as it is about memorizing definitions. Our Visual Quiz helps you find your way.

Contents

CONTENTS

CONTENTS

CONTENTS

PART

I

Learning the Software and Navigating AOL

The three chapters in this part get you rapidly up and running with America Online version 4.0, covering the most fundamental (and therefore most important) features. These include your online identity, your e-mail address, and your electronic "map," by which you will learn your way around AOL.

In these chapters you learn important concepts related to navigating the basic system. The foundation of the system is creating your own online identity from the public "name" you give yourself to the online profiles that let new online acquaintances know more about you. The next step is using your online identity to correspond with both AOL members and people outside of the AOL community. The final phase of the basic tour is perusing the myriad resources that America Online offers, including the help areas.

CHAPTER **1**

MASTER
THESE
SKILLS

▶ Installing the AOL Software

▶ Printing the Quick Reference Guide

▶ Detailing Your Phone Setup

▶ Finding Access Numbers

▶ Deciding on Your Billing Plan

▶ Picking Screen Name and Password

▶ Signing On

▶ Customizing the Preferences Area

Installing and Learning the Software

Setting up your computer for America Online is simple. You need only insert the installation disc, run the program, supply answers to a few onscreen questions, and then let the system walk you through setting up your account and billing information.

But easy doesn't necessarily mean fast. Reserve an hour for the entire installation (though depending on your computer and modem speeds, it could take less time than that). Before you insert the CD-ROM and start the installation, do the following:

▶ Have your credit card or checkbook handy. AOL will want to set up a billing method.

▶ Locate the registration number and temporary password on your distribution disc. They are probably printed inside the disc's cardboard jacket. If you received your software in another manner (such as from America Online's World Wide Web site), you may not need a registration number and temporary password.

▶ Start thinking about your screen name. This is the name by which everyone you meet and write to on AOL and the Internet will know you. It is the address to which your mail will be sent, and it is the name that will automatically appear on your messages in forums and in chat rooms. It can be up to ten characters long. Come up with several alternatives, in case somebody else is already using your first choice. Like license plates, all screen names are unique.

▶ Decide on a password of up to eight letters and/or numbers to replace the temporary password that came with the disc. While your screen name is your public persona, your password always remains private. Don't give it out to anyone; legitimate AOL staff will never ask you for it.

Installing the AOL Software

Your AOL experience begins by inserting the America Online version 4.0 CD-ROM into your CD-ROM drive. If you are using Windows 95 or 98, click the Start button on the taskbar and select Run from the menu. If you're using Windows 3.1, click the File menu of the Program Manager and select Run. For either, type **D:\Setup** (*D* being the letter corresponding to your CD-ROM drive) and then click OK. (Those of you on Macs can just double-click the Install AOL icon.)

A "Welcome to America Online" window appears and asks you to indicate whether you are joining AOL as a new member, upgrading to a new version of AOL, adding your existing AOL account to this computer, or adding an additional copy of AOL to your computer. Make your selection, click Next, and watch the system check to see if previous versions of AOL exist on your disk. A "Select AOL Directory" window appears next, suggesting the software be installed in `C:\America Online 4.0`. You can opt to have it put on a different directory with the Change Directory button, but it is not recommended.

The next display — entitled "Select AOL Startup Options" — notes that to make starting AOL easier, you can choose to have the AOL software automatically open each time you start your computer. Also, if you have Microsoft Office installed on your system, you can add an AOL shortcut icon to your Office toolbar. Checkboxes are provided for your selections.

If you do not want either of these options, make sure both checkboxes remain unchecked.

Now the software is ready to install. It checks your system to see how much space is free on your hard disk and reports how much space is needed to install AOL. If the amount of free space is less than the amount required, you need to click the Cancel button at this time and free up the necessary space on your hard disk before restarting the installation process.

TAKE NOTE

▶ IF YOU ALREADY HAVE AOL INSTALLED

You may already have America Online software on your computer. Many computers come directly from the manufacturer with AOL software pre-installed. Or you already may be a subscriber with a working version of the program in use. Does this mean you can simply skip this installation section? Maybe, but before you jump ahead:

▶ Make sure the version of the software you are using is the most recent. This book helps you teach yourself about AOL version 4.0.

▶ If in doubt about your software version, stay with me in this section, because installing the software for new subscribers and upgrading it for existing users employ the same painless process.

CROSS-REFERENCE

If you need to contact America Online about specific installation problems, see Appendix B about offline help.

FIND IT ONLINE

The AOL software's Offline Help section (under the Help option on the menu bar) has a section on problems with signing on to AOL.

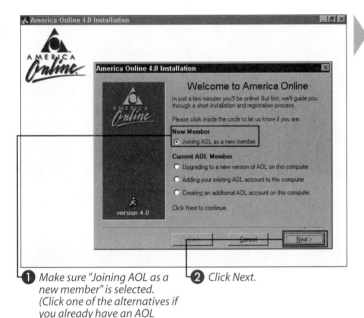

❶ Make sure "Joining AOL as a new member" is selected. (Click one of the alternatives if you already have an AOL account.)

❷ Click Next.

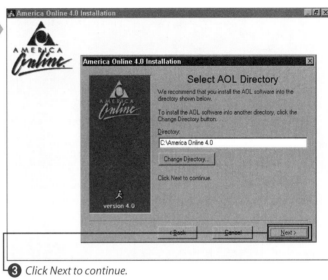

❸ Click Next to continue.

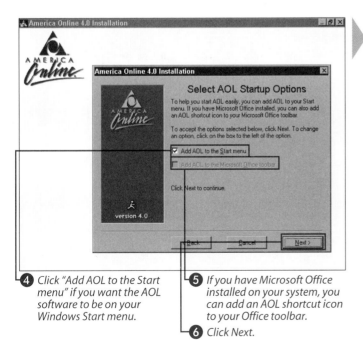

❹ Click "Add AOL to the Start menu" if you want the AOL software to be on your Windows Start menu.

❺ If you have Microsoft Office installed on your system, you can add an AOL shortcut icon to your Office toolbar.

❻ Click Next.

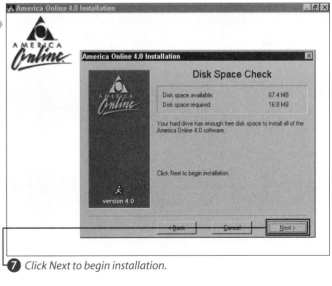

❼ Click Next to begin installation.

7

Printing the Quick Reference Guide

Now the software is ready to begin placing copies of its data onto your hard disk. The actual installation should take only a few minutes as the installer automatically copies the necessary files from the distribution disc to your system's hard disk in preparation for opening your account online.

When the file copying is finished, the software pauses to let you read or print the AOL Quick Reference Guide, which provides help with the rest of the setup and registration process, as well as hints for using the system. This useful five-page resource provides information on

▶ connecting to the service, finding access numbers, registering for the first time, choosing a screen name and password, and troubleshooting. Additional information on this is provided later in this chapter.
▶ basics, including background on keywords, the fundamentals of the software's menu bar and toolbar, searching features, and other ways to get around. Such navigation topics are covered in Chapter 3 and are then used throughout the rest of the book.
▶ communicating with others online through chat, Instant Messages, e-mail, and more. We take up electronic mail in Chapter 2 and "real-time" communication, such as chatting, in Chapter 4.

▶ particulars about important Member Services areas that provide online help, background on billing, e-mail usage tips, the Member Directory, more keywords, and the like. These features are also covered in the appendixes at the back of the book.

While the system provides an option to read the guide online, it's smarter to get a printout so you can have it handy for reference during the registration process.

TAKE NOTE

ABOUT DISK SPACE

As it prepares to copy files to your computer, the AOL software automatically checks your system to see how much space is free on your hard disk and reports how much space is needed to install AOL. If the amount of free space is less than the amount required for AOL's software, you need to click the Cancel button and free up the necessary space on your hard disk before starting the installation process again. Check the reference section of the printed material that came with your CD-ROM for the latest disk space requirements.

CROSS-REFERENCE

For more tips and shortcuts about navigating the system, see the Appendixes.

FIND IT ONLINE

The AOL software's Offline Help section (under Help on the menu bar) has a Troubleshooting section covering common installation problems.

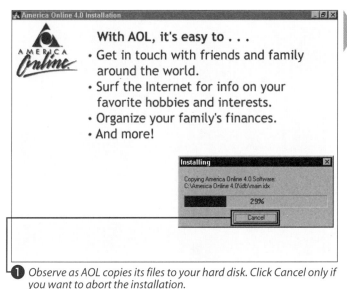

❶ *Observe as AOL copies its files to your hard disk. Click Cancel only if you want to abort the installation.*

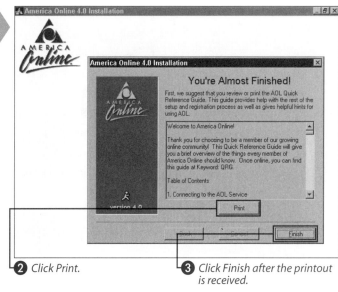

❷ *Click Print.*

❸ *Click Finish after the printout is received.*

❹ *Click Yes.*

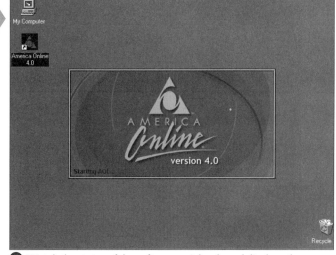

❺ *Watch the status of the software as it loads and displays the America Online logo.*

Detailing Your Phone Setup

Next, the program is ready to set up your modem and phone connections. While the software has an option for a customized setup, it's easier — and also much safer for all but advanced users — to accept the automatic setup.

The automatic setup enables AOL to search your computer for information about your modem and communications connections. AOL then automatically adjusts itself accordingly. With that, you need only look over the default setup to make sure it has correctly read your configuration.

AOL also needs to collect the following information about your phone and calling arrangements:

- ▶ The country from which you are connecting. (The default is the U.S.)
- ▶ Your area code.
- ▶ Whether you are using a Touch-Tone phone. If you are not, you need to uncheck the box in the screen displayed in the lower right.
- ▶ Whether you need a dialing prefix to reach an outside line and if so, the prefix. If you do need a dialing prefix, check the box in the lower-right screen and specify the code (such as **9,**) in the box. Keep the comma after the number — this indicates that the modem should pause briefly after dialing the prefix (a requirement for some phone systems).

▶ Whether you have a call-waiting feature on your phone and what code (such as *70) is used to turn off the service. If you have call waiting, decide if you want to turn it off while you are online (highly recommended). Click the checkbox at the bottom of the screen shown in the lower right to disable call waiting.

TAKE NOTE

▶ CORRECTING MODEM ERRORS

As you look over the modem configurations (see the figure in the upper right), if you find an error — such as in modem speed — click the Change Modem button and follow the directions.

▶ UNSELECTING OPTIONS

Here — and with *any* window with options in the AOL software — if you incorrectly clicked a mark on a checkbox, you can unselect it by simply clicking it again.

▶ EXTERNAL MODEMS NEED TO BE ON

If you have an external modem (one that is not built into your computer), take a moment now to make sure it is turned on and connected to your phone line and computer. At the end of these steps, your computer needs to automatically go online, so make sure the modem is not currently being used by another application, such as receiving or sending a fax, if it has that capability.

CROSS-REFERENCE

For more information about getting personal help with setup, see Appendix A.

FIND IT ONLINE

If you need to manually configure your modem, see the software's Offline Help section (under the Help option of the menu bar). Click the Index tab and enter **setup, configuring** in the query box, and click Display.

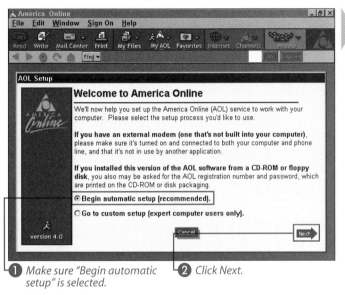

1 Make sure "Begin automatic setup" is selected.

2 Click Next.

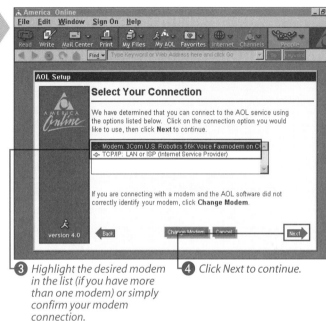

3 Highlight the desired modem in the list (if you have more than one modem) or simply confirm your modem connection.

4 Click Next to continue.

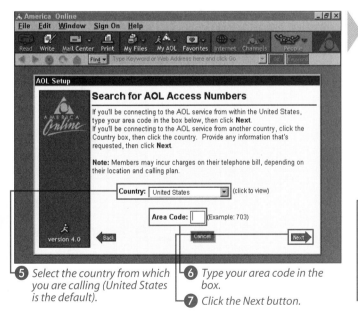

5 Select the country from which you are calling (United States is the default).

6 Type your area code in the box.

7 Click the Next button.

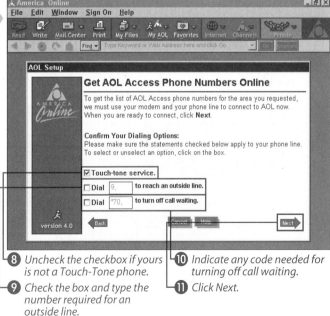

8 Uncheck the checkbox if yours is not a Touch-Tone phone.

9 Check the box and type the number required for an outside line.

10 Indicate any code needed for turning off call waiting.

11 Click Next.

Finding Access Numbers

Now the America Online software automatically dials its host computer to find local numbers for you to call to make your connections. Your job is to look for the closest (and therefore the cheapest) connection in your area. It shouldn't be too difficult as AOL maintains literally hundreds of local connection numbers around the country.

Because you have supplied the three-digit area code for your region, America Online immediately focuses on its numbers for your region and nearby communities. The goal here is to select at least *two* numbers that can be used to connect your computer to AOL's network. This way, the system will have at least one alternative number on file that it can dial if your primary number is ever busy or out of service.

The first number you select from the scrollable list should be the "best fit." Ideally, it is a local number for your city with the fastest speed your modem can accommodate. You can choose numbers that exceed your modem's speed, too!

Your city may be listed several times, each with a different number and/or modem speed. (For example, Charleston has several entries on the screen in the lower-left window.) You actually can (and should) select more than two numbers if there are multiple possibilities for your area. To get more details on a number, highlight it and click the More Info button — the maximum speed, network,

number, area code, city, state, and country are displayed. Each time you choose a number, the AOL software confirms your choice, adds it to your collection, and cycles back to the list to see if there are any more numbers you want to add. When you have added enough numbers, click Sign On to continue.

TAKE NOTE

▶ CAN'T FIND A LOCAL NUMBER?

If you can't find a local connection number in your region, you have the option to specify a different area code, which might help if you are near the border of your state. Also, note that AOL regularly adds new connection numbers.

▶ SURCHARGED NUMBER AVAILABLE

For those without local connections to AOL (or for those traveling with a laptop), AOL has dependable, high-speed connections with surcharged 800 and 888 access numbers. While these are convenient and reliable, remember they are NOT toll free. You can connect to AOL from anywhere in the U.S., Puerto Rico, and the U.S. Virgin Islands by using either 1-888-245-0113 or 1-800-716-0023.

▶ OOPS! INTERRUPTING THE SIGN ON

If you click the Sign On arrow (in the window in the lower left) before you mean to, you can abort the sign-on by quickly clicking the Cancel button on the connection screen, as seen in the lower-right window.

CROSS-REFERENCE
For more information about finding latest reports on new access numbers, see Appendix A.

FIND IT ONLINE
To find more about access phones and related topics, click Help on the menu bar, select Offline Help, click the Find tab, and enter **access** in the query box.

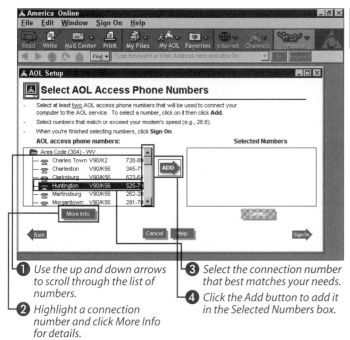

❶ Use the up and down arrows to scroll through the list of numbers.

❷ Highlight a connection number and click More Info for details.

❸ Select the connection number that best matches your needs.

❹ Click the Add button to add it in the Selected Numbers box.

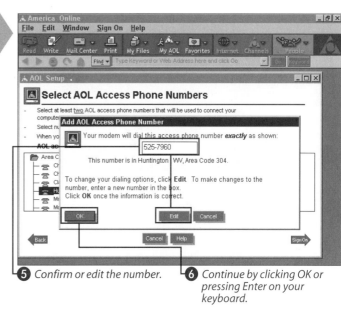

❺ Confirm or edit the number.

❻ Continue by clicking OK or pressing Enter on your keyboard.

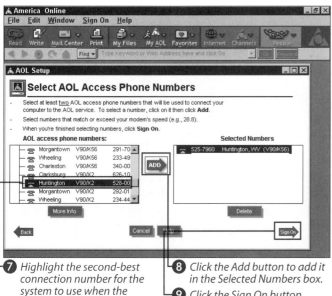

❼ Highlight the second-best connection number for the system to use when the primary number isn't available.

❽ Click the Add button to add it in the Selected Numbers box.

❾ Click the Sign On button.

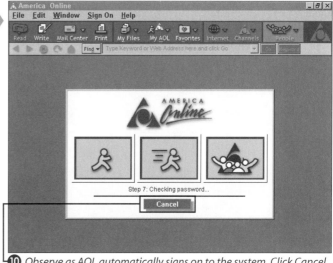

❿ Observe as AOL automatically signs on to the system. Click Cancel only if you wish to abort the sign-on.

Deciding on Your Billing Plan

After you have specified the numbers and the modem speeds you want to use for your connections when calling AOL, the software is set to do some bookkeeping. Here is where you use the information you prepared in advance, such as the credit card information, registration number, and temporary password.

Notice that the registration form displayed onscreen (upper-left figure) can be used both by new users and by existing members who want to upgrade their software. Options at the top of the window are as follows:

- ▶ You want to create a new or additional AOL account.
- ▶ You already have an AOL account you'd like to use.
- ▶ You are an AOL Instant Messenger user and you want to create an AOL account (more about Instant Messenger later in chapter 4).

If you are a new member, verify that the first option is checked, enter the registration number and temporary password (if requested), and click Next. In the resulting window, enter your personal information. If you are going to use a credit card, be sure that your address and phone match your credit card billing address and phone. Windows explaining how an AOL membership works appear next — read them

and click Next to continue. Now enter your billing information and then verify your billing address.

If you're an existing member, check the appropriate button and enter your screen name and password; the system then skips the remaining steps in this section, because you already have billing information, a screen name, and a password on file.

TAKE NOTE

▶ **BILLING CONSIDERATIONS**

Most AOL users choose to pay by major credit card, but there also is an Other Billing Options button. This includes direct withdrawal from your checking account. If you click this and select "Checking," the system then will ask for your bank name and city, the nine-digit transit number and your account number. AOL currently charges $5.00 a month for this electronic funds transfer.

▶ **VERIFICATION MAY TAKE TIME**

After you have made your billing selections, America Online verifies the data you have provided. If it encounters a problem, it informs you that registration is suspended until you can update the billing information. Also, if you decide to have your charges automatically deducted from a checking account, AOL may need a day or two to verify the account information. If so, an onscreen announcement is shown.

CROSS-REFERENCE

For more information about checking your billing and account information, see Appendix A.

FIND IT ONLINE

To get additional information about billing, see the software's Help section. Enter **billing** in either the Index or Find section's query box.

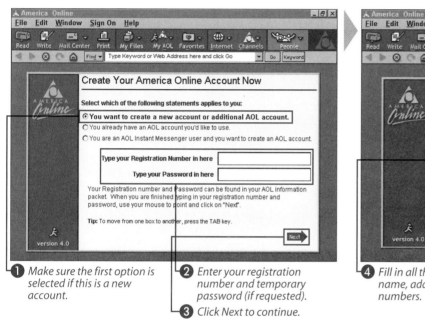

① *Make sure the first option is selected if this is a new account.*

② *Enter your registration number and temporary password (if requested).*

③ *Click Next to continue.*

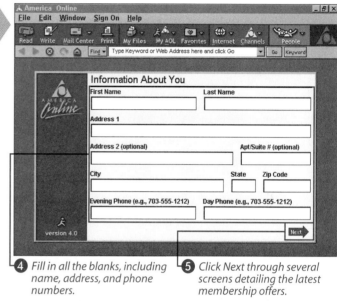

④ *Fill in all the blanks, including name, address, and phone numbers.*

⑤ *Click Next through several screens detailing the latest membership offers.*

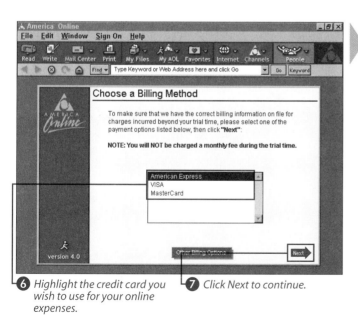

⑥ *Highlight the credit card you wish to use for your online expenses.*

⑦ *Click Next to continue.*

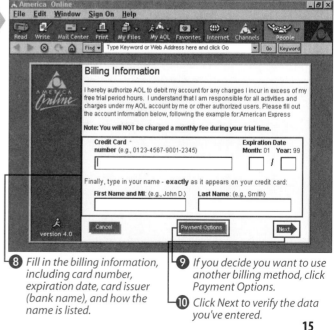

⑧ *Fill in the billing information, including card number, expiration date, card issuer (bank name), and how the name is listed.*

⑨ *If you decide you want to use another billing method, click Payment Options.*

⑩ *Click Next to verify the data you've entered.*

Picking Screen Name and Password

Now it is time for introductions. The system wants to know what it should call you, and more importantly, how it should introduce you to everyone else you meet and correspond with on America Online. This is all done through what is known as a *screen name*, which you get to choose for yourself.

This is an important decision, because your screen name is the name you use when you sign on to the system (enabling AOL to identify you and find your account), your electronic mail address (the name to which your friends and acquaintances send their letters), your nickname (the system automatically assigns it to everything you say in chat rooms), and your signature (placed on messages you post on the message boards of forums).

Actually, this is the first of up to five screen names you can create for your account. AOL permits a *master screen name* — the one you are creating now — and up to four additional screen names for use by other members of your household or by yourself. If you want, you can have one screen name for business use and others just for fun. Unlike the additional screen names I cover later, the master account name cannot be deleted without deleting the entire account — which is a big hassle — so take all the time you want now to get just the screen name you want. If the screen name is taken, you have the option of using an available name selected by the system or

trying another screen name. Don't be discouraged if the name you want is taken — be creative and try variations.

You also are prompted to create a password, the private key to your account. While all the world can know your screen name, no one but you should know the password.

TAKE NOTE

SCREEN NAME CONSIDERATIONS

Your screen name may be between three and ten characters long and you may use both letters, numbers, and spaces. Because this is your public persona, you might want to pick something that will be recognizable to friends, such as a variation on your name (ChasBowen), a nickname (OldSlide), a favorite pastime (GuitarGuy), or expression (Thats Life). NOTE: You might want to avoid using all capital letters, because online that is how some people indicate when they are SHOUTING about something.

PASSWORD CONSIDERATIONS

The password does not display on the screen as you type it. This is an extra bit of security, in case you are entering it in a public setting where someone may be peeking over your shoulder. Because you can't see what you are typing — and therefore are more prone to make a typographical error — AOL prompts you to enter the password a second time in the adjacent box. Click Next.

CROSS-REFERENCE
For information about Parental Controls to protect younger family members, see Chapter 16.

FIND IT ONLINE
For additional assistance with screen names and passwords, see the sections called, "Managing Your Account and Screen Names" and "Keeping Your Account Secure" in the Contents of the Offline Help (accessible from the Help option of the menu bar)

Ideas for Smart, Secure Passwords

▶ Don't pick any password that's easily guessed, such as your spouse's or children's names

▶ Use all eight characters, both letters and numbers.

▶ Random letters and numbers will be harder for a crook to guess, but they also may be harder for you to remember. Easier for you would be combinations that have some obscure meaning to you.

▶ Never use the password of *password*. You are not the first person to think of that. Traditionally it is the very first word would-be password thieves try.

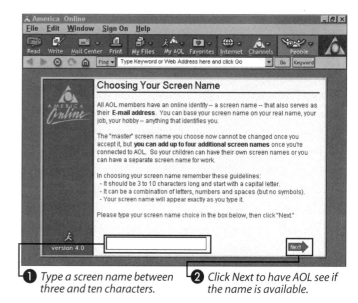

1 *Type a screen name between three and ten characters.*

2 *Click Next to have AOL see if the name is available.*

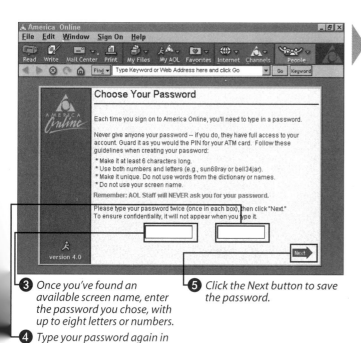

3 *Once you've found an available screen name, enter the password you chose, with up to eight letters or numbers.*

4 *Type your password again in the box on the right.*

5 *Click the Next button to save the password.*

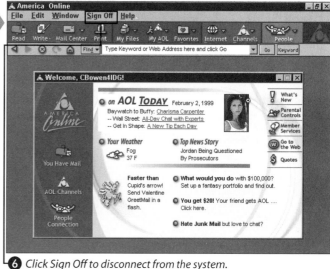

6 *Click Sign Off to disconnect from the system.*

Signing On

The installation program completes its work by placing a program icon on your desktop. From now on, to go online, you need only double-click that icon (or select America Online from the Start menu if you had it placed there earlier in the setup process). This summons the Sign On window.

To sign on to the system, make sure that the screen name and location you want are displayed in the Select Screen Name and Select Location fields, respectively. If they are not, click the down arrow and select the desired screen name and/or dialing location.

Next, click the Enter Password field and type in your password. As you learned in the previous section, for security reasons the password does not display as you type it. After that, click the Sign On button in the bottom right of the window (or just press the Enter key).

This brings up the connection displays. The AOL software calls the network and delivers your screen name and password. In a moment, you hear the spoken words, "Welcome," followed by another message: "You've got mail!" (if your volume is turned up and your computer is sound-capable). You learn all about electronic mail in Chapter 2.

TAKE NOTE

▶ **THREE PARTS OF THE INTRODUCTORY WINDOW**

Select Screen Name. The screen name you have created already should be showing in this box. The arrow on the right-hand side of the box can be clicked to display a drop-down list of other possible screen names. As you create more screen names for this account starting in Chapter 5, they will be available here, enabling you to select the one with which to sign on.

Enter Password. This field blank currently is blank, waiting for you to enter the password you have chosen for this screen name. Later in Chapter 4, you will see how to store a password so that you don't have to enter it each time you log on. This is handy if you are the only one likely to use this particular computer and AOL account. However, you might not want to do this if other people have access to your machine.

Select Location. This contains alternate connection data for various ways you might connect to AOL, such as from home, from work, and so on. This feature is particularly useful if you have AOL installed on a laptop computer, so you can create separate Location files for use in the cities to which you travel frequently. To create new Locations, click the Setup button at the bottom of the Sign On screen and then click the Connections Locations tab on the subsequent screen. Options there enable you to add, edit, and delete locations and connection numbers.

CROSS-REFERENCE

For more information about the Welcome window, see Chapter 3.

FIND IT ONLINE

To get additional information about logging on, click the Member Services icon of the Welcome screen and then select "Connecting to AOL" from the subsequent window.

Using the Welcome Window

The first major window you see after connecting to the system is the Welcome window (which lists today's highlights on the system and events going on today). Among points of interest:

▶ AOL Today, an updated report on events around the AOL community.

▶ Your local weather outlook and forecast. Click to search for cities and states, radar and satellite images, and weather news.

▶ Top news headlines. Click here for a display of other news resources.

▶ Assorted features from around the system.

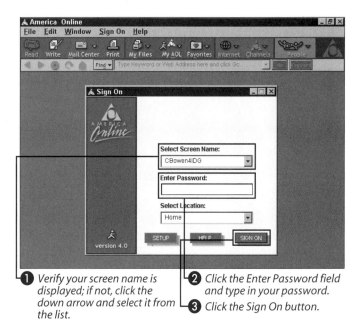

① *Verify your screen name is displayed; if not, click the down arrow and select it from the list.*

② *Click the Enter Password field and type in your password.*

③ *Click the Sign On button.*

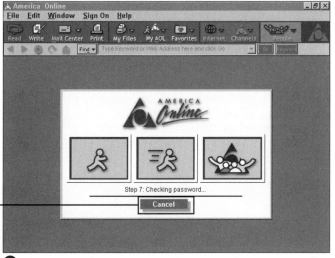

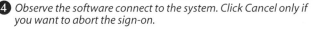

④ *Observe the software connect to the system. Click Cancel only if you want to abort the sign-on.*

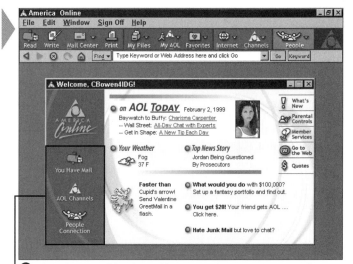

⑤ *Click the icon of the desired feature, such as e-mail, Channels, People Connection, Top News, weather, and so on.*

Customizing the Preferences Area

Customizing AOL has been the theme that has connected all the tasks in this first chapter.

To carry on this concept, wrap up Chapter 1 with your first visit to Preferences area. This powerful section controls customizing 14 aspects of your account and software, which you explore further in later chapters.

- ▶ **General** preferences include enabling online sounds, the size of displayed type, and so on.
- ▶ **Toolbar** controls the appearance and placement of the toolbar, as well as other aspects of navigation.
- ▶ **Mail** regulates e-mail performance, everything from saving incoming mail in your filing cabinet to automatically performing a spelling check before sending letters.
- ▶ **WWW** has options regarding how you see and use the Internet's World Wide Web.
- ▶ **Chat** customizes how the system performs when you are in an online chat room, determines if you are notified when people arrive and leave, and so on.
- ▶ **Download** controls options for how you can retrieve online software and specialized files.
- ▶ **Graphics** has options for receiving, viewing, and saving picture files on your hard disk.

- ▶ **Passwords** lets you change and store your main password.
- ▶ **Auto AOL** lets you schedule unattended mail pickup and delivery, automate message postings and file downloads, and the like.
- ▶ **Personal Filing Cabinet** controls the size and structure of your resources for saving incoming and outgoing e-mail, files, photos, and so on.
- ▶ **Spelling** sets your preferences for the built-in spelling, punctuation, and grammar checker.
- ▶ **Font** regulates size, color, and appearance of the type you use online.
- ▶ **Language** enables you to change the language in some of the online areas you visit.
- ▶ **Marketing** controls how and when you authorize AOL to include your name on membership lists.

TAKE NOTE

▶ **FINE-TUNING AOL**

You can continue to use Preferences even as you become more experienced with the service, returning time after time to fine-tune the software as you learn more about how you want the system to work for you.

CROSS-REFERENCE

For more information about the Preference area, see Chapters 2, 4, and 7.

FIND IT ONLINE

To get additional information online about the Preferences options, click the Member Services icon of the Welcome screen and then select "Getting Around & Using AOL" from the subsequent display.

Elements of the Interface

The top row of the AOL software features a menu bar, familiar to all Windows and Mac users. The menu bar gives you quick access to some of the most commonly used computing commands, as well as some special commands needed specifically on AOL.

Below the menu bar is America Online's colorful, powerful toolbar, made up of text and icons. This is where much of your online navigation begins, and it can even be customized to appearance and content that suit your specific needs.

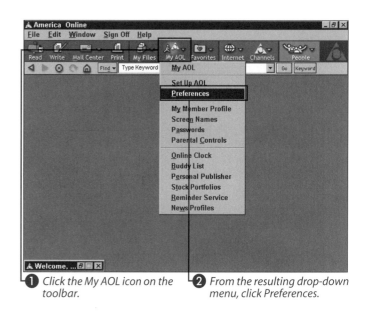

① Click the My AOL icon on the toolbar.

② From the resulting drop-down menu, click Preferences.

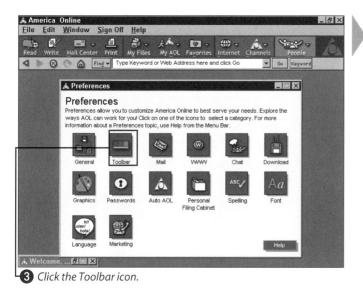

③ Click the Toolbar icon.

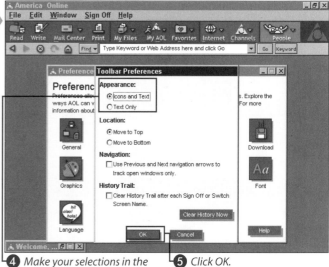

④ Make your selections in the Appearance area (either icons and text or text only) and Location (move to top or move to bottom).

⑤ Click OK.

Personal Workbook

Q&A

1 What is the maximum number of letters and numbers allowed in an AOL password?

_____

_____

_____

2 For billing, are there other options besides a major credit card for payment?

_____

_____

_____

3 How many screen names can be created with each America Online account?

_____

_____

_____

4 What is the significance of the master account screen name?

_____

_____

5 Where is the "control panel" for your AOL software?

_____

_____

_____

6 It's a good, clever idea to have _password_ as your password, right? Okay, if not, why not?

_____

_____

_____

7 How can you find a weather forecast for your area?

_____

_____

_____

8 Bonus Question: How do you abort a call to the network after you've launched the sign-on procedure but before the connection is made?

_____

_____

ANSWERS: PAGE 335

EXTRA PRACTICE

1 Click Options of the menu bar to see drop-down menus that give you quick access to some of the most commonly used commands.

2 Roll your mouse pointer over the toolbar and pause on an icon to see hidden text pop up describing its function.

3 All you need to use AOL is a general understanding of how to manipulate Windows screens. The essential topics — moving and closing windows, resizing, maximizing, and minimizing them, using vertical and horizontal scroll bars — can be picked up through ten minutes or so with your computer manual.

REAL-WORLD APPLICATIONS

✔ You can sign on to your account from another AOL member's house or office. Fire up your friend's copy of AOL and click the down-arrow beside the Select Screen Name field of the introductory screen. Tucked below the owner's master screen name is a "Guest" option. Select it, and the software lets you sign on and enter your own screen name and password.

✔ You can research your own questions about AOL and the software with the built-in help system. Select Help from the menu bar and click Offline Help from the menu. The database works like any other Windows help system

Visual Quiz

List the steps involved in displaying the menu shown here. And for what would it be used?

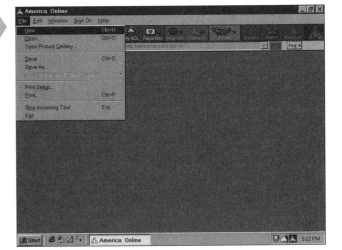

_____

_____

_____

_____

CHAPTER 2

Using Electronic Mail

Hands down, electronic mail is the favorite feature of America Online. As with the VCR in the 1970s, people immediately begin seeing applications for e-mail as soon as they hear the concept of sending and receiving letters online. Nowadays, millions of us write e-mail daily. Electronic letters, traveling almost instantly around the globe, link families, friends, lovers, business associates, new acquaintances, and friendly strangers. Because e-mail is so important to the online experience, America Online wastes no time getting you involved in e-mail. In fact, when you make your initial sign-on to your new account, the first message you hear after "Welcome" is "You've got mail!"

This chapter shows you everything you need to get started with e-mail, including

- ▶ reading and writing electronic mail online and using the electronic mailbox that comes with your account.
- ▶ working offline to compose text for delivery online.
- ▶ enhancing your text with formatting, including color, assorted typefaces and layouts, and pictures.
- ▶ spell-checking your text for accuracy.

Of course, there is more to e-mail than just reading and writing. AOL also provides you with an electronic Address Book for the names and addresses of your acquaintances, a digital filing cabinet for saving your correspondence, and options for sending computer programs and graphics. These advanced features can safely wait, and I cover them in Chapters 4 and 5. Right now, in spirit of getting you into the AOL swing of things as quickly as possible, I want to focus first on the "must-have" options. Reading this chapter, you become an expert at reading and writing your digital correspondence.

America Online maintains an electronic mailbox for you, in which all your incoming electronic mail arrives. To reach it, click the You Have Mail icon on the Welcome window and find your waiting letters are listed with the dates they were posted, the sender's screen names, and the subject. A bar cursor can be moved up and down with the keyboard's arrow keys. Or you can highlight a letter with the mouse. The first option button at the bottom of the window enables you to read the highlighted letter.

Reading Your First Letters

Do you remember your first real letter? Perhaps it was a warm letter from Grandma, or nothing more than fancy junk mail. Regardless, it was addressed and delivered to you! More mail has arrived for you, only this time it's a special delivery sent at the speed of light. You have e-mail!

To read the letter at the top of your online mailbox, highlight the first item with your cursor and then click Read. In a moment, the system opens a window and displays the contents. In this example, the first letter is from Steve Case, America Online's Chairman and Chief Executive Officer, with a welcome to the network.

All letters you receive are introduced by a header — this is a bit like the information on the outside of an envelope. The header includes the subject, the date and time it was posted, the sender's screen name, and your screen name. This information is supplied automatically by the system. Below the header, the actual text of the letter begins.

At the right of the letter is a scroll bar that works here the same way it works in all applications. Click the down or up arrows at the either end of the bar to move the text down or up one line. Click and drag the scroll bar box to go to a particular portion of the text. Click below or above the scroll bar box to page through the text one screen at a time. You can also use the down or up arrow keys on your keyboard to move through the letter.

At the bottom of the letter's window are numbers reminding you of how many new letters are in your mailbox and which one this is. (In the example, "1 of 4" means this is the first letter of four waiting for you.) There is also a Delete button to remove this letter from the mailbox permanently.

After you read Steve Case's welcome, click the Next button at the lower right of the window. This closes this letter and opens the next one in your mailbox. In the example, Keith Jenkins, AOL's Vice President of Member Services, also sends a welcome.

TAKE NOTE

THE FORMAT CHANGES SLIGHTLY

The format of the second letter is much the same as that of the first letter, but do you see two changes? They are at the bottom right of the window:

► First, the numbers are different (they read "2 of 4" in the example, meaning this is the second of four new letters in the mailbox).

► Second, another button has been added. The arrow labeled Prev enables you to go back to view the previous letter. Next enables you to continue to the next waiting message.

CROSS-REFERENCE

For more about Steve Case and his regular letters to AOL members, see Appendix A in the back of the book.

FIND IT ONLINE

For general background on the features of your mailbox, click the toolbar's Mail Center icon and then select Mail Center from the drop-down menu.

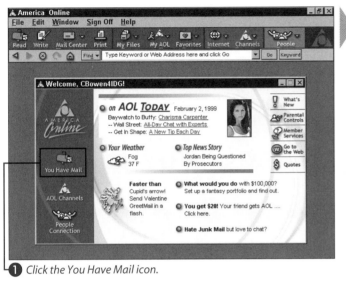

1 Click the You Have Mail icon.

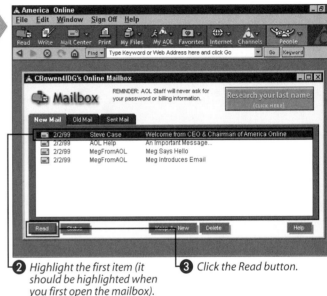

2 Highlight the first item (it should be highlighted when you first open the mailbox).

3 Click the Read button.

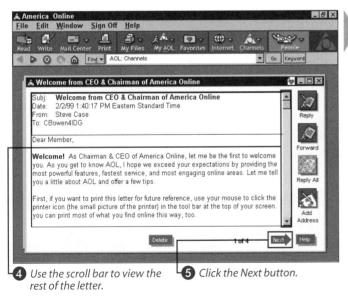

4 Use the scroll bar to view the rest of the letter.

5 Click the Next button.

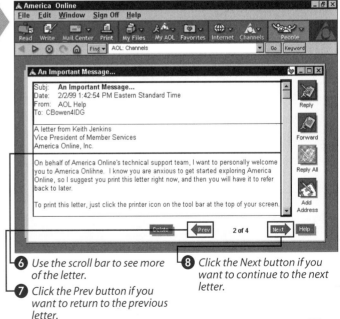

6 Use the scroll bar to see more of the letter.

7 Click the Prev button if you want to return to the previous letter.

8 Click the Next button if you want to continue to the next letter.

Printing and Other Actions

O f course, you don't have to do all your letter reading online. You also can get printouts to read the mail later offline.

There are three good ways to print the letter that's currently on the screen. First, you can click the Print icon on the toolbar, as seen in the upper-right window (this probably is the fastest way). Second, you can select File from the menu bar and click Print from the resulting drop-down menu, as is shown in the lower left. Finally, you can type Ctrl+P, the keyboard shortcut (that is, press P while holding down the Ctrl key, usually located in the lower left corner of your keyboard).

After you have your printout, return to the mailbox display by clicking the Read icon on the toolbar and notice that more changes have taken place. Where once there were four letters (in the example), there now are only two. What happened to the Steve Case letter and the Keith Jenkins letter? You purposefully did not delete them, but they are no longer in the mailbox.

Notice the mailbox window is set up to look something like a filing cabinet drawer, with tabs at the top of each window. The current window is labeled "New Mail." Under that is "Old Mail" and beneath that, "Sent Mail." The New Mail folder contains letters you have not yet read. Old Mail contains messages you have already read. The Sent Mail folder keeps copies of letters you send to other people.

Click the Old Mail tab to open it, and you find the Case and Jenkins letters are there.

TAKE NOTE

▶ **MAIL DISPOSITION OPTIONS**

Click back and forth between the New Mail and Old Mail folders and you see that the options at the bottom of the windows (shown in the lower-right window on the facing page) are the same:
▶ The Read option displays the contents of the currently highlighted letter.
▶ The Status option gives you background information on the highlighted letters, including when it was sent, by whom, whether it has been read yet, and if so, when.
▶ Keep as New enables you to keep the highlighted message among your list of waiting messages, even if you have already read it. This is handy if you want to use a particular message to remind you of an upcoming event or that you need to send a reply yet. Keeping it as "New" signals the "You've Got Mail" announcement each time you sign on.
▶ The Delete option permanently removes the current letter from the mailbox. The system asks you to confirm that you are sure you want to delete the highlighted message.
▶ Help gives you additional information about the mailbox.

CROSS-REFERENCE

For more information about alternate ways to travel the system, see Chapter 3.

FIND IT ONLINE

For online assistance with specific mail-related questions, click the Help button at the bottom of your mailbox display and select from the provided list of topics.

Alternate Ways to Reach the Mailbox

To reach your electronic mailbox, you can also try the following actions:

▶ Click the You Have Mail icon on the Welcome window.

▶ Select the Read icon on the toolbar.

▶ Click the toolbar's Mail Center icon for a menu of options that include Read Mail.

▶ Hold down the Ctrl key and press the letter R. This is referred to as a *keyboard shortcut*.

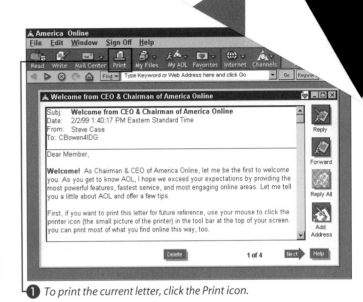

1 To print the current letter, click the Print icon.

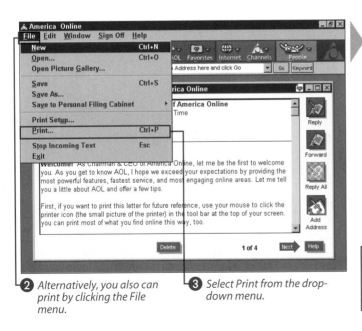

2 Alternatively, you also can print by clicking the File menu.

3 Select Print from the drop-down menu.

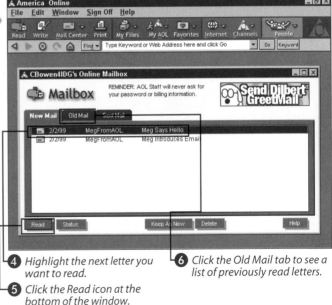

4 Highlight the next letter you want to read.

5 Click the Read icon at the bottom of the window.

6 Click the Old Mail tab to see a list of previously read letters.

etting a Mailbox Preference

How old is Old Mail? That is, how long will the system keep previously read letters?

The answer is up to you. As you saw in Chapter 1, much of America Online can be customized to suit your tastes and interests. This includes options related to the mailbox. You can specify that you want old mail saved from one to seven days after you have read it.

To do that, you use the Preferences area, the same section you use in Chapter 1 to manipulate the appearance and location of the toolbar. Again, you click the My AOL icon on the toolbar, illustrated the window in the upper left on the facing page, and then select Preferences from the resulting drop-down menu.

From the Preference screen (seen in the lower-left window), click the Mail icon to view a list of "switches" that can be "flipped" for the mailbox.

Look at the bottom of the window, where you see "Keep my old mail online — days after I read it." Up and down arrows appear beside the box with the number of days. Click the up arrow to raise the number from the current setting (the default is three days) or click the down arrow to the lower the number. When you have it set as you want it, click OK. If you feel more secure knowing your mail is available for a while online, in case you want to reread it or get a printout later, increase the number. On the other hand, if you want to keep your mailbox as clutter free as possible, reduce the number.

TAKE NOTE

▶ WHAT'S YOUR PREFERENCE?

▶ You must be online to change your Old Mail preferences. If you try it while not connected to the system, the option shown in the upper-right window is dimmed out.

▶ If you increase the number of days to retain mail, letters already deleted earlier do not reappear. The change applies only to future mail.

▶ Another of the switches on this Mail Preferences screen — "Perform a spell check before sending mail" — is covered at the end of this chapter when we take up spell checking and other refinements to your letters.

▶ When a piece of mail has been successfully sent, a confirmation message informs you and asks you to acknowledge it by clicking the OK button. If you find this message annoying, you can turn it off with the Preference box. Uncheck the box labeled "Confirm mail after it has been sent."

▶ Other important Preferences are covered in later chapters. For instance, those related to the Personal Filing Cabinet are discussed in Chapter 5, while those related to real-time chatting and privacy issues are covered in Chapter 4.

CROSS-REFERENCE

For more on using the Preferences area of the software, also see Chapters 1, 4, and 7.

FIND IT ONLINE

For assistance with setting controls, click the Help button on the bottom of the Preference screen and select "Online Mail Preference" from the list of topics.

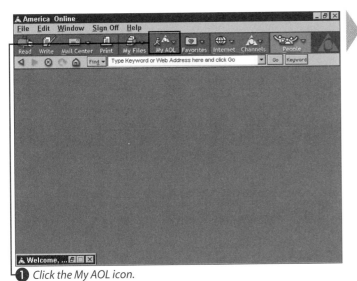

1 Click the My AOL icon.

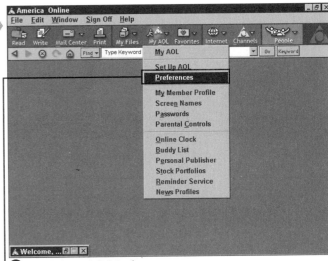

2 Highlight and click Preferences.

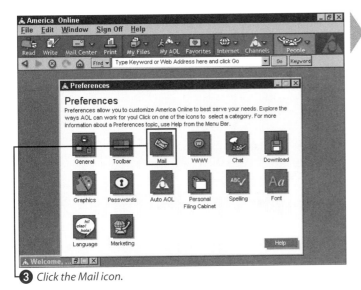

3 Click the Mail icon.

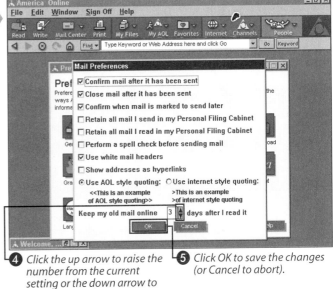

4 Click the up arrow to raise the number from the current setting or the down arrow to lower the number.

5 Click OK to save the changes (or Cancel to abort).

Addressing Letters

In the early days of cyberspace — say, at least ten years ago — composing e-mail was hard to explain. Every computer and every piece of communications software handled e-mail and text entry in general quite differently. Hundreds of thousands of words were published in books and magazine articles on the subject. One of the great civilizing effects of America Online's arrival has been the simplifying of e-mail writing. It couldn't be easier.

Start by clicking the Write icon on the toolbar (you can do this while signed on or not). The software responds by opening a fill-in-the-blank onscreen form, shown here in the upper-right window on the facing page.

In the Send To: box, enter the screen name of the person to whom you wish to send the message. Of course, if you are new in these parts, you might not know the e-mail addresses of anyone else yet. Fortunately, to practice you can actually write and send e-mail to yourself. Try it. In the Send To: box, enter your own address (that is, the screen name you created in Chapter 1).

Next, press the Tab key to reach the adjacent field. Copy To: is the field in which you can put screen names of other people to whom you would like to send copies of this note as a courtesy. Or you can leave it blank by just pressing the Tab key again.

Your cursor arrives at the subject box when you press the Tab key in the Copy To: field. In the Subject: box, enter the line you want to appear in the recipient's mailbox, such as, "My first e-mail and I'm already talking to myself" (without quotation marks).

Press the Tab key to reach the text entry box, where you can type your letter.

TAKE NOTE

MOVING FROM FIELD TO FIELD

Many AOL data boxes have multiple fields of data, like the Write Mail window. You can use the Tab key to move between the fields, from left to right and top to bottom. Also, Shift+Tab (hold down the Shift key and press the Tab key) moves you in the other direction, right to left and bottom to top. Besides the Tab key, you also can simply click the desired field with the mouse.

NOT ALL FIELDS ARE REQUIRED

As you will find with many of AOL's onscreen forms, not all fields require data. In this case, the only field requiring data is Send To: field. Subject: and Copy To: are optional. I strongly recommend you fill in the Subject: field — if you do not, your recipients see "(No Subject)" when your mail arrives.

LENGTH LIMITS FOR THE TEXT

Messages sent through AOL may be up to 30K, which is about 15 typewritten pages.

CROSS-REFERENCE
For information on finding screen names you can use as e-mail addresses, see Chapter 5's discussion of the Member Directory.

FIND IT ONLINE
To find more general assistance for the reading, writing, and saving of e-mail, click the Member Services icon on the Welcome window and then choose E-mail in the resulting window.

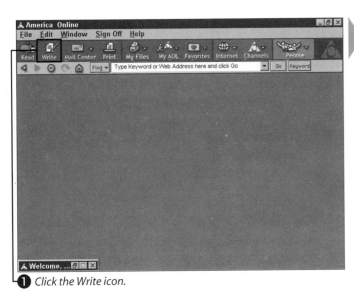

1 *Click the Write icon.*

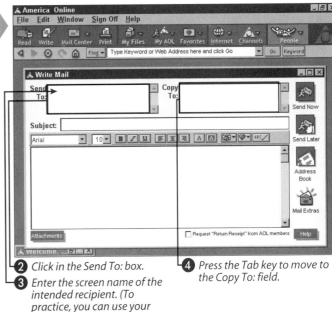

2 *Click in the Send To: box.*

3 *Enter the screen name of the intended recipient. (To practice, you can use your own screen name).*

4 *Press the Tab key to move to the Copy To: field.*

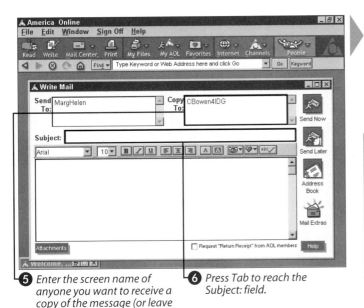

5 *Enter the screen name of anyone you want to receive a copy of the message (or leave this field blank).*

6 *Press Tab to reach the Subject: field.*

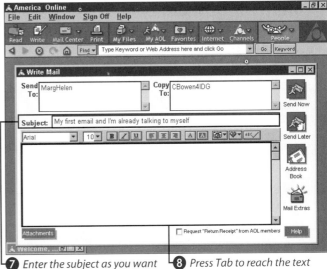

7 *Enter the subject as you want it to appear in the recipient's mailbox.*

8 *Press Tab to reach the text entry box.*

Writing and Sending a Letter

To compose the letter, once your cursor is in the text box, just type. You don't need to do anything special at the end of lines. AOL automatically wraps the words and sentences to a new line. Also, inside the text box, the Tab key produces a real tab and you can use the Enter key to reach a new line.

To read and make simple changes in the text, use the mouse to manipulate the scroll bar at the right of the window. Click the portion of the text you want to change. Use the Delete and Backspace keys to remove unwanted letters and words and then type in your changes.

When ready, click Send Now. If the Send Now button is dimmed, sign on first and then click Send Now. The system reports that your letter has been posted.

Multiple Addresses and Blind Carbon Copies

In the previous example, I used a single address in the Send To: field, but AOL can send the same e-mail to more than one person. In the Send To: field, separate the e-mail addresses of the recipients with commas. For example: `CBowen, KatCastner, DavePey, JoeDobbs`.

Also, the same format is used in the Copy To: field to send multiple copies of a message.

Sometimes you might not want everyone on a list of recipients to know who is getting the letter. That is a job for a "blind copy" option. Include the recipient's screen name in parentheses in the Send To: or Copy To: fields, as in (`CBowen, KatCastner, DavePey, JoeDobbs`). In fact, you can even combine regular recipients and blind copy recipients, like this:

`CBowen, KatCastner, (DavePey, JoeDobbs)`.

TAKE NOTE

ADDING A RECEIPT

▶ You sometimes might wonder if an important message did indeed reach its destination. For those times, you can request a return receipt. On the lower-right side of the Write Mail window is a checkbox labeled "Request 'Return Receipt' from AOL members." Click this box and then send your message as usual. You are automatically notified with e-mail when the recipient(s) opens that letter. (The feature works only when writing to other AOL members, not messages sent through the Internet to non-AOL subscribers.)

▶ If you forgot to request a receipt, you still can determine if your outgoing e-mail has been received and read yet with the Status option in the Sent Mail folder. Click the toolbar's Read icon to reach the mailbox and select the Sent Mail tab at the top. In the list of posted letters, highlight the one you want to check and then click Status at the bottom of the window. The system reports when it was sent and if and when the recipient(s) reads it.

CROSS REFERENCE

For information on automating the delivery of e-mail, see Chapter 5 for a discussion of your Address Book and Chapter 6 for information on Automatic AOL.

FIND IT ONLINE

To see a personalized, online tutorial about electronic mail, click Help ⇨ Member Services Online Help from the menu. Select E-mail from the resulting list of subjects and then click the 5 Minute Guide to AOL E-mail.

Basic Editing Options

Block: To select (or "block") text, click the left mouse button as you point to the beginning of the chosen place in the text. Holding down the button, drag the block to the end of the desired area and release.

Cut: To delete a large block of text, select it, click the Edit option of the menu bar, and then choose the Cut function.

Paste: Select a block of text and then cut it. Click the place in the text where you want the cut material to appear. Then either click Edit ⇨ Paste, or press Ctrl+V.

Undo: To undo an action, drop down the Edit menu on the menu bar and click Undo, or press Ctrl+Z.

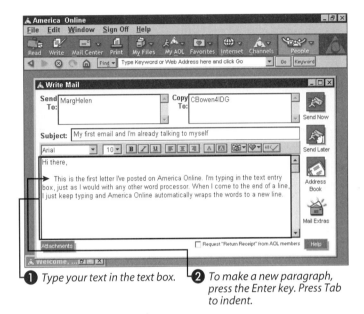

❶ Type your text in the text box.

❷ To make a new paragraph, press the Enter key. Press Tab to indent.

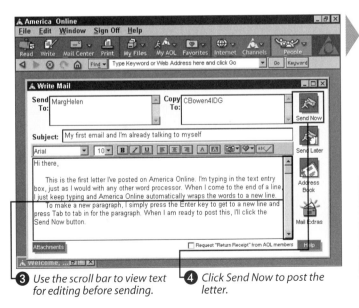

❸ Use the scroll bar to view text for editing before sending.

❹ Click Send Now to post the letter.

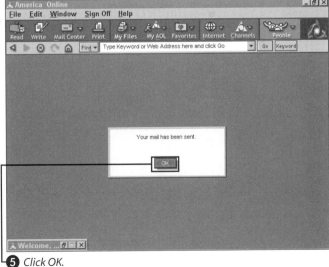

❺ Click OK.

Retrieving and Replying to Mail

Because you are both the writer and the recipient of the letter in this exercise, within seconds you hear, "You've Got Mail."

As you travel America Online, you hear this familiar, spoken message whenever you are online and a new letter arrives in your mailbox (unless you have unread mail there already). If you are offline when the letter arrives, you hear the message at your next sign-on.

To retrieve your message, click the toolbar's Read icon (or perhaps use the Ctrl+R shortcut if that seems convenient). When you arrive at your mailbox, you find that the letter you posted to yourself is there. To read it, highlight it and click Read.

And if composing e-mail is easy, replying is even easier, because you don't have to fill in as many fields. With the message still on your screen, click the Reply icon.

In the resulting window, notice the Send To: and the Subject: fields already have been filled in. You need only write your message in the text box and when you click Send Now, AOL sends it back, automatically addressed to the person who wrote to you.

CROSS-REFERENCE

For information on another form of message — the public notes posted in AOL forums — see Chapter 6.

FIND IT ONLINE

For help with copying the letters you receive in your mailbox, click the Member Services icon on the Welcome screen, choose E-mail for the resulting window, and then scroll the list of topics and click "Saving E-mail."

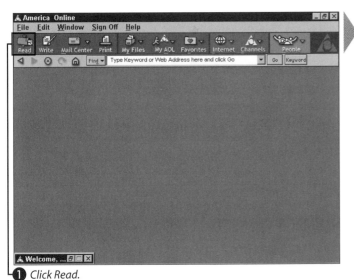

1 Click Read.

2 Highlight the mail you just sent yourself and click Read.

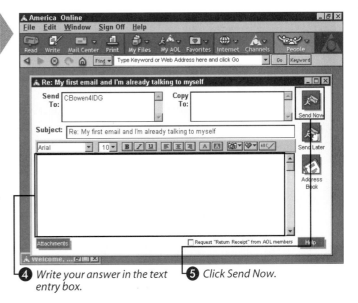

3 Click Reply.

4 Write your answer in the text entry box.

5 Click Send Now.

Composing E-mail Offline

One of the beauties of America Online is that the software often appears to think the way you do. For instance, it probably doesn't make sense to you to have to sign on to the network and then just sit there and write your letters. That doesn't make good sense to AOL either, so the software is designed to do much of its e-mail work "offline" (not connected).

To see how it works, disconnect from the system if you are now online (by clicking Sign Off on the menu bar and then selecting Sign Off from the down-drop menu). After you have disconnected, notice that the Write icon on the toolbar has not been dimmed out, which means it is still available to you.

Now click the toolbar's Write icon to see the familiar Write Mail window appear, ready to accept your letter. Enter the recipient's screen name in the Send To: field. If you want to send copies to other users, enter screen names in the Copy To: field. Describe the topic in the Subject: field. Write your text as usual and fix it using the editing options described earlier.

When you are ready to send your letter, click the Send Later button. Your letter is now stored in your offline mailbox for later posting. The software informs you that you can manage your online delivery with the Automatic AOL option in Preferences. I cover this powerful feature in detail in Chapter 6. This sophisticated option is not necessary for the simple task at hand, so just click OK.

When you are ready to actually post your letter(s), sign on to AOL as usual. This time when you arrive, you are greeted with a message that says you have mail waiting to be sent. Click the Send Now option in the lower-left corner of the new window. AOL now posts each letter you have written offline, quickly and efficiently. Continue online as long as you want and then disconnect with the Sign Off option on the menu bar.

TAKE NOTE

▶ WRITING MULTIPLE LETTERS

You can write more than one letter offline. If you have more to compose, click the toolbar's Write icon again, typing your message and clicking the Send Later option for each letter.

▶ MANAGING MAIL FOLDERS

If you used the Send Later icon by mistake, you don't have to mail your message on your next sign-on. Just click the Mail Waiting to be Sent button, shown in the lower-left figure on the facing page. The system then lists the letters awaiting delivery, with options for action. Highlight the letter you want removed. You can highlight it and either click Delete (to remove it entirely) or Edit (to make changes).

CROSS-REFERENCE
For more information on the Internet and its links to AOL, see Chapter 7.

FIND IT ONLINE
For help with offline mail composition, click the Help option on the menu bar, choose Offline Help from the drop-down menu, and enter **offline mailbox** in the query box.

Exchanging Mail Between AOL and the Internet

You also need to know how to send electronic mail from your AOL account to acquaintances on the Internet:

Click the Write icon of the toolbar as usual. In the Send To: field, enter the Internet address, such as cebowen@ramlink.net. Enter your Subject and text of your letter as usual and then click Send Now.

People can send mail to your Internet address, which is your screen name followed by @aol.com.

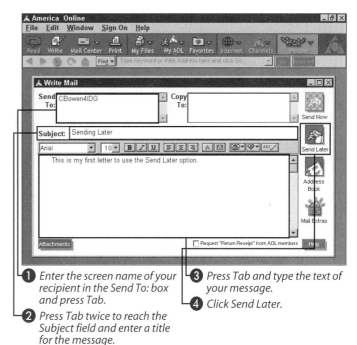

❶ Enter the screen name of your recipient in the Send To: box and press Tab.

❷ Press Tab twice to reach the Subject field and enter a title for the message.

❸ Press Tab and type the text of your message.

❹ Click Send Later.

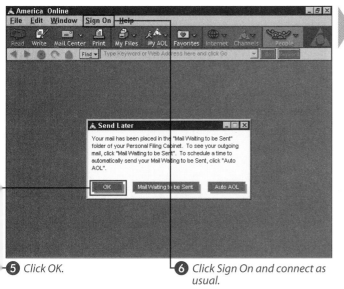

❺ Click OK.

❻ Click Sign On and connect as usual.

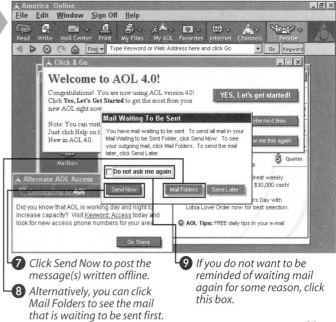

❼ Click Send Now to post the message(s) written offline.

❽ Alternatively, you can click Mail Folders to see the mail that is waiting to be sent first.

❾ If you do not want to be reminded of waiting mail again for some reason, click this box.

Creating Prettier Text

America Online enhances the basic editing tools to enable your letters to make a real statement. Dozens of different typefaces, many type sizes, and plenty of type styles are available for use in your text.

If you have already written your letter and want to transform all or some of it into a new typeface, select the block you wish to change, and then click the down arrow under the Subject line adjacent to the name of the current typeface. Click a new typeface from the list. The block of type is converted.

If you still are composing your text, you can change to a new typeface as you write. Click where you wish the new typeface to appear and then click the down arrow under the Subject line adjacent to the name of the current typeface. Click a new typeface from the list. Now as you type, your words appear in the new typeface.

Typefaces also can be put in different sizes. The default size is 10, but you can select a size ranging from 8 (quite small) to 72 (enormous). As with typefaces, you can select (block) existing type and change it to a new size — just click the down arrow beneath the subject field adjacent to the current size (it probably reads "10" right now). Or if you want to switch type sizes as your compose your letter, position your cursor with the mouse and then click the down arrow by the current size and choose a new size from the list. From then on, everything you type is in the new size until you change it again.

CROSS-REFERENCE

For more information on graphics and other binary files, see Chapter 6 for a discussion on uploading and the Download Manager.

FIND IT ONLINE

For more help with fonts and typefaces, click the Mail Center icon and select Mail Extras from the drop-down menu. Click Colors & Style from the resulting window.

Inserting Graphics in E-mail

Click the Write icon and fill in the addresses and subject line. Next, click the icon of the camera above the message field.

In the resulting drop-down menu, select either Insert a Picture or Background Picture. AOL displays its Open Image File Window, which you can navigate to reach the directory on your computer containing the image file you want to send. When you find the image you want to send, double-click its filename to insert it into your e-mail's message window.

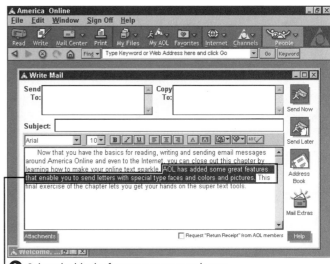

❶ Select the block of text you want to enhance.

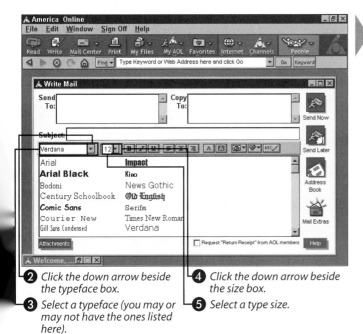

❷ Click the down arrow beside the typeface box.

❸ Select a typeface (you may or may not have the ones listed here).

❹ Click the down arrow beside the size box.

❺ Select a type size.

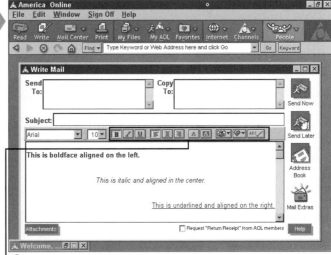

❻ Select any other desired format button, such as Boldface, Italic, Underlined, a particular text alignment, or a color.

Checking Your Spelling

No matter how smart and graphically pleasing you make your e-mail, spelling errors can undercut its effect. Fortunately, AOL version 4.0 has added a great face-saver for the spell-challenged: a built-in spelling checker works in tandem with your e-mail. To use the feature, click the toolbar's Write icon to address and compose your letter as usual. When you are ready to have AOL check the spelling for you, position the cursor at the beginning of the text and click the last icon below the Subject: line (the one with "ABC" and a check mark on it).

If the spelling checker finds a word it questions, it highlights it and offers possible corrections, which you can click if you want to use and replace. Other options invite you to cancel the checking, skip that one and/or other such spellings in the letter, replace that one and/or all other such spellings with the highlighted alternative, or learn the word (add your spelling to AOL's dictionary of words).

The spelling checker is such a popular feature that America Online has given it its own keyboard shortcut. Hold down the Ctrl key and press the equal sign (that is, Ctrl+=) to begin spell checking the onscreen document. You can also begin spell checking by clicking the Edit option in your menu bar and selecting Spell Check from the drop-down menu.

Customizing Your Spelling Checker

Misspellings are as unique as we are. With that in mind, you also can customize your spelling checker. From the toolbar, select My AOL ➪ Preferences, and then click Spelling. On the resulting window, you can make choices about the kind of errors you want the software to check for, including capitalization, doubled words, punctuation, the incorrect use of *a* and *an*, improper use of hyphens, and more. You can also change the dictionary (if you speak another language and another dictionary is available) and edit your personal dictionary.

In addition, an Advanced option enables you to view the rules the spelling checker applies for various errors and specify whether to turn the functions on or off. Select each option to see a description of its function in the box below it.

TAKE NOTE

▶ AUTOMATIC SPELLING CHECKING IS AVAILABLE

If you like AOL's spelling checker, you can make it automatic with each e-mail you send. Just click the toolbar's My AOL icon, select Preferences from the drop-down menu, click the Mail icon, and click the checkbox next to "Perform a spell check before sending mail." Click OK to save your change.

CROSS-REFERENCE

For information on other forms of automation, see Chapter 5 for material on the Personal Filing Cabinet, and Chapter 6 for a discussion of Automatic AOL.

FIND IT ONLINE

For more online help with using the spelling checker, click the Mail Center icon and choose Mail Center from the drop-down menu. Click Help on the resulting display and scroll the list of topics to find "Spell-Checking."

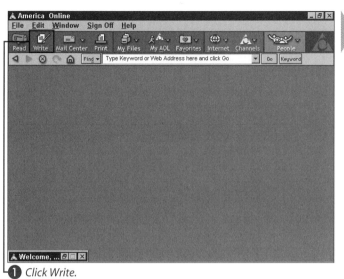

1 Click Write.

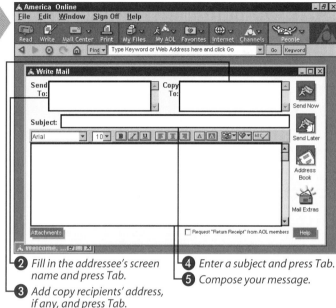

2 Fill in the addressee's screen name and press Tab.

3 Add copy recipients' address, if any, and press Tab.

4 Enter a subject and press Tab.

5 Compose your message.

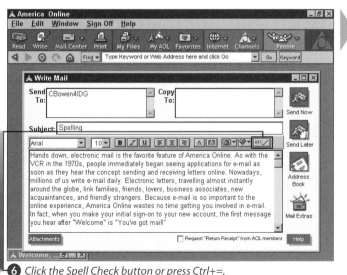

6 Click the Spell Check button or press Ctrl+=.

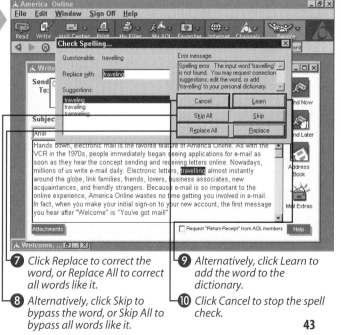

7 Click Replace to correct the word, or Replace All to correct all words like it.

8 Alternatively, click Skip to bypass the word, or Skip All to bypass all words like it.

9 Alternatively, click Learn to add the word to the dictionary.

10 Click Cancel to stop the spell check.

Exercising Mail Controls

Junk e-mail and other nuisance mail have become a problem throughout cyberspace. America Online's response — in addition to fighting mass electronic mailers in court — has been to give members multifunctioning Mail Controls that enable you to place restrictions on the exchange of e-mail for each of the screen names on your account.

To reach the Mail Control features, sign on to the system using your master account screen name, click the toolbar's Mail Center icon, and select Mail Controls from the drop-down menu. On the resulting window, click the Go to Mail Controls button.

A list of all screen names currently assigned to your account appears. Select the one for which you want to use Mail Controls and click the Edit button. Now click the button beside the setting you want to activate for this screen name. A dark circle appears within the button indicating it has been selected. You can select only one of these six alternatives:

- ▶ **Allow all mail.** This default setting authorizes AOL to deliver all e-mail addressed you.
- ▶ **Allow mail from AOL Members and addresses listed.** Select this to receive e-mail from any AOL member and only those Internet e-mail addresses that you specify in the box at the right of the window.
- ▶ **Allow mail from AOL Members only.** Choose this option to receive e-mail from any AOL member. You will not receive e-mail from Internet addresses.

- ▶ **Allow mail from the addresses listed only.** Select this to receive e-mail only from those AOL and/or Internet addresses that you specify in the box at the right.
- ▶ **Block mail from the addresses listed.** Choose this option to receive all e-mail except letters from those AOL and/or Internet addresses that you specify in the box at the right.
- ▶ **Block all mail.** Select this setting only if you do not wish to send or receive any e-mail whatsoever. Also, a checkbox at the bottom of the window can be marked if you don't want to send or receive any e-mail that contains an attached file, such as a program. This check box can be used in conjunction with any of the above Mail Controls settings.

TAKE NOTE

▶ LISTING E-MAIL ADDRESSES

If the setting you have selected allows or blocks specific addresses, type the first address in the box next to the Add button at the right of the window and then click Add to add it to the list below the data entry field. Repeat this step for each name to allow or block. You can add Internet domain names (`spam.com`, for example) to block all mail from that domain. To delete a name from the list, highlight it and use the Remove button. Remove All clears the list entirely.

CROSS-REFERENCE

For more on other forms of controls you can exercise over your account and data coming into your mailbox, see Chapter 16's discussion of Parental Controls.

FIND IT ONLINE

For online help with related security issues, click Help ⇨ Member Services Online Help, and then click "Online Safety & Security."

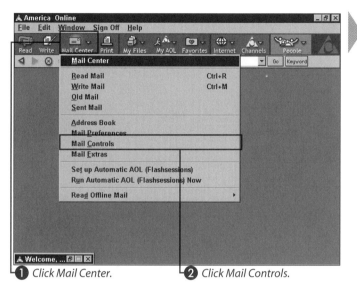

❶ Click Mail Center.

❷ Click Mail Controls.

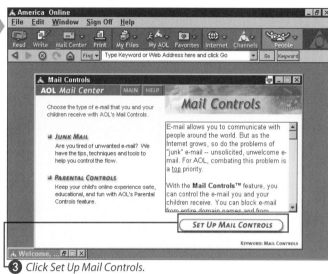

❸ Click Set Up Mail Controls.

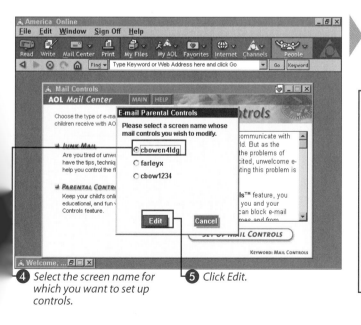

❹ Select the screen name for which you want to set up controls.

❺ Click Edit.

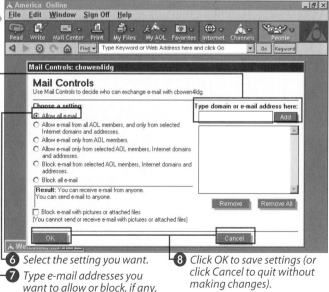

❻ Select the setting you want.

❼ Type e-mail addresses you want to allow or block, if any, and click Add for each.

❽ Click OK to save settings (or click Cancel to quit without making changes).

Personal Workbook

Q&A

1 How can you tell when a letter in your mailbox was sent to you?

_____

_____

_____

2 What are at least two ways to print a letter that's on your screen?

_____

_____

_____

3 What is the default for the number of days AOL keeps your previously read letters as "old mail," and how do you change that number?

_____

_____

4 What are at least two ways to reach your online mailbox window?

_____

_____

5 How do you address a letter to more than one recipient?

_____

_____

_____

6 How do you send e-mail to a non-AOL members through the Internet?

_____

_____

_____

7 How do you compose a letter to another AOL member containing different colors of type?

_____

_____

_____

8 Bonus Question: How can you check the spelling of a letter before sending it?

_____

_____

ANSWERS: PAGE 336

EXTRA PRACTICE

1 Offline, write an e-mail to yourself — that is, using your own screen name as the recipient — and set it for later delivery.

2 Sign on and notice the system's first order of business is to remind you of the pending letter and to ask your permission to send it.

3 View the contents of your Mail Folders to see how you can delete the pending message if you'd like.

4 Now direct the system to send the pending letter, noticing that in a moment you hear the "You've Got Mail!" message as it arrives in your mailbox (if your mailbox was previously empty).

5 Open your mailbox and retrieve the letter.

6 Send a reply to the practice letter.

REAL WORLD APPLICATIONS

✔ Among the first letters arriving in your mailbox probably will be those from Meg the AOL Insider. This valuable collection of tips, news, and advice is from AOL itself, and you are automatically signed up to receive a tip a day. If for some reason you don't want to receive the tips, though, see the bottom of any of Meg's messages for instructions on how to cancel your automatic subscription.

✔ While doing the exercises in this chapter, you probably got tired of typing in screen names in these Send To: fields (and optionally, the Copy To: field). Good automation is coming for this task. If you want to jump ahead to Chapter 5, you can get an advance look at the Address Book feature, which stores the e-mail addresses of your friends, family, and associates and saves you all that keyboarding.

Visual Quiz

How would you come to see a window like this one? Need a tip? Figure out why there is already a subject line present, but at the same time, the Send To: and message fields are empty.

_____

_____

_____

_____

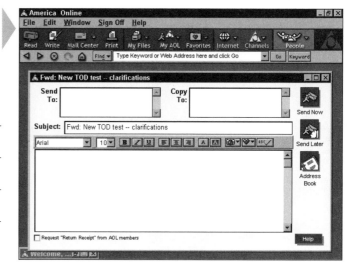

CHAPTER **3**

Exploring the System

Crossroads, in communities large and small, are where people come together for commerce, camaraderie, and communications. Intersections of highways and byways are where civilization takes root. If you want to learn about a town, start with Main Street. On America Online, the main street is the area called *Channels*, where all of the system's thousands of powerful resources come together.

But sightseeing is not this chapter's only mission. While you are getting your first look at Channels, you also will learn important things about how to navigate this enormous system, using resources such as *keywords* and *hyperlinks*, as well as the software's built-in history trail and options that store your favorite sites. The best way to discover the techniques is to learn by doing. This chapter breaks down the subject into these parts, letting you

- ▶ see the broad view of AOL and how it is built around nearly two dozen communities, much like neighborhoods of a large city.

- ▶ discover multiple ways of getting from here to there.
- ▶ customize the system further by starting your own list of favorite sites you find along the way.
- ▶ search databases and electronic directories for people, places, and things.

Our mission, then, has two goals. First, experiment with each new navigation technique, tools you will use throughout the rest of this book and in subsequent exploration of the system. Second, get your first good look at every key section on this massive system, and to help with that, I provide one-paragraph overviews of each channel as we come to it on this tour. By the end of the chapter, you will have used all the go-there tools and will have zipped in and out of every major AOL port of call.

Reaching the Channels

All aboard for the America Online main street tour! To begin, sign on as usual by double-clicking the AOL program icon on your desktop, entering your password in the Sign On window, and clicking the Sign On button. AOL automatically connects you, greeting you with the spoken "Welcome" and possibly the "You've Got Mail" messages, and bringing you to the familiar Welcome window you used in previous chapters. Click the middle icon on the left — AOL Channels — and the system displays its Channels window.

Consider each block on the Channels window as a signpost pointing to a unique AOL borough devoted to a specific interest or activity. There are 19 boroughs in this bustling AOL metropolis, and they are all open for exploration. Even better, there's no need for a parking space here.

Run your mouse cursor over the window and notice that the mouse's arrow pointer automatically changes to a hand with one finger pointing (also called the "helping hand") when it touches any of the signposts. As a regular Windows user, you probably already know that the pointing finger means each of these signs is "clickable." To "go" from here to the AOL channel devoted to Entertainment, for instance, you need only place your cursor on the Entertainment sign and click once with the left button on your mouse. These clickable items are called *buttons*, *links*, or sometimes *hyperlinks*.

Let your mouse pause on any of the signposts (with the arrow altered into the helping hand), and the system automatically describes each locale. For instance, roll the cursor onto the Travel sign and pause until the system displays a description ("Destinations, Online Booking, Ideas — and Bargains"). These helpful descriptions can be found throughout the service, too!

TAKE NOTE

ANOTHER WAY TO THE CHANNELS

Another way to reach a specific AOL channel is to check the toolbar's Channels icon and then select the channel you want from the drop-down menu.

REDUCING ONLINE ADS

As you probably have noticed now that you have signed on several times, America Online often greets you at sign-on with one or more pop-up advertisements for products you can order online. Buttons at the bottom of the ads give you options to order or decline ("No Thanks"). If you would like to reduce the number of pop-up ads you see, click My AOL on the toolbar and then select Preferences. Next, click the Marketing icon and select the option called "Popup." In a subsequent window, you can click a box marked "No, I do not want to receive special AOL members-only pop-up offers." By the way, even with the checkbox marked, you still may occasionally receive pop-up announcements from AOL itself about changes in the system and new features.

CROSS-REFERENCE

If you need a quick overview of the channels, see Appendix A.

FIND IT ONLINE

For online help with navigating the system, click Help ⇨ Member Services Online Help. From the resulting list, select Getting Around & Using AOL.

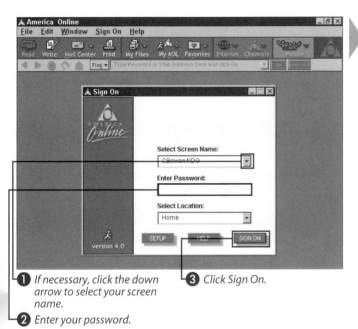

➊ If necessary, click the down arrow to select your screen name.

➋ Enter your password.

➌ Click Sign On.

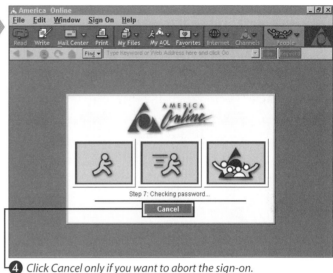

➍ Click Cancel only if you want to abort the sign-on.

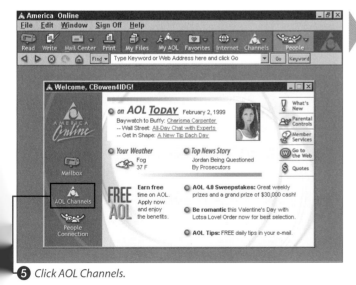

➎ Click AOL Channels.

➏ Click any of the 19 channels to reach that neighborhood of the system.

Learning the Parts of the Channels Menu

AOL may resemble a metropolitan city in many ways, but in at least one important way it differs: Getting around is much easier on AOL! Each channel you see in this chapter works largely the same way, making it easy to navigate all once you've learned just one. Take a moment to study the AOL Today channel window (in the upper-right corner on the facing page) and its components.

Underlined words and sentences usually appear as blue text and frequently are referred to as hypertext links. You see the same type of links on the Internet's World Wide Web in Chapter 7. Clicking these links takes you to articles or features described in the highlighted text.

Targeted items, identified by a button in the shape of a triangle, square, or circle, indicate a collection of material you might be interested in, from the horoscopes to the classified ads. You see the same or similar buttons all across the service — watch for the pointing finger cursor to appear.

Photographs, which most channel windows use in the form of thumbnail-sized graphics, usually bring up related stories or features to illustrate material when clicked.

A miniature channel list appears along the left side of each channel window you see. For example, if you are visiting the AOL Today channel and want to switch to the Lifestyles channel, you need only point to and click Lifestyles in the list at the left.

CROSS-REFERENCE
For more information about AOL's news-related features, see Chapter 8.

1 Click AOL Today to begin our tour.

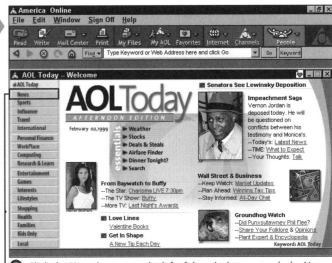

2 Click the News button on the left of the window to reach the News channel.

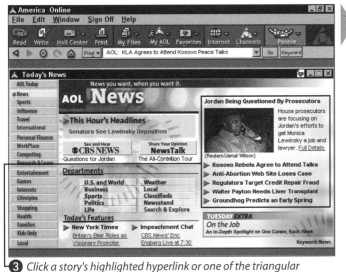

3 Click a story's highlighted hyperlink or one of the triangular buttons.

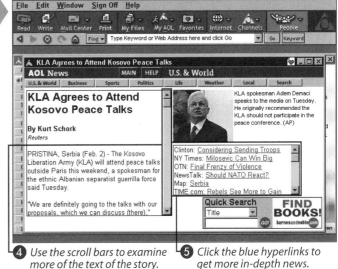

4 Use the scroll bars to examine more of the text of the story.

5 Click the blue hyperlinks to get more in-depth news.

Retracing Your Steps

This is a good place to stop for the first of several practice sessions in navigating America Online. You just saw how to click channel signposts on the main Channels window and on the miniature list at the left of each channel. Besides that, you also can travel these roads in reverse. Frequently when something is on your screen — in this case, a news story — you finish with it and want to get back to where you were, like the News channel window. As often is the case with AOL, there are several ways to do that. No one of them is the "right" one or the "best" one.

At the top of your screen on the toolbar are two arrow buttons directly below the Read icon. These are the Previous and Next buttons. **Previous** (the arrow that points to the left) can be clicked to go back to the window you were viewing before you made your last selection. **Next** (the arrow pointing to the right) is activated after you have used the Previous button at least once and allows you to backstep along a trail of previously viewed windows. The opposite of Previous, Next goes forward to the next window in a previously viewed series. To try them out, click the Previous button to remove the news story and return to the News channel.

Another useful navigation tool for retracing your steps also is on the toolbar. The *History Trail* keeps a list of all sites you have recently visited, enabling you to quickly return to any of them. Click the down arrow next to the white bar on the toolbar. Examine the drop-down list of recently visited sites. Highlight the page you wish to return to and click once. In a moment, AOL returns you to the requested page. To try this out, pull down the History Trail on your screen, find the AOL Today entry, and click it to move back to the first channel you visited.

TAKE NOTE

CLEARING OUT OLD HISTORY TRAIL ENTRIES

▶ The History Trail can be become a long list because it automatically stores sites visited on sessions prior to the current one. If you want to limit its records to the current session only, click My AOL ⇨ Preferences and click the Toolbar icon. In the resulting window, click the checkbox next to "Clear History Trail after each Sign Off or Switch Screen Name." Click OK to save your changes.

▶ Also on the Toolbar Preference window is an option to use previous and next navigation arrows to track open windows only. If you leave this option unchecked, you can go back to windows you've already closed. There is also a button that simply clears your history trail now (without resetting your Preferences).

CROSS-REFERENCE
For more information about setting your Preferences, also see Chapters 1, 2, 4, and 7.

FIND IT ONLINE
For History Trail help, click the Member Services icon on the Welcome window, click Find It Now, and enter **history trail** in the query box.

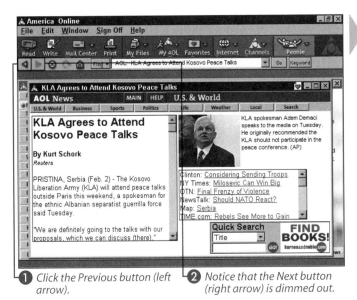

1 Click the Previous button (left arrow).

2 Notice that the Next button (right arrow) is dimmed out.

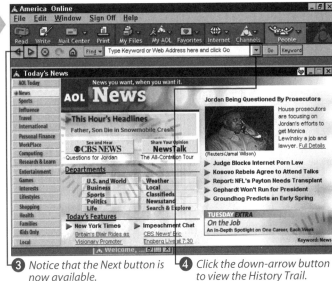

3 Notice that the Next button is now available.

4 Click the down-arrow button to view the History Trail.

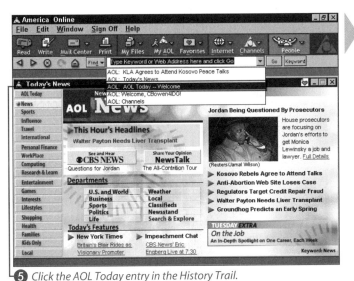

5 Click the AOL Today entry in the History Trail.

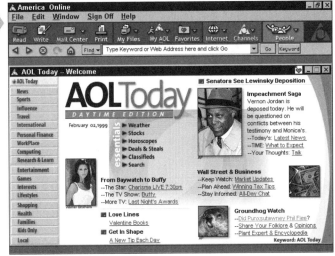

Using Keywords

Options in the previous section enable you to quickly retrace your steps online. What if you want to move ahead to a new window you haven't yet visited or just go back to one you have visited quicker? A navigational tool even bigger and better is ahead, completely independent of such buttons and History Trails.

Keywords are the transportation tool of choice for all savvy AOL members. Many pages throughout the massive America Online network have their own keywords — often more than one keyword, actually — operating like street addresses in a city. Only keywords are faster and easier. By knowing a page's keyword, you can jump right to it, bypassing scores of introductory pages and saving lots of time.

How to Use the Keyword Button

Keywords are such an important part of America Online that the new AOL version 4.0 software puts a Keyword option right on the toolbar at the top of screen. To use it, click the Keyword button on the toolbar to open a keyword window. In the "Enter word(s)" field, type the name of the AOL area you want to visit, such as AOL TODAY (for the AOL Today channel) or NEWS (for the News channel). Click the Go button to get under way.

To give this new concept a try, use the Keyword option to reach the next few stops on the Channels tour. For instance, the next stop is the Sports channel and its keyword is SPORTS. So, click the Keyword button, type **SPORTS** in the resulting window, and click Go (or just press Enter).

TAKE NOTE

▶ **HOW THIS BOOK LISTS KEYWORDS**

Throughout this book, keywords are listed in parentheses, as in (KEYWORDS). While the book uses all capital letters to set keywords apart from the rest of the text, you don't have to enter them in all caps. America Online's keywords are not case sensitive. Nor are they space sensitive, which means KEY WORDS would work fine too.

▶ **MULTIPLE DESTINATIONS**

In a few cases, the same keyword applies to more than one area of the system. If this happens, you are presented with a window displaying possible destinations. Click the icon or link to go to the site you want to visit.

▶ **CONTINUING THE TOUR WITH THE SPORTS CHANNEL**

This is the AOL Sports desk, for news, scores, statistics, discussion groups, and upcoming events. Standing departments are devoted to all major competitions, including basketball, baseball, football, golf, auto racing, tennis, with separate sections for professional and college sports and breaking news from the sports world. Also, don't miss the Grandstand, where fans talk, write, and at times, yell about the latest happenings on and off the field, court, rink, ring, and track.

CROSS-REFERENCE

For more information about AOL's Sports channel, see Chapter 8.

FIND IT ONLINE

You can get more background on the use of keywords from the system itself. From the menu bar, click Help ➪ Help with Keywords .

Watching for Keywords

Most pages on America Online list their keywords in the bottom-right corner of the screen. As you explore AOL, take note of the keywords associated with your areas of interest. Then when you want to return to that area, you can get there directly by using the keyword. Consider keywords one of the ultimate shortcuts to AOL features and Internet Web sites as well.

Fortunately, the keywords for most of the channels are the same as the channel names themselves. The keyword for the Shopping channel is SHOPPING, while the keyword for Personal Finance is PERSONAL FINANCE.

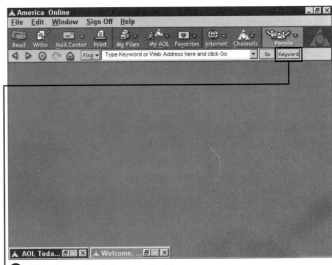

1 *Click the toolbar's Keyword button.*

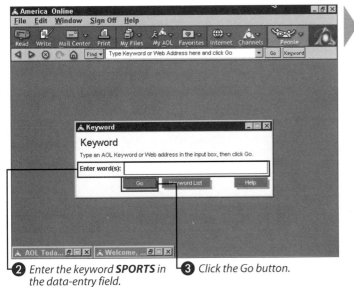

2 *Enter the keyword **SPORTS** in the data-entry field.* **3** *Click the Go button.*

4 *Notice the keyword for this page is listed in the lower-right corner.*

Learning Keyword Shortcuts

In addition to the Keyword button, there are handy shortcuts for entering keywords. For instance, besides clicking the Keyword icon, you also can enter keywords directly into the toolbar. Just click your mouse on the long, white data field beside the toolbar, which highlights the words currently there, type your desired keyword, and then either click Go or press Enter.

Also, you can quickly summon the Keyword window with a keyboard shortcut. Ctrl+K (hold down the Ctrl key and press the letter K) does the trick. Try this shortcut on the some of these stops as well.

On the next eight stops of the tour, you sample each Keyword method we've learned. The next site is the Influence channel, which has the keyword of INFLUENCE. Click the data field in the toolbar, enter the word **influence** and either press Enter or click Go. This brings you to the screen shown in the upper-left window on the facing page. Now follow along with the listed steps to reach the other windows.

TAKE NOTE

CONTINUING THE TOUR

▶ Influence channel. If the News channel is AOL's news section and the Sports channel is the sports page, then the Influence channel (keyword: INFLUENCE) is the system's combined editorial page and gossip column. Come here for

commentary and opinion, but also for personality profiles and celebrity happenings. It also has lively columns on arts and leisure, media and money, dining, and the general pursuit of The Good Life.

▶ The Travel channel (keyword: TRAVEL) enables you to make airline reservations, search for hotels and restaurants, talk to other travelers, and receive various on-the-road tips. Also come here when you are bargain hunting for travel ideas. A classified ad section specializes in travel-related subjects. Can't find what you're looking for on the menus? Try the Search & Explore option for specific requests.

▶ The International channel (keyword: INTERNATIONAL) serves armchair travelers and students, as well as those who are actually on their way for far-flung ports of call. It provides the day's top international news headlines and links to world business information, data on international cultures, and statistics on countries of the world. You'll also find international travel suggestions and miscellaneous material, such as religious information, photos from various countries, even music and recipes.

▶ The Personal Finance channel (keywords: PERSONAL FINANCE or MONEY), serves up stock market data, help with taxes, investment research, and income-planning strategies. Also see its resources on mutual funds, real estate, insurance, and banking. It also has resources for recording your own portfolio to facilitate quick lookup of a number of stocks.

CROSS-REFERENCE

For more information about AOL's Travel and International channels, see Chapter 9.

FIND IT ONLINE

Visit the Personal Finance channel (keyword: PERSONAL FINANCE) and click Search & Explore under its listing of departments.

1. Click the text-entry field in the toolbar and enter the keyword **TRAVEL**.

2. Click the Go button to move to the Travel page.

3. Click the text-entry field and enter the keyword **INTERNATIONAL**.

4. Press the Enter key to reach the next stop.

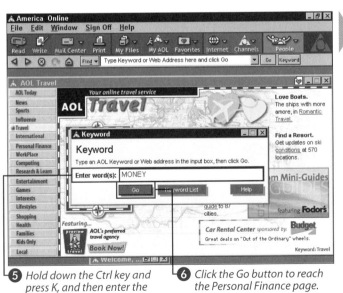

5. Hold down the Ctrl key and press K, and then enter the keyword **MONEY**.

6. Click the Go button to reach the Personal Finance page.

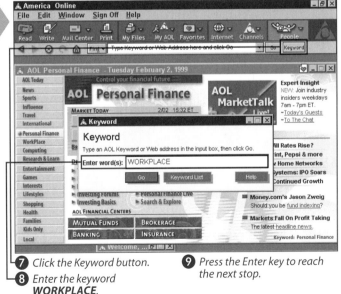

7. Click the Keyword button.

8. Enter the keyword **WORKPLACE**.

9. Press the Enter key to reach the next stop.

Summarizing the Keyword Options

Before we tackle another major navigational aid, get comfortable with the tools you've just met. To do that, practice with them on the next half-dozen channels on the tour. For each of the following sites I show you in this section, simply choose a different one of the navigation methods you have learned so far:

▶ Click the appropriate button on the left side of the window.

▶ Click the Keyword button and enter the site's keyword in the resulting window. (For the next six stops on our AOL tour, the keyword is the same as the site's name. In other words, to go to the WorkPlace channel use the keyword: **WORKPLACE**, or to reach the Computing channel, enter **COMPUTING**.) Remember to click the Go button or press the Enter key.

▶ Click the data field in the toolbar, enter the keyword there, and click the Go button or press the Enter key.

▶ Press Ctrl+K to reach the Keyword window, enter the keyword, and click the Go button or press the Enter key.

Remember, also, to stretch your wings by moving back and forth between previously visited pages with both the Previous and Next buttons on the left side of the toolbar. Practice using the History Trail list, which can be dropped down with the down-arrow button on the right side of the toolbar.

TAKE NOTE

▶ NEXT STOPS ON THE TOUR

▶ WorkPlace (keyword: WORKPLACE) is your online job center and employment counseling service. Whether you are looking for a first job, a better position, or just trying to get more out of the current job, this is the place to click for employment tools and services. Linked from here are professional forums, business research services, message boards, and a collection of career research tools.

▶ Computing (keyword: COMPUTING) links to all that wonderful technical knowledge you expect from the computer information service. Here is everything about your computer and its peripherals, along with answers to computer-specific questions regarding America Online. You can buy computer equipment and supplies here, too. The page includes downloadable computer software, a computer-oriented help desk, a newsstand of computer magazines with articles online, and message boards that cater to computer topics. Want to brush up on your technical knowledge? You can even sign up for online courses.

▶ Research & Learn (keyword: RESEARCH & LEARN) is the America Online reference desk, with encyclopedias, dictionaries, phone directories, and guides of all kinds. Links are provided to let you explore by subjects, such as history, science, education, business, health, geography, and language arts. And if you are in school and need some homework help, don't miss the popular Ask a Teacher service.

CROSS-REFERENCE

For more information about AOL's Computing channel, see Chapter 11.

FIND IT ONLINE

To get further background on AOL's educational services, visit the Search & Explore area of Research & Learn (keyword: RLSEARCH).

Finding the Keyword List

At least 10,000 keywords are used on America Online, and the number is growing daily. It isn't exactly practical, then, to want to print out the entire list for bedtime reading. Still, there are times when you may want to browse the list online, and AOL is happy to accommodate. To reach the latest list of AOL keywords, click the Keyword button and enter the keyword KEYWORD. (Alternatively, you also can click the Keyword List button at the bottom of the Keyword entry window.) A scrollable display lists the keywords either alphabetically or by channel. Double-click the part of the list you want to see. If you want to print that portion of the list, click the toolbar's Print icon.

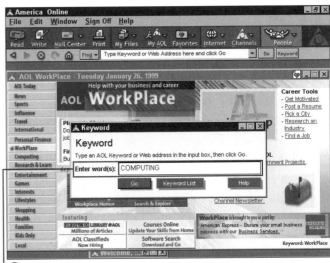

① *Press Ctrl+K, type the keyword* **COMPUTING**, *and press Enter.*

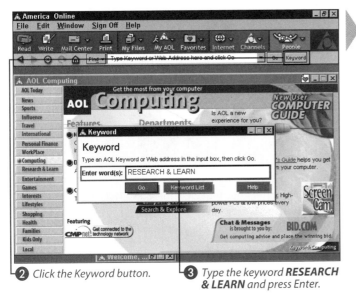

② *Click the Keyword button.*   ③ *Type the keyword* **RESEARCH & LEARN** *and press Enter.*

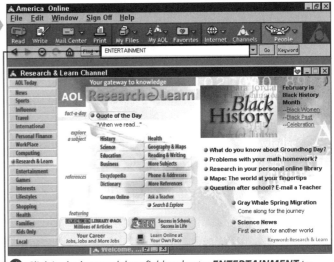

④ *Click in the keyword data field and enter* **ENTERTAINMENT** *to reach the next site.*

Creating and Using Favorite Places

As great as keywords are for instant navigation of the enormous America Online system, it quickly becomes a nuisance having to type them in each time you want to revisit a particular page or site. That is why the next great innovation in AOL navigation has been the automatic storage and retrieval of keywords and other addresses in the form of a feature called *Favorite Places*.

Favorite Places enables you to mark and return to sites on America Online (and on the Internet's World Wide Web) that interest you without having to enter a keyword. This service is as simple as visiting the site you like and clicking a special icon. To use, navigate to the site you want to save, using any of the navigation tools discussed earlier, and click the heart-shaped icon that appears in the upper-right side of the window's title bar. The system then acknowledges the Favorite Place request and asks if you want to either add the site to your Favorites, insert it in an Instant Message, or insert it in Mail.

Once a site has been saved in your Favorite Places list, you can return to it easily in one of two ways. First, you can click the toolbar's Favorites icon and select Favorite Places from the subsequent drop-down menu. In the resulting window, your marked sites are shown with hearts to the left of their names. Alternatively, you can click the site you want to visit and then either click the Go button or just press the Enter key.

You also can quickly remove a Favorite Place by calling up your list (as you see in the screen in the lower right), highlighting it, and clicking the Delete button.

TAKE NOTE

CONTINUING THE TOUR

Entertainment (keyword: ENTERTAINMENT) is the playground for those interested in television, movies, music, stage, and books. You find the latest reviews, and you can even become your own critic, right here. And check out the Entertainment Asylum for the latest news and near-news of the entertainment world. Also, the site specializes in today's hot news from Hollywood, Broadway, Nashville, and other entertainment capitals.

USE PRELOADED FAVORITES PLACES

The AOL version 4 software also comes with a great collection of preloaded Favorite Places of special interest to new users. To explore these picks, select the toolbar's Favorites icon and select the Favorite Places option at the top. Now double-click any of the folders (About AOL, Member Exclusives, Meeting People & Staying in Touch, and AOL's Top Picks) and you are shown additional selections. Each has the characteristic heart symbol to indicate it is a Favorite Place. Click the heart to highlight it and then click the Go button or press Enter to visit the site.

CROSS-REFERENCE

For more information about AOL's Entertainment channel, see Chapter 13.

FIND IT ONLINE

Visit the Member Services area (keyword: HELP), click the Find It Now option, and enter **favorite places** in the resulting query box.

1 Click the heart in the upper right of the window.

2 Click Add to Favorites.

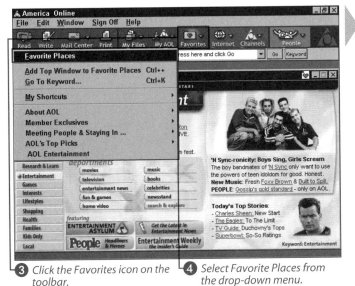

3 Click the Favorites icon on the toolbar.

4 Select Favorite Places from the drop-down menu.

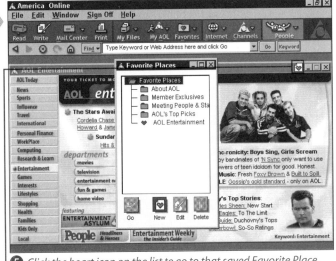

5 Click the heart icon on the list to go to that saved Favorite Place.

Reviewing All Navigation Tools

To practice with the navigation tools, including the Favorite Places options, I'll wrap up with a review of all major go-there options. And you have some of the best channels yet to come on this tour, neighborhoods devoted to fun and family, health, and more. Take your time as you explore these last areas and look for features you can add to your Favorite Places list.

More about Favorite Places

Your Favorite Places collection is not limited to only the main Channel pages we are seeing here. On the contrary, any window that has a tiny heart in the title bar — which is virtually all AOL windows — can be marked for your Favorite Places.

And there are some interesting additional uses for Favorite Places. For example, if you have found an interesting place on America Online (or the Internet's World Wide Web), why not share it with friends through e-mail? If you place a hyperlink reference in your letter, the reader can click the link and go directly to the information you have found, right as they are reading your e-mail.

To add a hyperlink to your e-mail, click the toolbar's Write icon to compose your letter as usual and then click the heart icon on the Write window's style toolbar (located above the message field). Now find the Favorite Places folder that contains the hyperlink you want to add. Another menu appears showing the hyperlinks in that folder. Click the hyperlink to add it to the e-mail.

By the way, if you are online while you are writing this letter, you also can just drag the heart icon from the title bar of any AOL window to your e-mail.

TAKE NOTE

▶ WRAPPING UP THE TOUR

▶ AOL Games (keyword: GAMES) lets you play online, alone or with friends, and you also can read up on the latest hot trends in cool computing adventures and simulations. The channel is divided into departments covering video games, computer games, the games store, and a newsstand featuring related magazines and online articles.

▶ Interests (keyword: INTERESTS) covers the complex issues of daily life, such as where to find just the right recipe, how to finance or fix the car, and how to make those home repairs and still keep your marriage intact.

▶ Lifestyles (keyword: LIFESTYLES) delves into the entire spectrum of human relations, from teens and seniors to beliefs, from romance to the end of romance, from ethics to self-improvement.

▶ Shopping (keyword: SHOPPING) caters to the bargain-hunter in all of us, dedicated to the great adventure of buying and selling. AOL has built a remarkable digital shopping mall with some of the top retail names, and they're ready to do business with you.

CROSS-REFERENCE

For more information about AOL's Interests and Lifestyles channels, see Chapter 14.

FIND IT ONLINE

To get additional information on the Games channel, visit its Search & Explore section (keyword: GAMES SEARCH).

1 Click the Interests button on the left of the window to reach the Interests channel.

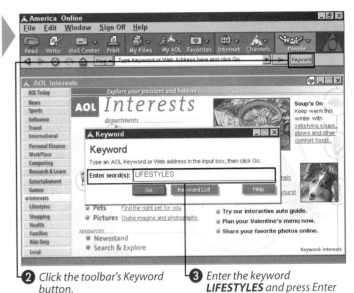

2 Click the toolbar's Keyword button.

3 Enter the keyword **LIFESTYLES** and press Enter to reach the next stop.

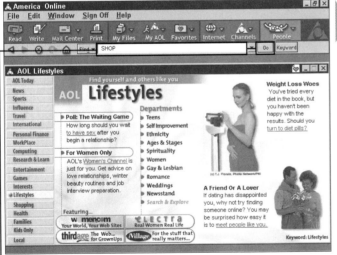

4 Click into the text-entry field, enter **SHOP**, and click Go to reach the Shopping channel.

5 Press Ctrl+K, type **HEALTH** in the resulting window, and press Enter to reach the next site.

Summarizing the Navigation Tools

Here are the AOL navigation tools you learned in this chapter:

▶ **Links.** These "clickable" portions of screens — underlined, highlighted words, pictures, buttons, and icons — connect to features elsewhere on the system.

▶ **Previous and Next buttons.** Located on the left side of the toolbar beneath the Read icon. They are used to retrace your steps, revisiting previously viewed AOL pages.

▶ **History Trail.** Viewed by clicking the down arrow next to the data-entry field in the middle of the toolbar, it lists all recently visited pages. Click the one to which you want to return.

▶ **Keywords.** The best of the navigation tools, keywords take you directly to features, often bypassing scores of windows and menus. To enter a keyword, either (1) type it in the text-entry field in the middle of the toolbar and click the Go button, (2) click the Keyword icon and enter it in the resulting Keyword window, or (3) press Ctrl+K and enter the word in the subsequent window.

▶ **Favorites Places.** Enhancing the keyword concept, this features lets you collect and store the locations of the pages you like the best. To save a site as a Favorite Place, click the heart icon that appears in the left side of a window's title bar. To revisit a stored site, click the toolbar's Favorites icon, choose Favorite Places from the drop-down menu, and on the resulting list, double click the site you want to see.

TAKE NOTE

▶ **THE TOUR'S LAST FOUR STOPS**

▶ Health (keyword: HEALTH) talks about subjects ranging from serious illnesses like heart disease and cancer to alternative medicines and self-help.

▶ Families (keyword: FAMILIES) provides help for parenting, with sections devoted to new moms and dads, kids, and teens.

▶ Kids Only (keyword: KIDS ONLY) is a special corner for youngsters, where they can find old favorites such as Disney Adventures and newcomers.

▶ Local (keyword: DIGITAL CITY) gives you local information about what is going on in communities all across the U.S., from Seattle, San Francisco, and Los Angeles to Boston, New York, and Philadelphia and dozens of communities in between.

CROSS-REFERENCE

For more about AOL's health- and family-related services, see Chapter 16.

FIND IT ONLINE

To find out what U.S. and international cities have online extensions on AOL, visit the Digital Cities channel (keyword: LOCAL) and click the City Index button under its departments.

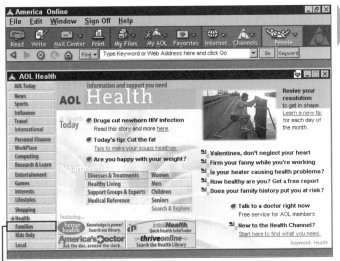

1 Click the Families button.

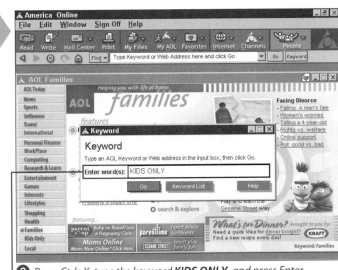

2 Press Ctrl+K, type the keyword **KIDS ONLY**, and press Enter.

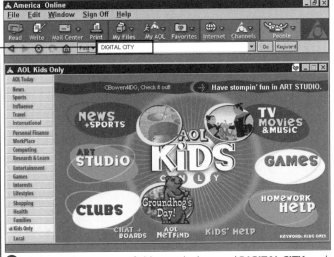

3 Click into the text-entry field, type the keyword **DIGITAL CITY**, and press Enter.

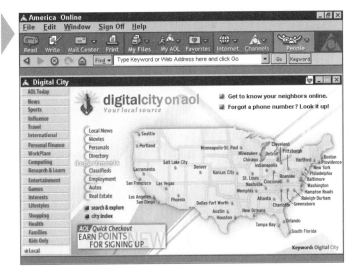

Searching with AOL Find

Entire books have been written just about the thousands of features on AOL. Some focus only on keywords. Earlier in this chapter, you saw how to search the super list of keywords right online (reaching the page with the keyword of KEYWORD). But being a smart traveler online means not relying so much on lists, but rather learning how to find the features you need as you need them.

Find Central (keyword: FIND CENTRAL) is America Online's bureau of missing persons, places, and things. Come to this diverse utility to search for AOL services and features, sites on the Internet's World Wide Web, screen names of other AOL members you can write e-mail to, online events, software you can retrieve, online yellow page listings in which you can search for goods and services, and electronic classified ads. You can use this multifaceted feature often during these chapters and later, as you tackle different subjects.

For now, the subject is finding AOL features. To use it, sign on to the network as always with the Sign On option on the menu bar. Navigate to Find Central by either entering the keyword FIND CENTRAL, clicking the Find icon on the left side of the toolbar and selecting Find Central from the resulting drop-drop menu, or going to the Channels window and clicking the Find option.

In the data field of AOL Find, type words or phrases that describe your subject. Click the Find button, located on the right of the data entry field. AOL then produces a new window listing the features that match your query. Scroll the list to examine the selections and double-click any that seem interesting. AOL offers a description of the area you have chosen, complete with a "hot list" (key features of the area), a full synopsis, and the keyword.

If, after you have read the description, you are interested in seeing the feature itself, click the Go There button at the bottom of the window.

TAKE NOTE

▶ AOL FIND IS AVAILABLE ON THE TOOLBAR

AOL Find is so useful that it also is on the toolbar. Click the Find button at the left side of the toolbar and notice that Find it On AOL is listed on the drop-down menu.

▶ GUIDE TO CHANNELING

AOL Find brings us full circle with the Channel Guide (keyword: CHANNEL GUIDE), a comprehensive directory of every area in each channel. When you just want to browse by subject, the Channel Guide provides simple, no-nonsense links to related areas.

CROSS-REFERENCE
For more about searching AOL databases, see Appendix A.

FIND IT ONLINE
To get additional help from the system in using search features, visit Member Services (HELP) and click the Using Search & Find option on the resulting list.

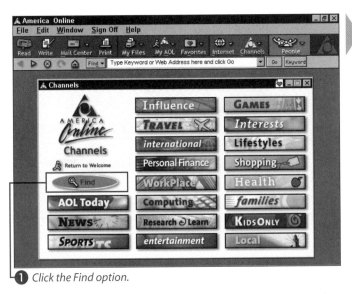

❶ Click the Find option.

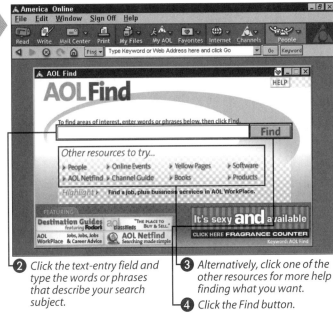

❷ Click the text-entry field and type the words or phrases that describe your search subject.

❸ Alternatively, click one of the other resources for more help finding what you want.

❹ Click the Find button.

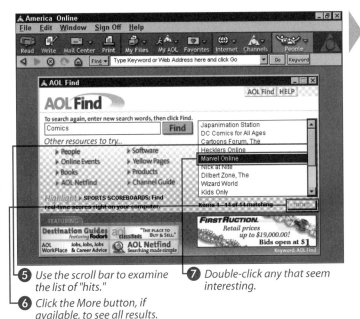

❺ Use the scroll bar to examine the list of "hits."

❻ Click the More button, if available, to see all results.

❼ Double-click any that seem interesting.

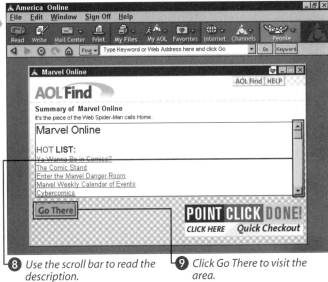

❽ Use the scroll bar to read the description.

❾ Click Go There to visit the area.

Personal Workbook

Q&A

1 What are at least two ways to enter a keyword?

_____

_____

_____

2 What does the History Trail feature do?

_____

_____

_____

3 Which channel would you visit if you were interested learning how to cook dishes from other countries?

_____

_____

_____

4 How do you save a page as a Favorite Place?

_____

_____

_____

5 What do you do to return to one of your Favorite Places?

_____

_____

6 What is the fastest way to go back to the page you were viewing just before the current one?

_____

_____

_____

7 What are at least two ways to get to the AOL's Find Central to search for keywords?

_____

_____

_____

8 Bonus Question: What is the keyword for the AOL's list of keywords?

_____

_____

ANSWERS: PAGE 336

EXTRA PRACTICE

1 With AOL Find (keyword: AOL FIND), search for HUMOR and note the number of features it found (often called "hits").

2 Now search for COMICS and note the difference in the number of hits.

3 After you have visited a few sites you've found through AOL Find, retry the Previous and Next buttons to move back and forth through previously viewed pages.

4 Finally, there's a familiar alternative to the Previous button. AOL screens are like any other cascade of Windows or Mac windows — you can remove (close) the latest window by simply clicking the *X* (or *close box*) in the upper right of the title bar.

REAL-WORLD APPLICATIONS

✔ If you don't how to spell a particular keyword, just take your best guess. AOL might be able to sort out what you are trying to spell. If the word you enter in the Keyword window is not actually a keyword, AOL reports the problem but may also display several keywords that approximately match what you entered. If you find what you are really looking for in the list, double-click the correct keyword and the system takes you to that page.

✔ America Online's search engines, including AOL Find, are not case sensitive (capitalization does not matter). Also, to speed up searching, you can leave out articles such as *a*, *an*, and *the*. They don't add anything to your searches.

Visual Quiz

How would you reach a display like this one? (Hint: It was the result of a navigational technique you learned earlier in this chapter.) Also, how could you use this display to reach yet another page on AOL?

_____

_____

_____

_____

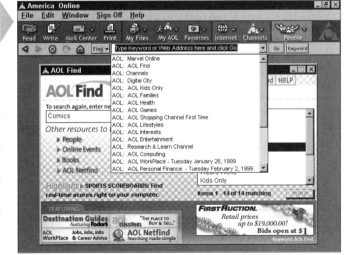

PART

II

Going Online Like a Pro

The chapters in this part cover America Online's more advanced features. These are the ones you probably have come to AOL for, from online chatting to the World Wide Web and other areas of the Internet.

The topics covered in these chapters involve how to automate AOL to get the most out of your time and money, and how to let the AOL version 4.0 software be your online assistant, keeping your records and storing your files for you. The Internet can be somewhat intimidating, but America Online makes it easy to glean information from the Web and newsgroups without getting lost. The Address Book, Member Directory, and Personal Filing Cabinet provide the necessary organization any newcomer needs.

This section of the book builds up to the concept of AOL channel navigation. The tools you master in this part — from searching databases to writing online text — will be put to greater use in Part III as you begin to explore each AOL channel in depth.

CHAPTER 4

Chatting Online

In the late 1970s, more than a decade before there even was an America Online, real-time conferencing already had been added to those primitive early computer networks. As one cyberspace pioneer told me, "We patterned it after CB (a tribute to the citizens band radio craze sweeping the nation at the time), and we thought it would be just an interest diversion." Most online systems in those days were largely populated by computer professionals and serious hobbyists more interested in online programming tools than chatting it up by keyboard. It was not unusual, the old pro said, to be logged on to the new conferencing area for an hour or more, just waiting for someone to come along and talk. Finally a message like this might appear:

    (FRED:) WHAT KIND EQUIP U USE?

Such clipped messages, mostly technical in nature, were the pre-AOL equivalent of "What hath God wrought?"

Many things indeed. Today you won't find a time, day or night, when someone isn't chatting on America Online. Usually, it is a great *many* somebodies, from all around the world. And the conversations are hardly limited to technical topics. Nowadays, tens of thousands of people captivated by the simple elegance of this powerful medium trip through AOL's People Connection chat rooms daily (and nightly). They talk about everything under the sun (and moon), coming to the People Connection to meet new people, to hang out with old friends, to visit with family, even to make business deals.

No wonder chat is among the most popular features on America Online today. The system has taken a simple idea — talking keyboard to keyboard with friends and strangers alike — and enabled it to evolve into a sophisticated medium that can accommodate all kinds of public and private conversations. The same resource that enables lovers to whisper sweet nothings in an out-of-the-way corner of cyberspace also facilitates public debates on politics, private meetings on business matters, and online classes on just about anything. In fact, there's no limit to what a chat room can inspire.

Getting Started in the Chat World

This chapter shows you not only how to talk the talk, but also how to use the many other features of the People Connection. You can join public chats already in progress, both those hosted by AOL volunteers as well as those operated by your fellow AOL members. You can enter private invitation-only chats. You can use search facilities to find interesting ongoing chats. You can create your own public and private chat rooms on any subject you choose. You can customize the system further by setting Preferences for chat and related features. You can keep tabs on your friends, new and old, and learn when and where to find them online. You can use Instant Messages to whisper with fellow Net surfers elsewhere in cyberspace. And there's more! It is all happening 24 hours a day, seven days a week in the People Connection.

Reaching the People Connection

All this chatting around the clock has made the People Connection one of AOL's most popular features, which is why it is one of the three services (along with e-mail and channels) accessible from the Welcome window that greets you upon sign-on. And that is not the only way to reach the feature. By the time you reach the end of the chapter, you will have mastered the art and science of the chat room.

To enter the People Connection, sign on to the system as usual and then either enter keyword: PEOPLE, click the People Connection icon at the bottom of the left column in the Welcome window (as shown on the facing page), or click the People icon on the toolbar and then select People Connection from the drop-down menu.

TAKE NOTE

THREE KINDS OF CHATS

America Online hosts different kinds of chats in its massive People Connection area:

▶ Featured chats. These public online forums are open 24 hours a day. Many of these chats are hosted by volunteers, called *hosts*, who greet members and strive to keep conversations in the chat room running smoothly. Topics vary greatly, depending on the forum. You will see how to search hundreds of featured chats by selecting the Find a Chat button on the main People Connection window.

▶ Member chats. These are named and created by AOL members themselves and are listed under the Member Chat categories in People Connection's Find a Chat area. You can participate in any member chat that strikes your fancy. Some of the chat world's most popular featured chats began as member chats.

▶ Private chats. These are member-created chats that are available by invitation only, though anyone can open one for themselves. Private chats are not listed anywhere in public view, offering AOL members a place for private meetings.

CROSS-REFERENCE

For more information about passwords, see Chapter 1.

FIND IT ONLINE

For assorted online articles about password maintenance, visit the Member Services area (keyword: HELP), click the Find it Now option, and enter **password** in the query box.

Storing Your Password

Getting tired of having to type your password each time you sign on? You can save time by storing your password in the software. To do that, click the toolbar's My AOL icon, select Preferences from the drop-down menu, and click the Passwords icon. Now just type your password in the indicated data-entry field. Click to place a check mark in the box labeled Sign On.

Now when you sign off the system and sign on again, the software supplies the system with your password automatically.

While this feature is a time-saver, use it with caution. Anyone with entry to your computer can sign on with your screen name and wreak havoc.

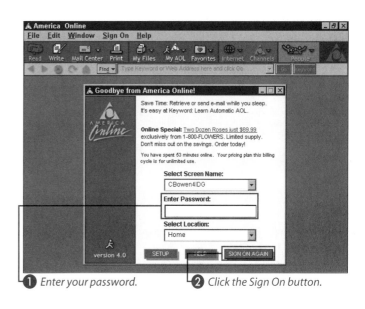

❶ Enter your password.   ❷ Click the Sign On button.

❸ Click the People Connection icon.

❹ Click the Find a Chat option.

Finding a Chat By Browsing

The People Connection's Find a Chat area is the central resource for all of America Online's chat rooms. Here you can browse and join featured and member chats, start your own member chat, and enter a private chat. You can also look through a list of scheduled chats and search a database of specific chats to find one that meets your interests.

The important Find a Chat window has two modes of operation to facilitate your chat browsing. When you first open the Find a Chat window, AOL displays a current list of featured chat categories and their associated chats. If, instead, you want to view the member chat categories, click the Member Chats button in the center of the window.

How to Browse Chats

To browse, select, and visit a chat, first select the mode of display you wish to use by clicking either the Featured Chats or Member Chats button at the top of the Find a Chat window. Now, use the scroll bar on the Categories box at the left of the Find a Chat window to examine the categories. Highlight a category and click View (or just double-click) to bring up a directory of chat rooms for that category, listed in the box to the right. You may need to click the More button below the list box to see all the chat rooms in a category.

Numbers to the left of the chat names indicate how many people are currently in that particular chat room. To see the screen names of each individual in a given chat room, highlight the chat in the list and click the Who's Chatting button below it.

To move to one of the chat rooms, highlight the name and then click the Go Chat button.

TAKE NOTE

CHAT ROOMS HAVE A LIMITED SIZE

If you try to visit a chat that is full — chat rooms have a 23-person limit — America Online displays a message asking if you want to be sent to a similar room. Click Yes to enter a similar chat room, or click No to select another room. You may continue trying to enter the full chat room — with patience, you should eventually be able to enter when another chatter leaves and a "seat" becomes available.

CHAT NOW IS RANDOM CHATS FOR THE ADVENTUROUS

If you are in the mood to chat but don't want to go to the trouble of locating a specific chat room through the Find a Chat window, you can click the Chat Now button in the main People Connection window. America Online picks an available chat room and tosses you in. It is not recommended for first-timers, but it can be fun for those who want to use People Connection as a global cocktail party.

CROSS-REFERENCE

A more formal version of chats is in use in many of AOL's forums. For information, see Chapter 6.

FIND IT ONLINE

For a general online overview of the People Connection feature, visit the main window (keyword: PEOPLE) and then click the Help button.

Categories of Chats

America Online creates and maintains the categories of chat rooms available for both the featured chats and the member chats. Some samples are:

▶ Town Square is for casual, impromptu chats.
▶ Arts and Entertainment is for books and movies, music and plays, and television and games.
▶ Friends is for like-minded people drawn to chats with names such as Cheers, Disaffected, Doers, Duuuude, Extremes, and Hey Girlfriend.
▶ Life is for chats by people who define themselves by their age or activities.
▶ News, Sports, and Finance is home to many a heated debate on current issues.

1 Click the Find a Chat option.

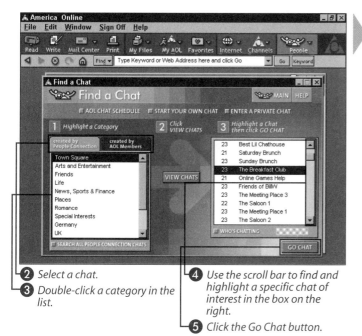

2 Select a chat.

3 Double-click a category in the list.

4 Use the scroll bar to find and highlight a specific chat of interest in the box on the right.

5 Click the Go Chat button.

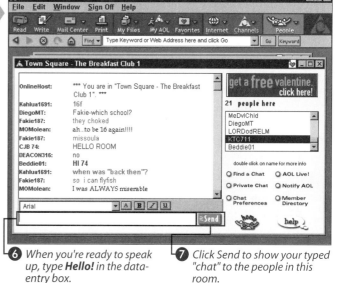

6 When you're ready to speak up, type **Hello!** in the data-entry box.

7 Click Send to show your typed "chat" to the people in this room.

Searching for Chats of Interest

The sheer number of categories and chats available on AOL is staggering. Finding the perfect chat can be next to impossible if you only browse category by category and chat by chat. In answer to this dilemma, AOL recently introduced an option that lets you search for a chat topic that matches your mood and interests.

To begin your search for the perfect chat, click the Search Featured Chats button on the Find a Chat window (seen in the lower left of the previous page). In the resulting query box, enter a word or words to begin the search. Separate words with *OR* to find chats that match at least one of the words. To filter out chats that contain a word, precede it with *NOT*. When ready, click the Search button below the data-entry field. In a moment, the system lists all chats and AOL Live events that match your query.

To learn more about one of the chats you found, highlight its name and then click the View Description button. These short descriptions give you a general idea of the topic, scope, and attitude of a chat. To enter that chat room, click the Go Chat button at the bottom of the description.

Viewing the Chat Schedule

The top featured chats — those featuring celebrities and newsmakers, for instance — are listed on a public schedule that is accessible from the Find a Chat window. To use it, click the Featured Chats Schedule on the lower-right side of the Find a Chat window. The resulting window invites you to select the chat schedule for today, this week, or special events, and to specify whether you are looking for morning, afternoon, or evening events. Click a chat that interests you to see a further description.

TAKE NOTE

▶ **AOL LIVE**

Chatting isn't just for the average Joe and Jane anymore. America Online has become the computer chat line to the stars, and a standing feature called *AOL Live* (keyword: LIVE) is the venue. This site offers nightly chats with actors and actresses, authors, famous attorneys, sports figures, and other celebrities.

AOL Live is designed for especially large groups of real-time talkers and listeners (up to 300 at a time). Structured events—speeches, panel discussions, roundtables, and so on—are scheduled in auditoriums, which are divided into two parts: the *stage*, where the hosts and guest speakers are, and the *chat rows*, where the audience "sits."

Special options in auditoriums enable those on the stage and in the audience to communicate. In general, audience chat is limited to the same chat row. If you find the chatter of other members distracting, you can use menu options to turn off the chat feature so that you see only the text that originates from those on the stage.

CROSS-REFERENCE

For more on entertainment features like AOL Live, see Chapter 13.

FIND IT ONLINE

To get more information online about finding chats, visit Member Services (keyword: HELP), click the Find it Now button, and enter **CHAT** as the search word.

A Window of Chat Opportunity

A special window is designed for chat communications in "real time."

▶ The largest portion of the window is reserved for the actual text of the chat. The first thing you see there is a message from OnlineHost, welcoming you to the chat room. (This is not a person, but a computer-generated message.) After that, the words from the real people begin to fill space.

▶ The bar just below the text box shows the typeface, color, and style (which you can change to add a bit of flair) currently used to format your chat text.

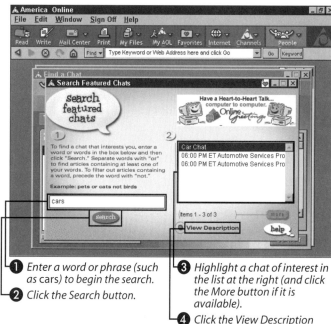

❶ Enter a word or phrase (such as cars) to begin the search.

❷ Click the Search button.

❸ Highlight a chat of interest in the list at the right (and click the More button if it is available).

❹ Click the View Description button.

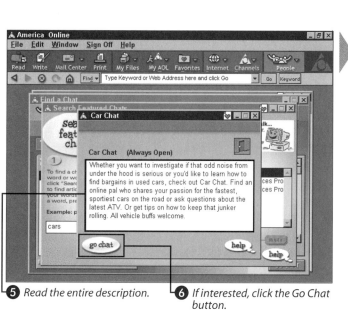

❺ Read the entire description.

❻ If interested, click the Go Chat button.

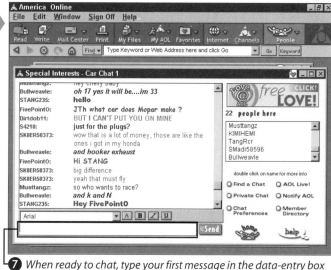

❼ When ready to chat, type your first message in the data-entry box and press the Enter key to send it.

Using Chat Window Options

Chat rooms are intimidating for many new arrivals. Conversations are all going on at once. Like a crowded room at a lively party, people may be communicating in groups of three and four, but their words add to the general din of the room. Whenever you enter a chat room, you land in the middle of a half-dozen ongoing discussions. And everyone already appears to know each other, while you feel as if you are sticking out like the ultimate outsider. Beyond that, some of the chat actually may be distasteful to you. Childish, provocative, raucous conversations are common in these freewheeling chat rooms. But there are options for civilizing the chat room.

Shutting Out the Noise

No matter how patient you are or how good you get at sorting out all the conversations going on at the same time in their weird shorthand, eventually you want to focus on selected talkers. It is never easy to carry on a good conversation with up to 23 people in the same chat room chiming in at the same time. That is why America Online added the Ignore option, so you can block out the comments of selected people in the chat room.

To block chat with the Ignore option, first examine the screen names of the participants listed in the box at the upper right of the window, using the scroll bar if necessary to look down the list. Double-click the name of the person you want to tune out. In the resulting window, AOL invites you to see that member's online profile, send him or her an Instant Message (a kind of electronic whisper I discuss later), or ignore him or her. Click the Ignore box, which places a check mark by the option.

Now you no longer "hear" (see) anything transmitted by that person in the chat room. If you decide you want to hear some of these people again, find their screen names in the box, double-click it, and remove the check mark beside the Ignore box.

TAKE NOTE

▶ **FINDING OUT MORE ABOUT YOUR COMPANIONS**

▶ After you have thinned out the herd a bit in order to concentrate on the conversations of a chosen few, you may find it useful to get some background on your fellow chat room visitors. Online profiles of many (but not all) AOL members are online, and they can be viewed during chats.

▶ To see them, start with the same steps you use with the Ignore option: Double-click the screen name of the person on whom you want background. This time, instead of clicking Ignore in the resulting window, click the Get Profile button.

▶ Online profiles list a member's screen names, location, birthday, marital status, hobbies, computer type, occupation, and more.

CROSS-REFERENCE

To learn about creating your own online profile, see Chapter 5.

FIND IT ONLINE

People Connection also has information on the chat lingo and on "netiquette." Visit the People Connection's Community Center (keyword: COMMUNITY CENTER) and select A Field Guide to People Connection.

Lurk and Learn the Lingo

Lurking, in chat room parlance, means waiting for a few minutes before you speak. This is the time-honored way of assessing whether you want to participate with these gathered talkers or click the Find a Chat button to seek out another venue.

After a few moments your mind sorts out the strands of the different conversations, zeroing in on the talkers' different tones and topics.

Not everyone loves a lurker. Sometimes one of the talkers already in the chat room may note your arrival and send you a public hello. It is polite for you to send back a simple "Hi."

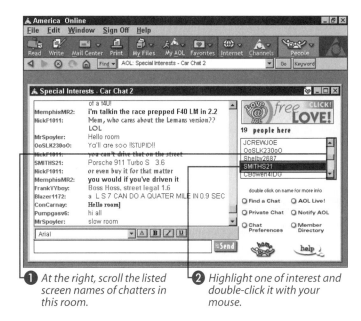

❶ At the right, scroll the listed screen names of chatters in this room.

❷ Highlight one of interest and double-click it with your mouse.

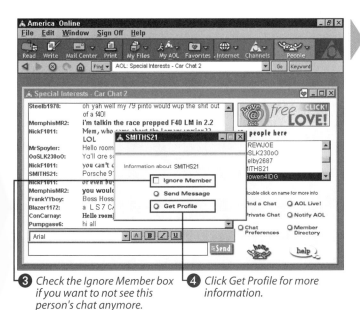

❸ Check the Ignore Member box if you want to not see this person's chat anymore.

❹ Click Get Profile for more information.

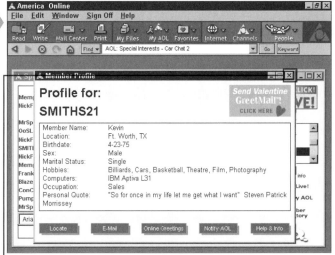

❺ When finished with the profile, click the X in the upper right to close the window.

Starting Your Own Chats

The People Connection offers a staggering array of chat rooms to choose from. Even so, you may not find your perfect chat listed among them. But rest assured the People Connection's popularity isn't due solely to the hundreds of featured and member chats already going on. You also can open your own chat room — as either a public facility or a private, invitation-only hideaway.

To create your own chat room, open the Find a Chat window and click the button labeled "Start Your Own Chat" on the right. Click the appropriate button to indicate the kind of chat room you want to open: *member chat* or *private chat*. Remember, a member chat is listed in the Find a Chat directory and other members are able to enter. If you select a member chat, you then are asked to choose a category name under which you wish your chat to be listed. Alternatively, you can choose a private chat that won't be listed anywhere. Other members can enter your private chat room only if they know the exact name.

You even get to name your new chat room. The chat name may contain numbers and/or letters, but it must begin with a number. You may not use punctuation marks or special characters (and it cannot contain vulgar language, of course). Once named, you can click the Go Chat button to enter your chat room. Your newly created chat room stays open as long as you or one of your visitors remains in it. If everyone leaves, the chat room closes (but can be created again if you wish).

Entering a Private Chat

If you have been invited to someone else's private chat, all you need to know is the name of the chat room and when you are expected to join. To reach the private chat, either click the Enter a Private Chat button on the Find a Chat window or, if you are already in a chat, click the Private Chat button at the right of the window. On the resulting window, enter the exact name of the private chat room. Click the Go Chat button and the room opens for you. If your party isn't already there, double-check your spelling of the room. Also keep in mind that you may have arrived before your party.

> **TAKE NOTE**
>
> **SHORTCUTS TO REACHING CHATS**
> Besides the People Connection window, the toolbar provides a shortcut to three important chat functions. Click the toolbar's People icon, and from the drop-down menu you can select Chat Now (to go directly to a randomly chosen chat room), Find a Chat (to browse and search chats), and Start Your Own Chat (to create a chat).

CROSS-REFERENCE
To learn more about AOL security issues, see the section on Parental Controls in Chapter 16.

FIND IT ONLINE
To get more information about safely chatting online, go to the People Connection (keyword: PEOPLE), click the Community Center option, and select A Field Guide to People Connection.

Calling the AOL Authorities

Occasionally you might witness chat room behavior you consider to be beyond mere rudeness, perhaps even a possible violation of the law. America Online makes it easy for you to report it to them.

To make a report, first get a copy of the questionable conversation by selecting the text and clicking Edit ⇨ Copy from the menu bar. Click the Notify AOL button at the right of the chat window (or go to keyword: NOTIFY AOL). Place the cursor in the box labeled Paste a Copy of the Chat Violation here. Click the mouse button once and then click Edit ⇨ Paste from the menu (or press Ctrl+V) to place the copied text in the box. Fill in the rest of the information in the form and click Send.

❶ Click Start Your Own Chat.

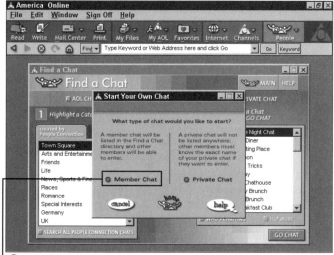

❷ Click Member Chat to create a public chat room (or Private Chat for an invisible chat room).

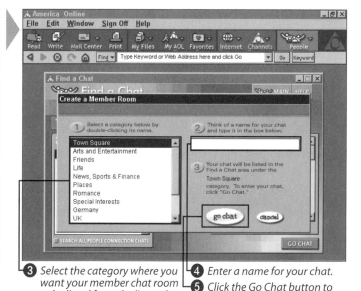

❸ Select the category where you want your member chat room to be listed from the list at the left.

❹ Enter a name for your chat.

❺ Click the Go Chat button to enter your new room.

Whispering with Instant Messages

How can you invite someone to a private chat without everyone else knowing the name of the chat room? E-mail is one way, if you and your friends or associates can plan in advance. But for those spur-of-the-moment private meetings, most America Online experts use the system's highly versatile system for electronic "whispering": *Instant Messages*.

Instant Messages — or *IMs* as they are known to their many fans — are private notes that can be sent to any AOL member who is currently signed on, regardless of whether he or she is in a chat room. Incoming Instant Messages are announced with a chime on the recipient's screen, along with an option for an easily entered reply.

Sending Instant Messages

To send an Instant Message, click the toolbar's People icon and select Instant Message, or use the Ctrl+I keyboard shortcut. Once the Send Instant Message window appears, enter the screen name of the person to whom you want to send your message in the top data-entry field. Be sure to type their exact screen name, spelled just as it appears in chat, e-mail, or their member profile.

You may click the Available? button to confirm that the person currently is signed on. If they are not, wait for another time. If your intended recipient is online, enter your message in the box at the bottom of the window and click Send. Note that as with e-mail and chat, you can use the formatting buttons to change the appearance of the text. The message appears on both the recipient's screen and your screen as a pop-up window.

If you receive an Instant Message, you can reply by clicking the Respond button at the bottom of the window. The system automatically extends the window, giving you the same data-entry space and formatting tools to write back. Write your message and click the Send button.

TAKE NOTE

WATCH OUT FOR PASSWORD THIEVES

It is a shame someone is always out to abuse a good thing, but Instant Messages sometimes are used to try to sucker new users out of their passwords. America Online officials *never* ask for your password online. If you receive an Instant Message—or a message in a chat room—asking for your password, it is a fraud.

INSTANT MESSAGES NOW CAN GO TO THE INTERNET

It used to be that Instant Messages could only be sent among America Online subscribers. Now, though, AOL lets you send IMs to non-AOL members who are on the Internet. Tell Internet friends to sign up for the free AOL Instant Messenger service at `http://www.newaol.com/aim`.

CROSS-REFERENCE

For more about other ways AOL interacts with the Internet, see Chapter 7.

FIND IT ONLINE

To get more information about using Instant Messages, select Show Me How from the People Connection window (or use keyword: SHOW ME HOW), and then select the Instant Message feature from the list.

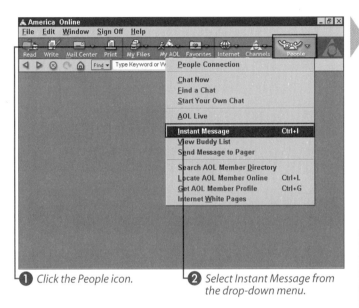

❶ Click the People icon.

❷ Select Instant Message from the drop-down menu.

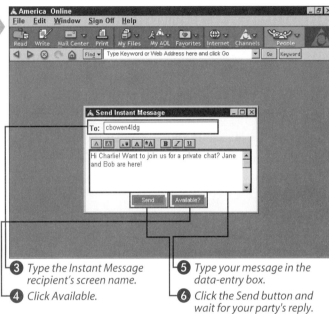

❸ Type the Instant Message recipient's screen name.

❹ Click Available.

❺ Type your message in the data-entry box.

❻ Click the Send button and wait for your party's reply.

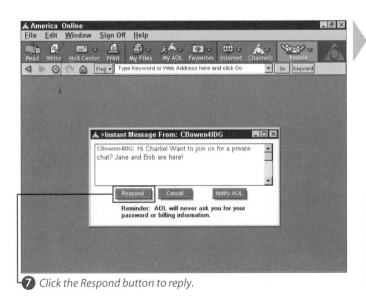

❼ Click the Respond button to reply.

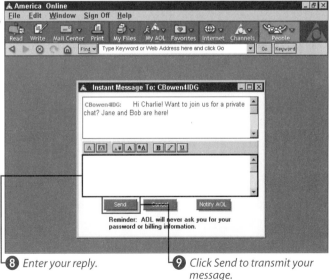

❽ Enter your reply.

❾ Click Send to transmit your message.

Tracking Friends with the Buddy List

All these real-time communication features depend on your knowing when your friends, family, and associates are online and available for chatting. AOL's *Buddy List* works hand-in-hand with Instant Messages because it enables you to watch for acquaintances to arrive on the system. Once you have the Buddy List set up, you can tell at a glance if any of your pals is online. The Buddy List also provides shortcuts to your favorite real-time chat features.

Setting Up the Buddy List

You can create as many lists as you like, or you can lump everyone into one great big Buddy List. To set a list up, click the toolbar's My AOL icon, select Buddy List from the drop-down menu, click the Create button, and follow the on-screen instructions. Be sure to click Save when finished to retain your changes. Other options on the Buddy List Setup window enable you to view, edit, and delete groups, as well as set preferences. Later you can return to the setup screen to make further additions and other changes to the Buddy List.

You can keep separate lists for business, school, friends, and other groups. You also can have a list devoted to friends with particular interests. For example, create a list called Hockey to record all your friends who are hockey fans. The Buddy List follows in each group with two numbers in parentheses (0/5);

the second number reports how many people are listed in the that group, and the first number tells how many are currently online. When one is currently present, the screen name is displayed, which you can highlight for action with one of the associated icons.

Your Buddy List also lets you find out what, if any, chat room a friend on the list is in by highlighting his or her name and clicking the Locate button. Or you can send an Instant Message to a friend by highlighting the screen name and clicking the IM icon. You can even invite all your Buddy List friends to a private chat room (handy for scheduling meetings with co-workers or parties with friends) by clicking the Buddy Chat icon.

TAKE NOTE

USING THE BUDDY LIST

When you first sign on, the Buddy List window automatically appears, telling you who in your groups currently is online. You can leave it open so you have a current, constantly updated list of all the people in your Buddy List groups who presently are online. Or you can close the window (by clicking the closebox in the right corner of the title bar). You can reopen your Buddy List at any time by clicking the toolbar's People icon and selecting View Buddy List, or by entering keyword: BUDDY VIEW.

CROSS-REFERENCE

If you missed the discussion on e-mail, backtrack to Chapter 2.

FIND IT ONLINE

For more help with setting up and using the Buddy List feature, enter keyword: BUDDY and then click the Help button on the resulting screen.

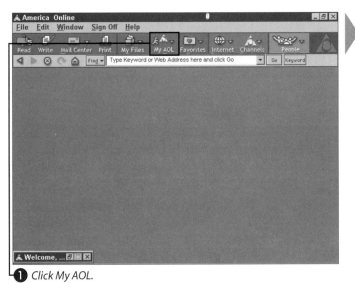

1 Click My AOL.

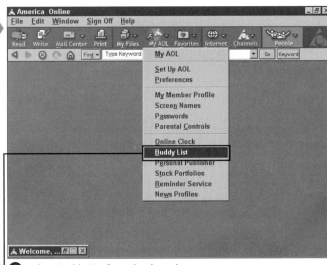

2 Select Buddy List from the drop-down menu.

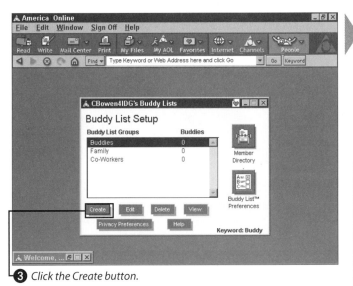

3 Click the Create button.

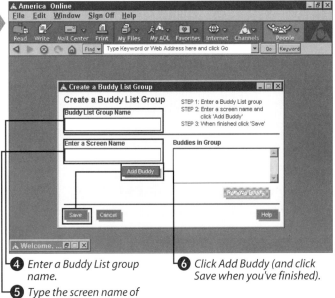

4 Enter a Buddy List group name.

5 Type the screen name of someone you want to add to the list.

6 Click Add Buddy (and click Save when you've finished).

Customizing the Buddy List

A whole new medium for communications is opened up in this chapter. Real-time communication — through public and private chat rooms, the digital whispering of Instant Messages, and the Buddy List — merge the power of the written word with the speed and spontaneity of the telephone. And the power doesn't stop there. You also can customize these options to better serve your needs.

Setting Your Privacy Preferences

Of course, wonderfully imaginative features such as the Buddy List and Instant Messages raise privacy concerns. Do you want anyone on the system to be able to know when you sign on and where you are chatting? Do you want to enable anyone to send you an Instant Message at any time you are online? The Privacy Preferences enable you to control who can contact you online.

To choose privacy settings, sign on to the system as usual and use the keyword BUDDY to reach the Buddy List Setup window and then click the Privacy Preferences button at the bottom of the window. You can choose from one of five scenarios listed at the top of the window:

▶ Allow contact with everyone, which is all AOL members and all Internet users who subscribe to the Instant Messenger service described earlier in the chapter.

▶ Block contact from Internet (Instant Messenger) users only.

▶ Block contact with only those people whose screen names you list in the data box at the right of the window.

▶ Allow contact with only those whose screen names you list in the box.

▶ Block contact with all AOL and Internet users.

The Sound Library

To play Buddy List sounds and other sound-enabled AOL features, you must download and execute the Buddy List Sound Installer found in the Sound Library.

▶ Click Go to Sound Library on the Buddy List Preferences window. The Buddy List Sound Installer installs BuddyIn and BuddyOut events and two WAV sound files.

▶ The default WAV files are a door opening and a door closing, used when members on your Buddy List sign on and sign off the service, respectively. You can customize your Buddy List sounds by selecting these sound events (BuddyIn and BuddyOut) in the Sounds section of your Windows Control Panel and pointing to any WAV file on your local drive.

▶ You can turn Buddy List sounds on and off by going to the Buddy List Preferences window found by clicking the Preferences button on the Buddy List Setup window.

CROSS-REFERENCE

For more on binary data such as sound (WAV) files and other downloadable program issues, see Chapter 6.

FIND IT ONLINE

To get more on hearing sounds on AOL, go to the Member Services desk (keyword: HELP), click the Find it Now button, and then enter **sound** in the query box.

TAKE NOTE

TO BUDDY OR NOT TO BUDDY

Two options at the bottom of the Buddy List Privacy Preferences window let you apply the settings to your Buddy List only, or to both your Buddy List and Instant Messages together. If you choose to apply these settings to your Buddy List only, you can still exchange Instant Messages with everyone, but only certain individuals can see you in their Buddy List.

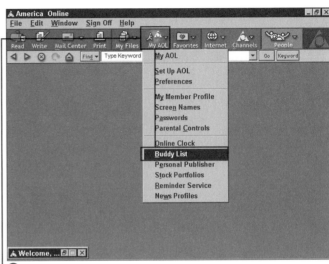

① Click the toolbar's My AOL and select Buddy List from the dropdown menu (or use keyword: BUDDY).

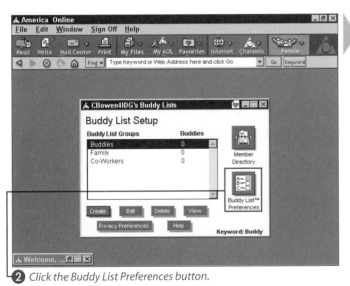

② Click the Buddy List Preferences button.

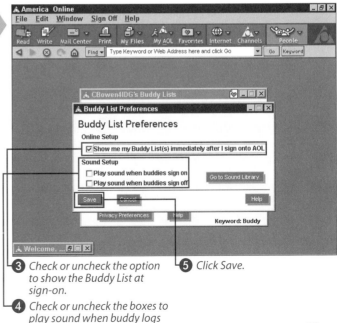

③ Check or uncheck the option to show the Buddy List at sign-on.

④ Check or uncheck the boxes to play sound when buddy logs on and off.

⑤ Click Save.

Setting Chat Preferences

You also can customize the appearance and function of AOL chat using the now-familiar AOL control panel, the Preferences window. Open your preferences as you have before by clicking the toolbar's My AOL icon and selecting Preferences from the drop-down menu. Now click the Chat button and, from the subsequent window, set your chat preferences. Your options are to have AOL

- notify you with online announcements when new members arrive and when they leave the chat room you are visiting. (Be warned — during a busy time, this can produce a lot of additional text for you to examine.)
- double-space incoming messages. (Some members find double-spacing easier to read than the chat rooms' default single-spaced display setting.)
- alphabetize the list of member screen names in your current chat room.
- enable chat room sounds. Note that the default setting has this option activated. However, in a busy session with a lot of messages sending sounds, this can make America Online sound something like a barn. If that isn't the effect you're going for, come here to deactivate the options.

When you have some or all of the options selected, click OK to save your changes.

TAKE NOTE

BEING SMART WITH REAL-TIME CHATTING

If your account is to be used by children in your household, you need to be aware that chat rooms are sometimes not especially kid-friendly places. In fact, news stories abound of predators prowling chat rooms on AOL and on the Internet, trying to lure children. But kids are not the only victims. Adults, too, have been swindled out of passwords, billing data, and personal information online. So, some final thoughts about safe Net surfing for you and your kids:

- Never give your password to anyone, even relatives and your best friends. It is yours only, like your banking card PIN number and your house key.
- Think twice about telling anyone online your home address, your telephone number, or any other personal information. Remind the kids never to give out the names of their schools, where their parents work, and so on.
- If someone says something to you in a chat room that makes you feel unsafe or threatened, call an online guide. Use the keyword NOTIFY AOL. You also should consider leaving the chat room or just signing off the system.
- Make sure the kids realize they must never meet someone in person they first met online without first asking a parent.
- Ask children to tell a parent about any threatening or bad language they see online.
- Finally, do not accept things from strangers, including e-mail, pictures, hyperlinks, Web addresses, and especially files. This goes for kids and adults.

CROSS-REFERENCE

There are additional sections on using the Preferences area for more customization in Chapters 1–4 and in Chapter 7.

FIND IT ONLINE

To get more help online with these and other settings in your Preferences, enter the keyword MY AOL.

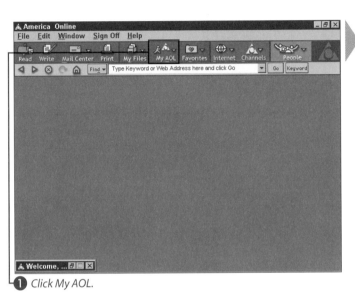

1 Click My AOL.

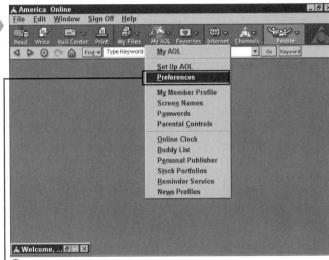

2 Select Preferences.

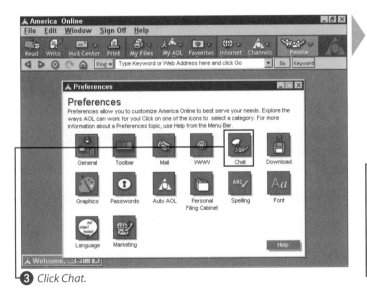

3 Click Chat.

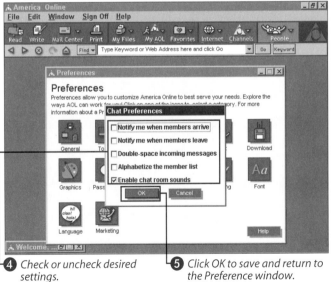

4 Check or uncheck desired settings.

5 Click OK to save and return to the Preference window.

Personal Workbook

Q&A

1 List at least two ways to reach the People Connection feature.

_____

_____

_____

2 What are the three types of AOL chats?

_____

_____

_____

3 Name at least three ways to reach an AOL chat room.

_____

_____

_____

4 How do you hide the text from a particular member in a chat room?

_____

_____

_____

5 How do you find a member's profile information in a chat room?

_____

_____

6 What steps do you follow to create your own public chat room?

_____

_____

_____

7 How do you send an Instant Message?

_____

_____

_____

8 Bonus Question: What is the purpose of the Buddy List feature, and how do you set it up?

_____

_____

_____

ANSWERS: PAGE 337

EXTRA PRACTICE

1 Just as you practiced e-mail techniques by sending letters to yourself, practice now sending Instant Messages to your own screen name to see how they appear to someone else.

2 Search for a chat of interest and attend. Lurk at first to get a feel for the conversation and then jump in!

3 Check out the list of chat abbreviations in the Appendix and see how many of them are in use in the chats you view.

4 Create your own chat room and see who drops in to say hello.

5 Create a private chat room to see how it looks different.

REAL WORLD APPLICATIONS

✔ Note you can send Instant Messages while you are in a chat room. In fact, the "whisper" nature of IMs makes them a perfect enhancement for the public conversation of the chat room.

✔ If you have trouble hearing sounds online, check your hardware. Computers must have sound board installed before they can play sound (WAV) files sent by members in a chat room.

✔ Note also that you can only hear a sound someone else plays if you also have that particular WAV file in your hard disk's America Online directory.

✔ You can save transcripts of chat room conversations. The Log Manager enables you to save conversations directly to your hard disk. I discuss this feature in the next chapter.

Visual Quiz

What is this screen? When do you see it? How can you turn it off and on? How do you set it up?

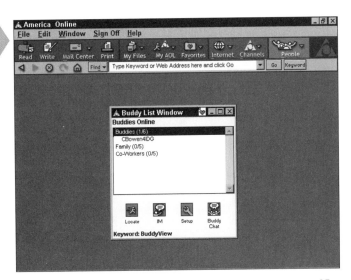

CHAPTER 5

Using Record-Keeping Tools

As you become more active online—meeting and chatting with old and new friends, sending and receiving e-mail, and finding electronic communities you want to explore—you may find yourself filling your pockets with paper notes: e-mail addresses, keywords, printouts of important messages, and notes about dates and times for online rendezvous. And *you* thought computers would mean less paper in your life. Actually, America Online can reduce the paperwork. Record-keeping tools built into the AOL software itself can be used to take the place of old-fashioned paper records. And you can use many of the built-in tools offline as well as online. In other words, in addition to being your connection to cyberspace, it also can work with you as your secretary and personal assistant in managing your online life.

This chapter focuses on outstanding AOL features—most of them greatly enhanced in version 4.0 of the software—such as

- an address book to keep all those e-mail addresses straight and to simplify your letter sending. After you've used an electronic address book for a while, you will wonder how you ever got by without one.

- a digital filing cabinet for electronic copies of online documents. This tool can store incoming and outgoing messages that you exchange privately with other members, as well as those you send and receive publicly in forums and on the Internet.

- an electronic stenographer who can log transcripts of sessions in chat rooms and other online text. This is like having a tape recorder built into the America Online software, except that it saves text of your conversations.

You also will enhance your online persona by creating your own biography online and by making more screen names, and will locate friends and acquaintances online through another of the system's powerful databases. In other words, it is here that you teach yourself how to authorize America Online to keep your records straight, freeing you to concentrate on the business and pleasure of communicating.

Managing Your Address Book

The Address Book can store the names and the screen names of your frequent correspondents, along with notes (phone numbers, addresses, descriptions, and so on) and even digital photos. You can enter the information manually or automate the process by collecting addresses from incoming e-mail messages. To reach your address book, click the toolbar's Mail Center icon and select Address Book from the drop-down menu.

Adding Names Manually

When you call up the Address Book the first time, the Name/Address field is blank, of course, since nothing has been added yet. To begin, click the New Person button at the bottom of the Address Book window and enter the person's information. Their first and last names go in the top two fields (you can leave one or both blank if you don't know them). The E-mail Address field is required, however, and can hold either the person's screen name or Internet address (but not both). Optionally, you can enter additional information in the Notes field, like other e-mail addresses, their home address, their birthday, or anything else you want to keep handy. Click OK to save the entry.

Now when you call up the Address Book (by clicking the toolbar's Mail Center icon and choosing Address Book), your new entry appears in the Name/Address box.

Adding Names from Incoming E-mail

You also can add addresses directly from e-mail you receive in your mailbox. Just click the Add Address icon that appears on the right side of your e-mail's window. The system brings up the New Person screen (shown in the lower-right window) with the name and screen name of the letter's sender already entered. You may click into any of the fields, in-cluding the Notes field, to edit and/or add information.

If you want to create an Address Book entry for an address that was copied on an e-mail you received, select the address before you click the Add Address icon and a new entry for that address is created. If you select multiple addresses, multiple Address book entries will be created — one for each.

> **TAKE NOTE**
>
> **ALTERNATIVE ROUTE TO ADDRESS BOOK**
>
> You can reach the address book from the Write Mail window while composing e-mail. An Address Book icon appears among those assembled on the right side of the window.

CROSS-REFERENCE
For more about writing and reading e-mail, see Chapter 2.

FIND IT ONLINE
To get online assistance, visit the Mail Center (keyword: MAIL CENTER), click the Help button, and choose Using Your Address Book.

Adding Pictures to Address Book

AOL's version 4.0 software enables you to add pictures to your Address Book entries, linking to graphics files elsewhere on your computer. Reach the Address Book from the Mail Center icon and select the existing entry to which you want to attach the picture. Click the Edit icon (or use the New Person icon to create a new entry). Click the Picture tab and click the Select Picture option.

In the Open Image File window, navigate to reach the directory on your disk that contains the image file you want to send. Double-click the image file's name.

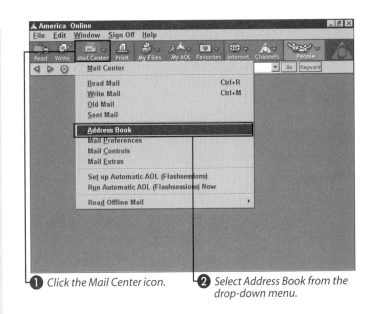

1 Click the Mail Center icon.

2 Select Address Book from the drop-down menu.

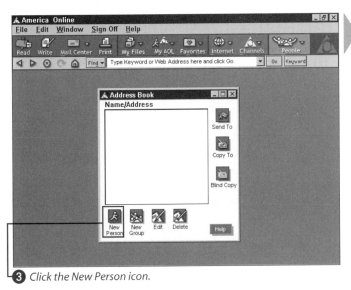

3 Click the New Person icon.

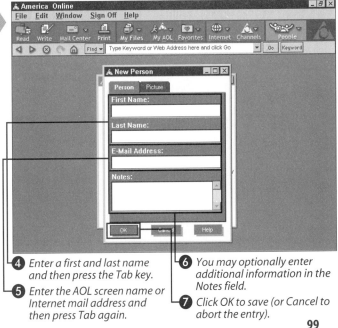

4 Enter a first and last name and then press the Tab key.

5 Enter the AOL screen name or Internet mail address and then press Tab again.

6 You may optionally enter additional information in the Notes field.

7 Click OK to save (or Cancel to abort the entry).

Using the Address Book to Send E-mail

Once screen names are added, your Address Book can greatly speed up the process of writing and mailing a letter. Your Address Book can also reduce the need to remember everyone's e-mail address, some of which are practically impossible to memorize. Storing addresses cuts down on those typing errors, too!

To write to someone who is recorded in your Address Book, click the Address Book icon at the right of a new mail window, as shown in the figures on the facing page. Once your Address Book is open, select a name from the Name/Address list and click the Send To button (or simply double-click the name). The address is automatically inserted in the Send To: field. If you have others in the Address Book to whom you also want the letter sent, repeat the previous step, and AOL adds each screen name you double-click, automatically separating each by the required comma.

Sometimes the trickiest part of using your Address Book is finding the entry you need. Happily, you can search for information stored in our Address Book — first names, last names, e-mail addresses, and even notes! Just select Find in Top Window from the Edit menu at the top of your screen, type in your search word or phrase, and click Find. A matching entry is highlighted when found. Click Find again to find another match.

Changing and Removing Entries

After an entry is made in the Address Book, you can alter it, amend it, or remove it. Just click the toolbar's Mail Center icon and select Address Book from the drop-down menu. Highlight a name in the Name/Address list and click the Delete icon to remove the entry (AOL asks you to confirm that you want it removed) or click the Edit icon to change the data. A quicker way to delete entries is to highlight them in the Name/Address list, click the right mouse button, and select Delete from the pop-up menu. (Mac users: hold down the Control key when you click the entry and select Clear from the pop-up menu.)

TAKE NOTE

▶ **SENDING COPIES AND BLIND COPIES**

The Address Book also can automate the sending of courtesy copies and blind copies. Just highlight a name in the Name/Address list and then click either Copy To or Blind Copy. AOL puts that address in the appropriate field.

▶ **A SHORTCUT FOR SENDING**

Here's a shortcut for sending e-mail. Start by calling up the Address Book (clicking the toolbar's Mail Center icon and selecting Address Book), then double-click the name of the person to whom you want to write. AOL opens the Write Mail display and automatically puts the person's screen name in the Send To: field.

CROSS-REFERENCE

A "real-time" equivalent of the Address Book's group function is the Buddy List, which lets you track friends online. For more about the Buddy List, see Chapter 4.

FIND IT ONLINE

Want somebody new to write to? AOL's Pen Pal service (keyword: PEN PAL) helps you find letter writers in the U.S. and around the world.

Creating Group Mailing Lists

If you regularly send e-mail to a group of recipients, automate the addressing process by creating a group mailing list. It puts in all the addresses you want at one time.

Click the toolbar's Mail Center icon and select Address Book. Click the New Group icon, and in the Group Name: field, type the name you want to assign this group. In the Addresses field, enter the screen names and/or Internet addresses of the people you want included in this mailing list, separating each name with a comma, as in MargHelen, KatCastner, AmiCakes, DavePey.

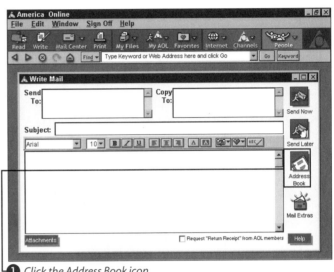

1 Click the Address Book icon.

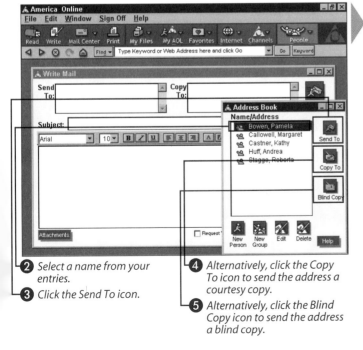

2 Select a name from your entries.

3 Click the Send To icon.

4 Alternatively, click the Copy To icon to send the address a courtesy copy.

5 Alternatively, click the Blind Copy icon to send the address a blind copy.

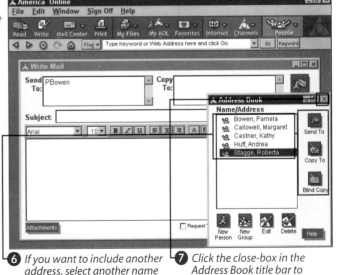

6 If you want to include another address, select another name and click Send To, Copy To, or Blind Copy. Repeat as necessary.

7 Click the close-box in the Address Book title bar to remove it from the screen when finished.

Accessing Your Personal Filing Cabinet

The Personal Filing Cabinet enables you to instantly organize incoming electronic mail, files you have downloaded (retrieved), unread messages from AOL forums and Internet newsgroups, letters you have written to be posted later, and messages you have written for forums and newsgroups.

This chapter introduces the Personal Filing Cabinet and shows its use in connection with electronic mail. Later chapters return to show the Personal Filing Cabinet's use in conjunction with the Internet and AOL forums. As you will later see, the Personal Filing Cabinet is especially valuable for storing your incoming and outgoing messages from America Online forums and the Internet. It's like having a personal secretary carefully maintaining file folders for all your important correspondences.

To reach your Personal Filing Cabinet, click the toolbar's My Files icon and select Personal Filing Cabinet from the drop-down menu. You can also access the specific sections in other ways. To see your stored mail, click the toolbar's My Files icon and select Offline Mail. To get a list of your files, select Download Manager from the same menu. And to see your stored postings, select Offline Newsgroups, also from the same menu. You can also quickly access specific portions of your stored mail by clicking the toolbar's Mail Center icon, selecting Read Offline Mail, and selecting an option from the drop-down menu.

Password Protecting the Filing Cabinet

Each screen name created on your account has its own Personal Filing Cabinet and each can require the password to protect its contents from prying eyes. You need to be signed on to AOL in order to create your Personal Filing Cabinet password. To begin, click the toolbar's My AOL icon and select Preferences from the resulting menu. In the Preferences window, click the Passwords icon. Enter the password for the current screen name (if it is not already entered) in the Password field, and then click a check mark under the Personal Filing Cabinet column. Click OK to save your changes. As noted in the previous chapter, the same window is used to store the account password to speed up sign-on.

Now when you open your Personal Filing Cabinet, you are asked to enter your password. Enter the same password you set for your screen name itself and click Continue.

TAKE NOTE

▶ **CAN'T REACH THE FILING CABINET AS A GUEST**

The Personal Filing Cabinet can't be reached if you have signed on to America Online as a "guest" rather than with your usual screen name and password.

CROSS-REFERENCE

The Personal Filing Cabinet also is used extensively with AOL forums. For more on this application, see Chapter 6.

FIND IT ONLINE

For more help online with setting up and using your Personal Filing Cabinet, use the appropriate Member Services area (keyword: PFC).

Parts of the Filing Cabinet

The Personal Filing Cabinet has three general collections of folders:

▶ **Mail** includes saved incoming mail, letters waiting to be sent, and mail you have sent earlier.

▶ **Newsgroups** includes saved messages from AOL and the Internet (called *postings* among Internet regulars), your messages waiting to be posted, and messages you have posted earlier.

▶ **Download Manager** organizes files you have retrieved and files you want to retrieve later.

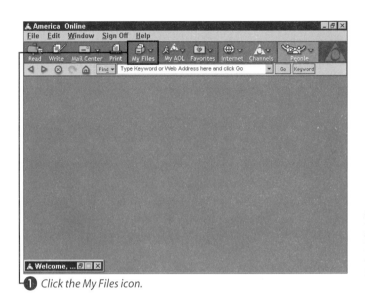

① *Click the My Files icon.*

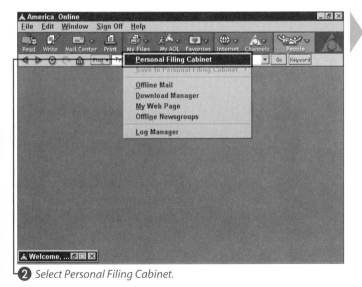

② *Select Personal Filing Cabinet.*

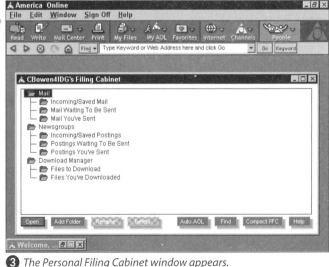

③ *The Personal Filing Cabinet window appears.*

Saving Incoming and Outgoing E-mail

The Personal Filing Cabinet can serve as your offline mailbox, because it can be instructed to automatically save your incoming e-mail. Just click the toolbar's My AOL icon, select Preferences from the drop-down menu, choose the Mail icon, and click the options on either or both of these selections:

▶ "Retain all mail I send in my Personal Filing Cabinet." Choosing this option means copies of letters go into the Personal Filing Cabinet as you click the Send icon to post an e-mail.

▶ "Retain all mail I read in my Personal Filing Cabinet." Selecting this option means copies of mail you receive go into the filing cabinet as you read them in your online mailbox.

Messages saved in your Personal Filing Cabinet are also preserved in the Old Mail and Sent Mail folders of your online mailbox. In other words, you still can retrieve them and reread them online. They will remain in the online folders until the system automatically deletes them either when the time limit has expired or when you delete them manually (whichever comes first).

Reading E-mail in the Offline Mailbox

Once saved in your Personal Filing Cabinet, copies of your e-mail — either letters you have received or those you have posted — can be read in the Offline mailbox. To do that, just click the toolbar's Mail Center icon, select the Read Offline Mail option from the drop-down menu, click either "Incoming/Saved Mail" or "Mail You've Sent," and double-click the letter you want to read.

You can also read a letter in your "Mail Waiting To Be Sent" folder if it hasn't yet been sent (once it is sent, it is automatically moved to your "Mail You've Sent" folder). You can make changes to waiting mail. Just make your changes, close the window, and save the changes when AOL asks.

Mac users have a few unique features in the Personal Filing Cabinet. Click the labels at the top to reorganize your letters by name, by address/location, and by date. You can even reverse the order by clicking the arrow icon in the upper right-hand corner.

TAKE NOTE

▶ **ANOTHER WAY TO READ AND DELETE SAVED MAIL**

You also can read saved e-mail directly from the Personal Filing Cabinet. Click the toolbar's My Files icon, choose the Personal Filing Cabinet option, open the appropriate folder, and then double-click the subject of the letter you want to read. To remove a letter from the Personal Filing Cabinet, highlight it and click the Delete button. You can also highlight a letter and right-click with your mouse to delete it.

CROSS-REFERENCE

The Personal Filing Cabinet also has uses in offline reading of messages from Internet newsgroups. For more about this, see Chapter 7.

FIND IT ONLINE

For more help with offline mail reading, select the menu bar's Help option, choose Offline Help (or AOL Guide on the Mac), and, in the resulting query box, enter **mail offline**.

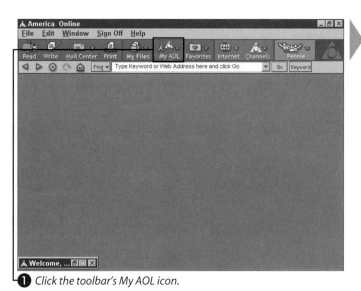

1 Click the toolbar's My AOL icon.

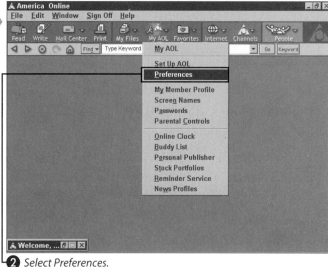

2 Select Preferences.

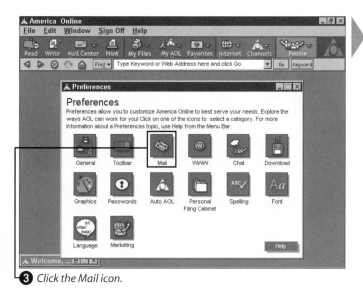

3 Click the Mail icon.

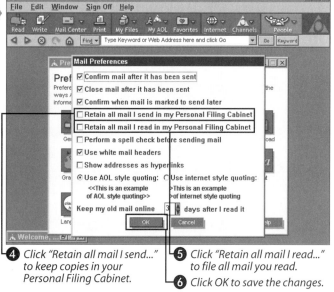

4 Click "Retain all mail I send..." to keep copies in your Personal Filing Cabinet.

5 Click "Retain all mail I read..." to file all mail you read.

6 Click OK to save the changes.

Searching the Personal Filing Cabinet

Unlike the bulky, low-tech filing cabinets in your office or school, the America Online Personal Filing Cabinet can instantly be searched for material. Looking for that letter from Uncle Jake or that message you wrote to your mom? The Personal Filing Cabinet's Find option is the tool to use.

To begin, click the toolbar's My Files icon and choose the Personal Filing Cabinet option. Subjects of the letters saved in the various folders are displayed. You can search through all letters and all folders, or just search a particular folder by opening it (and only it) first. Click the Find button at the bottom of the screen. In the "Find what:" field, enter the word or words you are seeking. In the Scope of Search section, indicate whether you are searching all folders or only the currently opened folder(s). In the Type of Search area, select either full text (that is, contents of the folders) or titles (subjects) only. Decide whether to check the "Match case" checkbox at the left of the window — leave it unchecked unless upper/lowercase is important to the search word or phrase you have entered. Click the Find Next box to find the first folder that has the reference.

You can click Find Next again to find the next reference or click Cancel to end the search. If you found a letter with the word or phrase you specify, the subject is highlighted on the screen after the Find box is removed. Double-click it to read the letter.

Mac users have a similar Find feature, with the added capability of entering a name or address to search on, instead of, or in addition to, the contents.

TAKE NOTE

ADJUSTING THE SIZE OF THE FILING CABINET

The Personal Filing Cabinet may seem to have come equipped with all the folders you need, but as you use the system, you may discover you need more. To create new folders, click the toolbar's My Files icon and then choose the Personal Filing Cabinet option. In the resulting window, click the location for the new folder. If you select an existing folder, the new folder is created inside it. If you select an existing document, the new folder is inserted before that document.

ANOTHER WAY TO CHANGE THE SIZE

You also can regulate the size of your Personal Filing Cabinet. Click the toolbar's My AOL icon, select Preferences, and then choose Personal Filing Cabinet. You can set AOL to issue warnings when your filing cabinet reaches a certain size or has a certain amount of free space.

RECOVERING SPACE

To recover unused space in the filing cabinet after a period of additions and deletions, click the toolbar's My Files icon, select Personal Filing Cabinet, and then click the Compact PFC button on the resulting window.

CROSS-REFERENCE
For more on AOL search strategies, see the Appendix.

FIND IT ONLINE
For further online help with the Personal Filing Cabinet, visit the Member Services area (keyword: HELP), click the Find It Now option, and then enter **filing cabinet** in the query box.

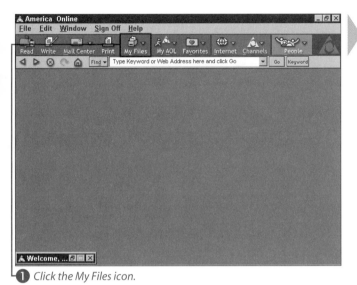

1 Click the My Files icon.

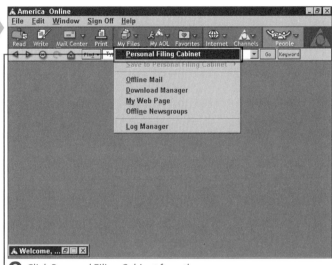

2 Click Personal Filing Cabinet from the menu.

3 Click the Find button.

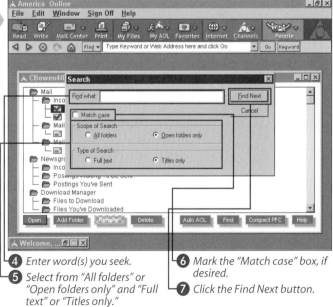

4 Enter word(s) you seek.

5 Select from "All folders" or "Open folders only" and "Full text" or "Titles only."

6 Mark the "Match case" box, if desired.

7 Click the Find Next button.

Logging Online Chats

Imagine you are in a chat room or in a private Instant Message session when suddenly your friend starts telling some classic jokes. You say to yourself, "Gee, I wish I had a copy of this so I could tell the folks at the office." Or you are visiting message boards in your favorite forums and you see notes that you want to copy. Or you find articles in AOL news resources or on the Internet, and once again, you want to save them for further reference.

What you need in these situations is a log of what you are seeing online. This is a job for the Log Manager, America Online's built-in tool for transferring online text to a file you can read or print offline.

Opening and Closing the Log

In practice, the Log Manager most often serves as a kind of electronic stenographer, capturing transcripts of online chats. To begin, visit a chat room and click the toolbar's My Files icon and select Log Manager from the drop-down menu. In the Chat Log section of the dialog box, click the Open Log button. Notice the name of the log file. It usually is something picked up from the system, such as `Town Square-Lobby 32` with the `.log` suffix. Close the Log Manager window and continue the chat as usual. Then when you are ready to put away the log and end the transcribing, click the toolbar's My Files icon and select Log Manager from the drop-down menu

again. Click the Close Log button and close the Log Manager window.

You may also keep the Log Manager window open while you are logging. In fact, the open window can serve as a reminder that you are logging while it keeps the controls handy.

TAKE NOTE

READING AND PRINTING A LOG

To read a log file, click File ➪ Open from the menu. Navigate to the directory on your disk that contains the log file. It is probably in the AOL directory's `\DOWNLOAD` folder. Look for the filename you noted when the logging began (it will be a file with a name such as `Town Square-Lobby 32.log`) and double-click it to view it. If you would like to print the log as well as view it on your screen, click the toolbar's Print icon.

If the log file does not appear on your screen when you open it, that usually indicates that the file is very large. Open it within a word processor or a text editor (like WordPad) instead.

APPENDING LOGS

If you have closed a chat log and wish to resume it in the same file, follow the steps outlined in the previous section, but click the Append Log button in the Chat section. This puts the new text at the end of the existing transcript.

CROSS-REFERENCE

The Log Manager can be used to get transcripts of news articles and other online files. For that information, see Chapter 8.

FIND IT ONLINE

For further assistance with logging transcripts, select Log Manager from the My Files menu and then click Help in the resulting window.

Logging Instant Messages

You can log conversations you conduct through the "whispering" of Instant Messages. To do that after initiating an IM session, click the toolbar's My Files icon and select Log Manager from the menu. In the Session Log section of the window, click the Open Log button. Click the Save button to begin the transcript. Now click the Log Instant Message check box.

When you are finished with the IM conference and want to end the transcript, click the toolbar's My Files and select Log Manager. Click the Close Log button.

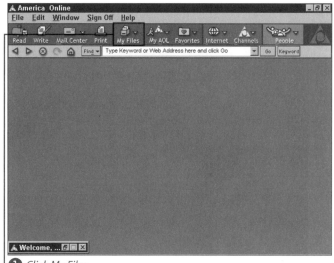

① Click My Files.

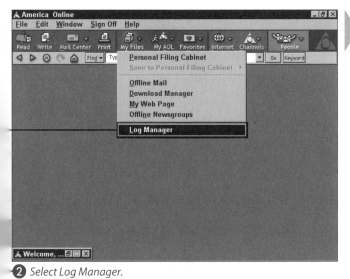

② Select Log Manager.

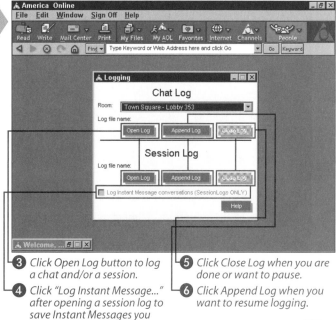

③ Click Open Log button to log a chat and/or a session.

④ Click "Log Instant Message..." after opening a session log to save Instant Messages you send and receive.

⑤ Click Close Log when you are done or want to pause.

⑥ Click Append Log when you want to resume logging.

Searching the Member Directory

While chatting in the previous chapter, you learned how to gather additional information about people in chat rooms by highlighting a screen name and then clicking the Get Profile option. This feature actually linked you briefly to a powerful AOL database called the Member Directory (keyword: DIRECTORY) which also can be used apart from the chat rooms whenever you want to locate a fellow member's online "profile" of autobiographical data.

To use the Member Directory to find a member profile, you first must be signed on to the system. Click the toolbar's People icon and select Search AOL Member Directory from the drop-down menu. The resulting window offers a Quick Search with a number of fields. You can enter a word or phrase — such as **tennis** or **mountain climbing** — in the Search field at the top of the window. Keep in mind that your search words must be at least three characters long. AOL uses the data you enter to search the entire profile of each member on file when you click the Search button.

When your results appear, double-click one of the names to see a profile, click More to see additional findings, or Cancel to end the search. A red arrow next to a name indicates that member is currently online. Options at the bottom of each profile include Locate (to see if the person profiled is currently online and available for an Instant Message) or E-Mail (to write him or her an electronic letter).

If you aren't finding what you want, add more information (for fewer results) or less information (for more results). Remember that not every member has a profile either.

TAKE NOTE

ENHANCING YOUR SEARCH STRATEGY

Because America Online has millions of subscribers around the world, many of whom have taken the time to create a profile for inclusion in the Member Directory, simple searches often are too generic. They can take way too long to perform and produce more results that anyone wants to sort through. Smart folks, then, enhance their searches. An asterisk (*) can be used to indicate that any number of characters can follow the indicated word. For example, "comput*" finds profiles containing computers, computing, computations, and so on. A question mark (?) can replace a single character. The word "gr?y" finds profiles containing "grey" as well as "gray." A space functions as AND, so "horse riding" works the same as if "horse AND riding" were entered.

SHORTCUT FOR GETTING A PROFILE

If you already know the screen name of the person you are seeking, you can bypass the Member Directory with the keyboard shortcut of Ctrl+G (for *Get a Members Profile*). Enter the screen name in the resulting data field, and the system displays the online profile of that person.

CROSS-REFERENCE

For more about searching AOL databases, see Appendix B.

FIND IT ONLINE

To get additional information about using the Member Directory, visit the feature (keyword: DIRECTORY) and click the Help & Info button on the introductory screen.

Narrowing the Search

If your search produces too many "hits," narrow it with the Optional Fields option:

▶ **Member name** searches for the profiles of specific persons.

▶ **Location** seeks out members who indicate a specific state and/or city.

▶ **Country** looks for members specifically in the U.S., Germany, France, Switzerland, the United Kingdom, Canada, or Japan.

▶ **Language** seeks out members who speak a specific language.

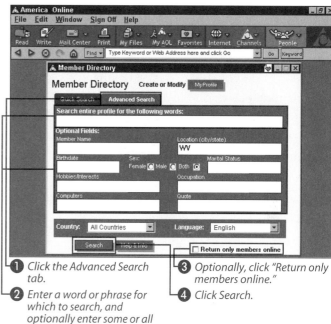

1 Click the Advanced Search tab.

2 Enter a word or phrase for which to search, and optionally enter some or all additional fields.

3 Optionally, click "Return only members online."

4 Click Search.

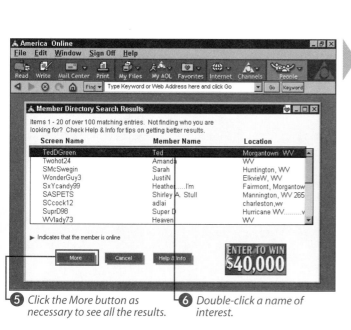

5 Click the More button as necessary to see all the results.

6 Double-click a name of interest.

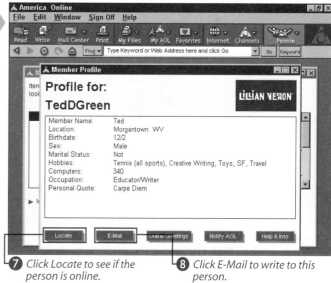

7 Click Locate to see if the person is online.

8 Click E-Mail to write to this person.

111

Creating Your Member Profile

Not everyone wants to be in the Member Directory, but if you become a regular in chat rooms, in e-mail, or in the forums (discussed in the next chapter), you probably want to have at least a little information on file. Here is where you create your digital persona and control how much or how little about yourself is shared with the AOL community.

Your screen name is not automatically included in the Member Directory. It appears there only after you have created a member profile for yourself. You can add as much or as little personal information as you want to display. To create a profile that others can find in the Member Directory, sign on to AOL as usual, click the Keyword option, and enter **PROFILE** as the keyword. Now Click the My Profile button on the Member Directory window.

Fill in as many or as few of the data fields as you like in the window. You can enter your name, city, state, country, birthday, sex, marital status, hobbies, computers used, occupation, and a personal quote. In the interest of safety — especially with profiles for children or teens — consider entering only a first name (or nickname) and leaving the location generic or blank. If you include your birthday, members can search for people of a particular age group. Sharing hobbies is a good way for folks with similar interests to find you. Listing your computer lets people with similar technology background and experience locate

you. The personal quote field works great as a conversation starter (like a fellow writer quoting an old banjo picker who said, "If you were born to hang you'll never drown, so let the big cat jump!").

When you have the form as you want it, click the Update button to have it filed in the Member Directory. The system reports it will be available for searchers within about 24 hours (though it often takes much less time to update). To see your profile as others see it, click the toolbar's People icon, select Get AOL Member Profile, and type in your screen name.

TAKE NOTE

▶ RULE OF THUMB: START SLOWLY

▶ You can come back to modify or delete your Member Profile later by entering keyword: PROFILE and then making changes or using the Delete option. Since the information in the profile is in your hands, you might want to start by filing only brief information and then adding to the data as you feel more comfortable in this electronic environment.

▶ And even after you are a happy online traveler, don't take unnecessary risks. Never put information like your street address or telephone number in your profile, unless perhaps your account is used primarily for business and you want to give your company's information.

CROSS-REFERENCE

Member Profiles can be searched while you are in chat rooms. For more about that, see Chapter 4.

FIND IT ONLINE

For online background on creating your Member Profile, visit the feature (keyword: PROFILE) and click the Help & Info button at the bottom of the screen.

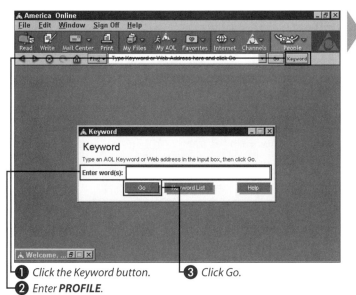

❶ Click the Keyword button.

❷ Enter **PROFILE**.

❸ Click Go.

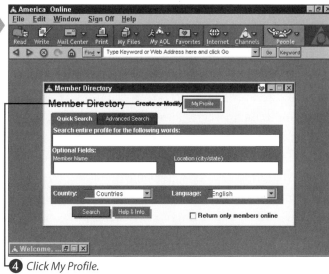

❹ Click My Profile.

❺ Enter your first name or a nickname.

❻ Indicate your sex if you like.

❼ Enter any additional information you want to share with others.

❽ Click Update.

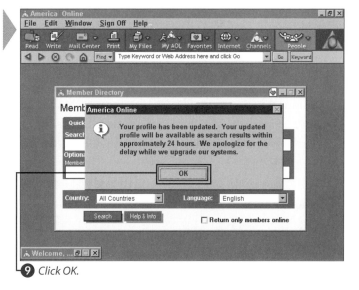

❾ Click OK.

Establishing Multiple Identities

In Chapter 1, you learned that the master screen name—the one you originally created—cannot be deleted or changed without canceling your account altogether. However, you can create up to four additional screen names for your account, each with its own password, mailbox, Personal Filing Cabinet, Favorite Places list, and member profile.

Multiple screen names enable up to five family members to use the same account with relative privacy (the master screen name controls passwords and security options for all screen names on that account). If the account is being used by you alone, you may want to create additional screen names for work and home, for various online activities like interacting in chat rooms and visiting with friends in forums, or for exchanging e-mail with friends and relatives.

To create an extra screen name, sign on to the system (if you are not already there), use keyword: NAMES and click the "Create a Screen Name" option. When prompted, enter a screen name of three to ten letters, as you do in Chapter 1 when you create your master screen name. You can use letters, numbers, and/or spaces, but the first character must be a letter, and it is automatically capitalized after creation. If the name is already in use by another account or is a restricted name, you are prompted to select another name. Once you find a unique screen name, you are prompted to enter the password for your new screen name. As you now know, the system does not display the password as you type, and it prompts you to enter the password twice to avoid the possibility of typing errors. When finished, your new screen name's information is added to your AOL software on your hard drive.

By the way, no matter how many additional screen names you create and which one you or a member of your household uses for an AOL session, the time is billed to your master account.

TAKE NOTE

▶ SIGN-ON ALTERNATIVES

Additional screen names give you more sign-on options:

▶ When new screen names are added to your account, AOL automatically adds them to the Sign On window. To sign on with a different screen name, run the AOL software as usual and click the down-arrow button to view your other screen names on the Sign On window. Click the one you want and then click the Sign On button.

▶ You can change screen names without disconnecting from the system. Just click the Sign Off option on the menu bar and Select the Switch Screen Name option.

▶ Each new screen name has its own mailbox and Personal Filing Cabinet and can create unique member profiles when signed on.

CROSS-REFERENCE
For more about creating screen names, see Chapter 1.

FIND IT ONLINE
For help with screen names and scores of other AOL topics, visit Meg the AOL Insider (keyword: AOL TIPS).

Modifying Screen Names

Use the NAMES keyword to alter your additional screen names:

▶ To erase a screen name, select "Delete a Screen Name" from the Screen Names window. Once deleted, that name cannot be created by anyone else for at least six months.

▶ To restore a screen name you deleted in the last six months, select that option from the window and pick one from the resulting list. The Personal Filing Cabinet for that screen name may still be available on your hard drive.

▶ Use keyword: PASSWORD to change passwords for additional screen names.

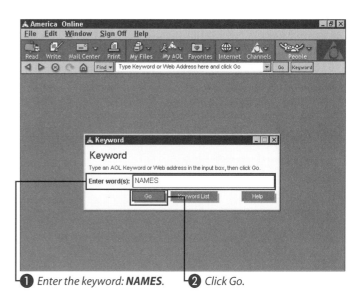

1 *Enter the keyword: **NAMES**.*   **2** *Click Go.*

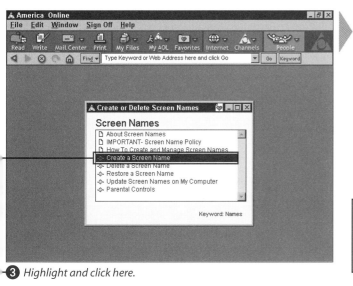

3 *Highlight and click here.*

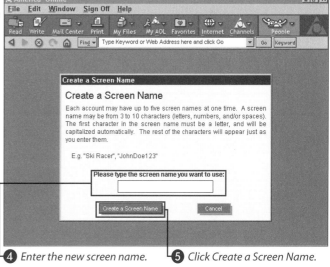

4 *Enter the new screen name.*   **5** *Click Create a Screen Name.*

Personal Workbook

Q&A

1 How can you use incoming e-mail to add names to your Address Book?

_____

_____

2 What do you do to add pictures to entries in your Address Book?

_____

_____

_____

3 How do you use your Address Book to automatically address a letter you are sending?

_____

_____

4 What procedure do you follow to create a group of related addresses in your Address Book?

_____

_____

_____

5 How do you reach your Personal Filing Cabinet from the toolbar?

_____

_____

_____

6 What are the three main parts of your Personal Filing Cabinet?

_____

_____

_____

7 How can you automatically save all incoming mail in your Personal Filing Cabinet?

_____

_____

_____

8 Bonus Question: How can you use the Log Manager to make a transcript of a chat session?

_____

_____

ANSWERS: PAGE 338

EXTRA PRACTICE

1 Set your Personal Filing Cabinet to save incoming e-mail and then write a few letters to yourself to see how it works.

2 Visit a chat room and give the Log Manager a try by capturing the chat.

3 Create a new screen name for your account.

4 Create a Member Profile, either for your master screen name and/or for the new screen name.

5 Search the Member Directory for people with hobbies similar to yours or from your state or city.

6 Set up your Address Book with a group of addresses of friends or relatives online.

REAL-WORLD APPLICATIONS

✔ If a transcript made by the Log Manager is larger than 30K, you will not be able to read it within America Online. Instead, use a word-processing program to read it and print it. WordPad, built into your Windows software and available under Accessories, should do the trick.

✔ Your Address Book can be especially useful in managing those long Internet addresses, like `cbowen@tso.ix.net`. The Internet is notoriously persnickety about typos, even upper and lowercase letters. But once the address is correctly saved in the Address Book, you never have to worry about typographical errors again.

Visual Quiz

What is this screen? How would you reach it, and what would you do with it when you got there? Hint: Remember the mention of groups at the end of an earlier task?

_____

_____

_____

_____

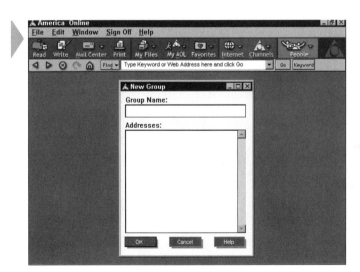

CHAPTER 6

Using Forums and Automating AOL

More than 20 years ago, two clever Chicago electronics hobbyists — Ward Christensen and Randy Suess — made a big place for themselves in personal computing history. A phone call started it all, as they chatted about how members of their computer club ought to be able to stay in touch between meetings through their computers. The result was their creation of the Computer Bulletin Board System (CBBS). The CBBS became the first digital version of the plain cork bulletin board you still find in any grocery story or Laundromat.

BBSes (the *C* got dropped in the generic term) changed the face of computing. Thousands of these individual bulletin boards still operate around the world in computer clubs, libraries, schools, and family basements. But the bigger impact of BBSes has been the evolution of super message boards operating on commercial information services and the Internet, inviting people around the world to come together in a corner of cyberspace to compare notes, share software and other files, and chat in real time. Message boards have become the town squares for the various neighborhoods of America Online. What you learn in this chapter will be of value to you as you further explore the system in later chapters.

On America Online, the BBS tradition lives on in its scores of *forums*. These discussion groups or electronic clubhouses are devoted to topics ranging from genealogy to world religions, from photography and cooking to computer technology and favorite television shows. More importantly, though, AOL also has greatly improved the quality of digital life in these online communities. For instance, this chapter shows you how to thoroughly automate AOL. Without your even needing to be in the room, you can enable your computer to

- pick up and deliver messages on the message boards.
- automatically retrieve files you want from selected forum libraries.
- send your outgoing letters and save the incoming mail letters for your perusal offline when you have time later.
- find and download software and other files for use when you are offline.

Reaching a Message Board

To check out a typical forum — and have a valuable future resource for answers to questions about using America Online — visit the Help Desk. Not to be confused with AOL Member Services, the Help Desk is a unique forum devoted to making life better for new members and for people who are new to computing in general. To reach the Help Desk, sign on to AOL as usual and enter the keyword HELP DESK. Most forums have their own keywords and all have their own addresses which can be saved in your Favorite Places list for future visits, using techniques illustrated in Chapter 3.

Reading and Writing on the Message Boards

The heart of all forums is the message board center, where members posts notes to discuss aspects of the group's central interest. In most forums, an option on the main window links you to the intersection of all its message boards. In the Help Desk, a Message Boards button is provided on the right side of the window. Other forums may put the link elsewhere on the window, so be prepared to scan for a related button or list item.

Here in the Help Desk, you can click the Message Boards button to reach a list of the various message boards available, arranged by topic. Look over the list of message boards, scrolling the box in the center of the window. Other forums may present their message board list in different formats — lists with icons or checkboxes, for instance — but the concept remains the same. The Help Desk's message board topics cover the gamut: Every operation system and computing arena is represented here. A good topic to start with is the one titled "Computing for Beginners."

TAKE NOTE

KEY PARTS OF ALL AOL FORUMS

While the topics that hold these communities together are diverse, the elements of the forums are the same throughout the system. Learn the structure of one forum and you know how to use them all. Forums have these components:

▶ Message boards are used to gather information, share comments and experiences, ask and answer questions, introduce people with common interests and goals, debate issues (and make peace). Writing and reading messages here is much like electronic mail except that, where e-mail is private communications, the messages in forums are public, open to all to see.

▶ Libraries hold the treasures of the forum, including free and shareware programs, files that answer frequently asked questions, and transcripts of earlier messages that preserve the wisdom of members who have passed this way before.

▶ Conference rooms are private, standing chat rooms where you converse with fellow forum members away from the hubbub and partying of the People Connection chat facilities.

CROSS-REFERENCE

For information about Internet forums — called newsgroups — see Chapter 7.

FIND IT ONLINE

To get an online overview of forums, visit the Help Desk (keyword: HELP DESK) and select "Welcome to the PC Help Desk" from the introductory screen.

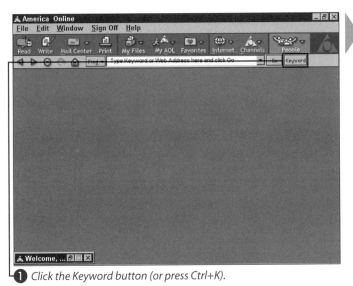

1 Click the Keyword button (or press Ctrl+K).

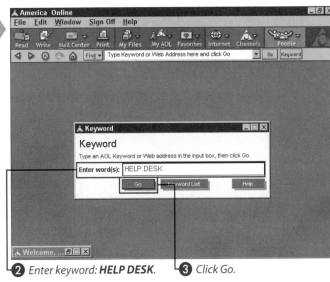

2 Enter keyword: **HELP DESK**.   **3** Click Go.

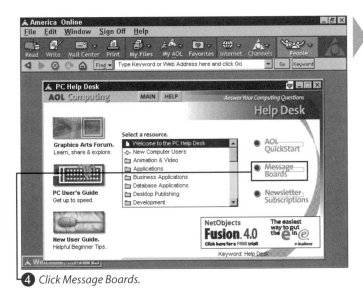

4 Click Message Boards.

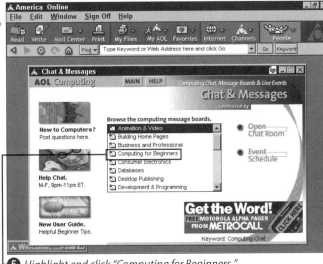

5 Highlight and click "Computing for Beginners."

Reading Messages

To understand how AOL message boards are organized, it is helpful to recognize a hierarchy of three distinct parts. The first, *topics*, is the board's broad categories, such as "AOL Software Tips & Tricks," "AOL Connections," "Downloading," and so on. The second, *subjects*, is the groups of messages that are posted within each topic — each subject topic may contain dozens of individual groups of messages. The third, *posts*, is the individual messages that make up each subject, which may have anywhere from one to scores of individual posts.

Upon first entering a message board, AOL shows you an overview of the message board by listing all topics and the number of subjects in each. To dive down to the next levels and progress to more refined lists of material, open one of the topics for a list of all subjects in this topic and the number of postings in each. You can now get a list of all posts in a subject or begin reading the first message in a subject.

AOL formats its posts (messages) like e-mail. The header at the top provides the subject, the date and time of the posting, and the screen name of the sender. But they also have additional information, such as a line at the top identifying the number of messages within the current subject. In the example, the line reads, "Message 1 of 5 Subject 10 of 182." So there are five posts in this subject (called "Selected printed") and 182 subjects in this topic.

TAKE NOTE

▶ READING MORE

After you have read a post, you may click the button at the bottom of the window to read the next post or previous post in the current subject. You also can jump to the first post in the previous or next subject or reply to the current message by writing and posting a public answer or comment. Or click the *X* in the window's title bar to close this message and step back a level to the subject list.

▶ REPLYING

When you find a message to which you want to respond, click the Reply button at the bottom of the window. AOL presents you with a new window, automatically filling in the subject and the name of the person to whose message you are replying. Write and edit your message in the text-entry field, just as you would with e-mail. Style icons above the text box enable you to control text color and type size, to emphasize with boldface, italic and/or underlining, and to align text either left, right, or center. When the text is as you want it, click the Send button at the lower right of the window.

CROSS-REFERENCE

For more about writing messages, see the discussion of e-mail in Chapter 2.

FIND IT ONLINE

To get additional online help with using forum boards, go to Member Services (keyword: HELP), click Find it Now, and then enter **message boards** in the query box.

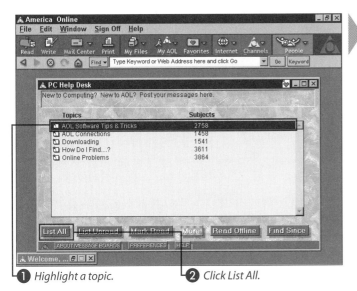

1 Highlight a topic.

2 Click List All.

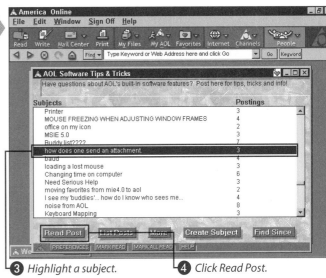

3 Highlight a subject.

4 Click Read Post.

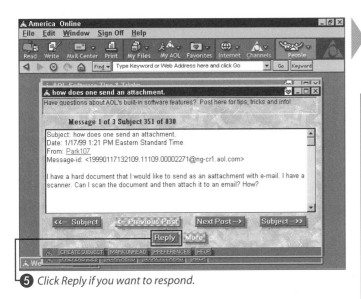

5 Click Reply if you want to respond.

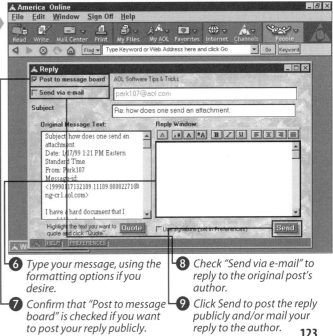

6 Type your message, using the formatting options if you desire.

7 Confirm that "Post to message board" is checked if you want to post your reply publicly.

8 Check "Send via e-mail" to reply to the original post's author.

9 Click Send to post the reply publicly and/or mail your reply to the author.

Finding Posts

Most forum fans these days read their messages offline, using the Automatic AOL feature I introduce later in this chapter. But obviously, before you can do that, you need to do some online exploring to find out which forums you want to target with this automated service. This means you need to sample messages, ideally over several online sessions. A good way to do that is to use the Find Since option, which enables you to target messages that have been added since your last visit.

Begin by visiting a message board, highlighting the topic or subject you wish to search, and selecting the Find Since button at the bottom right of the window. You have several options for finding posts. You can find messages posted since the last time you read this particular board with "New (Since last visit)." You can find posts dating back a certain number of days with "In last ___ days" (fill in the blank up to 9999 days). Or you can find posts between a range of dates with "From ___ to ___" (fill in the blanks with dates in the mm/dd/yy format). The last two options find all posts in your date range, whether you have previously read them or not. When you're ready, click the Find button to list the subjects or posts that meet your specifications. Keep in mind that the higher up in the message board hierarchy you are, the more posts you will find.

The Find Since option is great at finding new or dated posts, but what if you're more interested in the content of posts? Though there is no Search function for AOL's message boards yet, you can use the Find in Top Window option (under the Edit menu) to find text in a topic list, subject list, or within a post itself.

TAKE NOTE

▶ MARKING AND UNMARKING MESSAGES

As you climb up and down the three levels of the message boards — from the topics to subjects to posts and back again — AOL offers you some basic bookkeeping options:

▶ List Unread, which displays a list of subjects or posts in the highlighted topic that you have not yet read or that contain unread messages

▶ Mark Read, which tells the system you are finished with (that is, have "read") all the messages in the highlighted topic or subject

▶ Mark Unread, which tells the system you are not finished with the messages in the highlighted subject or topic

Use these options as alternatives to the Find Since feature as a means of locating messages of interest. You might click the List Unread button when first visiting a new topic or subject, and then use Mark Read to bookmark what you have seen as you move through the posts.

CROSS-REFERENCE
For help in finding forums of interest, see Chapter 3's discussion about AOL Find.

FIND IT ONLINE
To get more help with reading and writing messages, visit any forum message board and click the Help button at the bottom of the screen.

Creating Your Own Subject

To create your own subject, examine the list of board topics and click the one in which you want your subject to appear. Then click the Create Subject button at the bottom right. The system automatically fills in the Send to: field with the name of the topic you have chosen.

In the Subject: field, describe the contents of your message. Click into the text box and enter and edit your message. When you have the message as you want it, click the Send button in the lower right of the screen to direct AOL to post your new subject. Others will be able to read it and reply to it shortly.

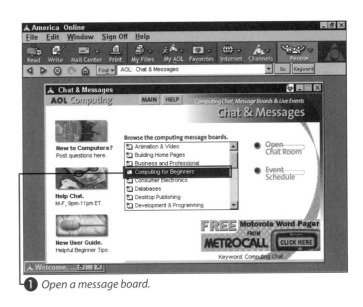

1 Open a message board.

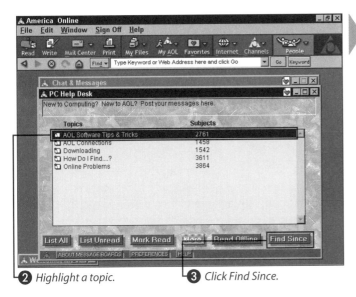

2 Highlight a topic.

3 Click Find Since.

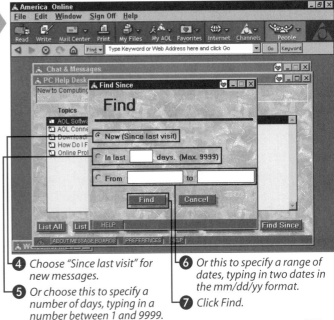

4 Choose "Since last visit" for new messages.

5 Or choose this to specify a number of days, typing in a number between 1 and 9999.

6 Or this to specify a range of dates, typing in two dates in the mm/dd/yy format.

7 Click Find.

Setting Message Board Preferences

Customization is everywhere these days. And AOL is no exception. At the bottom of each message board window is a Preferences button that enables you to customize how you view all message boards. Settings here determine the order in which you view the messages, how many are available to see, and even how your own name appears at the end of messages you post.

Your first customization option is to create and save a signature. A signature is a short, personalized note automatically attached to the end of your messages. Commonly, signatures contain a name, a title, a World Wide Web address, or a favorite quote. Design the signature in the box at the left of the window, using the formatting buttons above the box to select colors, sizes, styles, alignment, and so on.

More options let you specify the Sort Order, listing subjects with the oldest first, the newest first (default), or alphabetically. The second set of Sort Order options lets you view message boards as they are defined (default), as all threaded (listing both subject groups and postings), or as all unthreaded (listing only postings, no subject groups).

You can also limit the age of the messages that appear — the default is 30 days, which you can change to 0 to see all messages ever posted in a message board. Note for future reference that you can limit the number of messages downloaded by Automatic AOL (the default limit is 300 messages). Be sure to click OK to save your settings.

Targeting a Message Board for Automatic AOL

After exploring a forum for a while, you may decide that you want to regularly follow activity on several of its message board's broad topics. This makes them prime candidates for offline reading through the Automatic AOL feature discussed soon. An option on the topics window — the Read Offline button — lets you identify a message board for this special attention. When you find a message board you wish to follow more closely offline, highlight the topic and click the Read Offline option. The preferences you set in the previous section also determine how many messages are retrieved by Automatic AOL and in which order they appear. Repeat the process for each topic of interest.

> ### TAKE NOTE
>
> ▶ **MY BOARDS**
> After you have used the Read Offline option to mark at least one message board topic for offline retrieval, use keyword: MY BOARDS to see a list of your marked boards. Other options let you read and remove boards.
>
> ▶ **LIST POSTS**
> An alternative to the Read Post option is List Post, which lists relevant information regarding each message in that subject. This includes screen names of the individual message authors, length of each message, as well as the date and time of each posting.

CROSS-REFERENCE
For more information about real-time conferencing, see Chapter 4.

FIND IT ONLINE
To get online help with Preferences, click the Help button at the bottom of the Preferences screen.

Chatting in Forum Conferences

Many forums ask members to observe special protocols as a way to avoid confusion. Imagine dozens of people gathered to hear a specific presentation all trying to talk at the same time, and you'll understand the necessity for protocols.

▶ If you have a question, first send only a question mark. Press the ? key and click Send at the bottom of the chat display. The host calls on you when it's your turn to type in your actual question.

▶ Let the host know when you want to make a comment (as opposed to a question) by sending an exclamation point (!).

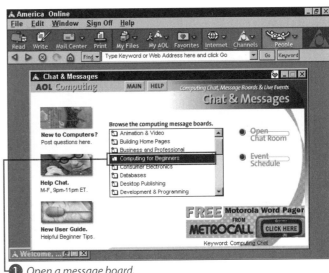

1 *Open a message board.*

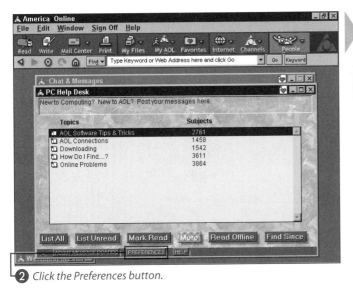

2 *Click the Preferences button.*

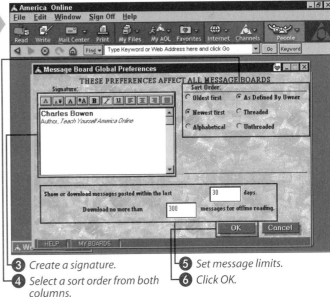

3 *Create a signature.*
4 *Select a sort order from both columns.*
5 *Set message limits.*
6 *Click OK.*

Downloading Files

Another important component of forums is the software library, where you can download all kinds of files, including programs, pictures, articles, instructions, and sometimes even complete books. Tens of thousands of files are available for you to browse and retrieve.

One easy way to find files for downloading is to start with specific forums. Most forums have links to software libraries filled with material of interest to their unique members. The Genealogy Forum (keyword: GENEALOGY) has software devoted to family histories, family tree programs, tips and ideas for library research, for instance. Use the toolbar's Find icon to locate the forums you like, explore them, and link to their software libraries.

Using File Search

To take a more general approach to the hunt, search the system at large with File Search (keyword: FILE SEARCH). This search utility simplifies the process enabling you to search many forum libraries at the same time for specific kinds of files and then download them immediately without having to visit each forum. Use the keyword and select Shareware when prompted for the type of files you wish to search.

File Search gives you a lot of choice for finding files. The Timeframe options let you choose to search software from either All Dates, the Past Month, or the Past Week — the default (All Dates) gives you the broadest range of files. The Categories option allows

you to check as many of the boxes as you want, including Applications, Development, DOS, Education, Games, Graphics & Animation, Hardware, Music & Sound, OS/2, Telecommunications, and Windows. Note that if you leave all category boxes unchecked, all categories are searched. Optionally, you can also enter a search word or phrase to narrow the search further by describing what you are looking for with keywords. When you have your choices made, click the Search button. The resulting list shows the initial 20 files found — click the List More Files button to get the next 20. When you find a file of interest, highlight it and click the Read Description button.

Continued

TAKE NOTE

COMPRESSED FILES

Most large files or collections of files are compressed into a single, smaller file known as a ZIP file (because they appear online with .zip as the extension, as in `baseball.zip`).

▶ The AOL software automatically processes the majority of zipped files downloaded from the AOL software libraries. You can have your AOL software do this by clicking the toolbar's My AOL icon, choosing Preferences, and then selecting Download.

▶ In the resulting window, make sure there is a check mark to the left of the item reading, "Automatically decompress files at sign-off." Click OK.

CROSS-REFERENCE

For help with searching on AOL, see the Appendix.

FIND IT ONLINE

Downloading is such a popular AOL pastime that a Download Info Center has been established to field assorted questions. To reach this area, use the keywords DOWNLOAD INFO CENTER.

Downloading Files

Overview of File Transfer

With AOL, downloading can be as simple as two steps:

▶ View the description of files and find one you want. (Read the entire description, because any special handling, additional software, or specific hardware needed for the program is outlined in the Needs and Equipment lines.)

▶ Click the Download Now button.

AOL also offers a sophisticated Download Manager feature, discussed in a moment. The Download Manager enables you to manage more than one download in a session and oversee the entire process from a single window.

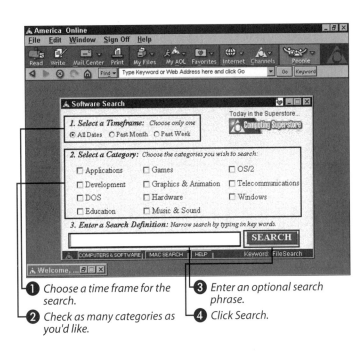

① Choose a time frame for the search.

② Check as many categories as you'd like.

③ Enter an optional search phrase.

④ Click Search.

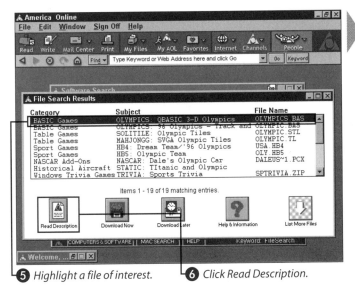

⑤ Highlight a file of interest.

⑥ Click Read Description.

⑦ Click Download Now to retrieve.

⑧ Click Related Files to see other files in this library.

Downloading Files

Continued

Examining and Retrieving Files

Whether you reach a list of files through File Search or by examining the software libraries of a specific forum, the options for examining and actually downloading files from the list are identical. To use them, highlight the name of a file that interests you and click the Read Description icon. Each file description includes the subject, author name, screen name of the person who actually uploaded (contributed) it to the library, contribution date, the filename, the estimated download time, and the number of other members who have downloaded it so far. Also described is any special equipment and instructions for using the file, along with the type (free or commercial shareware) and comments from the contributor.

If you decide you don't want a file, click the close button in the upper right of the window's title bar to close the window and return to the list of files. Or, if you want the system to find other similar files for you, click the Related Files button at the bottom of the file description window.

If you decide you do want a file, you can retrieve it in one of two ways. The first is to use the Download Now button on the left on the bottom of the display to retrieve it immediately. Your computer shows you where it plans to save the file (the default is AOL's \DOWNLOAD folder on your hard disk) and the filename it is using. Click the Save button to begin the file transfer. Alternatively, if you want to retrieve the

file later, use the Download Later button. The file is automatically added to a list of files to be downloaded later.

TAKE NOTE

▶ LOCATING DOWNLOADED PROGRAMS

To use software you have downloaded from America Online, all you need to do after the download is to sign off and then do the following things:
- ▶ Click the toolbar's My Files icon and select Download Manager.
- ▶ Click the Show Files Downloaded button (or look in the Completed Downloads folder if you're on a Mac).
- ▶ Highlight and click the name of the file you want to locate on your computer.
- ▶ Click the Show Status icon to see where the file was placed when you downloaded it.
- ▶ By default, all the files you download are placed in the \DOWNLOAD folder of the disk, but you can change this destination with the Download Manager's Select Destination button (or the Save To button on the Mac). On Windows, most downloaded programs can be run from program manager by clicking FILE ⇨ RUN and entering the filename when prompted. On Windows 95, a shortcut is to use the Start Menu and select Run, entering the filename when prompted. On the Mac, double-clicking the file generally does the trick.

CROSS-REFERENCE

For more about computer-related topics and forums, see Chapter 11.

FIND IT ONLINE

For more online help with download, visit Member Services (keyword: HELP) and select Downloading Files & Attachments from the resulting list.

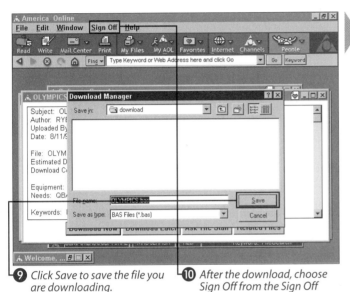

9 Click Save to save the file you are downloading.

10 After the download, choose Sign Off from the Sign Off menu and log off the system.

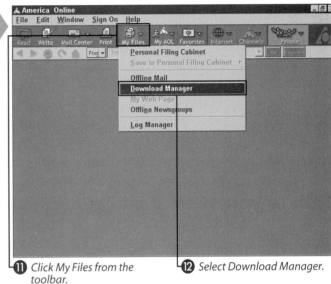

11 Click My Files from the toolbar.

12 Select Download Manager.

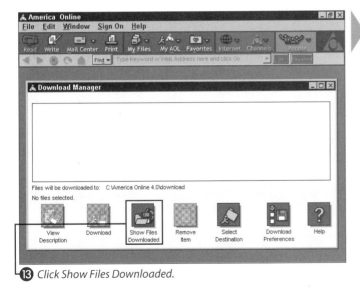

13 Click Show Files Downloaded.

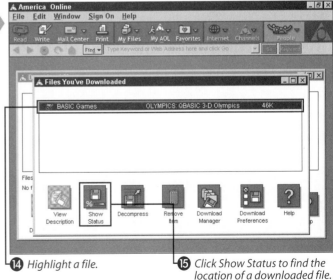

14 Highlight a file.

15 Click Show Status to find the location of a downloaded file.

Changing Download Preferences

Like many AOL features, the Download Manager can be customized by throwing a few switches. Set its preferences by clicking My Files, selecting Download Manager from the drop-down menu, and clicking the Download Preferences icon.

Options abound for the Download Manager. You can choose to "Display image files on download." While the default is on, some users prefer to click it off to save time online and just view graphics files later when they have signed off the system.

Another option is to "Automatically decompress files at sign-off." As noted, many files stored online have been compressed and archived to save you download time. The software defaults to automatically unpacking the programs when you sign off. I suggest you leave this option marked just as it is.

Consider the option to "Delete ZIP files after decompression." "ZIP" in this case refers to those original compressed files from which AOL automatically extracts files at sign-off (assuming you leave the previous option marked). You can either keep the original ZIP files as a backup or delete them. Click this option on if hard disk space is at a premium on your system.

Yet another option is to "Confirm additions to my download list." As noted, the Download Later button on file descriptions adds files to the Download Manager's list for later retrieval. This option simply specifies whether you are notified by AOL each time something is added to that list.

You can also configure your software to "Retain information about my last ___ downloads." The Download Manager maintains a list in your Personal Filing Cabinet of the items you have retrieved in the "Files You've Downloaded" folder. If you would rather not use disk space to keep such a list, uncheck this box.

"Use this directory as default for downloads." The default directory is the AOL \DOWNLOAD folder. For convenience, you probably ought to keep that as the destination directory. If you need to change it for some reason, you can enter a new path in the data-entry field at the bottom of the window or use the Browse button to find another directory.

TAKE NOTE

YOU CAN INTERRUPT DOWNLOADS

Most files can be retrieved in a minute or two. If you are downloading a really long file and get impatient with how long it is taking — or if you decide that you don't want the file after all — click the Finish Later button.

After a moment, the download stops. If you plan to resume the download later, don't delete the partial file that has been transferred to your computer already; the Download Manager needs to be able to find it when you want to resume the download later. If you really want to scrap the file, use the Download Manager's Remove Item icon to delete the partial file.

CROSS-REFERENCE

For a list of keywords to major forums, see the Appendix.

FIND IT ONLINE

For more help with the Download Manager, select the Help menu, select Offline Help, and then enter **download manager** in the query box.

Using Download Manager

If you have several files to retrieve from various places around AOL or just one that is especially long and will take a lot of time, consider using the Download Manager.

When you click the Download Later button after reading a file's description, you automatically add that file to the list being compiled by the Download Manager. After you have marked all the files you want, you can use the Download Manager to retrieve them all at one time, either while you are online or later as part of a scheduled visit to the system with Automatic AOL.

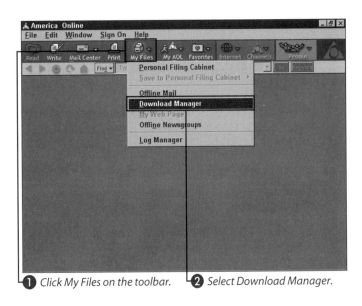

① *Click My Files on the toolbar.*   ② *Select Download Manager.*

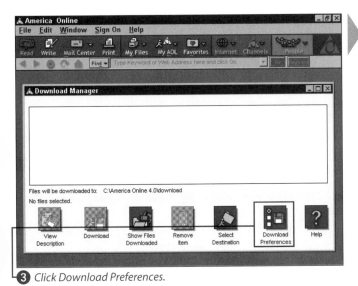

③ *Click Download Preferences.*

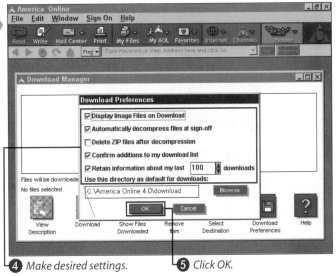

④ *Make desired settings.*   ⑤ *Click OK.*

Uploading Files

When you have become a regular in one or more forums, you may want to start contributing — or *uploading* — files to its libraries. Uploading is an excellent way to give something back to the community, and AOL encourages this by keeping any time spent uploading from being charged to your bill. If you are new to uploading, mention this in a note to the forum's operators. Often forums have online help files to guide newcomers through any conventions for contributing to that particular forum.

How to Upload

Forums that are accepting new files in their libraries display an Upload icon among the options visible when you are viewing files for descriptions and possible downloads. To upload a file from your computer, visit the forum and go to the appropriate section of its software library. That could be either a library with a topic that fits the file you wish to upload, or a special library just for uploading files.

Clicking the Upload icon produces a window for you to provide information about the file you are contributing. Enter data regarding the file's subject, author, any special equipment needed to use the file, and a description of what it does. The more information you provide, the more likely members will want to download it, so be generous. Designate the file to be uploaded with the Select File button. When all information is entered, click the Send button, and AOL takes it from there, transferring a copy of the file from your computer to AOL's system.

After the file is received, the forum's staff reviews it and decides whether to add it to the library for others to retrieve. It is checked for viruses and for functionality, making sure it does what it claims to do. This may take a few days as forums often are staffed by volunteers. If your file is released to the public, it appears at the top of the library it belongs in. Check back often to watch the download count rise!

TAKE NOTE

▶ **FOUR KINDS OF FILES ONLINE**

Forum libraries (and the resources on the Internet) offer four different kinds of software for downloading:

- ▶ Public domain programs. These files are uncopyrighted and completely free for you to use and copy.
- ▶ Freeware. These programs are copyrighted but offered free for personal use. Check the software's license agreement to determine if it can be used commercially and redistributed freely.
- ▶ Shareware. These copyrighted programs are distributed for free evaluation for a limited time period. After that evaluation, the user is required to either pay a registration fee or delete the program.
- ▶ Demoware. These are marketing versions of commercial software that give users a demonstration of some features and are not fully functional working programs.

CROSS-REFERENCE

For help with writing text online, see Chapter 2.

FIND IT ONLINE

For additional online help with uploading, visit Download 101 (keyword: DOWNLOAD 101) and select Uploading from the list of topics.

1 *Find and click the forum's File Libraries option.*

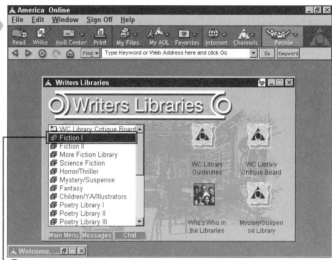

2 *Highlight and click the desired library.*

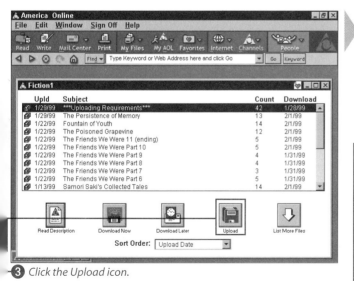

3 *Click the Upload icon.*

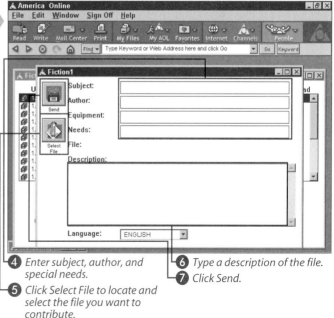

4 *Enter subject, author, and special needs.*

6 *Type a description of the file.*

7 *Click Send.*

5 *Click Select File to locate and select the file you want to contribute.*

Setting Up Automatic AOL

Automatic AOL can be used to automate the downloading and uploading of files, as well as the sending and retrieving of e-mail and postings. It can even save you time by signing on and perform these tasks when you are not even around.

With Automatic AOL (known to a previous generation of AOL members as *FlashSessions*), each screen name you create for your account has its own incoming and outgoing mailboxes and Download Manager. And Automatic AOL works in concert with the Personal Filing Cabinet for an easier way to read and write postings for message boards and newsgroups (discussed in the next chapter). To get started, click the toolbar's My AOL icon and select Preferences.

Automatic AOL is best known for its mail features, evidenced by the first three options in the Preferences window. The first, "Send mail from the 'Mail Waiting to be Sent' folder," tells Automatic AOL to send any waiting mail—I recommend that you leave this one checked. The second, "Get unread mail and put it in 'Incoming Mail' folder," retrieves any mail waiting for you and stores it in your Personal Filing Cabinet—I suggest you click this one to activate it. The third, "Download files that are attached to unread mail," directs Automatic AOL to retrieve any files that might be attached to e-mail you receive. This third option isn't for everyone. You shouldn't download files mailed by strangers. If you leave this option unselected, you can still sign on and manually download files attached to e-mail. I recommend leaving it unchecked.

Automatic AOL can also send and receive your message board and newsgroup postings. "Send postings from the 'Postings Waiting to be Sent' folder" tells Automatic AOL to post any forum messages (and notes to Internet newsgroups) you have written for automatic delivery. "Get unread postings and put in 'Incoming Postings' folder" retrieves unread messages from forum message boards (and Internet newsgroups) that you marked to read offline.

Files saved to your Download Manager are also retrieved by Automatic AOL. "Download files marked to be downloaded later*" enables Automatic AOL to automatically retrieve any software library files you have placed in the Download Manager by clicking the Download Later button. I suggest that you select this one.

Once your preferences are set, click the Select Names icon to the left of the selections, and in the subsequent display, check the screen name(s) and enter password(s) to be used by Automatic AOL when it automatically logs on.

TAKE NOTE

SIMPLIFYING SETUP

Clicking the Walk Me Through icon enables the system to simplify the setup by posing easy questions for each setting.

CROSS-REFERENCE

For more background on electronic mail, see Chapter 2.

FIND IT ONLINE

To get a further overview of Automatic AOL and its features, visit Member Services (keyword: HELP), click the Find It Now option, and then enter **Automatic AOL** in the query box.

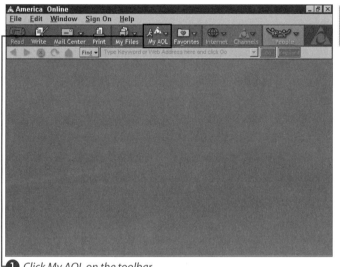

1 *Click My AOL on the toolbar.*

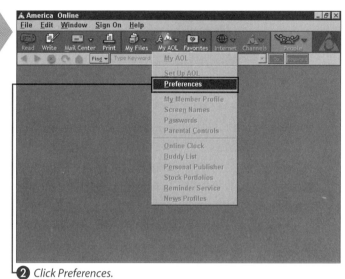

2 *Click Preferences.*

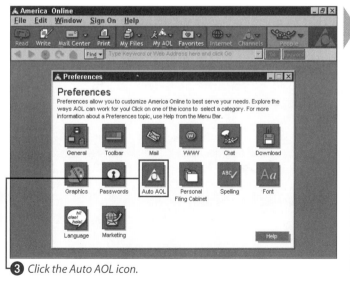

3 *Click the Auto AOL icon.*

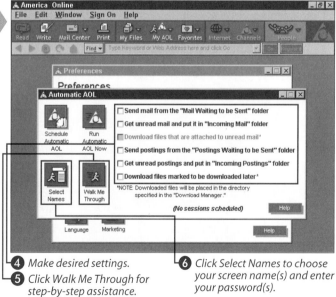

4 *Make desired settings.*

5 *Click Walk Me Through for step-by-step assistance.*

6 *Click Select Names to choose your screen name(s) and enter your password(s).*

Running Automatic AOL

Automatic AOL is really a kind of built-in software robot that does your bidding. It can carry out your commands either while you sit and watch or at some scheduled time, hours or even days after you have left the keyboard.

At any time, you can direct your robot to get busy. Begin by clicking the toolbar's Mail Center icon and selecting Run Automatic AOL Now. Alternatively, you can click the Run Automatic AOL Now icon on the Automatic AOL window. If you want to review or change your Automatic AOL setup, click Set Session. If you want to remain signed on after the Automatic AOL session is done, click the checkbox beside "Stay Online When Finished." When ready, click Begin, and Automatic AOL whisks about its tasks. It is fascinating to watch the first time, but I recommend you do something else while it works—you can't use other AOL functions while Automatic AOL is in progress.

Scheduling Automatic AOL to Run Later

For Automatic AOL to really shine, you need to give it permission to go online on your behalf at some scheduled time in the future. To schedule it to run later, click the toolbar's Mail Center icon and select Set up Automatic AOL (or just use keyword: AUTO AOL). The first time you use the option, you may see a screen asking which mode of operation you wish; select Expert Setup.

If you haven't already set your preferences, select or change the tasks you want performed by Automatic AOL and then click the Schedule Automatic AOL icon. Check the Enable Scheduler box to alert your Auto AOL robot that it has a schedule. Now select the days, times, and frequency you want Automatic AOL to run. Note that you can pick any hour of the day to start Automatic AOL, but there are only two, pre-set times during each hour to choose from—AOL does this purposefully to balance load on the system. To save your settings, click OK. Now just make sure the AOL software is running on your computer at the scheduled times (and is not already online).

TAKE NOTE

OFFLINE VERSUS ONLINE

If you already are online, Automatic AOL runs only for the screen name with which you currently are signed on. So if you want to activate Automatic AOL for more than one screen name created for this account, sign off before activating Automatic AOL. Passwords for your screen names must be stored, as described at the beginning of Chapter 4, for Automatic AOL to be able to sign on when you are not around. If you choose not to store your password, you have to manually sign on to AOL with each screen name and start Automatic AOL while you are online.

CROSS-REFERENCE
For information on writing e-mail offline for later online delivery, see Chapter 2.

FIND IT ONLINE
To get additional information about Automatic AOL, visit the My AOL site (keyword: MY AOL).

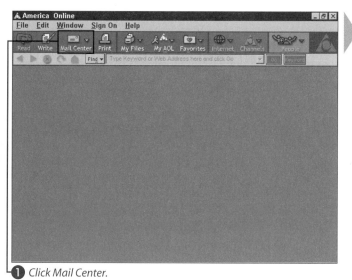

1 Click Mail Center.

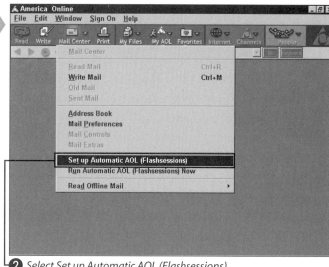

2 Select Set up Automatic AOL (Flashsessions).

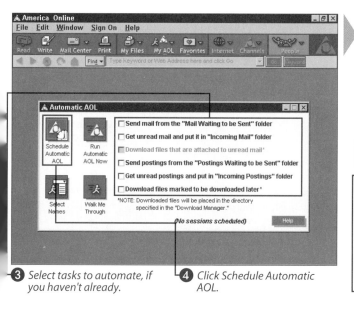

3 Select tasks to automate, if you haven't already.

4 Click Schedule Automatic AOL.

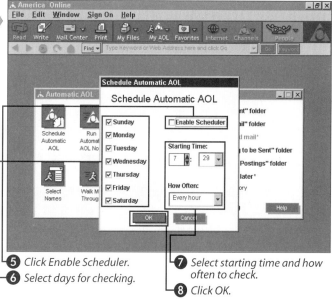

5 Click Enable Scheduler.

6 Select days for checking.

7 Select starting time and how often to check.

8 Click OK.

Using Auto AOL Offline

Once Automatic AOL has been put through its paces — either on a time-delayed basis or with you in attendance — you have data waiting for your attention, such as newly arrived e-mail or messages from favorite forums. This section shows how to deal with what Automatic AOL has brought home.

To read and respond to e-mail collected by Automatic AOL, click the toolbar's Mail Center icon and then select Read Offline Mail. Click Incoming/Saved Mail, and then, in the resulting display, double-click the e-mail you want to read. If you then want to respond, click the Reply (or Forward) button and enter your message as usual. Click the Send Later icon to post the letter on your next sign-on or at the next Automatic AOL session (if you have one scheduled and have checked the appropriate Automatic AOL Preferences option).

To find files collected by Automatic AOL, click the toolbar's My Files icon, select Download Manager, and click Show Files Downloaded. Highlight a file and click Show Status to find its location on your hard drive.

Reading and Replying to Captured Message Board Posts

To read message board posts gathered by Automatic AOL, click the toolbar's My Files icon and then select Personal Filing Cabinet. In the Newsgroups folder, double-click the message you want to read. Once a message is open, additional options make it easier to move about in the collected data. You may reply to the entire group or to the specific author of the note you are reading, delete the message from your Personal Filing Cabinet, or create a new message in that topic. You can also read the previous or next message, the previous new next thread of messages, or the next group of threads.

If you want to reply to a message, highlight any section of original text you want to quote and then click either Reply to Group (to send the response to the message board or newsgroup) or Reply to Author (if you want to send private e-mail to the writer of the original post). Compose and edit your response and then click Send Later.

CROSS-REFERENCE

For more about your Personal Filing Cabinet, see Chapter 5.

FIND IT ONLINE

For online assistance with the filing cabinet, go to Member Services (keyword: HELP), click the Find It Now button, and enter **filing cabinet** in the query box.

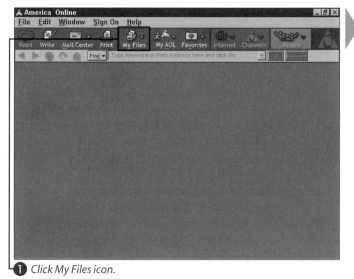

1 Click My Files icon.

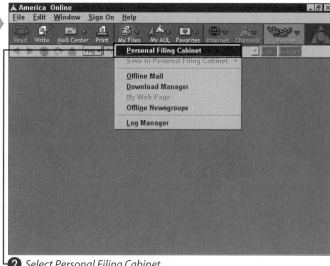

2 Select Personal Filing Cabinet.

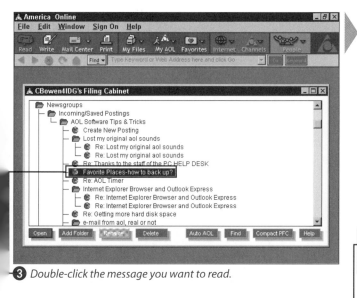

3 Double-click the message you want to read.

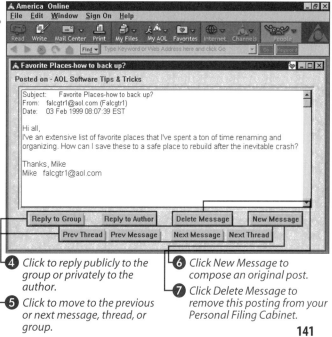

4 Click to reply publicly to the group or privately to the author.

5 Click to move to the previous or next message, thread, or group.

6 Click New Message to compose an original post.

7 Click Delete Message to remove this posting from your Personal Filing Cabinet.

141

Personal Workbook

Q&A

1 What are the three levels of a message board?

_____

_____

_____

2 How do you reply to a message on a message board?

_____

_____

_____

3 How do you customize AOL message boards?

_____

_____

_____

4 What special AOL feature is called into play by the Download Later option button?

_____

_____

_____

5 How can you interrupt a download in progress?

_____

_____

_____

6 What option do you select if you want to contribute a file to a forum's library?

_____

_____

_____

7 How do you set up the Automatic AOL feature?

_____

_____

_____

8 Bonus Question: How do you read offline the messages retrieved for you by Automatic AOL?

_____

_____

_____

ANSWERS: PAGE 339

EXTRA PRACTICE

1 Practice hunting down files (keyword: FILE SEARCH). For instance, see if you can locate the file used as an example in this chapter by searching for recreational computer programs with the Olympic Games as a theme.

2 Give Automatic AOL a spin, enabling it to pick up messages for you as you watch.

3 Also, write e-mail to yourself and then schedule an unattended Automatic AOL session for an hour from now to see how it picks up the letter.

4 Use the AOL Find feature you see in Chapter 3 to locate forums of interest you can visit.

5 Browse the forums' message boards and find discussions in which you can participate.

6 Check out the forums' libraries for files to download.

REAL-WORLD APPLICATIONS

✔ If you download a file by mistake or got the wrong file, or if the download gets interrupted by system problems and won't resume, you can request a credit from the AOL customer service department. Use the keyword: CREDIT. Fill in the resulting form with information on when the problem occurred, the reason for the problem, and the number of minutes lost. Then click the Send Request button.

✔ Not all message boards are organized exactly the same. Some are *threaded* message boards, meaning messages begin with an original post and move on to each reply before beginning discussion on a new subject or topic. Other message boards, especially those on the Internet seen in the next chapter, are unthreaded. Here posts move from subject to subject to subject, without regard to topics. On unthreaded message boards, subjects are listed only in chronological order.

Visual Quiz

What does this screen signify? How can it interact with another major feature of the AOL software?

_____

_____

_____

_____

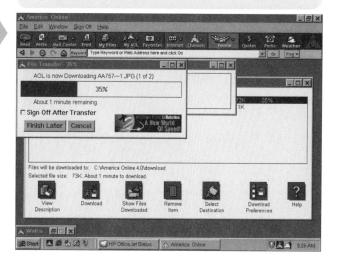

CHAPTER **7**

MASTER
THESE
SKILLS

▶ **Making the Internet Connection**

▶ **Navigating the Web**

▶ **Finding Things on the Web**

▶ **Finding People**

▶ **Using Yellow Pages**

▶ **Creating Your Own Web Pages**

▶ **Finding and Joining Newsgroups**

▶ **Reading Messages Online**

▶ **Reading Messages Offline**

▶ **Using Internet Extras**

Exploring the Internet

Not so long ago, books about America Online put their discussions of the Internet and the World Wide Web in their very back pages. Some authors thought the Internet was too complex for most of us. Some publishers saw the Net as too big to be covered as just part of a book. Some in the online community even wanted us to be "protected" from the wild and wooly Internet because it was notoriously unregulated, cyberspace's version of the unruly Old West.

Times change. In the past few years, tens of millions of people around the world started surfing the Internet. Many of them now actually explore the Web before they even see America Online. Internet e-mail addresses now appear on business cards and Web site locations are added to television commercials. Even political candidates invite us to rally with them on the Internet. And, while of course the Net is still huge — more enormous than ever — and just as unregulated and unpredictable, it also is less complex. That is, in part, because of America Online's efforts to incorporate the Web into mainstream computing. With AOL version 4.0, America Online

- ▶ offers its best Web browser to date as part of the AOL software. It is powerful and yet easy to use.
- ▶ adds an Internet icon on the toolbar for seamless Web connections.
- ▶ expands its tools like the Find command and the Favorite Places feature to locate and save Web sites as well as AOL pages.
- ▶ broadens the scope of the Personal Filing Cabinet and the Automatic AOL options to simplify your participation in Internet message boards, called newsgroups.
- ▶ simplifies its facilities for creating and publishing your own Web pages.

So the Internet has become mainstream, and nowadays the Net is actually the reason many people get online in the first place. In other words, the bottom line is: The time has come to let the Internet step up to the middle of the book.

Making the Internet Connection

The Internet Connection is the rallying point for AOL members wanting to explore the World Wide Web and other Internet features. One of the first Internet gateways to appear anywhere, the Internet Connection continues to offer a user-friendly interface to the world beyond AOL. While AOL doesn't own or maintain the Internet itself, it acts much like your local highway commissioner by providing good access to the Interstate. The Internet Connection is the equivalent of convenient, easy on-ramps to the best destinations on the Information Superhighway.

By far the most popular Internet destination these days is the Web (short for World Wide Web). AOL not only makes the Web simple to reach, it integrates it fully into your software. While those outside of AOL may need to spend time and money gathering together software components, you have everything you need already in your AOL software. In fact, the software makes the transition from AOL to the Web so seamless that you may never know you've left AOL.

The first two figures on the facing page show you how to reach the Internet Connection and the World Wide Web beyond it. For an even faster connection, you can bypass both windows and go to the Web directly with keyword: WEB. As you travel the Web, the address (also called an URL) of the page you are currently viewing is always displayed.

The Web page itself is usually a combination of text and pictures, and sometimes even sound and animation. *Hyperlinked* ("clickable") text is found throughout the Web. Roll your mouse cursor over any of the blue, underlined words and phrases, and over any of the icons, and your cursor changes into a pointing hand. As on AOL, you can click once with your mouse to activate a hyperlink.

TAKE NOTE

USING AN INTERNET SERVICE PROVIDER

If you use an Internet Service Provider (ISP) to connect to the World Wide Web and other Internet features, you also can use it to connect to America Online instead of your local AOL access number: First, set up your AOL software to use TCP/IP. Begin by staying or getting offline, clicking the Sign On option on the menu bar and then clicking Setup on the Sign-On screen. Choose the Create a location … option and then click Next. In the Add Location window, click the "Add a custom connection" option and then click Next.

To use your new ISP location, make your connection with your ISP as usual and then load the AOL software. On the Sign On screen, click the down arrow beside the Select Location box and then click "My Internet Provider" (or whatever you called the new location). Click Sign On to connect.

CROSS-REFERENCE

For more information about sign-on options, see Chapter 1.

FIND IT ONLINE

To get help online with Internet Connection, visit Member Services (keyword: HELP) and click the Internet & World Wide Web option on the resulting screen.

Some Internet definitions

▶ Web page or Web site. A display created on the Web with databases, articles, pictures, and other data, as well as links to other sites on the Internet.

▶ Web browser. This software enables you to connect to and "surf" the World Wide Web.

▶ HTML. Short for *Hypertext Markup Language*. The technical name of the universal language of the Web used to create those hyperlinked pages.

▶ URL. Short for *Uniform Resource Locator*. A unique address assigned to a page on the Web. It is the equivalent of a keyword on AOL.

▶ Search engine. An online utility for finding specific Web sites by names and subject.

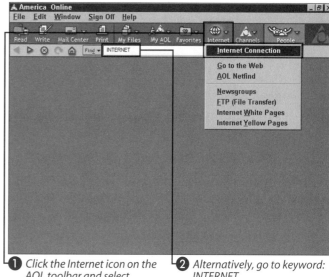

❶ *Click the Internet icon on the AOL toolbar and select Internet Connection.*

❷ *Alternatively, go to keyword: INTERNET.*

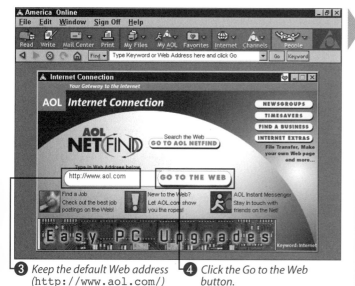

❸ *Keep the default Web address (http://www.aol.com/) in the center of the window, or type in a new one.*

❹ *Click the Go to the Web button.*

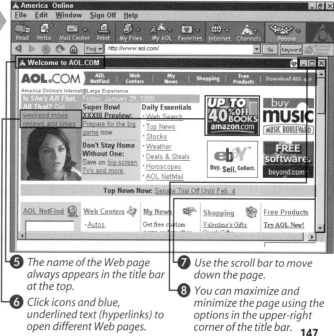

❺ *The name of the Web page always appears in the title bar at the top.*

❻ *Click icons and blue, underlined text (hyperlinks) to open different Web pages.*

❼ *Use the scroll bar to move down the page.*

❽ *You can maximize and minimize the page using the options in the upper-right corner of the title bar.*

Navigating the Web

America Online has so fully integrated the World Wide Web into AOL life that all of the navigation techniques you learned in Chapter 3 also work on the Web, making it easy to step back and forth between AOL and the Web. Even getting to the Web works in the same way. Just as you use keywords to get to AOL pages, you can use URLs (Web addresses) to get to Web pages. You can even enter an URL into the toolbar's data field or the keyword window (Ctrl+K) just like you enter an AOL keyword.

Once you arrive at a Web page, the left (back) and right (forward) arrow buttons in your AOL toolbar continue to function just as they do with AOL pages. The back button returns you to the previous pages you visited (Web and AOL alike). The forward button sends you forward until you reach the last page you visited. If you want to go back again, say six or seven pages, you don't need to click the back arrow six or seven times — just use your History Trail. Click the down arrow next to the data field in the center of the toolbar and the list of all of Web and AOL pages you visited recently appears, beginning with the most recent page. Simply click on the one you want and you're whisked back there without any intervening steps.

Remember that anything displayed in blue, underlined text — either on the Web or on AOL — is a link that you can click for a new page. Icons and some pictures also are "clickable." Drop-down menus transport you to new pages as well. Click the down arrow next to a menu to produce the list then select your destination. There are also data-entry fields for searching information such as stock quotes and so on.

As you reach a new Web page, notice again that the new URL appears in the data field in your toolbar and that the page is structurally similar to previous ones. It has a scroll bar, hyperlinks, drop-down menus, and data entry fields for searching, though, of course, the information itself is different. Where the News page dealt with newspapers and stocks, this Entertainment page covers TV and movies.

TAKE NOTE

USING DROP-DOWN MENUS

Web page menus that drop-down with a list of selections may require an extra step. Some menus activate upon selection, while others may require you click another button (like Go! or Search) to get things going.

SAVING FAVORITE PLACES

As on AOL itself, the title bar of each page on the Web includes the familiar heart icon. Click it to save it as a favorite place.

CROSS-REFERENCE

For background on navigation techniques, from keywords to the History Trail, see Chapter 3.

FIND IT ONLINE

To get further Web background online, go to the Internet Connection screen (keyword: INTERNET), click Internet Extras, and then select Internet Help from the subsequent display.

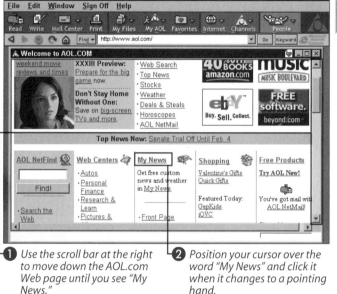

1 Use the scroll bar at the right to move down the AOL.com Web page until you see "My News."

2 Position your cursor over the word "My News" and click it when it changes to a pointing hand.

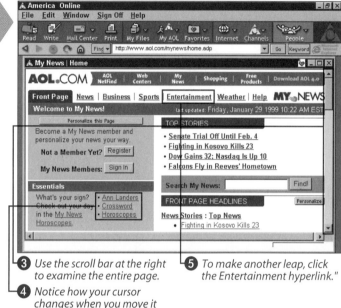

3 Use the scroll bar at the right to examine the entire page.

4 Notice how your cursor changes when you move it over hyperlinks and buttons.

5 To make another leap, click the Entertainment hyperlink."

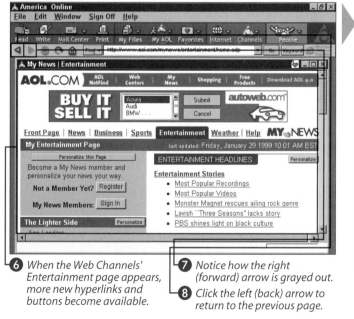

6 When the Web Channels' Entertainment page appears, more new hyperlinks and buttons become available.

7 Notice how the right (forward) arrow is grayed out.

8 Click the left (back) arrow to return to the previous page.

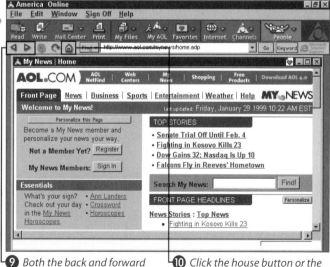

9 Both the back and forward arrows are active when you return to the My News page.

10 Click the house button or the back arrow again to return to the AOL.com Web page where we started.

Finding Things on the Web

The World Wide Web truly is global, adding hundreds of thousands of pages each week, and much larger than America Online. AOL is to the Internet as your town is to the nation, or maybe even to the world itself. For that reason, we need facilities — called *search engines* — for locating information on the Web. AOL has created its own, called AOL NetFind.

AOL NetFind uses Excite Incorporated's clever *Intelligent Concept Extraction* technology to find more of what you are looking for on the Web by searching for the concepts as well as the words. In other words, like most search facilities you have used, AOL NetFind looks for documents that contain the exact words you enter in the data-entry field. It then takes things a step further by also looking for the ideas most closely linked to those words. This increases your chances of finding what you seek in this massive reservoir of data. Once AOL NetFind has found something, you can redisplay the results to your liking and fine-tune your search further — all with just the click of your mouse.

AOL NetFind is more than just a good search engine, though. Each week they reveal the most popular searches and the best Web sites — just the thing when you're not sure where you're going. Those of you who know what you want can explore AOL NetFind Tips, a collection of searching secrets for finding exactly what you seek (keyword: NETFIND TIPS). There is more to AOL NetFind searching, too, like specific business, individual, e-mail, newsgroup, and kid searches. You can even extend your search overseas — AOL NetFind offers links to Canada, Germany, and the United Kingdom, with more to come.

Feel confident to explore and "Net surf" by clicking links and icons — you now know how to get back to familiar ground using your usual navigation techniques. If you exhaust AOL NetFind's resources or just want to venture further afield, search on "search engine" for a list of other searching pages. More explorations abound at Excite (`http://www.excite.com/`), Yahoo! (`http://www.yahoo.com`), and Lycos (`http://www.lycos.com`). You can type these and any other URLs directly into the AOL keyword box for smooth surfing.

TAKE NOTE

MANY WAYS TO FIND AOL NETFIND

▶ Use keyword: NETFIND.
▶ Click the Go to AOL NetFind button on the Internet Connection window.
▶ Click the toolbar's Find button and select Find it on the Web from the drop-down menu.
▶ Click the Internet icon on the toolbar and then choose AOL NetFind from the menu.
▶ Enter the Web address http://www.aol.com/netfind in the keyword box.

CROSS-REFERENCE
For more about search strategies, see Appendix C.

FIND IT ONLINE
To get further assistance online with AOL NetFind, visit Member Services (keyword: HELP), click the Find It Now button, and then enter NETFIND in the query box.

Performing Advanced Searches

You often have to be more specific in your search strategies in order to home in on just the subject of interest. Use words that are as specific as possible to what you are looking for.

▶ Put quotation marks around entire phrases you want searched.

▶ Use *AND* or a plus sign *(+)* to narrow searches by requiring matches that contain two or more specific words or phrases, as in *"ice cream" AND business*.

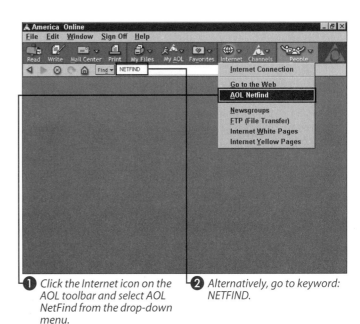

① *Click the Internet icon on the AOL toolbar and select AOL NetFind from the drop-down menu.*

② *Alternatively, go to keyword: NETFIND.*

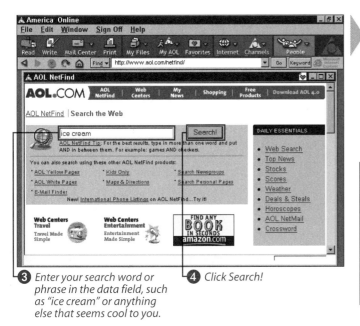

③ *Enter your search word or phrase in the data field, such as "ice cream" or anything else that seems cool to you.*

④ *Click Search!*

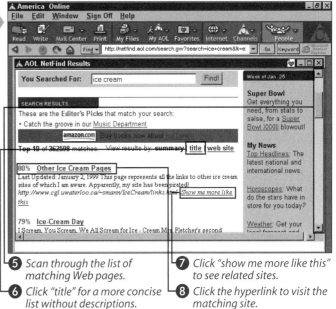

⑤ *Scan through the list of matching Web pages.*

⑥ *Click "title" for a more concise list without descriptions.*

⑦ *Click "show me more like this" to see related sites.*

⑧ *Click the hyperlink to visit the matching site.*

Finding People

AOL NetFind also can locate people, using Web resources that operate like enormous searchable phone books. You can search for and find a person's street address and phone number, as well as zip code. If they have registered online, you can even find other information such as e-mail addresses and associated Web sites. In keeping with the phone book metaphor, this resource is known as the AOL White Pages.

Finding the AOL White Pages is considerably easier than locating the real phone book that is rarely near the phone. You can get to the AOL White Pages through the Internet icon on your toolbar or via keyword: WHITE PAGES. It is also available through AOL NetFind — just click the White Pages link at the left of the screen.

Once the White Pages are open, fill in as many of the data fields as you can. The First Name field is optional — you can leave it blank or enter just the first few letters to narrow the search. The Last Name field requires at least the first letter of a name — it is best to type as much of the name as you know in order to limit the number of retrievals. The City field can be left blank — if you do enter something here, make sure you spell out the full city name, no initials like *L.A.* or *N.Y.C.* The State field also is optional — use either the two-letter postal code, the state's full name, or the first few letters of the state's name. Clicking the Find! button activates the Search.

AOL White Pages lists its findings, with names, addresses, cities and states, zip codes, and phone numbers. Some listings also have e-mail addresses and other data. The results are in alphabetical order by last name, with further sorting by first name, middle name/initial, and address if necessary. Only the first eight matches are displayed, so be sure to click "next" at the bottom if it is available.

TAKE NOTE

EXERCISING PRIVACY OPTIONS

Data listed in the Find a Person facility comes from publicly available U.S. white page listings, along with U.S. and international listings that people have submitted. You can add your entry to the database by clicking the "Add Your Listing" link at the bottom of any of the Find a Person screens. You will get a password that enables you to modify the entry. But what if you want your listing in the database hidden? Click the "Modify Your Listing" link on any Find a Person screen. When prompted, enter the password. On the subsequent screen, scroll down the display until you see Privacy Options, where you can then check "Please don't show my listing or my e-mail address."

CROSS-REFERENCE

For information about find fellow AOL subscribers, see the discussion of the Member Directory in Chapter 5.

FIND IT ONLINE

For online assistance with locating tools, go to Find Central (keyword: FIND CENTRAL) and click the Help button.

Searching and Sending to E-mail Addresses

AOL NetFind's E-mail Finder can't find every e-mail address ever used but it can find many of them:

▶ Click the "E-mail Finder" link on the AOL NetFind screen.

▶ Type a last name and as much of the first name as you know.

▶ Click the Find button or press the Enter key.

▶ Search the list to see if the person you seek is there. If so, click the hyperlinked name and AOL takes you to the Mail Center, opens the Write Mail screen, and automatically puts the e-mail address you have clicked into the Send To: field.

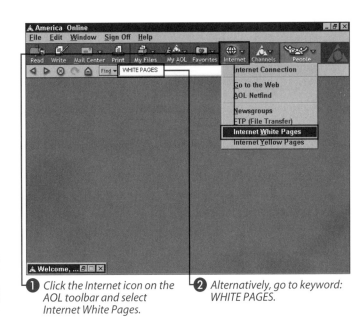

1 Click the Internet icon on the AOL toolbar and select Internet White Pages.

2 Alternatively, go to keyword: WHITE PAGES.

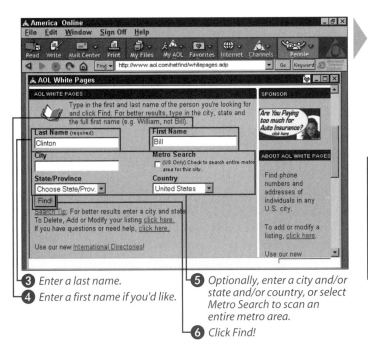

3 Enter a last name.

4 Enter a first name if you'd like.

5 Optionally, enter a city and/or state and/or country, or select Metro Search to scan an entire metro area.

6 Click Find!

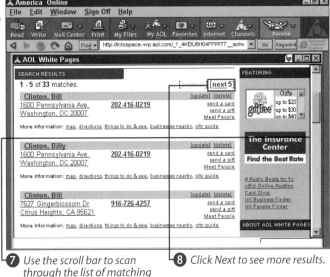

7 Use the scroll bar to scan through the list of matching names and addresses.

8 Click Next to see more results.

Using Yellow Pages

Looking for a business or service somewhere in the nation? Why make a trip to the library to get out-of-town yellow pages? AOL NetFind locates businesses for you with the AOL Yellow Pages. With it you can find street addresses and phone numbers for United States businesses. AOL Yellow Pages even draws you maps to show you how to get there!

You can search by business category (such as *hotel*) or by business name (such as *Hilton*). Be sure to click one of the buttons under the field to indicate whether you are searching by business category or by name. The City field is optional — you can leave it blank or enter the full name of the community (no abbreviations). The State field is required if you are searching by category — it needs either the two-letter postal code, the state's full name, or the first few letters. Click the Find! button after you have filled in the information.

When the Yellow Pages lists its findings, it provides names, addresses, and phone numbers. There are even hyperlinked options for maps, which are created to order for each business location. The maps come complete with navigational controls that let you zoom in, zoom out, move about, and label features. The Yellow Pages also gives you options for driving directions to the business from any starting point you indicate. You can even save time by entering your intermediate destinations and letting it plan out the fastest route to each location. Just click the hyperlinked "directions" text displayed with the listing and follow the instructions on the screen.

TAKE NOTE

▶ SHORTCUT TO THE YELLOW PAGES

In a hurry to find a business address and map? A shortcut to the Find a Business feature is on the toolbar. Click the Internet icon and then select Internet Yellow Pages from the drop-down menu. Find a Business is also a clickable button on the Internet Connection screen. You can even get to the Yellow Pages from the White Pages (and vice versa).

▶ TIME SAVERS DO A DOZEN USEFUL JOBS

As you surf the Web, you will find scores of useful databases and calculators for simplifying tasks. America Online gets you started with Time Savers (`http://www.aol.com/NetFind/timesavers`), which you can reach by clicking the Time Savers button on the main Internet Connection screen. The selection grows and changes all the time, but generally the time savers include links to Web sites that help with taxes, finding a new or used car, changing jobs, planning a night out (or a night in), buying a computer, managing your investments, and finding a new home. Listed on the AOL NetFind display, each Time Saver is hyperlinked for direct access to the Web site.

CROSS-REFERENCE
For more about finding businesses, see Chapter 10.

FIND IT ONLINE
To get more online help with Web searching, go to Member Services (keyword: HELP), select Internet & World Wide Web, and then choose the topic "Searching the Web" from the resulting list.

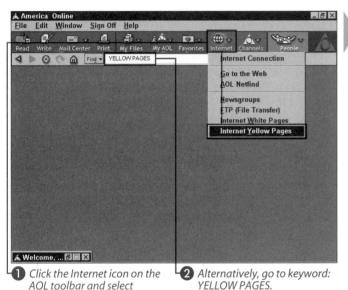

1 Click the Internet icon on the AOL toolbar and select Internet Yellow Pages.

2 Alternatively, go to keyword: YELLOW PAGES.

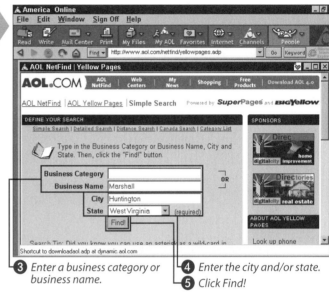

3 Enter a business category or business name.

4 Enter the city and/or state.

5 Click Find!

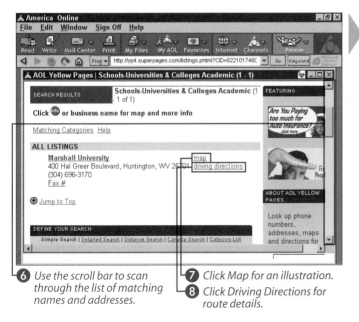

6 Use the scroll bar to scan through the list of matching names and addresses.

7 Click Map for an illustration.

8 Click Driving Directions for route details.

9 Click the arrows to move the focus of the map.

10 Click a zoom button to zoom in or out.

Creating Your Own Web Pages

Want to make your own big splash in cyberspace? AOL's Personal Publisher software enables you to quickly create and manage a Web page complete with text and graphics, hyperlinks, background colors, and patterns, just like the ones you have seen earlier in this chapter. The Web page creation feature requires a small add-on to your AOL software. To get the free add-on, use keyword: PERSONAL PUBLISHER or click the toolbar's My AOL icon and select Personal Publisher from the drop-down menu. Click the Download Now button on the window that pops up to get the add-on and follow the on-screen instructions. When the download is complete, the system may bring you to the Welcome to Personal Publishing window where you can begin your first Web page. If it does not, you can use keyword: PERSONAL PUBLISHER to reach the site where you can create your own Web page.

When you click the Create button to begin building your home page, you are asked to choose a *template* to define your layout. A template is a sample Web page with predetermined styles for headlines and photo placement and so on. Highlight one of the template names in the box at the left and then click the Preview button to see what it looks like. If you don't like it, click the Return button to return to the list and pick another. When you have sampled the template you want to use for your own home page, click the Begin button to retrieve a copy of the template and save it on your computer.

Personal Publisher continues to walk you through the template step-by-step, customizing the content as you see fit. The system prompts you for each piece of information it needs. Throughout the process you can preview your home page in progress (click the Return button to resume the work) or step back to change things you did in previous steps. When you have worked your way through the seven to nine steps and have the page the way you want it, click Done. Enter a filename when you are prompted (`index.htm` is recommended).

Continued

TAKE NOTE

WHERE'S THE PAGE SAVED?

Your page is saved on your computer's hard disk within your AOL folder and can be opened again at any time from the Personal Publisher site (keyword: PERSONAL PUBLISHER).

BUT WHERE DOES IT "GO?"

Every AOL member has space automatically reserved on a server connected to the Internet. When you publish your page, it is placed into a directory that contains, among other things, folders labeled with your screen name and the template name. You can see and access this FTP directory (FTP is described in more detail later in this chapter) at keyword: MY PLACE.

CROSS-REFERENCE
For more about resolving computing issues, see Chapter 11.

FIND IT ONLINE
To get more background on Personal Publisher, go to Internet Connection (keyword: INTERNET), click Internet Extras, and select Personal Publisher from the next screen.

Typical Data Needed by Templates

Generally you are asked for the following information when creating templates:

▶ A title and headline for the page

▶ Background style and colors

▶ A picture, either of your own or from clip art available online, clicking one from a selection presented on the screen

▶ Real text to replace the sample text in the template with what you really want the page to say

▶ Hyperlinks to other Web sites you want to connect to, copied from your Favorite Places list

▶ Extras, such as links to your e-mail address

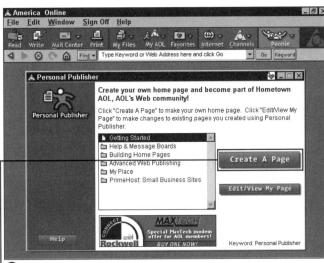

① *Click Create A Page.*

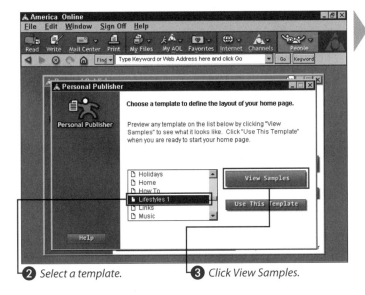

② *Select a template.*   **③** *Click View Samples.*

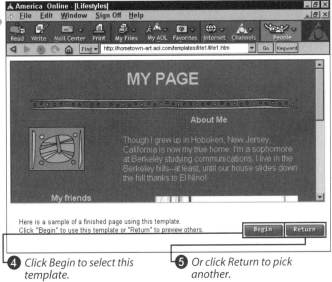

④ *Click Begin to select this template.*   **⑤** *Or click Return to pick another.*

Creating Your Own Web Pages

Continued

Modifying Your Pages

Your page is created, but you think it may need some polishing before it is ready for publishing and a world debut. Personal Publisher can also help with modifications. Just use the PERSONAL PUBLISHER keyword to return to the main window and click the Manage Your Pages button. Note that your page has been saved in a folder on your disk.

Managing your page is easy. You can preview your page again, rename your page, and edit the page itself. Follow the on-screen instructions for making modifications and then click Save to keep the changes. When you have the page as you want it, click the Publish button and notice that the system lists the page's name, summarizes its number of graphic elements and total size, and offers a checkbox to include a menu of any other pages linked to this page. Click the Publish button to continue. The system automatically communicates with the Internet to post the page for you.

Once published, you are invited to include your page at Hometown AOL, the community of home pages on AOL. Simply choose a category, a subcategory, and then pick the community that best fits your home page. Type in a description when prompted, click OK, and that's it! You're now a homesteader at Hometown AOL.

The ability to self-publish to the world on the Web is empowering and addictive. If you become hooked,

rest assured that AOL provides plenty of room to grow. In fact, every screen name has up to 2 megabytes (MB) of space on AOL's computers for their Web pages (that's up to 10MB per account). When you're ready, AOL's high-octane Web publishing system is standing by at keyword: AOL PRESS.

TAKE NOTE

▶ TELLING YOUR FRIENDS WHERE TO FIND YOU

When your creation has been successfully published, the system provides you with the address (URL) of your home page. You can share this with your online friends who will want to see your new online home. And, of course, you can view it yourself online, using the URL as a keyword. Once your page is published, you still can return to make refinements and add more pages. Use the Manage Your Pages button on the main window to unpublish the page and to make editing changes.

▶ WEB HAS HELP WITH THE WEB

America Online's Web sites also link to a growing collection of helpful articles on how to use the Internet and the World Wide Web. Reach it by clicking any links identified as NetHelp or go directly there with the URL http://www.aol.com/help/home.html. The site has links to resources about the Web in general, searching options, newsgroups, mailing lists, Web publishing, downloading software from the Net, and more.

CROSS-REFERENCE

For more about online learning, including computing topics, see Chapter 12.

FIND IT ONLINE

For more about publishing online, visit the AOL NetFind help page (http://www.aol.comnethelp/home.html) and click the "Web Publishing" link.

Let AOL Teach You More about Web Publishing

America Online is providing lots of background for teaching yourself about the basics of Web publishing. Here are some online resources:

▶ The Computing channel's On The Net department (keyword: ON THE NET) has Web publishing tools, support, and related topics for reading and downloading.

▶ Web Publishing Help Central (keyword: MY PLACE HELP) for information on Personal Publisher.

▶ The Personal Publisher welcome page (keyword: PERSONAL PUBLISHER) has a scroll box full of background articles.

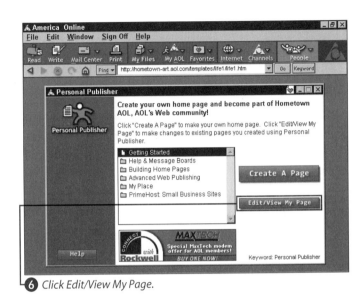

6 Click Edit/View My Page.

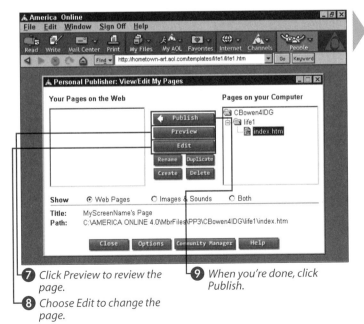

7 Click Preview to review the page.

8 Choose Edit to change the page.

9 When you're done, click Publish.

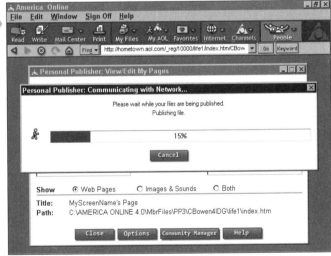

10 Personal Publisher puts your page on the Web.

Finding and Joining Newsgroups

Internet *newsgroups* (also called Usenet) are bulletin boards, much like the message boards in AOL forums. Currently more than 20,000 newsgroups operate, most of them unmoderated, so the tone and use of language is purely up to the participants. Anyone can join, or "subscribe" to, a newsgroup (usually without any fees involved), enabling him or her to read and to contribute to the messages. Messages in newsgroups are received and made available on Internet-linked computers and bulletin boards systems around the world.

To get started, reach the Newsgroup's page either by entering keyword: NEWSGROUPS or by clicking the Newsgroups icon on the Internet Connection window. You also can reach newsgroups by clicking the toolbar's Internet icon and selecting Newsgroups from the drop-down menu. Begin by clicking the Add Newsgroups icon. Scroll the resulting list of available choices and open any category you want to browse. The most active categories (alt, comp, news, rec, and so on) are listed at the top. After that, the rest of the list is alphabetical. Numbers at the right of the display tell you how many topics are in each category, anywhere from one to thousands. On subsequent visits here, you can use the Latest Newsgroups button to open a window of any newsgroups added since the last time you used the option. Open a topic to see the actual newsgroups within that topic, along with the number of subjects in each, to get an idea of how busy the newsgroup is.

To determine if you have indeed found a newsgroup you want to subscribe to (that is, to add to your personal newsgroups), browse the subjects and read a few messages. If you like it and want to return another time, subscribe to it and add it to your personal newsgroup collection. All newsgroups you subscribe to are available upon future visits when you click the Read My Newsgroups button.

If you find the task of wading through all 20,000 newsgroups overwhelming, try searching first. The Search All Newsgroups button on the main window sorts through the newsgroup names and descriptions and returns lists of matches. It even offers the option of reading the newsgroups' posts or subscribing to the newsgroup itself right then and there. Our old friend AOL NetFind provides newsgroups searches on both newsgroups and newsgroup messages, too.

TAKE NOTE

AOL TRANSLATES

▶ The Internet Names icon displayed through the newsgroups features links to AOL's Net-speak translation service, converting newsgroup names into plain English for easier reading by those unfamiliar with the Internet.

▶ For instance, the Internet name for "artificial intelligence" is "comp.ai.") If you would rather see the original Internet-style name of the latest newsgroups, click the Internet Names icon.

CROSS-REFERENCE

For more about AOL's own message boards, see Chapter 6.

FIND IT ONLINE

For additional online help with understanding newsgroups, visit the Newsgroup Center (keyword: NEWSGROUPS).

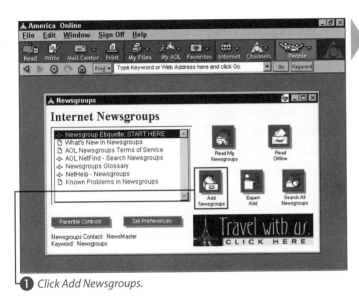

1 Click Add Newsgroups.

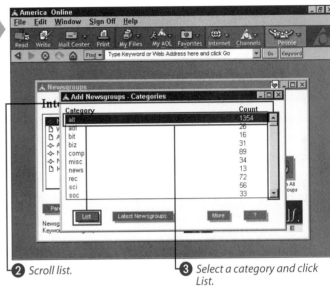

2 Scroll list.

3 Select a category and click List.

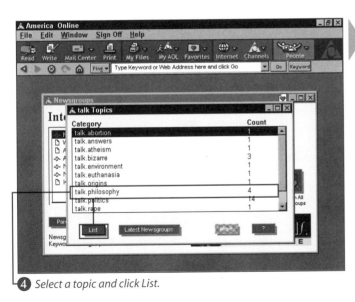

4 Select a topic and click List.

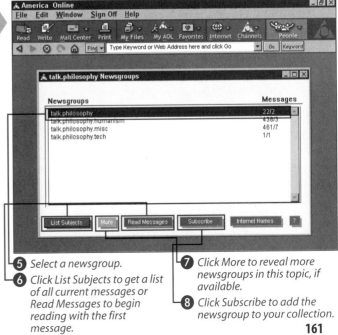

5 Select a newsgroup.

6 Click List Subjects to get a list of all current messages or Read Messages to begin reading with the first message.

7 Click More to reveal more newsgroups in this topic, if available.

8 Click Subscribe to add the newsgroup to your collection.

Reading Messages Online

You can check your favorite newsgroups during any online visit. Just drop by the Newsgroups area at keyword: NEWSGROUPS and click the Read My Newsgroups icon. This button produces a list of the newsgroups you have added to your personal collection. Don't worry if you haven't subscribed to any newsgroups yet. AOL has thoughtfully added some newsgroups to your list, such as `aol.newsgroups.help` (for newsgroup questions and answers), `aol.newsgroups.test` (for posting test messages), and `news.groups.reviews` (for descriptions and ratings of newsgroups). You can remove any newsgroup, including any of these preinstalled ones, by highlighting its name and then clicking the Remove button.

To dive into a newsgroup, highlight the newsgroup you want to visit and click the List All option to see all the subjects being discussed. Incidentally, the first time you go to a newsgroup, the number of unread messages is the same as the total number, so you can click either List Unread or List All. On subsequent visits, use List Unread to see the new messages (plus any messages you haven't already read in previous visits).

Finding a subject of interest is just the beginning. Open it and you'll discover you now have several options, similar to those you use with AOL message boards described in the previous chapter. You can see the previous or next message in this subject and view the previous or next subject in this newsgroup. You can mark the message as "unread" so you can read it again the next time you go to your newsgroups. You can reply to the group if you want to add your own public message to this thread in response to one you are reading. You can post a new message when your remark is not a direct reply to another message but is still connected to the newsgroup's topic. Last but not least, you can e-mail the author a private note. Before you post your first message in a newsgroup, consider a practice post or two in the `aol.newsgroups.test` newsgroup mentioned earlier.

TAKE NOTE

CREATING A CLEAN SLATE

Messages in the newsgroups were piling up before you got here, adding to the new ones coming all the time. Some newsgroups collect literally hundreds of messages a day. Messages posted before you subscribed continue to show up as "unread" clutter whenever you use the List Unread button.

▶ Some users like to occasionally clear the decks of all old messages, particularly when they first subscribe to a newsgroup. This gives them the feeling of having a fresh start.

▶ AOL provides icons labeled Mark All Read throughout the newsgroups section. Click the icon, and the next time you visit that newsgroup, you will see only those messages posted since your last visit, producing a much shorter list of postings.

CROSS-REFERENCE
For more about the organization of message boards, on AOL and on the Internet, see Chapter 6.

FIND IT ONLINE
To get more information about reading messages from newsgroups, visit the Newsgroup Center (keyword: NEWSGROUPS).

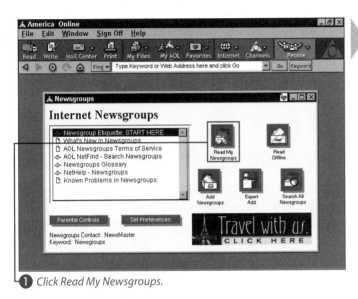

1 Click Read My Newsgroups.

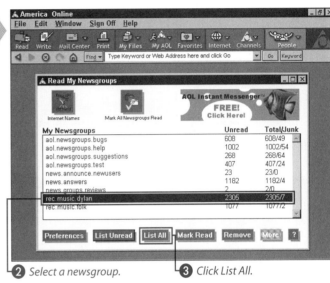

2 Select a newsgroup.   **3** Click List All.

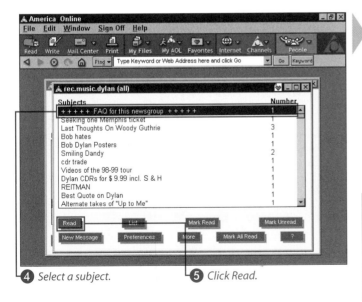

4 Select a subject.   **5** Click Read.

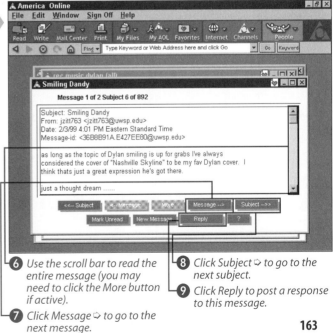

6 Use the scroll bar to read the entire message (you may need to click the More button if active).

7 Click Message ➪ to go to the next message.

8 Click Subject ➪ to go to the next subject.

9 Click Reply to post a response to this message.

Reading Messages Offline

Newsgroups have a way of becoming a regular stop on your daily online rounds. Unfortunately, finding the time to stop every day to find, read, and reply to the dozens or even hundreds of new postings is difficult. Luckily, you can read and write messages in your personal newsgroup collection offline much as you do with message boards. The Automatic AOL feature can be activated to collect the messages that you then can read and reply to when you are not connected to the system.

To get it all set up, go to the Newsgroups window (keyword: NEWSGROUPS) and click the Read Offline icon. From the resulting list of newsgroups, click the name of the newsgroup you want to read offline. From here you can add the newsgroup to the list at the right of the display, add all your newsgroups to the list, or remove one or all of the newsgroups that have been previously added. It may be tempting at first to add all your favorite newsgroups, but try to start with one or two to get a feel for the daily volume.

You now are ready to have Automatic AOL gather your newsgroup messages on its next online session, as described in the previous chapter. To make sure Auto AOL is set up to send and retrieve newsgroup messages, click the toolbar's My AOL icon, select Preferences from the drop-down menu, and then choose Auto AOL in the Preference windows. Click the checkboxes beside the options you want Auto AOL to perform (send postings and/or get unread postings). Click Select Names and choose the screen names and passwords for Automatic AOL. Now just schedule an Automatic AOL session, as described in Chapter 6.

TAKE NOTE

▶ USING THE FILING CABINET

After Automatic AOL has captured messages from your selected newsgroups you can read and respond to them offline. Click the toolbar's My Files icon and select Personal Filing Cabinet. In the Newsgroups folder, double-click the message you want to read. If you want to reply, click either the Reply to Group icon for a public response or the Reply to Author icon for a private e-mail answer. (Incidentally, if you want to quote from the original message in your reply, highlight the section of text to select it before clicking the icon.) Compose your message and click the Send Later icon, which in turn tells Automatic AOL to post it on its next scheduled session.

▶ A HANDY SHORTCUT

A shortcut to your newsgroups folders for offline reading is on the toolbar. Click the My Files icon and select Offline Newsgroups from the drop-down menu. You then go directly to the folders for Incoming/Saved Postings, Postings Waiting to be Sent, and Postings You've Sent.

CROSS-REFERENCE

For more about using your Personal Filing Cabinet, see Chapter 5.

FIND IT ONLINE

To get online help about the offline message reader, visit the Newsgroup Center (keyword: NEWSGROUPS).

Setting Newsgroup Preferences

You have control over how newsgroups perform for you. Go to the Newsgroups display (keyword: NEWSGROUPS) and click the Preferences icon. Then in the Newsgroups Preference screen, make adjustments to the following:

▶ Headers
▶ Name Style
▶ Sort Order
▶ Filtering
▶ Signature

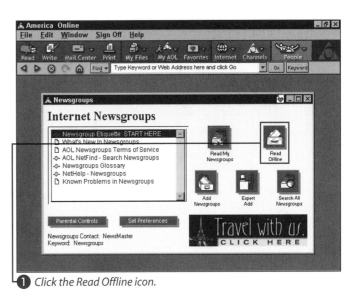

1 Click the Read Offline icon.

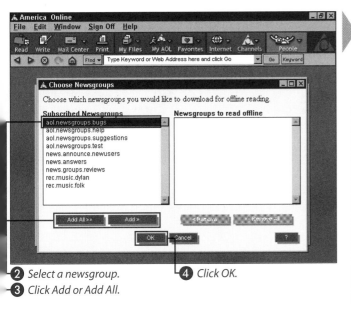

2 Select a newsgroup.
3 Click Add or Add All.
4 Click OK.

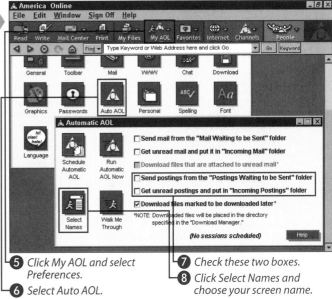

5 Click My AOL and select Preferences.
6 Select Auto AOL.
7 Check these two boxes.
8 Click Select Names and choose your screen name.

Using Internet Extras

In the years before the World Wide Web and 20,000 message boards called newsgroups, there was still an Internet, full of bulletin boards and messages, software, and databases. And all of those original Internet services, with strange-sounding names like *gopher* and *FTP*, are still around and available on AOL as Internet Extras.

Gophers

Before the Web, the hottest technology for finding your way around the Net was the gopher, which located databases and collections of articles and software. Hundreds of free databases still are available on the Internet in gopher format, devoted to topics as diverse as home brewing, NASA news, recipes, Congressional contact information, college slang, and the works of Shakespeare. These databases are "indexed," meaning that they can be searched for information using keywords and phrases.

America Online's Gopher service (keyword: GOPHER) is different from those usually found on the Internet, adding more structure to make navigating the system easier. AOL also has selected certain gophers that it thinks are especially interesting or useful and listed them as "Gopher Treasures." Scroll a list of topics (use the More button to expand the list) and double-click any topic of interest, and then let AOL take you to it. If you want to search for gophers beyond the AOL treasury, click the Search button or browse other lists on the Internet using the Gopher Directory button.

Mailing Lists

Electronic newsletters abound. Some are one-way communications, operated by a moderator who compiles the newsletter from assorted sources. Others invite everyone to contribute messages and replies. These are like message boards or newsgroups, except that they come to you rather than you having to go to them.

America Online has a list of more than 3,000 of these "mailing lists" on the Net (keyword: MAILING LIST). Usually all you have to do to sign up for one is to send a subscription e-mail to a designated online address requesting inclusion. After that, the newsletter pops up in your online mailbox to be read like any other letter. Click the Browse the Directory icon to link to the Web and search for mailing lists of interest. Follow online instructions for signing up.

TAKE NOTE

TALKING THROUGH TELNET

Many old computer bulletin board systems (see Chapter 6) first got onto the Internet through *telnet*, which enabled callers in one community to jump to boards and other sites all around the nation without hanging up and redialing a long-distance number. AOL's Telnet center (keyword: TELNET) connects to some of the best.

CROSS-REFERENCE

For more about downloading, see Chapters 6 and 11.

FIND IT ONLINE

To get additional online help with the Internet Extras, visit Member Services (keyword: HELP), click the Internet & World Wide Web option, and then on the next window select "FTP, Gopher, Telnet."

Finding FTP Sites

Use AOL's FTP site (keyword: FTP) to search FTP sites. There are, though, serious considerations to make before taking this particular journey:

▶ FTP is a direct connection between your computer and another system somewhere out on the Internet, without helpful lists and prompts.

▶ The FTP landscape is unregulated. Many of them are above board and honest, with some actually operated by government and scientific agencies. Others, on the other hand, traffic in a variety of cyberspace contraband, from pornography and hate material to counterfeit and pirated software.

▶ The sites aren't necessarily secure.

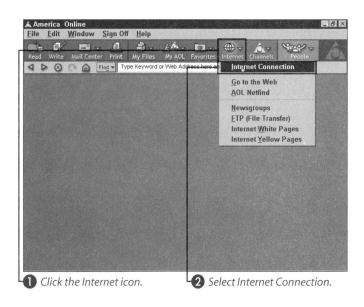

1 Click the Internet icon.

2 Select Internet Connection.

3 Click Internet Extras.

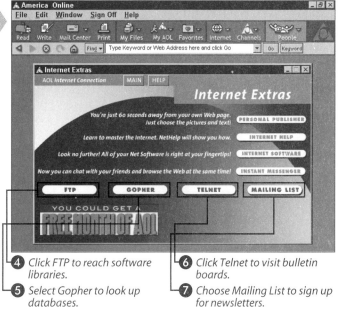

4 Click FTP to reach software libraries.

5 Select Gopher to look up databases.

6 Click Telnet to visit bulletin boards.

7 Choose Mailing List to sign up for newsletters.

Personal Workbook

Q&A

1 Name two ways to reach the Internet Connection.

_____

_____

_____

2 How is AOL's main Web page (www.aol.com) similar to windows on AOL itself?

_____

_____

_____

3 What does HTML mean?

_____

_____

_____

4 What is an URL?

_____

_____

_____

5 Name at least three ways to reach AOL's NetFind search engine.

_____

_____

6 How can you use AOL to find electronic mail addresses on the Internet?

_____

_____

_____

7 Where do you go on AOL to find links to Internet newsgroups?

_____

_____

_____

8 Bonus Question: What add-on software program can you obtain to publish your own pages on the Web?

_____

_____

_____

ANSWERS: PAGE 339

EXTRA PRACTICE

1 Use AOL NetFind to search for Web pages devoted to your hobbies, your occupation, your state and city, and the like.

2 Visit the AOL White Pages and look your own listing and that of friends and relatives.

3 With the AOL Yellow Pages, check listings for area businesses.

4 Call up maps of local firms and see how accurate they are.

5 Search for newsgroups that cover your particular interests.

6 Use Automatic AOL to retrieve newsgroup messages for you that you can then read in your Personal Filing Cabinet.

REAL-WORLD APPLICATIONS

✔ While AOL NetFind is a good search engine to practice with if you are new to the World Wide Web, remember that there are many of other popular search engines in use that you can reach. Check out Yahoo (`http://www.yahoo.com`), Infoseek (`http://www.infoseek.com`), Lycos (`http://www.lycos.com`), and HotBot (`http://www.hotbot.com`).

✔ Newsgroup names are hierarchical, with elements of the name separated by periods. So, `alt.politics` discusses general political topics, while `alt.politics.democrats` is a different group intended specifically for Democrat topics, and `alt.politics.democrats.clinton` focuses on the Clinton Administration.

Visual Quiz

Where are you when you see a screen like this one? What do you think the numbers at the right represent? How would you go about reading and replying to a message here?

_____

_____

_____

_____

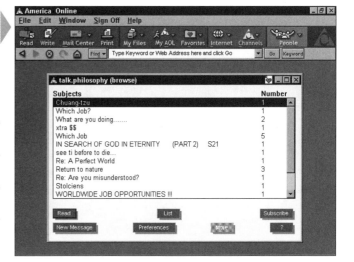

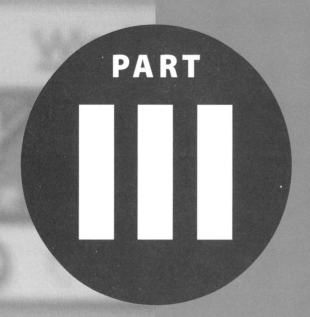

PART
III

Getting the Most out of AOL Channel Surfing

The nine chapters in this part take you to the next level of America Online. Using all the skills and techniques learned in the first part of the book, you are prepared to explore AOL's diverse neighborhoods, and not by merely wandering aimlessly, but by taking the direct route to the features and services you want right now.

Visiting cyberspace is sometimes described as "Net surfing." But let's be honest; most busy people don't have the spare time for surfing or Web *browsing*. In a busy life, you need a system that conserves, rather than consumes, your leisure time. That is why the goal of these chapters is to show you the best that each of AOL's 19 channels has to offer, how to reach them, and how to use them as the need arises.

CHAPTER 8

MASTER
THESE
SKILLS

▶ Visiting AOL Today

▶ Locking In on the News Channel

▶ Saving News Articles with the Log Manager

▶ Checking the Weather

▶ Sampling the Sports Channel

▶ Using the Influence Channel

▶ Creating News Profiles

Getting Your News

Throughout the unregulated Internet and its bright and feisty World Wide Web, rumors run rampant. Horrendous lies can be told on the prettiest pages. In a medium where everyone can be a publisher — even those with ulterior motives and hidden agendas — truth, accuracy, and accountability sometimes seem to be on the run. After a while, you long to come back to some of the traditional news reporting, where double-checking facts and attributing the sources of information are the rule, not the exception.

America Online has such places, resources where the day's news arrives from international wire services, from major newspapers and magazines, from broadcasters, and from Web correspondents. In this chapter, I start with four of my favorite channels:

▶ AOL Today (keyword: AOL TODAY) is your best first step on the entire system for a quick hit of the day's or evening's news, as well as links to old favorites, from horoscopes to stock quotes. AOL Today is much like the town crier, giving you a quick look at what's hot and happening on the system.

▶ The News channel (keyword: NEWS) provides a rundown of the hour's headlines, news features, photos, and searchable databases of news of interest. This is your own personal newsroom.

▶ The Sports channel (keyword: SPORTS) is a sports desk that never quits, with all the scores in all the events, breaking news from sports around the world, and links to sports chat rooms for fans to interact with one another. If you like events on fields, courts, rinks, or diamonds, you're going to love this channel.

▶ Influence (keyword: INFLUENCE) is the system's editorial and op-ed page, with commentary and opinion, in addition to gossip and personality profiles and columns on the media, money, and more. Here's where news meets commentary.

This chapter also introduces you to News Profile, a feature that enables you to automatically gather stories of interest and have them waiting for you in your online mailbox when you sign on. It's like having a news editor working just for you.

Visiting AOL Today

AOL Today changes at least twice daily — offering daytime and evening editions — with links to timely features around the system, highlights of breaking news and stories, and tips to help with everything from taxes to vacation planning. The site is so popular, many members add it to their Favorite Places list.

To visit AOL's welcome center, sign on to the system as usual, go to the Channels screen (keyword: CHANNELS), and click the AOL Today icon. Alternatively, you can take the express route by simply using keyword: AOL TODAY.

Reviewing Navigation Techniques

Here is a summary of the AOL navigation tools you learned in Chapter 3:

- ▶ **Links.** These "clickable" portions of windows — underlined, highlighted words, pictures, buttons, and icons — connect to features elsewhere on the system. You recognize them because your mouse cursor changes from an arrow to a hand when it rolls over one.
- ▶ **Previous and Next buttons.** Located on the left side of the toolbar beneath the Read icon, these buttons are used to retrace your steps, revisiting previously viewed AOL pages.

- ▶ **History Trail.** Viewed by clicking the down arrow next to the data-entry field in the middle of the toolbar, the history trail lists all recently visited pages.
- ▶ **Keywords.** The best of the navigation tools, keywords take you directly to features, often bypassing scores of menus and windows. To enter a keyword, either (1) type it in the text-entry field in the middle of the toolbar, (2) click the Keyword button on the toolbar and type the keyword in the resulting window, or (3) press Ctrl+K and type the keyword in the subsequent window. You can then click the Go button or press Enter to activate the keyword. Most AOL areas have their own keyword.
- ▶ **Favorites Places.** Collect and store the locations the pages you like the best. To save a page as a Favorite Place, click the heart icon that appears in the right side of a page's title bar. To revisit a stored site, click the toolbar's Favorites icon, choose Favorite Places from the drop-down menu, and double-click the site you want to see from the resulting list.

TAKE NOTE

▶ **ESSENTIALS**

In the middle of the AOL Today window are links to "essentials," standing favorites ranging from Sports Scores to Horoscopes.

CROSS-REFERENCE

For a refresher on navigation techniques and the overview of AOL Channels, see Chapter 3.

FIND IT ONLINE

For more information online about AOL Channels, go to Member Services (keyword: HELP), click the Find It Now icon, and then enter **channels** in the query box.

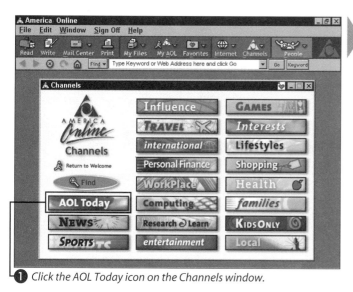

1 Click the AOL Today icon on the Channels window.

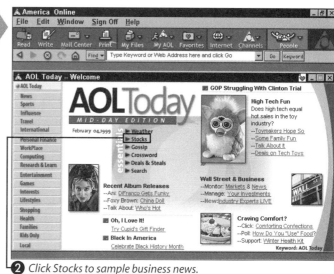

2 Click Stocks to sample business news.

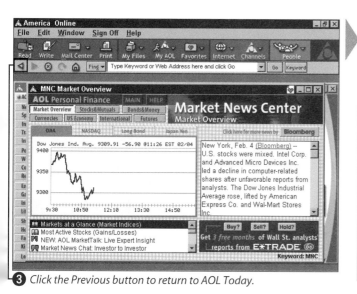

3 Click the Previous button to return to AOL Today.

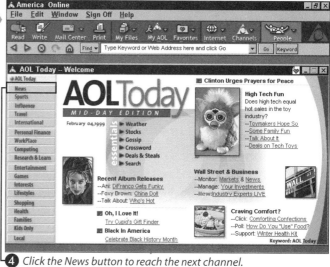

4 Click the News button to reach the next channel.

Locking In on the News Channel

The News channel, where America Online constantly takes stock of the world's news, is reached with the keyword NEWS. The resulting window gives a word and picture representation of what is making the world perk up at this moment, topped with a rundown of the biggest headlines of the moment. Click any of the red arrows at the right of the window to see highlights of specific stories. Or to get an even better fix on the day's news, browse a number of News channel departments.

Browsing is fine for following what is happening today, but if you are researching earlier stories, take a different approach to your data retrieval and search the database of news stories. Generally, more than 50,000 news stories are available for searching at any one time. Updated around the clock, the database contains reports from Associated Press, Reuters, the Business Wire, the PR Newswire, and the SportsTicker. Stories remain available for at least three days, and the procedure for finding specific news is simple.

To begin a news search, click the "Search & Explore" button on the main News channel window or enter the keyword NEWSSEARCH. On the resulting window, click the Search icon. In the next window, enter the word or words that describe the story for which you are looking and click List Articles (or press the Enter key). Remember, you can include words like AND or NOT to narrow your search. AOL lists titles of the stories that match your search word or phrase. Use the scroll bar at the right to see more. AOL also reports how many hits were located, noted above the list box. Use the More button at the bottom of the window to retrieve the next set of stories found. To view any story, double-click the title.

TAKE NOTE

▶ NEWS PARTNERS

A number of major U.S. and world news services are partners with America Online's news operations and have pages of their own. Among them are
- ▶ ABC News (keyword: ABC NEWS), with reports from TV correspondents around the world, video and audio clips online, highlights of the day's stories, and so on.
- ▶ *The New York Times* (keyword: TIMES), with its daily front page, book reviews section (keyword: NYT BOOKS), business news (keyword: NYT BUSINESS), and more.
- ▶ *Newsweek* magazine (keyword: NEWSWEEK), including its famed columns like My Turn, Perspectives, Transitions, and The Last Word.

More links to electronic editions of newspapers plus a number of major print magazines are in the Newsstand area. Use the keyword MAGAZINE and view the scrollable list of current titles, which include publications such as *Atlantic Monthly*, the *Chicago Tribune*, *Entertainment Weekly*, *National Review*, and *Christian Science Monitor*. You can also find deals on subscriptions here.

CROSS-REFERENCE

For more about search strategies, see the Appendix.

FIND IT ONLINE

For a different overview of what is available, visit its Search & Explore department (keyword: NEWSSEARCH) and click the "Tour Through the New Design" option.

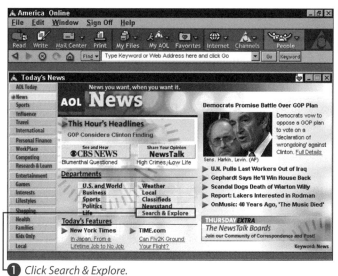

1 Click Search & Explore.

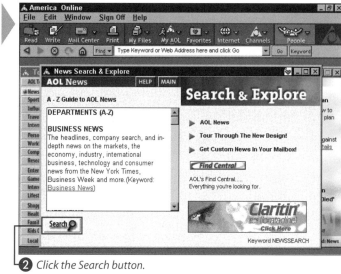

2 Click the Search button.

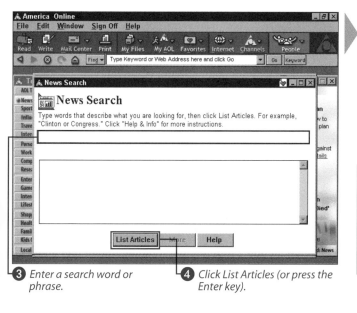

3 Enter a search word or phrase.

4 Click List Articles (or press the Enter key).

5 Highlight and double-click an article to view.

Saving News Articles with the Log Manager

The power and flexibility of AOL's news surpasses that of a traditional newspaper in many ways. You may, however, find yourself missing the ability to clip an article and share it with someone, or even just the chance to read your news on the morning bus ride. If so, AOL once again comes with features that give us article "clippings" and news "print." News and other text you find online can be saved to disk with the Log Manager, discussed initially in Chapter 5. And all online text can be printed!

To clip a story or several stories in any order you wish, visit the News channel and locate the news stories you'd like to save through browsing or searching. Now click the toolbar's My File icon and select Log Manager from the menu. In the Session Log section of the window, click the Open Log button. In the resulting window, note that the system is creating a file called `session.log`. Click the Save button to begin the transcript. Now just open the articles, stories, and other text as you usually would. You don't even have to scroll down to view all the text — the software reads it all just by opening the window. When you've finished capturing, click the Close Log button in the Log Manager window.

Reading What You've Captured

To read the captured file, click File on the menu bar and choose the Open option. Double-click the filename (such as `session.log`). AOL opens the log file for you. If the file does not open, it is probably too large for AOL to display — use a word processor or Windows NotePad to open it instead.

If you want to print the transcript, click the toolbar's Print icon.

Appending Logs

If you have closed a log and wish to resume logging to the same file, follow the steps outlined for a new log but this time click the Append Log button. Locate and select your log file in the next window. Now AOL logs the new text at the end of the existing file.

TAKE NOTE

EDIT MENU ALTERNATIVE

When it comes to saving articles found online, you might find the Edit menu's Select All option an easier alternative than the Log Manager.

Open the story you want to save and click your mouse once on a blank line in the display (so AOL knows you are "pointing" at it). Now click Edit ⇨ Select All, which highlights all the text in the article. Click File ⇨ Save and, when prompted in the resulting window, enter a filename for the highlighted material.

Now you can read and/or print the material by clicking File ⇨ Open and then double-clicking the file you created.

CROSS-REFERENCE

For more about the Log Manager, see Chapter 5.

FIND IT ONLINE

For additional information, click the Help option on the menu bar and select Offline Help. Click the Index tab and enter **log** in the query box.

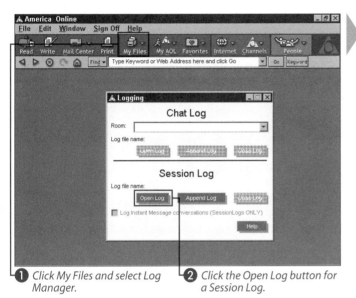

① Click My Files and select Log Manager.

② Click the Open Log button for a Session Log.

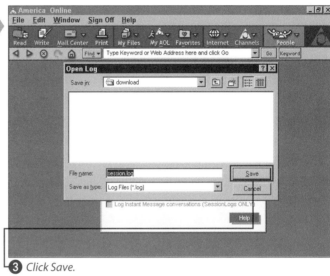

③ Click Save.

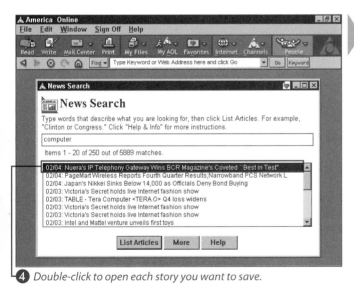

④ Double-click to open each story you want to save.

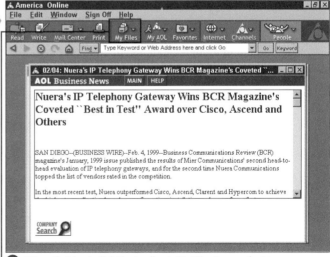

⑤ When finished, click the toolbar's My Files icon, select Log Manager, and then click the Close Log button.

Checking the Weather

You don't need a meteorologist if you have AOL. The online weather center (keyword: WEATHER) covers local forecasts and current conditions. You can find what you are looking for in a number of ways, from keyword searching for your own city, state, or zip to specially prepared reports on recreation and business travel, international weather, forecasting for the classroom, and more.

To use the weather feature, go to the News channel and click the Weather icon. (Alternatively, you can simply click the toolbar's Weather icon or go to keyword: WEATHER.) In the data-entry field, enter a city, state, telephone area code or zip code, and click the Search button. Double-click the name of your city from the resulting list and the next window lists temperature, current conditions, winds, the comfort index, barometric pressure, visibility, and five-day forecast.

Back on the Today's Weather window are links to weather news, national and regional maps, satellite and radar images, forecasts and conditions in other locations in the U.S. and internationally, business travel, and weather news for the classroom. The Weather channel is an excellent source for information on major weather news, like hurricanes and winter storms. You can often find invaluable resources — such as track maps, storm surge patterns, and safety tips — that just aren't readily available offline.

Reaching Other News Departments Directly

Here are other important news areas:

▶ Business News (keyword: BUSINESS NEWS) has breaking news and in-depth financial reports from *The New York Times, Business Week* magazine, ABC News, and others.
▶ Politics (keyword: POLITICS NEWS) has reports and commentary on officeholders, campaigns, and Washington controversies.
▶ U.S. & World News (keyword: US & WORLD NEWS) covers national and international stories, including science, health, environment, crime, and courts.

TAKE NOTE

▶ **PLAYING IT SAFE**

If the weather has rained on your parade one too many times, check AOL's Recreation Weather before your next outing. Get the latest forecasts on storm fronts, boating conditions and sunburn (UV) indexes (in the summer), and skiing conditions (in the winter). You can even calculate your local heat or wind chill index. To get there, click the Recreation Weather icon at keyword: WEATHER.

CROSS-REFERENCE
For more about business news, see Chapter 10.

FIND IT ONLINE
To get online help with using the system's assorted weather features, visit the weather center (keyword: WEATHER) and click the Help icon.

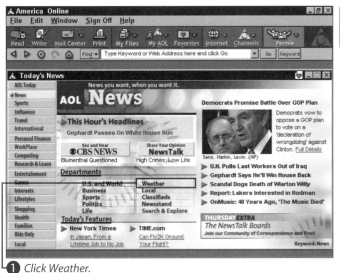

1 Click Weather.

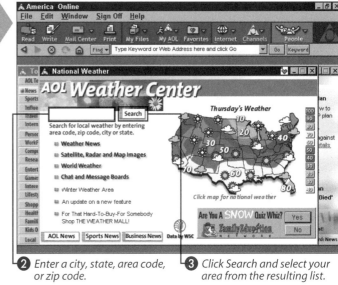

2 Enter a city, state, area code, or zip code.

3 Click Search and select your area from the resulting list.

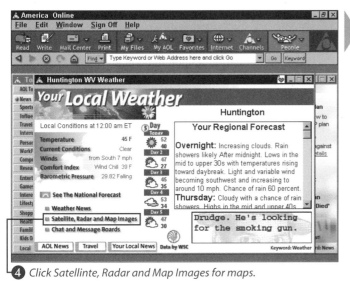

4 Click Satellinte, Radar and Map Images for maps.

5 Click the X (Close Window button) to remove the map from your screen.

Sampling the Sports Channel

America Online's Sports channel (keyword: SPORTS) is like a multilevel daily sports section in your newspaper, except that the information changes literally by the minute as new scores and breaking stories come in from the world's various sports venues. The Sports channel is divided into three main departments:

▶ Top Stories (keyword: SPORTS NEWS) has the hour's breaking news and latest photos from the most popular sporting events, such as pro and college basketball, hockey, baseball, football, auto racing, golf, tennis, and soccer.

▶ The Scoreboard (keyword: SCOREBOARD) gives the latest scores and enables you to follow dozens of games at once, and much more in the way of statistics. For instance, baseball fans can look up batting averages of righties and lefties in specific ballparks, as well as how selected teams have performed against specific pitchers. You also can examine box scores for every previous game particular teams have played against each other this season.

▶ The Grandstand (keyword: GRANDSTAND) invites fans of all sports to talk, write, and yell about what's happening on favorite fields, courts, rinks, rings, and tracks. Message boards and chat rooms buzz with sports talk, while software libraries are full of sports-related programs, photos, and articles.

To follow your favorite teams, click the Scoreboard button and, on the resulting window, choose your sport. Icons on any scoreboards show information on upcoming games, game recaps, box scores, and more. You also can view games in progress. For instance, in baseball, you can list a pitch-by-pitch button to see play-by-play cover. You can even move a copy of the details to your desktop by clicking the Mini Scoreboard tab.

Options vary depending, of course, on the sport you are viewing, but generally there are additional buttons for player stats, standings, roster, leaderboards, schedules, weather prediction for game time, and so on.

TAKE NOTE

▶ OTHER HIGHLIGHTS

The Sports channel also provides a number of original sports services, such as

▶ Fan Central (keyword: FAN CENTRAL), devoted to whatever The Next Big Thing is, from the Kentucky Derby, the World Series, the NBA Championship and the Stanley Cup Finals to Wimbledon, the Indy 500, the Masters, and the U.S. Open.

▶ Athlete Direct (keyword: ATHLETE DIRECT), an opportunity to interview your own favorite sports stars in live chat room conferences.

CROSS-REFERENCE
For health and fitness topics, see Chapter 16.

FIND IT ONLINE
For a different view of the Sports channel's hottest features, visit its Search & Explore section (keyword: SPORTS SEARCH) and click the Best of AOL Sports icon.

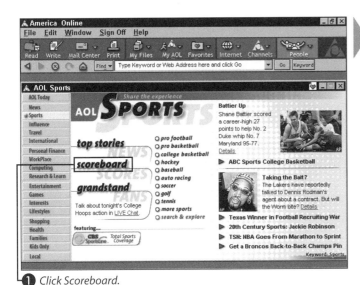

1 Click Scoreboard.

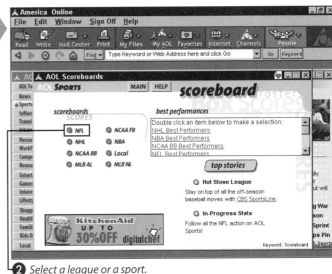

2 Select a league or a sport.

3 Click an icon for game info, recap, or box score.

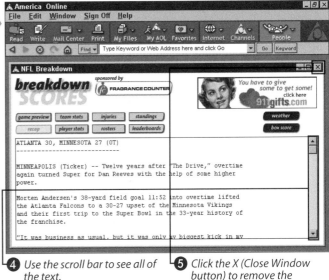

4 Use the scroll bar to see all of the text.

5 Click the X (Close Window button) to remove the window from the screen.

Using the Influence Channel

Influence (keyword INFLUENCE) is the home of interpretation, comment, satire, and elaboration on the news. The channel is devoted to digging beneath the day's headlines, debating current issues and events, and seeking out critics of movies, books, plays, music, and television. They're not adverse to finding the skinny on celebrities and politicians and getting ahead of trends in fashion, design, and entertainment either.

"Influence is not for rich folks who spend in an afternoon what most of us take home in a year," says the channel's managers. "Influence is not about a world that's defined by 20 square blocks in Manhattan and a few choice neighborhoods in Los Angeles. Influence is not for people who are so refined they would never touch anything so common as a mouse. We don't exclude those people. In fact, we welcome them — all 300 of them — but the real audience for Influence is the rest of us."

Five departments make up the Influence channel:

▶ Seen & Heard (keyword: SEEN AND HEARD) covers cultural movers and shakers, personalities in arts, entertainment, media, and business. Who's moving up, and who's moving out?

▶ The Good Life (keyword: THE GOOD LIFE) reports on the best in travel, style, design, entertaining, and gourmet dining from such resources as *Elle* and *Metropolitan Home*.

▶ Arts & Leisure (keyword: ARTS AND LEISURE) has the good word on works by paintbrush, pencil, or piano. Look here for exclusive book previews; comprehensive coverage of theater, music, and dance; and live online interviews with stars.

▶ Media & Money (keyword: MEDIA AND MONEY) has personalities behind the bylines. This is incisive commentary on the media itself by such sources as *The New York Observer* and *Salon*.

▶ The Inner Circle (keyword: INNER CIRCLE) invites like-minded AOL members to talk about books, design, arts, movies, and other culture topics about which you are passionate. The department also has a Culture Planner to help you learn what, where, and how to see the latest events around the country

TAKE NOTE

INFLUENCE ALSO IS SEARCHABLE

You also can search the Influence channel. Enter the keyword **INFLUENCE SEARCH** and you can locate material published in the past 24 hours, week, month, or year.

CROSS-REFERENCE

For more about movies and other entertainment topics, see Chapter 13.

FIND IT ONLINE

To see what's turning heads these days in the Influence channel, visit its Search & Explore area (keyword: INFLUENCE SEARCH) and then click the Best of AOL Influence icon.

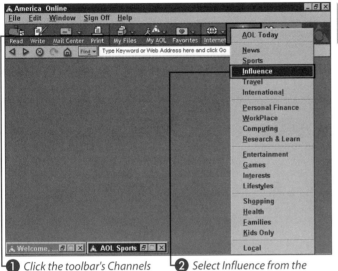

1 Click the toolbar's Channels icon.

2 Select Influence from the drop-down menu.

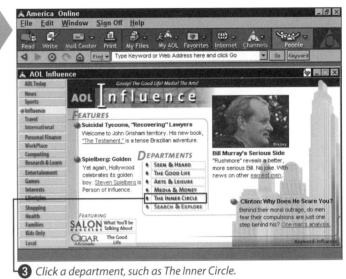

3 Click a department, such as The Inner Circle.

4 Click The Inner Circle Index.

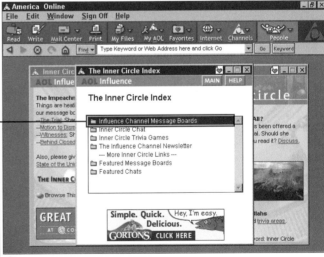

5 Select a feature to explore.

Creating News Profiles

Have you ever dreamed of having personal assistants who could shift the day's news and pull out just the stories they knew you would find interesting? America Online can be that assistant. A feature called News Profiles (keyword: NEWS PROFILES) automatically searches AOL's many news resources to locate articles that match any subjects in which you have previously indicated an interest. It then e-mails the full text of the reports to you.

You can create up to five different online news profiles for each screen name. Each is a separate automated search of the news resources and can deliver up to 50 articles a day to your mailbox. Profiles you create automatically search the news wires for the searchwords you specify.

To set up, use the keyword NEWS PROFILES to reach the main News Profiles window and click the Create a Profile button. In the first data-entry field, use the Backspace (Delete) key on your keyboard to erase the default title ("News Profile 1," as shown in the window on the facing page). Enter a new title for this profile so you can differentiate it from others when you later want to make modifications to it. In the second field, enter the maximum number of stories you want to receive each day. The default is 10, but you can set it as high as 50. Click the Next arrow to reach the first of three windows — General, Required, and Excluded — devoted to selecting searchwords or phrases you want to use in customizing this

profile. List as many words as you would like in each box, separated by commas. If you want a set of words to be searched together as a phrase, enclose them in single quotation marks, as in '*Digital Equipment Corp.*' Also, case is ignored, so the profile makes no distinction between *Ford* and *ford*. The Wildcards button in the lower-left corner of each window explains how to narrow your search with special punctuation marks.

Continued

TAKE NOTE

▶ THREE CRITERIA

New profiles seek three kinds of searchwords and phrase:

- ▶ **General search words.** These are words that you want to appear in the articles. A computer news profile, for instance, may include general words such as *modem, Internet,* and *keyboard.*
- ▶ **Required search words.** These are words and phrases that must appear in articles to be clipped. In the Computer News folder, you might list the word *computer* as a required word. This enables News Profiles to find articles specifically about computer keyboards (as opposed to musical keyboards).
- ▶ **Excluded search words.** These include words and phrases that would force the exclusion of stories being clipped. If you were not interested in news about Apple Computer, Inc. in your Computer News folder, for example, you could list "Apple" in this field.

CROSS-REFERENCE
For more about automating your e-mail, see Chapter 6.

FIND IT ONLINE
For additional information on creating news profiles, go to Member Services (keyword: HELP), click the Find It Now option, and then enter **news profile** in the query box.

Don't Overload Your Mailbox

Each America Online screen name's mailbox can hold no more than 550 pieces of mail at one time. Once your mailbox is full, News Profiles automatically turns off your profile and stops collecting articles for you. You must then manually turn the profile back on, using the Manage Your Profile option on the main News Profile screen. Also, once the total amount of mail in your online mailbox reaches 550 items, AOL begins to automatically delete the excess, starting with previously read mail and then unread mail.

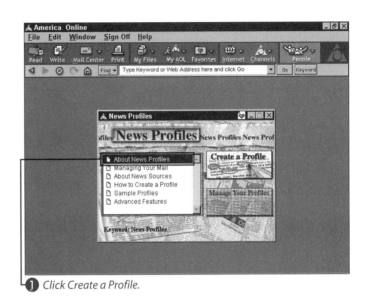

1 Click Create a Profile.

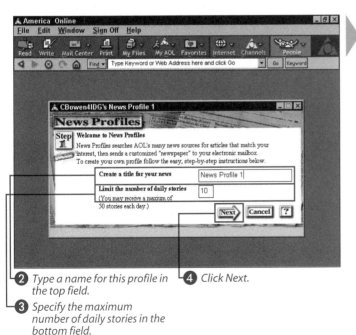

2 Type a name for this profile in the top field.

3 Specify the maximum number of daily stories in the bottom field.

4 Click Next.

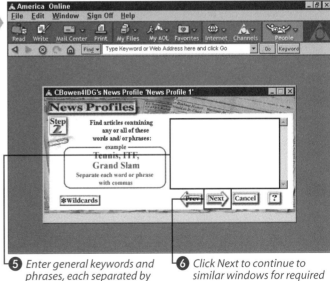

5 Enter general keywords and phrases, each separated by commas, in the box on the right.

6 Click Next to continue to similar windows for required and excluded words.

Creating News Profiles

Continued

Specifying Your News Wires

Once you have your general, required, and excluded keywords and phrases specified, you are ready to wrap up the creation of your news profile.

Picking up where we left off on the previous task, the next window asks you to choose the news sources from which you want to gather information for this profile. Use the Add and Remove buttons to include or exclude highlighted sources to or from your list. Your choices can include any or all of these resources:

▶ **AP International News.** Breaking news and in-depth stories from around the world

▶ **AP National News.** Reports from around the country, including extensive coverage from the nation's capitol

▶ **AP Weather News.** Covering severe weather that strikes anywhere in the world

▶ **AP Business News.** Wall Street updates and the latest government economic figures

▶ **AP Entertainment News.** Stories from Hollywood, TV and elsewhere

▶ **AP Sports News.** Coverage of professional sports around the world

▶ **The Business Wire and the PR Newswire.** Press releases and announcements from corporations and organizations

If you want to add all news sources in a category, just select the category name and click the Add button.

Summarizing Online

After you have specified your news sources, click the Next button to receive a summary and review of the profile you are creating. Look over the title, the number of daily articles, search terms, and sources. If you need to make changes, use the Prev and Next buttons to step back to the appropriate points in the process. When you have your profile as you want it, click Done.

Once a profile has been created, the system begins immediately monitoring the news wires on your behalf, sending stories that meet your criteria to your mailbox, where they wait like any other incoming e-mail. You can pick up the stories manually or with Automatic AOL.

TAKE NOTE

▶ **NO SURCHARGES**

There is no additional charge for using News Profiles. As always, you pay only for the time your computer spends online.

▶ **MAIL FROM NO ONE**

All stories sent to you by News Profiles appears in your mailbox as if they were letters sent by the screen name "AOL News." This is not an active screen name on America Online, however. If you write back to it, no one will read the message, so don't bother.

CROSS-REFERENCE

For more about using your online and offline mailboxes, see Chapter 2.

FIND IT ONLINE

For more assistance with maintenance of your news profiles, click Manage Your Profiles on the main window (keyword: NEWS PROFILE) and then click the question mark (?) on the resulting window.

Modifying a Profile

Click the Manage Your Profile button in the News Profile window. The system lists each profile, the number of stories it has located, and whether it is turned on.

Highlight a profile and click one of the following buttons:

▶ On/Off toggles the status on or off. Use this option to stop or restart a profile's collecting of stories.

▶ Delete erases the profile.

▶ Edit changes the contents. AOL then opens an Edit Profile window and invites you to review and/or change the general keywords, required words, excluded words, selected sources of information, profile title, and the limit on the number of stories to collect.

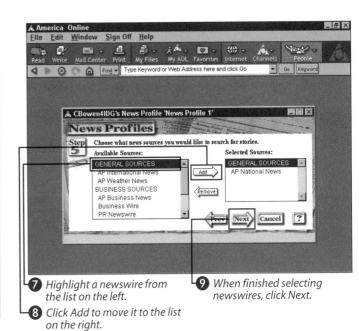

7 Highlight a newswire from the list on the left.

8 Click Add to move it to the list on the right.

9 When finished selecting newswires, click Next.

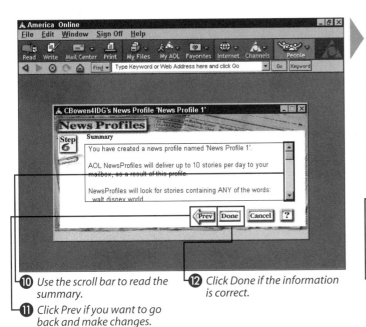

10 Use the scroll bar to read the summary.

11 Click Prev if you want to go back and make changes.

12 Click Done if the information is correct.

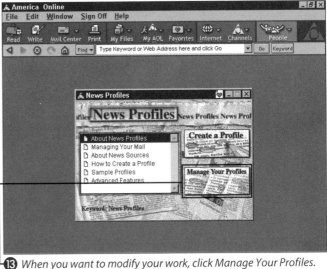

13 When you want to modify your work, click Manage Your Profiles.

Personal Workbook

Q&A

1 Where is your first stop online for celebrity gossip?

_____

_____

_____

2 How do you go about searching for a story from the day's news?

_____

_____

3 Where can you find weather forecasts for the nation?

_____

_____

_____

4 How can you reach the electronic extension of major magazines online?

_____

_____

5 Where's the best place to find the hour's top sports news?

_____

_____

_____

6 Where do other sports fans gather and talk about their favorite fields, courts, rinks, rings and tracks?

_____

_____

7 How do you find latest trends and raves in dining, drinking, lodging, and design?

_____

_____

8 Bonus Question: How can you assign America Online to be your personal editor, automatically gathering news for you?

_____

_____

_____

ANSWERS: PAGE 340

EXTRA PRACTICE

1 Search the news database for recent stories about your state, your alma mater, your company, and/or your family name.

2 Check the AOL Today and the News channel several different times of the day and see how the windows are routinely changed to keep up with events.

3 Get the recap of last night's sports events and previews of coming games.

4 Use the Sports channel's play-by-play feature to follow sports events in progress.

5 Look up reviews of this weekend's new movies.

6 Create a news profile to capture upcoming stories about events in your state.

REAL-WORLD APPLICATIONS

✔ If you're a crossword puzzle fan, note that the best of the field is on AOL with *The New York Times'* crossword puzzle (keyword: NYT CROSSWORD). In fact, tomorrow morning's puzzle is available online every night at 10:00 Eastern Time. It is played on Across-Line. Download the software here, follow the online instructions, and do the daily puzzles.

✔ Say you have just heard on the radio that a story you're interested in was reported by the Reuters news service. You can search the News channel archives specifically for Reuters stories. In the data query field, use the news service's identifiers in your search strategy: Associated Press (AP), Reuters (RTR), Business Wire (BSW), PR Newswire (PRN), and SportsTicker (STK).

Visual Quiz

What would you be doing when you saw this window? How would you reach it? What would you do from here?

_____

_____

_____

_____

_____

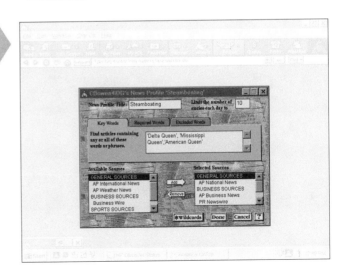

CHAPTER 9

Using the Travel and International Channels

The first time I ever said "Oh wow" in front of a computer screen was when someone showed me how I could use a home computer to make my own flight and hotel reservations. Of course, I have said my oh-wow's many times since then. These days, it is almost an everyday occurrence. And each time brings back a little of the original excitement, when I first realized that personal computers were going to do much more than merely change the way I did my taxes or wrote my articles.

Personal computers empower us, enabling us to take a little more control over decisions that affect our lives. If there are still people in your household or office who are unconvinced of this, bring them along this time as you tour America Online's travel-related features. By the end of this chapter, you will be on your way to becoming your own travel agent, whether you are journeying just down the road or to the other side of the globe.

With this chapter, you learn about

▶ staying abreast of the latest hot travel deals for business travel and family vacations.

▶ researching the world with an up-to-date, online atlas.

▶ locating memorable getaways, like a quaint little bed and breakfast that could become the highlight of a special trip.

▶ sharing data with travel experts and fellow members who have been where you want to go.

▶ setting up an online account to plan your trips, research flight schedules and accommodations, and even make your own reservations.

▶ checking out America Online's ever-expanding collection of international resources, from facts about foreign countries to help with other languages.

Tuning In the Travel Channel

America Online's Travel channel (keyword: TRAVEL) serves all aspects of life on the road, in the air, and on the water. It helps you plan and enhance that dream vacation, book the flight, reserve the rooms, rent the car, and just get out there.

Topping the channel's list of hot features is the trip planner. The Destination Guide answers the eternal question of where to go and what to do (keyword: DESTINATIONS). Start with the basic idea of the trip you want, then let the guide help you flesh it out with maps, background information, and photos.

You can browse travel ideas in the United States, Africa, Asia, Australia and the South Pacific, Canada, the Caribbean, Central and South America, Europe, Mexico and the Middle East. The site has details on cruises, family travel, food and wine adventures, gay and lesbian travel, golf resorts, outdoor experiences, romantic travel, trips for seniors, and more. Also available on the site are tools for currency conversion, articles on fares and schedules, frequent flyer mileage, languages, maps, and vacation packages.

And check out the Destination of the Week (keyword: DESTINATION FOCUS) which highlights a different site regularly and comes complete with tips for planning your escape to this wonderland.

Calling All Bargain Hunters

Once you have decided where to go, the challenge becomes doing it without spending the family fortune. That is why Travel Bargains (keyword: TRAVEL BARGAINS) probably ought to be your next stop. The site specializes in information on low-cost airfares, inexpensive car rental, and budget lodging. It also has the low-down on money-saving travel clubs and other cost-cutting strategies. Check out the Bargain Box (keyword: BARGAIN BOX) for great deals instantly and Cruise Bargains for sales on the high seas. Also, check out the AOL's Travelers Advantage club (keyword: TA). For a $1 three-month membership, you get discounts, upgrades, and other travel amenities, such as dining discounts.

TAKE NOTE

OTHER HIGHLIGHTS

▶ Reservations Center (keyword: RESERVATIONS) provides the specific tools for booking flights, hotels, trains, and rental cars, and choosing vacation packages.
▶ Travel Interests (keyword: TRAVEL INTERESTS) offers special travel destinations, tips, and advice tailored to your own unique interests.

CROSS-REFERENCE

For other kinds of bargain hunting, see Chapter 15's discussion about online shopping features.

FIND IT ONLINE

Interested in global shopping? Use the keyword: INTERNATIONAL STORE for information on maps, atlases, luggage, and food.

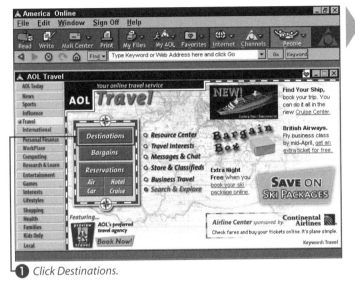

1 Click Destinations.

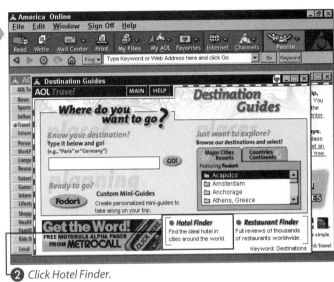

2 Click Hotel Finder.

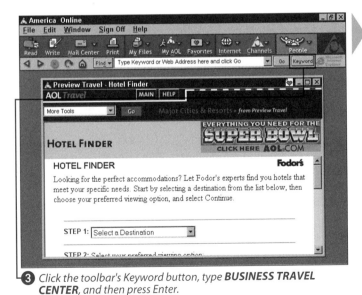

3 Click the toolbar's Keyword button, type **BUSINESS TRAVEL CENTER**, and then press Enter.

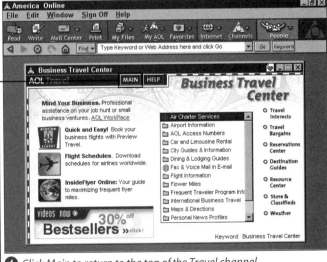

4 Click Main to return to the top of the Travel channel.

Finding Low Air Fares

Planning your next trip is a lot easier if you know the lowest available airfares between popular destinations, and America Online has just the ticket for the research. Farefinder, a service of Preview Travel, tracks and compares airfares daily for all major airlines in and out of the United States.

You can reach the Farefinder from the main Travel channel window or through the keyword: AIRFARE FINDER. There are more than 40 major U.S. cities from which you can find a low fare—choose one from the list in the lower right of the window to begin your search. AOL displays a list of the lowest available fares between your chosen city and other cities (both domestic and international) in their database. Those fares marked with "low!" are at least 5 percent lower than the average round-trip fares for corresponding itineraries found by Farefinder during the past three months. Just click a fare on the list to see the specifics.

Fares are subject to change, but the results of the search can give you some baselines for finding similar airfares on your own chosen travel dates.

AOL's Partners in Travel

A number of major travel publications and service companies have joined forces with America Online to provide information and travel products.

▶ Bed & Breakfast Guide (keyword: B&B) summarizes more than 20,000 bed-and-breakfast establishments around the world.

▶ Cruise Critic (keyword: CRUISE CRITIC) reviews the best cruises, offering news, bargains, tips, guides, and destinations.

▶ Inside Flyer Online (keyword: INSIDE FLYER) focuses on frequent flyer miles and points. This is the site for news of special deals and flight bargains.

▶ Lonely Planet Guides (keyword: LONELY PLANET) concentrates on those off-the-beaten-track destinations for intrepid travelers. The guides are noted for their lively writing, road reports, and global news.

▶ Outdoor Adventure Online (keyword: OUT-DOOR) helps with planning outdoor adventures, with tips on lodging and products for campers and hikers.

▶ Travel America (keyword: TRAVEL AMERICA) provides details of tourist activities in states and cities around the nation.

CROSS-REFERENCE

For information on finding other magazines and news resources online, see Chapter 8.

❶ Hold down the Ctrl key and press K, and then type the keyword FAREFINDER.

❷ Click the down arrow and select a city.

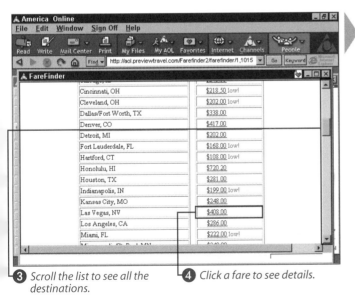

❸ Scroll the list to see all the destinations.

❹ Click a fare to see details.

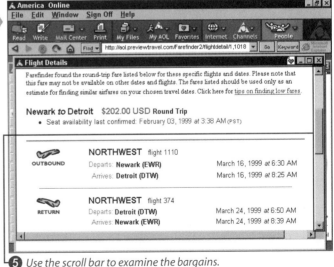

❺ Use the scroll bar to examine the bargains.

Setting Up a Preview Travel Account

After you have done your research — dreamed up your ideal vacation, plotted your next business trip, planned the ultimate family getaway, talked with the experts so you know what to expect, where to go, what to see — you are ready to let America Online handle the paperwork. The Travel channel's Reservations Center (keyword: TRAVEL RESERVATIONS) can arrange your flights, train tickets, car rentals, and lodging. It can even set up an entire vacation package. All the other details — such as dining and events — can be planned here, too. Best of all, you can use the resources to research schedules and prices without actually making purchases. This is all done through AOL's full-featured online travel agency called Preview Travel, which offers members the opportunity to set up an account free of charge.

To create a Preview Travel account, begin by clicking the Reservation Center button on the main Travel channel window to reach the main window. Click the Preview Travel icon and select Enter Preview Travel on the next window (or use keyword: PREVIEW TRAVEL). In the resulting window, click the graphic in the center which proclaims, "Book Here! No service fee." (See the window in the lower left on the facing page.)

Preview Travel has service terms, naturally. Read over them using the scroll bar at the right of the window to move through the text — if you agree with the terms of service, click the Accept Terms button to move on. Now enter your account identification by typing a special user name and password to use when you visit the site. You can use your current screen name if you like (the default) or create a new name (up to 15 alphanumeric characters). Type a password that is both easy-to-remember and hard-to-guess, enter it twice as indicated on the window, and click the Continue button.

Continued

TAKE NOTE

SPECIAL TRAVEL INTERESTS AND NEEDS SERVED

AOL also has a number of travel features dedicated to special interests and subjects, such as

▶ Family Travel Network (keyword: FAMILY TRAVEL NETWORK), covering family getaways, road trips, and kid-friendly accommodations.

▶ Honeymoon Travel: The Knot (keyword: KNOT), helping you plan the perfect honeymoon, with advice from experts and other couples. Find the most romantic destinations here.

▶ Independent Traveler (keyword: TRAVELER), providing invaluable advice from fellow travelers around the world. If you need to know before you go, this is the place!

▶ Over the Rainbow (keyword: OVER THE RAINBOW), presenting an online guide for gay and lesbian travel, with advice on vacation ideas and travel spots around the world.

CROSS-REFERENCE

Interested in the weather on the other end of your journey? See Chapter 8 for information getting forecasts anywhere on the map.

FIND IT ONLINE

For additional help using Preview Travel, visit the main window (keyword: PREVIEW TRAVEL) and click the various resources and links on the right side of the window.

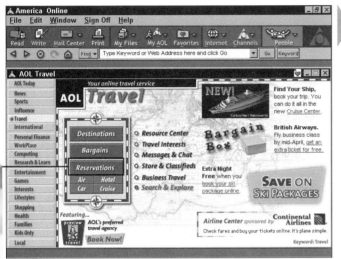

❶ *Click Reservations (or go to keyword: TRAVEL RESERVATIONS).*

❷ *Click Preview Travel and then click the Enter button.*

❸ *Click here to sign-in (or register if you are a new user).*

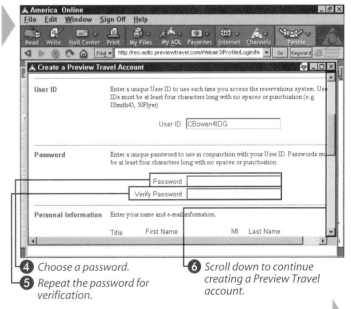

❹ *Choose a password.*

❺ *Repeat the password for verification.*

❻ *Scroll down to continue creating a Preview Travel account.*

Setting Up a Preview Travel Account *Continued*

Storing Your Background Information

It can be frustrating to have to reenter basic data every time you want to order special goods or services online. Preview Travel is one site that has addressed this situation. To make future travel planning easier, Preview Travel asks you to supply some bookkeeping information, including your name and address, age, day and evening phone numbers, and e-mail and fax numbers.

Preview Travel also records your travel preferences, such as regular departure city and home airport, seating and meal preferences, preferred class of service, and your favorite airlines, if any. This information is used later as a starting point for your reservations. The system also stores your frequent flyer account numbers, a huge help if you often misplace these. Once you've entered your information, be sure to name and save your travel profile as indicated. The default name is Personal, but you can enter a different name for the profile (up to 12 characters).

Once your personal travel profile is created, the reservation system is at your disposal. Future visits may require that you log back into the reservations system with your name and password — just click the same graphic in the center to begin again. After successful log-in, Preview Travel greets you with a list of your profiles. Options let you create, change, and delete profiles, as well as make air, car, and hotel reservations.

TAKE NOTE

▶ **YOU CAN CREATE MULTIPLE PROFILES**

You can create up to five different profiles with one screen name, which can be used in making arrangements by type (business travel, group travel, family travel), by style (first class all the way or as low as you can go) or even by destination (the monthly business meeting or your favorite weekend getaway) — you decide!

▶ **IF YOU FORGET YOUR PASSWORD**

Preview Travel requires a password for creating, viewing and editing travel information and plans. If you forget your password, click the Retrieve Password button on the window that requests your password. Preview Travel then sends Internet e-mail with your password, so be sure your mail controls (keyword: MAIL CONTROLS) are set up to allow mail from the Internet.

▶ **OTHER AOL TRAVEL FEATURES**

AOL also has several databases to help you research possible destinations.
▶ Travel File (keyword: TRAVEL FILE), providing data on more than 100,000 worldwide, discount vacation packages.
▶ Wine Country (keyword: WINE COUNTRY), helping with ideas for travel in California's wine country (Napa, Sonoma, Lake, and Mendocino counties).

CROSS-REFERENCE

If you're planning a vacation with the kids, you might also want to check out the Families channel. See the discussion in Chapter 16.

FIND IT ONLINE

For ideas on vacation packages, check out the AOL Traveler's Advantage Club (keyword: TA), which links to data on cruises, resorts, adventures, and event travel.

Making Reservations

When you have established at least one travel profile, you can use it to make and review reservations for your trips. Just visit the site, using the keyword: PREVIEW TRAVEL and, if prompted, enter the password you created for this account. In the resulting window, seen in the lower-right figure, highlight the profile you want to use (if you have created more than one) and then select the option for action, either

▶ Air Reservations for airline tickets with optional car and/or hotel reservations, or

▶ Hotel or Car Reservations Only, for hotel and/or car reservations without airline tickets.

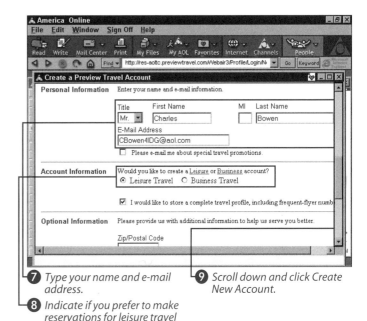

7 Type your name and e-mail address.

8 Indicate if you prefer to make reservations for leisure travel of business travel.

9 Scroll down and click Create New Account.

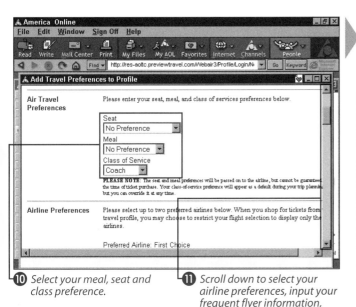

10 Select your meal, seat and class preference.

11 Scroll down to select your airline preferences, input your frequent flyer information, make hotel and car rental preference and enter your billing address.

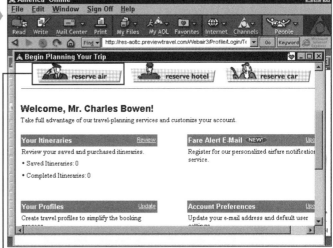

12 Once your account has been created and your travel profile saved, click Reserve Air to get started.

Booking Air Reservations

To have schedule flights, visit Preview Travel (keyword: PREVIEW TRAVEL), log in, and click the Air Reservations button at the bottom of the window. Verify the name of the primary passenger and indicate the number of passengers traveling on this itinerary.

Itinerary Planning is next. Specify your departure and arrival cities, the departure date and time, preferred airlines, and so on. Any preferences you entered into your travel profile — such as departure city and favorite airlines — appear in this window for your convenience.

Verify your departure and arrival locations (cities and airports) in the next two windows. Highlight the airport (if more than one is listed) and click the Select button. You also may re-enter the city name and select the Find button to locate another airport.

Preview Travel now does its magic, locating all available flights that meet your specifications and displaying them onscreen. Direct flights are listed first, sorted from least to most expensive, followed by flights with connections, again sorted by price. Each flight with a bullet to the left indicates either a direct or connecting flight with no plane changes. Connecting flights are listed on a separate line without a bullet, displaying the second flight and any additional segments.

Is this a one-way or round-trip flight, or a trip with multiple stops? Indicate the type of trip and review a selection of fares. If you find a winner and want to buy a ticket, click Select Fare and follow the directions for entering a credit card number and billing address. After the purchase is complete, you have an opportunity to print a complete record of the transaction (highly recommended).

You can always return to Preview Travel later and view your pending trip plans — use the View Travel Plans button on the right of the main window to log in. If you have more than one travel profile, your plans are sorted by profile name. Car and hotel reservations may be canceled online, but airline reservations cannot. You can, however, call Preview Travel (1-800-232-1586) or send them e-mail to change or cancel any reservations.

TAKE NOTE

ADDITIONAL INFO

On the Flight window, you can perform a number of functions:

▶ Get additional information on any flight by highlighting it and clicking the red Flight Details button on the middle-right of the window. This reports the number of stops, on-time record, aircraft type, meals served (if any), and so on.

▶ Choose a flight from the Available Flights list by highlighting and double-clicking (or clicking the indicated the button below the list). Flights you have selected then appear in the list box below Selected Flights.

▶ Remove a flight from the Selected Flights box by highlighting it and double-clicking and then clicking once on the indicated button.

CROSS-REFERENCE

Is this a business trip you're planning? You might also be interested in the tips from AOL's financial neighborhoods. See Chapter 10 for details.

FIND IT ONLINE

If you're as interested in airplanes as you are in air travel, visit the Aviation & Aeronautics department (keyword: AVIATION), where you can meet up with other aircraft enthusiasts.

Using the Fare Display

The Fare Display window lists options for your itinerary. If you selected a coach fare, the lowest available fare is displayed in the first list. In the second fare list you find the unrestricted full coach fare (the one that has no penalties imposed for changes to your itinerary after ticket purchase). From here, you can click

▶ The Rules button for details on the fares.

▶ The Flight Details button for more information on the selected flight.

▶ The Fare Shop button to compare prices on alternate dates.

▶ The Select this Fare button to choose the fare and move on to the Passenger List window.

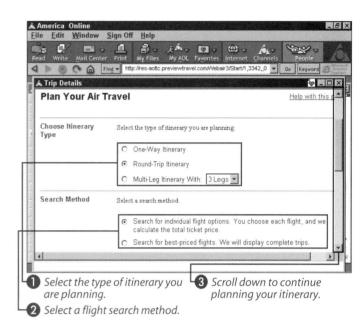

① Select the type of itinerary you are planning.

② Select a flight search method.

③ Scroll down to continue planning your itinerary.

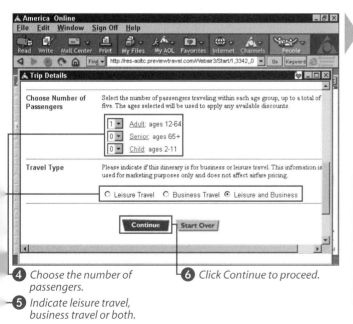

④ Choose the number of passengers.

⑤ Indicate leisure travel, business travel or both.

⑥ Click Continue to proceed.

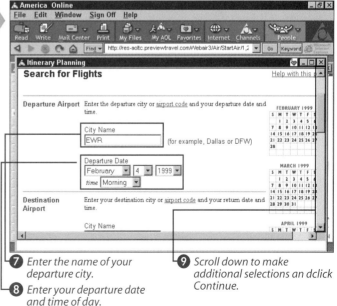

⑦ Enter the name of your departure city.

⑧ Enter your departure date and time of day.

⑨ Scroll down to make additional selections an dclick Continue.

Making Hotel Reservations

Have you dreamed of a relaxing resort that serves drinks by the pool, or perhaps a full-service business hotel with conference facilities? Preview Travel also can handle hotel reservations, either as a part of an airline reservation package or by themselves. To make hotel plans, visit Preview Travel (keyword: PREVIEW TRAVEL), log in and click the Hotel or Car Reservations button at the bottom of the window. In the next window, choose Hotel from the list of options, scroll down to enter your password (if prompted), and click the Continue button.

Begin by specifying the name of your destination city when prompted. Alternatively, you can type the state, country or zip to further qualify the search. Click the Continue button, and Preview Travel lists all matching hotels from its database. Each hotel is listed with two buttons: click Hotel Info (located to the immediate left of the hotel name) for details about the establishment and then click Check Availability for details on dates and rates. Indicate your check-in and check-out dates, the number of adults staying in the reserved room, any preferences, special rates, or corporate discount numbers.

From here, Preview Travel presents a selection of rooms, descriptions, and rates based on your specifications (or lets you know that no rooms were available and invites you to try again). If you find a room and rate, select the room you want and click the Room button to the left. Preview Travel then summarizes the request and prompts you for your credit card information. If everything appears in order, fill in the card data and click the Reserve Hotel button at the bottom. Alternatively, you can click Cancel to stop the process and not reserve a room or click New Hotel Search to start over again.

TAKE NOTE

RESERVING CARS

To reserve a rental car at your destination, click the Car button. In the next window, enter your data for the city where you would like to pick up and drop off the car, time of rental, including the pickup and drop-off dates, any preferred car size and type, a preferred rental agency, and the number of rental car options you would like to display. Click continue and then choose from a supplied list an airport for your pickup and drop-off location. Then click the Continue button. The system then lists the available rental car offers for agencies you have specified in that city, with the daily dollar amounts, car sizes and types and details (such as automatic transmission, air conditioning, and so on). Select the one you want and click the Continue button. The site summarizes the offer. If it is what you wanted, click the Continue button. Alternatively, you can click New Car Search to perform another search or Cancel to stop altogether.

CROSS-REFERENCE

If you're looking for information on the finest in lodging, dining and travel, check out The Good Life in the Influence channel. See Chapter 8 for background.

FIND IT ONLINE

An alternative to lodging is house swapping, a regular topic in the AOL Classified Ads. See Chapter 15 for details.

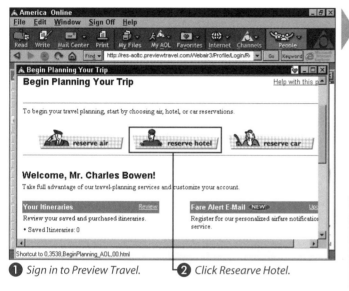

❶ Sign in to Preview Travel.

❷ Click Researve Hotel.

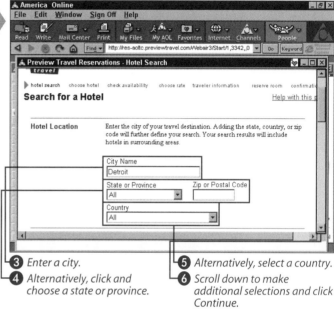

❸ Enter a city.

❹ Alternatively, click and choose a state or province.

❺ Alternatively, select a country.

❻ Scroll down to make additional selections and click Continue.

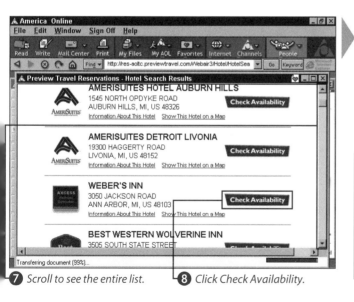

❼ Scroll to see the entire list.

❽ Click Check Availability.

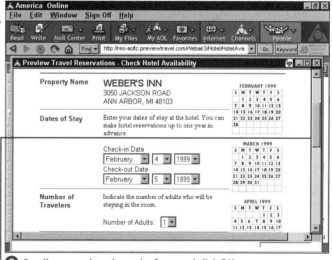

❾ Scroll to complete the entire form and click OK

Exploring the International Channel

An old song spoke fondly of "far-away places with strange-sounding names." If that is your travel dream, you can start rehearsing for that road trip right now. The International channel (keyword: INTERNATIONAL) is a perfect illustration of how America Online is not just for Americans anymore. With services in North America, Europe and Asia, AOL now brings you local content about people and places all around the world. Whether you are ready to actually travel to foreign ports or are still in the planning stages, the International Channel makes for interesting online visits right now. Already, it has links to people and cultures in Austria, Canada, France, Germany, Sweden, Switzerland and the United Kingdom, and the list grows daily. Each country contributes local content.

An Online Atlas

For students, travelers, and wanna-bes, the International channel is a full-featured world atlas. Click on a point on the world map displayed on the International channel's opening window and AOL zooms in on that region of the world, with links to relevant message boards, chat rooms, and online newsletters — even information on AOL access numbers in that region. The International channel also indicates when local AOL installations are up and running, such as AOL Sweden, AOL Germany, AOL Switzerland, AOL Japan, AOL Austria, AOL UK, AOL France, and AOL Canada.

Forums offer features and articles from and about countries in various parts of the world. Click on South America, for instance, and find information on Argentina, Bolivia, Brazil, Chile, Columbia, Ecuador, Guyana, Paraguay, Peru, Suriname, Uruguay, and Venezuela. Each area offers maps, business analyses, the national anthem, links to Internet newsgroups and web sites, a picture of the country's flag, and related material.

CROSS-REFERENCE
If you are learning another language, explore the AOL's educational resources for assistance. See Chapter 12 for information.

FIND IT ONLINE
Each continent in the online atlas has its own keyword: Australia and the South Pacific (OCEANIA), Asia (ASIA), Europe (EUROPE), the Mid East (MIDDLE EAST), Africa (AFRICA), North America (NORTH AMERICA) and South America (SOUTH AMERICA).

Chatting in Other Languages

The Bistro (keyword: BISTRO) offers real-time chatting in more than 15 different languages. It is a world cafe devoted to many languages and cultures. The Bistro also is the home for the International channel's hosted chats and special events. Among the languages that have been heard in the Bistro are Arabic, Chinese, French, Gaelic, German, Hindi, Korean, Polish, Russian and Tagalog. Each language has its own chat schedule. Check in at least once a week to view a schedule of upcoming events and guests.

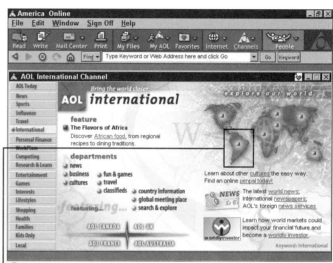

1 *Go to keyword: INTERNATIONAL and click a country to reach the atlas.*

2 *Click the Chat Rooms button or go to keyword: BISTRO.*

3 *Click a button to reach a language-specific message area.*

Personal Workbook

Q&A

1 How can you use the Travel channel to find the bargains on travel and vacation packages?

_____

_____

_____

2 What if you're focusing specifically on airfares? How can you find the latest, lowest costs?

_____

_____

_____

3 Suppose you're going camping in a new area. What's an AOL site that can help you plan?

_____

_____

_____

4 So, you're getting married! If you've still got time for a little online research, which AOL service is especially designed for honeymooners?

_____

_____

5 If you're planning a ski getaway, where can you go online for tips and travel hints?

_____

_____

_____

6 Where can you go to speak and read French online?

_____

_____

_____

7 If you are a globe-trotter (or a global wanna-be), where can you get a quick hit of international travel news?

_____

_____

_____

8 Bonus Question: How can you use America Online to find a electronic pen pal in Spain?

_____

_____

ANSWERS: PAGE 341

EXTRA PRACTICE

1. Use Preview Travel to research a hypothetical round-trip from Boston to Chicago, with a stop in Cincinnati.

2. Look up hotels available in Cincinnati for the dates of your imaginary trip.

3. Use the online atlas to look up information about the United Kingdom and some of its larger cities.

4. Look up the lowest fare you can find for a flight from Atlanta to Los Angeles.

5. Find someone to talk to online who is in Sweden.

6. Look for the latest bargains on cruise vacation packages.

REAL-WORLD APPLICATIONS

✔ As AOL becomes increasingly international, interesting new global features roll out. For instance, Family Heritage (keyword: TELL US) asks you to share family stories and learn about cultural roots and immigration.

✔ World Culture (keyword: INTL CULTURES) features the life stories, customs, and pastimes of people all around the world. Students should see the section on the meanings behind festivals and traditions and hear the sounds of traditional music. Don't miss the recipes for international dishes.

Visual Quiz

If you see this window, what AOL channel are you using? How did you get to this window? Why would you use it?

_____

_____

_____

_____

_____

CHAPTER **10**

Minding Your Money

The time has come to take control of your resources and how they are managed and distributed.

America Online invites you to take more of a direct and personal interest in the managing and nurturing of your nest egg. This chapter explores exciting personal finance utilities and services ranging from stock and fund performance lookups and online brokerage firms to online banking and bill-paying services. In particular, everything you need to know to set up and use AOL's powerful, built-in electronic stock portfolio software is right here at your fingertips.

Recognizing that money needs to be earned before it can be invested, America Online offers career centers for enhancing your current job, finding a new and better job, and improving your work environment. You can even teach yourself how to start your own business, market your existing one, and network with colleagues and associates in your field.

With this chapter, you learn about

▶ managing your money and following the stock market from your computer, even automating the process of buying and selling securities online.

▶ creating your own electronic portfolio that helps you follow the success of your investments, enabling you to instantly see how the ups and downs of the market affect your own holdings through up-to-the-minute information, statistics, charts, and histories.

▶ exploring the world of online banking for savings, checking, paying bills automatically, transferring funds electronically, and more.

▶ building your career online through job search resources, advancement techniques and opportunities, online conferences and courses, survival tips on self-employment, and more.

▶ talking shop in professional forums devoted to more than 100 different lines of work, from carpentry and medicine to design and consulting.

▶ conducting business research with searchable databases of newspapers, journals, periodicals, and reports, finding the latest information on thousands of companies and corporations either for investment or possible employment.

Reaching the Personal Finance Channel

The Personal Finance channel is like the business section of a major newspaper, but with several important improvements. The channel updates throughout the day and into the evening with developing and late-breaking business news stories. And while the Personal Finance channel provides those all-important daily market gauges — the Dow Jones Industrial Average, the Standard & Poor's 500, the Nasdaq indices, and so on — it also has interactive tools to get you involved, from stock portfolios to electronic bank accounts. The channel also invites you to talk with fellow investors and experts from around the world, producing a never-ending financial summit meeting.

You reach the Personal Finance channel with keyword: PF. Alternatively, you can click Personal Finance on the Channels window or select it from the drop-down menu under the toolbar's Channels icon.

The Motley Fool

The Motley Fool (keyword: FOOL) is AOL's megahit in the financial world. The Fool (as it is affectionately known) is a lively, irreverent publication conceived by David Gardner, Tom Gardner, and Erik Rydholm in 1993, and it has been amusing, informing, and educating investors ever since. Don't miss it for features such as The Fool's School, with its 13 Steps to Investing Foolishly, and the Hall of Portfolios for high-performing portfolios. The Fool is a "rich" area

with a great deal of information — if you get turned around, try Fool HQ Information or The Help Desk located in the list box on the main window for tips, answers, and indexes.

TAKE NOTE

▶ **RESEARCH RESOURCES**

Of course, at the heart of wise investing is research, research, research. And America Online puts all the tools you need at your fingertips.

▶ Company Research (keyword: COMPANY RESEARCH) provides the tools for delving into the history and performances of thousands of U.S. companies, with unlimited access to reports on earning estimates, financial statements, company snapshots, mutual fund reports, current and historical stock quotes, and more.

▶ Investing Basics (keyword: INVESTING BASICS) offers an online reference shelf for beginners on how to avoid investing mistakes.

▶ Business and Market News (keyword: AOL BUSINESS NEWS CENTER) gives you all the breaking financial reports from the major wire services. Also you can track market activity and economic data (keyword: AOL MARKET CENTER).

▶ Market Day (keyword: MARKETDAY) provides a single comprehensive market briefing, with highlights from the news and business centers elsewhere online. Market Day is updated throughout each business day, at market open, midday, and market close.

CROSS-REFERENCE

For more on finding news online, see Chapter 8.

FIND IT ONLINE

For a further overview of the Personal Finance channel, see the Search & Explore area (keyword: PFSEARCH). Click the Best of AOL Personal Finance option.

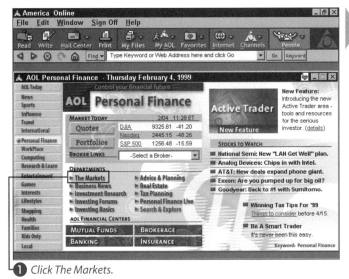

1 Click The Markets.

2 Click Keyword on the toolbar, type **BUSINESS NEWS**, and press Enter.

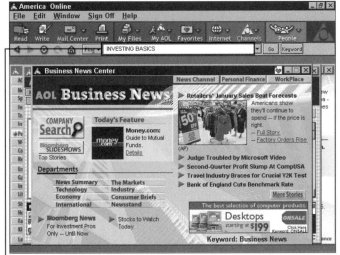

3 Type **INVESTING BASICS** into the data-entry box on the toolbar and then press Enter to reach the basics.

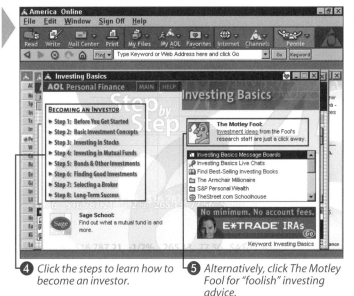

4 Click the steps to learn how to become an investor.

5 Alternatively, click The Motley Fool for "foolish" investing advice.

Creating Stock Portfolios

Central to the whole idea of the Personal Finance channel is the tracking of security prices on the various stock exchanges. You create electronic portfolios of stocks and mutual funds and then have the system monitor the latest stock prices, keeping track of the number of shares you bought, the most recent price or average, the price change, the original purchase price, and the total gain or loss to date. In fact, you can create more than one portfolio — you could have one for stocks you actually own, another to follow the company you work for, and still others for stocks you are watching or craving.

To create a stock portfolio, click the Portfolios button on the Personal Finance window or use keyword: PORTFOLIOS. Click Create Portfolio on the resulting window, name your new portfolio (up to 25 letters and spaces), and click OK.

For your portfolios to monitor your selected stocks, mutual funds, and money market funds, you need to work with their market symbols. The Lookup button at the bottom of the My Portfolios window lets you find a stock or fund either by symbol or by name, automatically adding the information to a portfolio if you wish. To use it, click Lookup and enter the symbol or the first few characters of the name you want to find. (If you choose to use a name, be sure to click Name above the data-entry box.) Click Lookup.

America Online looks up the stock or fund you are seeking and, if it finds more than one, lists all possible matches. Find the one you want using the scroll bar and the More button at the bottom of the window as needed, highlight it, and click Select. AOL gives you details on the last available price, the change, the high, low and opening prices, volume, 30-day average, year high and low, and more. To add the stock or fund to one of your portfolios, click Add to Portfolio and specify the following information: the exchange, number of shares you own (or wish you owned), purchase price you paid, purchase date, and any commissions or fees. Select the desired portfolio from the drop-down menu at the bottom and then click OK to add the shares to your portfolio.

TAKE NOTE

OTHER OPTIONS

To use other options on the Portfolio Summary screen, highlight the name of a portfolio and click Delete Portfolio to remove it, Rename Portfolio to change its name, or Display Portfolio to display its contents.

MULTIPLE PORTFOLIOS

You may create up to 20 portfolios for each screen name and each portfolio can hold up to 100 stocks.

CROSS-REFERENCE

For tips on other kinds of record keeping online, including the Personal Filing Cabinet and the Address Book, see Chapter 5.

FIND IT ONLINE

For more about creating your portfolio, visit the main screen (keyword: PORTFOLIO) and click the Help button at the top of the window.

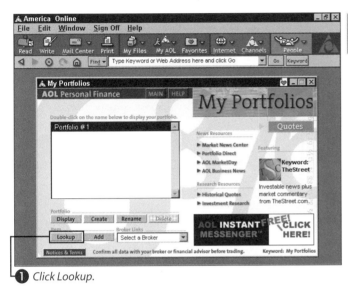

1 Click Lookup.

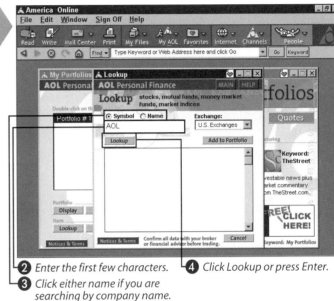

2 Enter the first few characters.

3 Click either name if you are searching by company name.

4 Click Lookup or press Enter.

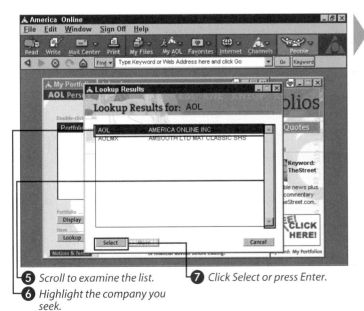

5 Scroll to examine the list.

6 Highlight the company you seek.

7 Click Select or press Enter.

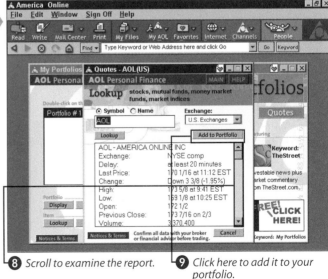

8 Scroll to examine the report.

9 Click here to add it to your portfolio.

Using Your Portfolio

ow that your portfolio is bursting with stocks, mutual funds, or money market funds, you can watch it go to work. Return to My Portfolios (use keyword: PORTFOLIOS or click the toolbar's My AOL icon and then select Stock Portfolios from the drop-down menu). In the resulting window, either double-click the portfolio you want to examine, or highlight it and click the Display button. The Portfolio Display provides a line for each stock in this portfolio with summary data, including the stock symbol, the number of shares, the last price or average volume, the amount of change since the previous business day, the original purchase price, the net gain or loss, and the total value.

Portfolio Display options at the bottom of the window include the following:

▶ **Details.** Click to get a summary of the highlighted security and fund's performance, latest news regarding this particular company (click any to read them), and charts of the stock's activity.
▶ **Add.** Click to add another stock or fund to the portfolio. As earlier, you are prompted for the stock symbol, number of shares, and purchase price.
▶ **Edit.** Click to make changes to the item(s) you have highlighted, including split information.

▶ **Transfer.** Click to move the highlighted stock to another portfolio.
▶ **Delete.** Click to remove the highlighted stock.
▶ **Refresh.** Click to update your portfolio with the most current available quotes. This is useful when viewing the portfolio during daytime weekday hours when the stock market is open and prices are changing rapidly.
▶ **Print.** Click to make a hard copy of the portfolio.
▶ **Download.** Click to save a copy of your portfolio in a delimited format or in Quicken- or Metastock-compatible files.
▶ **List All.** Click to see the list of all your portfolios.
▶ **Customize Columns.** Click to add, remove, or rearrange columns of data in the Portfolio Display window.

CROSS-REFERENCE

For more about computer-related topics, see Chapter 11.

FIND IT ONLINE

To get online assistance with all kinds of questions related to stock quotes, visit the Quotes window (keyword: QUOTES) and click Help at the top.

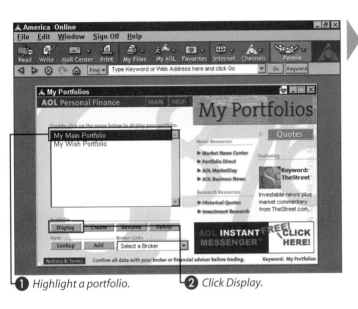

1 Highlight a portfolio.　**2** Click Display.

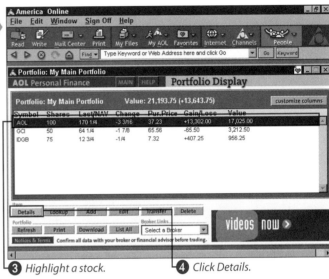

3 Highlight a stock.　**4** Click Details.

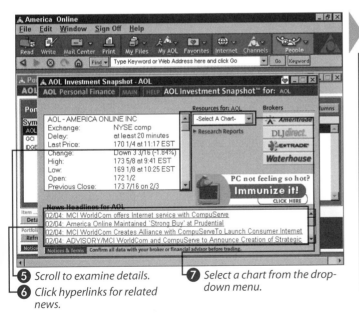

5 Scroll to examine details.

6 Click hyperlinks for related news.

7 Select a chart from the drop-down menu.

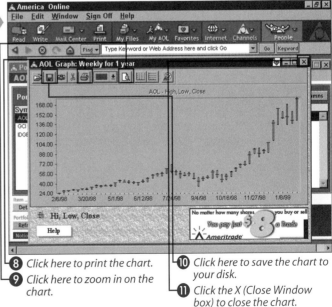

8 Click here to print the chart.

9 Click here to zoom in on the chart.

10 Click here to save the chart to your disk.

11 Click the X (Close Window box) to close the chart.

Learning Online Investing

America Online can do more than merely track your stocks. It also can help you invest right online, where commissions are historically lower than those at traditional brokerage houses. The Brokerage Center (keyword: BROKER) has links to major brokers, plus investing tools, backgrounders, research resources, and insightful columns. Among the brokerage houses with online sites are Ameritrade (keyword: CERES), DLJ/direct (keyword: DLJ DIRECT), E*Trade (keyword: E*TRADE), Charles Schwab (keyword: SCHWAB), SureTrade (keyword: SURETRADE), and Waterhouse Securities (keyword: WATERHOUSE).

Mutual Fund Center

You also can track the activities of mutual funds online from the AOL Mutual Fund Center (keyword: MUTUAL FUNDS), which has links to major players, fund research reports, fund screening, and more. Fund companies online include Fidelity Investments (keyword: FIDELITY), HighMark Funds (keyword: HIGHMARK), The Kaufmann Fund (keyword: KAUFMANN), Scudder (keyword: SCUDDER), and T. Rowe Price (keyword: T ROWE).

A major feature in the Mutual Funds Center is Sage (keyword: SAGE), a place where people gather to learn about mutual funds, hear from the experts, and share their knowledge. A dedicated chat room is open nightly from 7 a.m. to 11 p.m. eastern time.

Also a message board stands ready to exchange comments with fellow members outside the chat room. Fielding questions are certified financial planners Alan and Stephen Cohn. The site also offers a school teaching the basics of mutual funds and even has a quiz to help you test your mutual fund knowledge. In addition, Sage provides hyperlinks to the best mutual fund data on the Internet.

TAKE NOTE

▶ **OTHER FINANCIAL FEATURES**

The Personal Finance Channel has other investor tools reached by keyword, including
▶ American Association of Individual Investors (keyword: AAII), presenting message boards, downloadable software and more, all geared towards empowering the individual.
▶ Company News (keyword: COMPANY NEWS), enabling you to search by stock symbol for news of specific companies.
▶ Decision Point Timing and Charts (keyword: DP), teaching analysis skills for investors.
▶ Disclosure (keyword: DISCLOSURE), offering a database of public company data, including filings with the Securities and Exchange Commission.
▶ FundWorks (keyword: FUNDWORKS), presenting a forum on mutual funds with daily chats and interviews, articles and messages.

CROSS-REFERENCE

Speaking of spending money, for information about online shopping, see Chapter 15.

FIND IT ONLINE

For tips and guidance about electronic brokerages, click the "How to Invest Online" option on the main Brokerage Center screen (keyword: BROKER).

How to Trade Online

Not everyone is ready to trade stock through computers, but Wall Street is full of legends who saw the next wave and caught it. For now, there are compelling reasons to consider trading here:

▶ It is convenient. You trade any time of the day or night and anywhere you can get to a computer.

▶ You save money. Most online commissions are below those of traditional brokers.

▶ It is secure. America Online works with all participating financial institutions to secure the fund transfers.

▶ You are in control of your money, deciding when and where to invest, doing your own financial research.

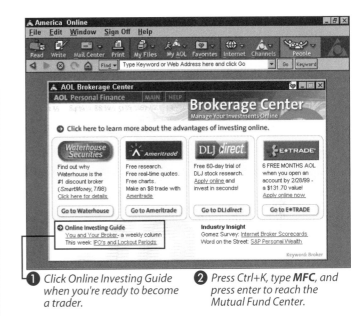

1 Click Online Investing Guide when you're ready to become a trader.

2 Press Ctrl+K, type **MFC**, and press enter to reach the Mutual Fund Center.

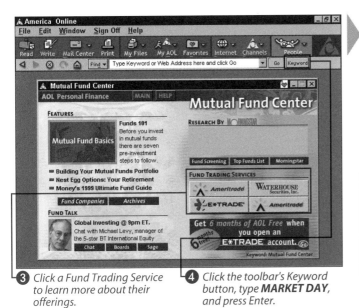

3 Click a Fund Trading Service to learn more about their offerings.

4 Click the toolbar's Keyword button, type **MARKET DAY**, and press Enter.

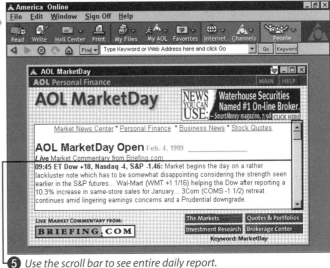

5 Use the scroll bar to see entire daily report.

Getting Started with Online Banking

Nothing better illustrates how computers have given us more control over our wealth and well-being than the booming electronic banking services. These interactive, online banks let you to track all account activity, set up automatic payment of your bills, transfer money from one account to another, apply for a loan online, and communicate with the bank itself. All this and more is available at your fingertips from the comfort of your home, any time of the day or night.

America Online offers the best in electronic banking with the Online Banking Center (keyword: BANKING), which now has more than 20 participating financial institutions, each with a variety of services. Many offer free online banking and some charge a minimal fee to add automatic bill-paying features. Shop around online for the banking service that best meets your needs. Start by visiting the central banking area, using keyword: BANKING. For background information on the latest bank additions and services, click the Getting Started button at the top of the window. Now return to the Banking Center and browse the available banks. If you don't see a bank you are looking for, click the More Banks button at the bottom of the window. Each bank you visit has a demo of the services you can reach online, a detailed introduction explaining their available services, instructions on how to access the services (that is, by the Internet or by specialized banking software,

and so on), and a list of the latest costs for basic services and added features (if any). If you decide to open an account with one of the banks, you receive a unique password and utilize special e-mail services for communicating with the institutions.

Of course, America Online covers traditional banking too. Its highly regarded Bank Rate Monitor (keyword: BANK RATE) tracks the latest lending rates, as well as those on auto loans, credit cards, mortgages, CDs, and more.

TAKE NOTE

▶ SOME MORE FINANCIAL SERVICES

Additional money-related sites:
- ▶ Business Week Online (keyword: BW) offers the electronic extension of one of the nation's best known business publications.
- ▶ Checks and Balances (keyword: PF NEWSLETTER) publishes a weekly newsletter on managing your money.
- ▶ Economist Intelligence Unit (keyword: EIU) forecasts and analyzes the political, economic, and business environments in more than 180 countries.
- ▶ MoneyWhiz (keyword: MONEYWHIZ) answers tricky, real-life financial problems through online articles, message boards, and chats.
- ▶ Tax Planning (keyword: TAX) provides tax news, forms and schedules, downloadable software, chats, and related services.

CROSS-REFERENCE
For more on using AOL's Internet links, see Chapter 7.

FIND IT ONLINE
To learn more about electronic banking, visit Member Services (keyword: HELP), click the Find It Now button, and enter **banking** in the query box.

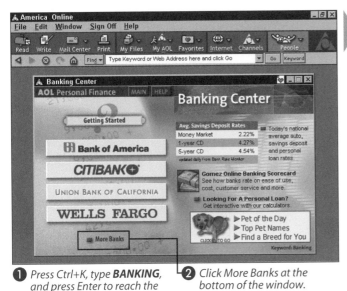

① Press Ctrl+K, type **BANKING**, and press Enter to reach the Banking Center.

② Click More Banks at the bottom of the window.

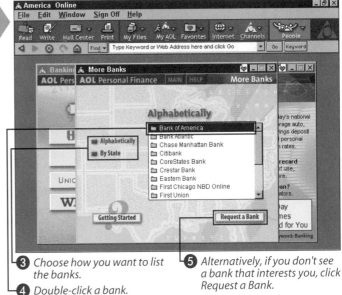

③ Choose how you want to list the banks.

④ Double-click a bank.

⑤ Alternatively, if you don't see a bank that interests you, click Request a Bank.

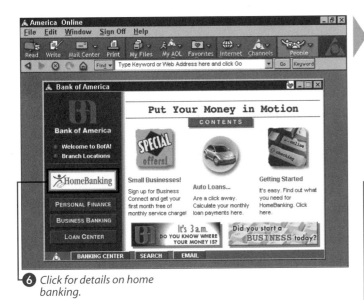

⑥ Click for details on home banking.

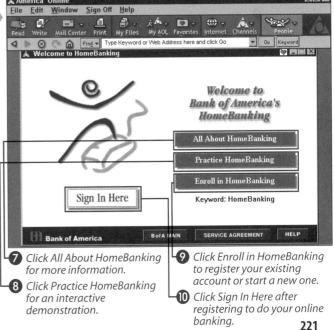

⑦ Click All About HomeBanking for more information.

⑧ Click Practice HomeBanking for an interactive demonstration.

⑨ Click Enroll in HomeBanking to register your existing account or start a new one.

⑩ Click Sign In Here after registering to do your online banking.

Working with the WorkPlace Channel

While you can exercise extensive control over the distribution of your money, you don't have as much say over the income itself. Or do you? America Online's WorkPlace channel (keyword: WORKPLACE) is dedicated to the proposition that you can get more out of your existing job, find a better job, and/or start an entirely new career or business. It all starts with know-how, and the know-how starts here.

One of the best features of the WorkPlace channel is AboutWork (keyword: ABOUTWORK), a focal point for people and services that can help you find a job, keep your job, advance your career, make more money, and get more satisfaction out of your work week. Of particular interest is their forum on home-based business that offers expert tips, coaching, information on hot home businesses, government resources, tax guides, and more.

Linking Up with Professional Forums

For many people, one of the secrets to a happy, successful career is creating and using a network of colleagues you can rely on for advice, support, and tips. Your starting point for building such a personal network of friends and associates in your line of work could be right here through the WorkPlace channel's Professional Forums.

To begin networking, visit the WorkPlace channel (use keyword: WORKPLACE) and click the Professional Forums button to reach the crossroads for more than 100 work-specific gathering places. Use the scroll box at the right to examine the list of group and individual forums, which range from those devoted to accountants to those for veterinarians. Double-click one of interest to reach a subsequent window where the first item in the scroll box will be "WELCOME! — Read This First." Begin there to learn more about the group and how you can make the most of it.

Every professional forum offers a set of helpful articles, message boards, software libraries, and Web sites. They also have regular chats and even a Chat Reminder Service to help busy professionals keep up with their schedule.

TAKE NOTE

▶ OTHER CAREER BUILDERS

America Online also has these fast-track career features:

▶ Advancing in Your Career (keyword: ADVANCING YOUR CAREER) provides tips and advice on successful careers.

▶ Career Research (keyword: CAREER RESEARCH) offers a central rallying point for information on staying competitive in the job market.

CROSS-REFERENCE

For information on using AOL Classified Ads for business and job hunting, see Chapter 15. And for help with using AOL forums in general, see Chapter 6.

FIND IT ONLINE

To get a further overview of the WorkPlace channel, visit its Search & Explore page (keyword: WORKPLACE SEARCH) and click the Best of AOL WorkPlace option.

1 Click the toolbar's Channels icon, select WorkPlace, select "All Professions A-Z" from the drop-down menu in the resulting window.

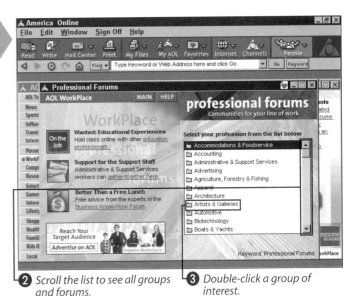

2 Scroll the list to see all groups and forums.

3 Double-click a group of interest.

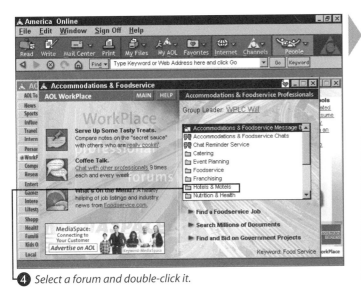

4 Select a forum and double-click it.

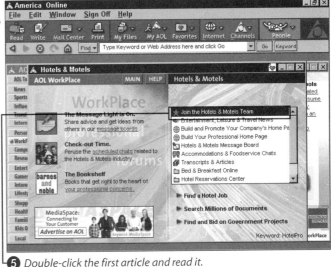

5 Double-click the first article and read it.

Finding Business Services

Essential to many businesses is the need to find other companies. Whether locally or across the country, companies that can be called on in a hurry for service and assistance for everything from copying and shipping to stepping in on a big project are valuable indeed.

The Business Research Center (keyword: BUSINESS RESEARCH) offers links to such businesses through key directories and business guides, not to mention business journals, periodicals, newspapers, and analysts' reports. Click the Business Research Site Index for links to data on copyrights, patents and trademarks, business associates, references, funding organizations, demographics, business magazine article archives, franchisers, glossaries, suppliers, and more.

The WorkPlace channel provides a suite of business tools, from those used in creating and running your own business to career building when you work for someone else. Stop by (keyword: WORKPLACE) and check out these business resources:

▶ Your Business (keyword: YOUR BUSINESS) provides the facilities for getting your own company off the ground.
▶ Your Career (keyword: YOUR CAREER) aims to help you, whether you are looking for a job or switching careers.
▶ The CCH Business Owner's Toolkit (keyword: CCH) offers tutorials and tools to help business owners strengthen their positions.

▶ Business Services (keyword: BUSINESS SERVICES) provides one-stop information shopping for online business services ranging from American Express to America Online itself.
▶ Dilbert (keyword: DILBERT) relieves the stress and tension with uncanny commentary and cartoons on the modern workplace.

TAKE NOTE

▶ **HELP WITH RUNNING BUSINESS**

The WorkPlace offers valuable startup, sales, and marketing advice. Take a look at these resources:
▶ Business Know-How Forum (keyword: BUSINESS KNOW HOW) offers strategies on starting and marketing a business. Author Janet Attard hosts and covers issues such as which business are hot and which should be avoided, how to work from home, and how to know when to incorporate.
▶ Doing Business Online (keyword: DOING BUSINESS ONLINE) reports the scoop on the Web as a business opportunity.
▶ Sales and Marketing (keyword: SALES & MARKETING) gives tips for selling your services and products.

CROSS-REFERENCE

For information on using the AOL Yellow Pages to find business, see Chapter 7. And to get more on other research topics, see Chapter 12.

FIND IT ONLINE

For general research projects, visit the Research Zone (keyword: RESEARCH ZONE), which covers directories, writing questions, libraries, and more.

1 Type **business research** in the toolbar's data-entry box, click Go, and click the drop-down menu in the resulting window.

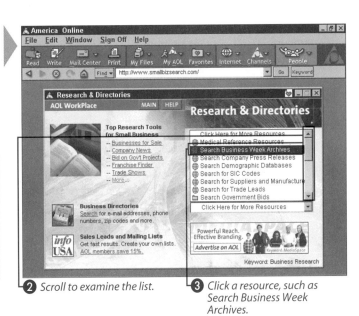

2 Scroll to examine the list.

3 Click a resource, such as Search Business Week Archives.

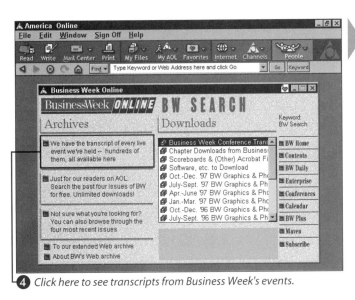

4 Click here to see transcripts from Business Week's events.

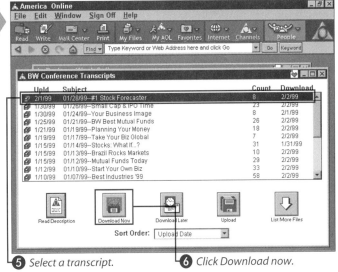

5 Select a transcript.

6 Click Download now.

Personal Workbook

Q&A

1 For what purpose is Hoover's Business Reports used?

_____

_____

_____

2 Who or what is The Motley Fool?

_____

_____

_____

3 How many stock portfolios can be created for each screen name?

_____

_____

_____

4 Where can you find a graph that charts recent performance of one of your stocks?

_____

_____

_____

5 A friend tells you about a hot stock. How can you quickly check its historical performance?

_____

_____

_____

6 You want to get into investing, but you need some pointers for starting. Where can you turn for the basics?

_____

_____

_____

7 Where can you can look for an online forum that serves veterinarians?

_____

_____

_____

8 Bonus Question: Where can you find online help with writing a resume for a job?

_____

_____

_____

ANSWERS: PAGE 341

EXTRA PRACTICE

1 Create a wish list portfolio of stocks you want to buy as soon as your ship comes in.

2 Use the portfolio manager to track the history of your wish list.

3 Print charts of selected stock histories.

5 Find company news about one of your stocks.

6 Take a demo of an online banking system.

REAL-WORLD APPLICATIONS

✔ You can speed up access to your portfolio by adding it to your Favorite Places list. Simply click the red heart-shaped icon in the upper-right corner of the Portfolio Details window.

✔ The Banking Center (keyword: BANKING) has an Interactive Calculators button that links to a site on the World Wide Web dedicated for nifty special-needs calculators, such as those for figuring auto loans, credit debt, interest rates, and the like.

✔ If your entrepreneurial plans include creation of a commercial site on the Internet's World Wide Web, check out AOL PrimeHost (keyword: PRIMEHOST), which is designed to help companies create an Internet presence.

Visual Quiz

How would you reach a window like this? How do you get a printout of it? How would you save it on your hard disk? How do you zoom in to enlarge a portion of the window?

_____

_____

_____

_____

_____

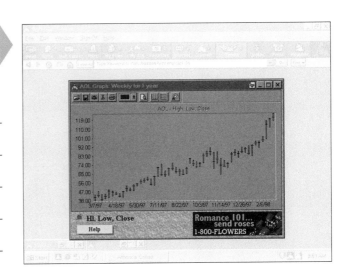

CHAPTER 11

Using the Computing Channel

It used to be that no matter how big or small your town, most of its computer users knew each other. It had to be that way. As with the first automobile owners and drivers, early pioneers of computer technology had to stick together. When something went wrong with your computer, you usually had to turn to a wizardly friend for assistance. Computer user groups sprang up around the world, complete with special interest groups devoted to specific hardware and software, newsletters, and online computer bulletin systems, as described in Chapter 6. Here is where the knowledge was shared, closeted among the techno-geeks who never thought twice about getting up early on Saturday morning for their user group meeting. Tips for solving problems, ideas about making the machines run better, reviews of the newest computers and peripherals — all were circulated in these user groups. So, whether you were thinking of buying a new machine or hoping to get more mileage out of an old system, your local user group was *the* place to start.

Nowadays, many more people use personal computers, yet fewer join a local computer user group (if they even have one in town any longer). This decline may be the result of the growth in computers themselves. Computers have become appliances, like telephones and televisions — and who belongs to a TV user group? At the same time, personal computer technology has become more complex, spurring the need for even more technical assistance.

Cyberspace is filling the void. America Online's Computing channel (keyword: COMPUTING) is a vast computer user group. It is specific enough to be "local" and serve your unique needs. At the same time, it is cosmopolitan enough to serve a global audience around the clock.

In this chapter, you learn how the Computing channel can teach you new computer technologies through online workshops and classrooms, answer your computer questions, serve up tasty tips, and help you with computer-buying decisions.

Taking Online Computing Classes

Today's classroom no longer needs four walls and a blackboard — you may now only need a computer and a modem. Online learning is the latest development in the sharing of technical information that has been central to the personal computer revolution since its early days. Online computing classes now teach everything from how to navigate America Online to how to create and polish a world-class Web page for the World Wide Web.

Electronic classes are taught by experts, and you can attend right from the comfort of your home. Classes are open to all ages and experience levels. Most require nothing more than your computer and AOL. Schedules posted online tell you what is offered and when each class is held. If you miss a class, you can view transcripts to catch up on what was covered in your absence. You can also supplement your electronic studies with resources from the software libraries that include tutorials and AutoClasses designed to help you learn at your own pace.

Browsing the Class Schedule

One way to find a class of interest is to browse the schedule of upcoming sessions. To begin, sign on to the system as usual and use the keyword ONLINE CLASSROOM to reach the area. Click the Class Schedule button to see what is coming up today and over the next few weeks. If you find a topic of

interest, click the hyperlink (the blue underlined text) to receive a detailed description of the class, plus any requirements and recommendations. Also on the window is an Enter Classroom icon, which is activated during the hours the class is in session. There is no need to register for a class in advance.

CROSS-REFERENCE
For other electronic classrooms and online courses, see Chapter 12.

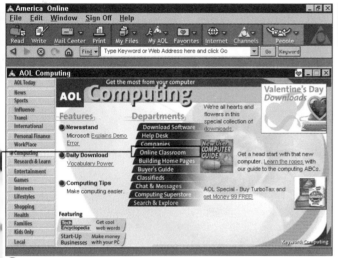

❶ Click Online Classroom or go to keyword: ONLINE CLASSROOM.

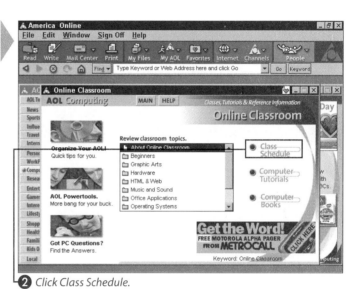

❷ Click Class Schedule.

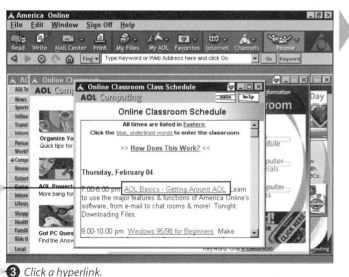

❸ Click a hyperlink.

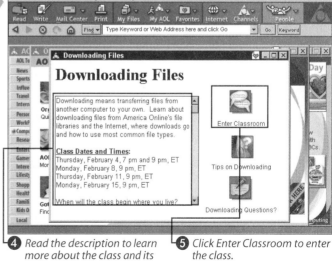

❹ Read the description to learn more about the class and its topic.

❺ Click Enter Classroom to enter the class.

Reading Class Transcripts

Although attending a live online class enables you to interact with the instructor and fellow students, it isn't for everyone. The hours may be inconvenient. You may have just missed a class on a topic you need to learn now. Or you may simply learn at different pace. If any of this sounds familiar, the Online Classroom has anticipated your needs. You can monitor the class simply by reading the instructor's transcripts.

To see a transcript, begin by clicking the Online Classroom button on the main Computing Channel, or use the keyword ONLINE CLASSROOM to reach the Online Classroom window. Now click the Class Transcripts button at the right, and in the resulting window, double-click the topic of interest (beginners, graphics & desktop publishing, hardware, multimedia, office applications, programming, Web & Internet, or Windows). From the resulting list of transcript titles, double-click the document you want to see.

Once the transcript is on your screen, you can read it by moving up and down the document with the scroll bar at the right of the window. You can also print it by clicking the toolbar's Print icon and save it by clicking File on the menu bar and selecting Save from the drop-down menu. If you're seeking a particular topic or answer, use the Edit menu's Find in Top Window option to search the text of the transcript.

Reading a transcript in advance is also a great way to prepare for a live class. Feel free to read transcripts from previous classes and prepare questions ahead of time.

TAKE NOTE

COMPUTER MAGAZINES

The Computing Newsstand links you to all kinds of computer publications — from *Computer Shopper* to *Wired* magazine — as well as to computer-oriented general news resources such as ABC News' Sci/Tech area and *Business Week's* Computer Room. Use the keyword COMPUTING NEWSSTAND to reach it.

COMPUTING HELP WITH AMERICA ONLINE

Remember Meg, the AOL Insider who wrote introductory e-mail to you when you first signed up as a member? A database of all Meg's tips is available to browse through. Use the keyword MEG or AOL INSIDER to reach today's tips. From there, you can click a button to flip through all of Meg's tips.

CROSS-REFERENCE

For background on using forums, see Chapter 6.

FIND IT ONLINE

To learn more about electronic computing classes, visit the site (keyword: ONLINE CLASSROOM) and select the article called "About Online Classroom" from the list box.

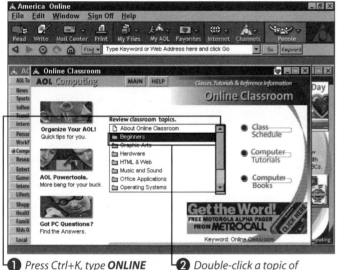

① Press Ctrl+K, type **ONLINE CLASSROOM**, press Enter, and scroll the list in the resulting window.

② Double-click a topic of interest.

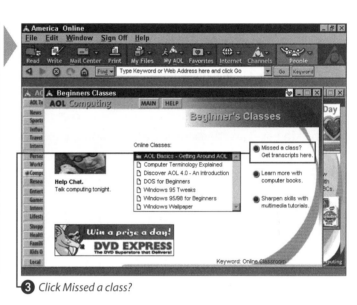

③ Click Missed a class?

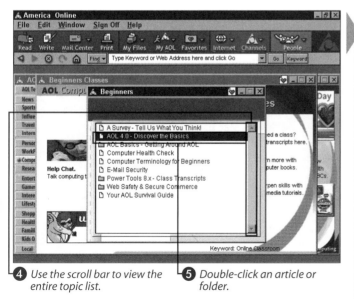

④ Use the scroll bar to view the entire topic list.

⑤ Double-click an article or folder.

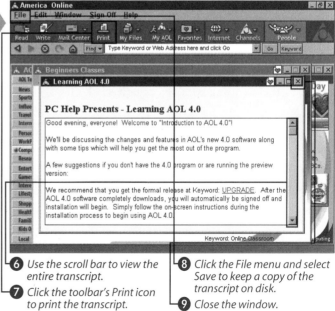

⑥ Use the scroll bar to view the entire transcript.

⑦ Click the toolbar's Print icon to print the transcript.

⑧ Click the File menu and select Save to keep a copy of the transcript on disk.

⑨ Close the window.

Getting Computer Tips

Of course, you don't have to rely only on classrooms for your computer wisdom. The Computing Tips area (keyword: COMPUTING TIPS) also provides a treasure trove of tricks on how to get your computer working faster, better, and easier. Topics range from how to clean a dirty mouse or CD-ROM to what you need to know to protect yourself from computer viruses and Trojan Horses.

To reach the resource, click the Computing Tips button on the main Computing channel window or use the keyword COMPUTING TIPS. Depending on the version of America Online you are running—Mac or PC—the resulting window will display computing tips for your type of computer:

▶ **PC User's Guide.** Information relating to Windows-based computers
▶ **Mac Tips.** Help with Apple Macintosh systems
▶ **AOL Tips.** Suggestions on navigating and using the features of America Online

In the resulting window, double-click one of the listed topics, such as general personal computing tips, Windows 95 tips for beginners, and so on. AOL displays a list of relevant tips that can be open or logged to file, like any other text described in Chapter 8. Hyperlinks in the text point to other useful resources and utilities that complement the information.

Youth Tech Serves Compu-kids

America Online also has a special corner for computer-savvy kids. Youth Tech (keyword: YT) is designed by and for computer-using teens and includes games, contests, and surveys. Chat rooms and Techie Pals give teens a place to make online friends and create e-mail relationships. Also featured are regular lists of cool sites on the World Wide Web and "Bits of Bytes," a daily source of computer industry news. Also included here are the Techie Terms Dictionary and tech tips from "The Daily Know-It-All."

TAKE NOTE

▶ **MAJOR COMPUTING FEATURES**

The Computing Channel provides many ways to talk to other computer users, ask questions of experts, and research more about the Net:

▶ Computing Live (keyword: COMP LIVE) offers live chat rooms all day long, inviting conversation about hardware and software as well as the day's issues in the computer industry. The area has a daily schedule of featured chats for gadget lovers, Mac users, game players, and assorted experts.
▶ The AOL Help Desk (keyword: HELP DESK) devotes its forum to computing in general and to AOL-specific questions and answers. It, too, hosts nightly chats and offers an active message board, as illustrated in Chapter 6.

CROSS-REFERENCE
For more features for kids and teens, see Chapter 16.

FIND IT ONLINE
To learn even more about the ins and outs of the AOL software, visit Member Services (keyword: HELP) and click Error Messages in the resulting window.

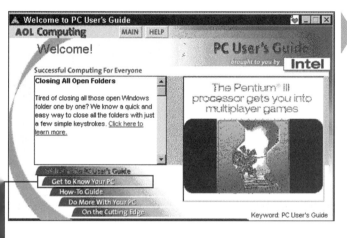

1 Press Ctrl+K, type **COMPUTING TIPS**, press Enter, and select a topic that appears on the lower-left of the resulting window. For example, choose Get to Know Your PC.

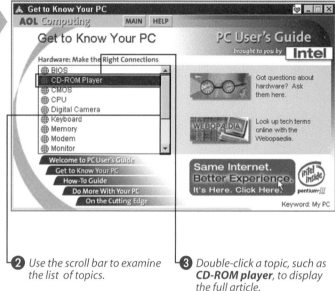

2 Use the scroll bar to examine the list of topics.

3 Double-click a topic, such as **CD-ROM player**, to display the full article.

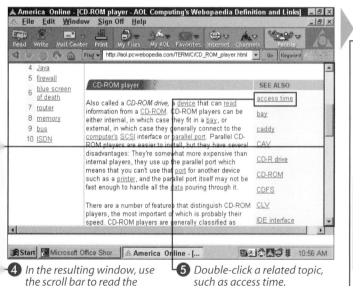

4 In the resulting window, use the scroll bar to read the article you chose.

5 Double-click a related topic, such as access time.

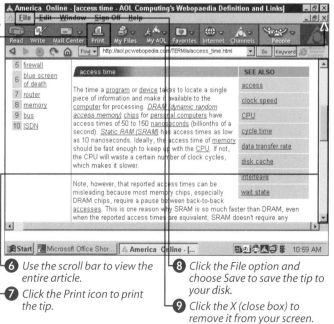

6 Use the scroll bar to view the entire article.

7 Click the Print icon to print the tip.

8 Click the File option and choose Save to save the tip to your disk.

9 Click the X (close box) to remove it from your screen.

Shopping for Computers and Peripherals

For some computer users, the biggest technical question is what to look for in the next computer or peripheral they buy. America Online has excellent utilities to help the computer shopper, from a buyer's guide that gives you the skinny on what is available, to a computer superstore where you can actually make your purchases online.

The Buyer's Guide (keyword: BUYERS GUIDE) has reviews from leading computer magazines on new computers and all kinds of peripherals, including the latest modems and printers. You can browse categories for the latest ratings on hardware and software. To use the feature, sign on to the system (if you are not already there) and use the keyword BUYERS GUIDE to reach the main window. Notice the two tabs in the center of the window that enable you to view material on either hardware or software:

▶ Hardware (the default) includes reviews of desktop computers, digital cameras, modems, personal digital assistants, notebook computers, monitors, printers, scanners, removable storage, and more.
▶ Software includes reviews of programs for business, games, graphics, home/hobby, education, utilities, Internet suites and tools, operating systems, Web publishing, and more.

Click the folder of interest, and the system offers further breakdowns in subjects. After you have further narrowed the list search by making any additional choices listed on subsequent windows, AOL displays a list of articles and reviews. Use the scroll bar at the right of the window to examine the list, and double-click any items of interest.

Once you have read the review, you often have the opportunity to actually buy the hardware or software online. Examine the window for a Click to Purchase option, as shown in the example on the facing page. Such links connect you to AOL's many online stores or to a site on the Internet where you can place a mail-order purchase.

TAKE NOTE

HELP WITH EQUIPMENT

There are even more features devoted to product reviews and information on equipment:
▶ Consumer Electronics (keyword: CE), providing news and reviews of the latest audio, video, communications, and personal electronics.
▶ Family Computing Forum (keyword: FC), offering product reviews, software, and computing tips — all with a family focus.
▶ Gadget Guru (keyword: GADGET), reporting on the latest and greatest products available. The Products by Category option in the list box in the lower left of the main window steers you towards the Computer reviews.

CROSS-REFERENCE

For more about online shopping, see Chapter 15.

FIND IT ONLINE

To get more help with shopping and other Computing channel topics, visit the PC Help Desk (keyword: HELP DESK), as described in Chapter 6.

1 Press Ctrl+K, type **BUYERS GUIDE**, press Enter, and click either the Hardware or Software tab on the resulting window.

2 Double-click a subject.

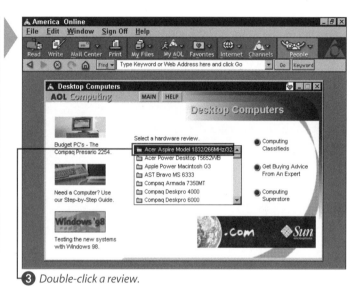

3 Double-click a review.

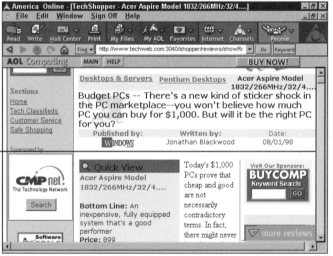

4 Use the scroll bar to see the eniter review.

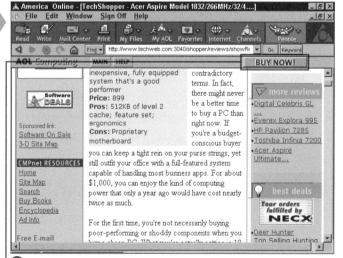

5 Click Buy Now! if you want to purchase the product.

Exploring the Superstore

When shopping is on your mind, don't miss the Computing Superstore (keyword: SUPERSTORE). The Superstore carries all manner of hardware (computers, modems, monitors, printers, scanners and digital cameras, and more) as well as software for work and play. You can browse or search for products, get full descriptions and prices, and then order online with a credit card for home delivery.

To visit the store, use the keyword SUPERSTORE to reach the main window. From here, you can choose a category from the list on the left of the window to explore further. Superstore categories include hardware (computers, modems, printers, digital imaging devices, and other peripherals) and software (games, educational programs, virus protection, utilities and other software). If you're not sure which category fits the bill, search for a specific product with the option at the bottom of the window. AOL prompts to you enter the name of a manufacturer or product type to start the search. Follow onscreen instructions to zero in on the product you are seeking.

Once you've found an item that interests you, whether by browsing or searching, click it to see more information. Descriptions vary, of course, depending on the type of product you are viewing. For instance, computer descriptions list specifications such as the speed of the processor, the size of the memory and hard disk, the speed of the CD-ROM drive and modem, the type of graphics, whether or not the monitor is included in the price, a written description, what software is included, and so on.

If you like what you see, click the option to put the item in your electronic shopping cart. When you've finished shopping, pay for your order online by entering a credit card number and mailing address when prompted.

TAKE NOTE

▶ ASSORTED COMPUTER-RELATED FORUMS

Here are some major computer-related forums on the system:

▶ DOS Forum (keyword: DOS) devotes a forum to the PC disk operating system (DOS) and related topics.

▶ Games Forum (keyword: PC GAMES or MAC GAMES) offers downloads of new games and previews for your PC or Mac.

▶ Graphics Arts and CAD Forum (keyword: MGR) focuses on the Mac with coverage of arts, 3D, and general graphics topics.

▶ Graphics Arts Forum (keyword: PGR) offers a PC equivalent forum with more than 14,000 software files to download.

▶ OS/2 Form (keyword: OS/2) devotes itself to the OS/2 operating system for PC users.

▶ PDA/Palmtop Forum (keyword: PDA) covers all aspects of personal digital assistants.

CROSS-REFERENCE

For background on downloading, see Chapter 6.

FIND IT ONLINE

For online assistance with downloading and other issues related to the software, visit the Software Help Center (keyword: SOFTWARE HELP) and select a topic from the list box.

Getting Your Daily Download

Chapter 6 introduced the idea of downloading software that you locate either via File Search (keyword: FILESEARCH) or through the software libraries of the individual forums. The Daily Download area (keyword: DAILY DOWNLOAD) spotlights a different program each day, either freeware, shareware, or commercial software. Use keyword: DAILY DOWNLOAD to reach the main window describing the file of the day. Click the hyperlink to retrieve it.

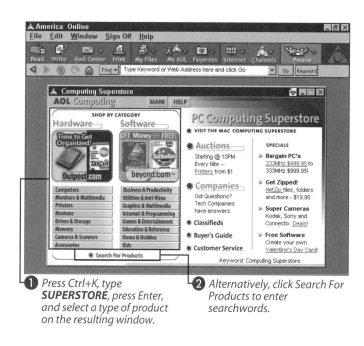

1 Press Ctrl+K, type **SUPERSTORE**, press Enter, and select a type of product on the resulting window.

2 Alternatively, click Search For Products to enter searchwords.

3 Select a product's hyperlink or picture for more information.

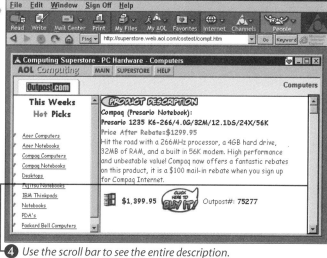

4 Use the scroll bar to see the entire description.

Finding Computer Companies Online

You've been around the block in the Computing channel. You've seen how the channel's resources can help you answer computer problems and find equipment to buy. It is now time to learn how to use the same channel to solve problems and get information about the very companies who sold you the computer equipment in the first place.

If you are looking for hardware or software companies, the Computing channel's Companies area (keyword: COMPANIES) may be able help you contact providers directly. The area has contact numbers and addresses for computer-related companies around the world, all searchable from the same starting point. Whether you are an old hand at computers or the newest user on your block, this resource is particularly valuable because the specifics of computer makers and software publishers change so rapidly. The Companies area gets you on the fast track for product support, tips and tricks, announcements of new products and upgrades, facts about companies and their sales, special offers, links to company Web sites, details on demos, upgrades and software patches, and more.

To use this valuable resource, sign on to AOL (if you are not already online) and use the keyword COMPANIES to reach the main window. At the top of the window's center panel, select one of the two tabs to browse either:

▶ Companies A to Z, for an alphabetic listing from Activision to Zoom Telephonics.
▶ By Category, for a subject listing including business, development, education, games, graphics and presentation, hardware, multi-media, music and sound, telecommunications, utilities, and windows. Double-click any category to get a list of companies.

Click a company's name from the resulting list to view a wide range of information about the company. Most areas contain an overview of the business, the latest news, technical support numbers and information, schedules of upcoming workshops and clinics, product information, price lists, software library, service centers, and so on.

TAKE NOTE

ADDITIONAL COMPUTER SERVICES

Also on the Computing Channel are several more related computer services, all reachable by keyword. Two examples are

▶ Computing Classifieds (keyword: COMPUTING CLASSIFIEDS), which offers a special place for members to buy and sell new and used hardware, software, and peripherals
▶ Education and Technology Forum (keyword: MED), which focuses on learning with the Apple Macintosh, serving beginners and experts alike

CROSS-REFERENCE
For assistance with search strategies in AOL database, see the Appendix.

FIND IT ONLINE
To get more help with the company database, visit the area (keyword: COMPANIES) and select the article called "About This Area" from the list.

Keyword Searching for Companies

If browsing the lists by name and/or category doesn't turn up what you need, try a keyword search. Use the keyword COMPANIES to reach the Companies window and click the Company Search button at the right. In the resulting window, type the words that describe the company for which you are searching. For instance, you might enter MICROSOFT AND GAME to find selected entertainment products. Now just click List Articles to find matches. Double-click a title in the resulting list to see the actual company or product.

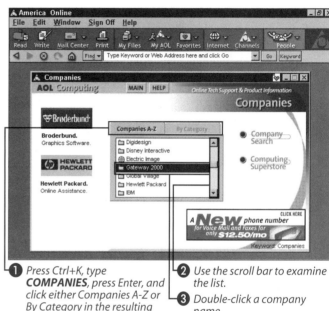

❶ Press Ctrl+K, type **COMPANIES**, press Enter, and click either Companies A-Z or By Category in the resulting window.

❷ Use the scroll bar to examine the list.

❸ Double-click a company name.

❹ Double-click a folder.

❺ Highlight an article.

Personal Workbook

Q&A

1 Where can you find the schedule of online computing classes?

_____

_____

_____

2 How do you save a transcript of a class you missed to disk?

_____

_____

_____

3 What do you do to find an online list of computer-related message boards?

_____

_____

_____

4 How can you locate tips to assist you in helping your mom learn to use her Macintosh computer?

_____

_____

5 What is Youth Tech?

_____

_____

_____

6 You're in the market for a new computer and you want to check reviews of some of the newest systems. Where do you go computer shopping online?

_____

_____

_____

7 What is the Daily Download?

_____

_____

_____

8 Bonus Question: How would you go about learning whether the manufacturer of your modem has an area on AOL?

_____

_____

_____

ANSWERS: PAGE 342

EXTRA PRACTICE

1 Research whether there are online classes about Web page design.

2 Check the class transcripts section to see whether you can find some early Web-oriented classes.

3 Look into the computing tips database for hints on using your AOL Address Book.

4 Locate a forum devoted to multimedia subjects.

5 Do comparison shopping on how much computing power you can buy with $1,500.

6 Determine which modem makers have information in the computer database.

REAL-WORLD APPLICATIONS

✔ Some people find online classes more fun in a group. See if other AOL acquaintances are interested in taking a class with you. You can use e-mail to share notes and transcripts.

✔ Online shopping often is useful as an extension of "real world" shopping. Some members like to test out computers in person at an electronic store and then compare the prices online for the same system, taking the best offer of the two.

✔ The company database can be a valuable source of contact numbers. Most of the companies have information on technical support, so be sure to check the makers of all the equipment you currently own and then build your address file.

Visual Quiz

How would you reach this window? Based on similar windows you have used in earlier chapters, how would you use this one? Or if you go here by mistake, how do you remove it from your screen?

_____

_____

_____

_____

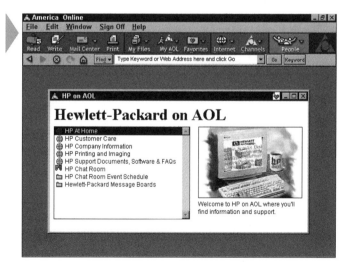

CHAPTER **12**

MASTER
THESE
SKILLS

▶ **Getting Homework Help for Youngsters**

▶ **Helping Older Students**

▶ **Enrolling for Online Studies**

▶ **Using Online Encyclopedias**

▶ **Using Online Dictionaries**

▶ **Finding Directories**

Aiding Education

People who design encyclopedias and assorted directories, reference works, and textbooks must have been dreaming of something like America Online long before the rest of us even got here. Imagine the problem of dealing with constantly changing information and knowing that as soon as you get it into print, it immediately begins to get out of date.

New scientific discoveries are made. Old government leaders step down. New books, films, and songs win the top awards. Old sports records are toppled. How in the world do you hope to keep your reference material current and relevant when the printed page is so quickly outdated? The answer, of course, is online. Reference material published digitally, on the fluid pages of cyberspace, can be easily updated as new material is available. And the readers get it immediately, rather than having to wait a year or more for a revised edition.

No wonder the online world is attracting enterprising students and teachers who realize the immediacy of this medium makes it a great boon to education. Whether you are a student in school or a smart adult who makes learning a lifetime pursuit, the vast databases and references available online can make you a success.

America Online has been at the forefront of the information revolution since its early days, offering all the education and data you crave. The Research & Learn channel (keyword: RESEARCH & LEARN) has educational materials and reference sources of all kinds:

- A full-featured electronic encyclopedia, enabling you to search the entire multi-volume work with a keyword or a phrase.
- Homework helpers who field questions on special message boards for students from grade school to college and beyond.
- Electronic classes you can take online to learn all kinds of subjects.
- Online dictionaries, a thesaurus, and other writing tools.

Getting Homework Help for Youngsters

Wouldn't it be wonderful to have a teacher on call? Imagine you're working your way through your economics homework, you get stuck on the definition of *gross national product,* and you call on your digital homework helper. Or you're writing a term paper and you suddenly realize you don't quite understand what ought to go in the bibliography, so you dial into an online English instructor. Or your school days are behind you, you're on the road with your business, and you need to know how to figure a percentage of increase or decrease, so you call on a digital math helper. On America Online, these are not fantasies, but daily realities. Ask a Teacher is a centerpiece of the Research & Learn channel, with a volunteer staff that answers more than 10,000 such questions a day.

Tutors are online from 4:00 p.m. until after midnight (Eastern Time) to help students with homework, and for the rest of us, to help solve life's little mysteries. Post a question on a designated message board and get an answer from a teacher within the next 48 hours. You also can brainstorm with other students. Topics discussed online include English, mathematics, science, social studies, foreign languages, and more. To reach the resource, use the keyword ASK A TEACHER. The resulting screen divides the work into age groups, from elementary school to college and beyond. Click the appropriate button to continue.

Realizing that successful students develop good study habits early in their schooling, America Online has given special attention to assistance for elementary school children. If you are an elementary school student or a parent helping your child learn to use the system for homework, you can get assistance from a teacher either by clicking the Elementary School button of the Ask a Teacher window or by entering the keyword KO HH (which stands for Kids Only Homework Help). On the resulting window, click the Ask a Teacher button. Now type your question in the center box and send it to the volunteer Homework Help teachers by clicking the appropriate subject button at the bottom of the window. Available subjects are English & Reading, Science, Math, and Social Studies. Within the next 48 hours, you should receive a reply by e-mail in your regular online mailbox (though, of course, more complex questions may take a little longer).

TAKE NOTE

MORE HOMEWORK HELP FOR KIDS

▶ Direct links to major reference works such as the Merriam-Webster Dictionary and Thesaurus and Compton's Encyclopedia.
▶ Tutoring Rooms and special message boards for asking questions and working out problems.
▶ Games and adventures in the Explore area, with puzzles, riddles, and links to museums and contests.

CROSS-REFERENCE
For more about the Kids Online channel, see Chapter 16.

FIND IT ONLINE
To get an overview of the Research & Learn channel, visit its Search & Explore section (keyword: RL SEARCH) and click the Best of Research & Learn option.

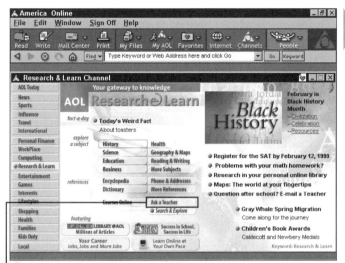

1 *Press Ctrl+K, type* **RESEARCH & LEARN**, *press Enter, and click Ask a Teacher on the resulting window.*

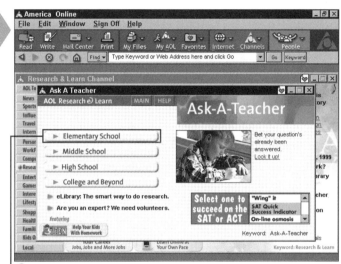

2 *Click Elementary School.*

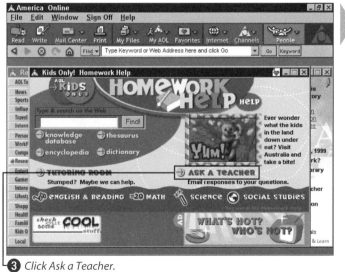

3 *Click Ask a Teacher.*

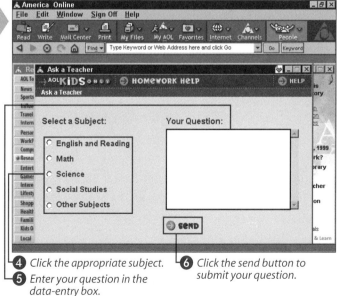

4 *Click the appropriate subject.*

5 *Enter your question in the data-entry box.*

6 *Click the send button to submit your question.*

Helping Older Students

Older students (from junior high school all the way to college and beyond) have their own variation on Homework Help. It has more options for searching answers to previously asked questions, for interacting with teachers in live discussion areas, and for writing e-mail on more advanced topics. Use the keyword ASK A TEACHER and click either Middle School, High School, or College and Beyond to begin.

Click Look Up Answers to get answers to the questions most frequently asked of the Ask a Teacher staff. The reference material from the Academic Assistance Center is arranged like a table of contents on specific topics, including art and music, business and finance, computers, education, English, foreign languages, geography, government and politics, health and medicine, history, law, math, science, social science, and sports and leisure activities. If you don't find the answer you seek, click the question mark to search the Knowledge Database.

Click Post a Question to find message boards relating to math, American and world history, geography, social sciences, physical science, earth and life sciences, English and literature, foreign languages, law and business, computer science, medicine and health, fine arts, and education. Often, someone else has asked your question already and the answer has been posted. If not, post your message and a volunteer teacher or another visitor to the board will answer, usually within 24 hours. Remember, the answers are posted publicly

on the board, not sent to you by e-mail, so you need to check back in to retrieve the reply.

Click Live Teacher Help if you need help right now. Between 4 p.m. and midnight (Eastern Time), five "tutoring rooms" are open for live chats with volunteer teachers discussing English, math, science, history, and miscellaneous topics. Each room can assist only a limited number of students at a time, so you may find some rooms closed.

Click E-mail a Teacher to pose a question for the volunteers. Enter your grade and age in the upper portion of the form, and then enter the specific questions below that. You will receive at least one answer by e-mail, maybe more. While this resource may take several days to produce a reply, it generally results in a more detailed answer than do the other options. It is a good resource to use when starting a report or term paper.

> ## TAKE NOTE
>
> ### ▶ SPECIAL COLLECTIONS
>
> The Academy Assistance Center (which hosts Ask-A-Teacher) offers a delightfully rich compilation of educational collections. Click About Ask-A-Teacher on the main window, and then double-click Collections in the list box. Collections include World Geography on AOL, History Resources, Student Puzzle Center, and Remembering Anne Frank.

CROSS-REFERENCE

For more background on writing e-mail, see Chapter 2. For more on real-time conferences, see Chapter 4.

FIND IT ONLINE

To get general online assistance with the tutorial features, click the About Ask a Teacher button and select the article entitled "The Art of Getting Help."

What Do I Say?

When filling in the Teacher Pager text box or the E-mail a Teacher form, put in as much information about the question as you can. There is more space than it appears, because the box scrolls up as you write, giving you more blank space. Be specific. Don't type, "I'm having trouble with English." Instead, type "We're studying the parts of speech, and I can't figure out the difference between verbs and adverbs."

The staff is there to help you get over the stumbling blocks and the confusing parts.

You can even ask the staff to review your reports for you and make suggestions for improvements.

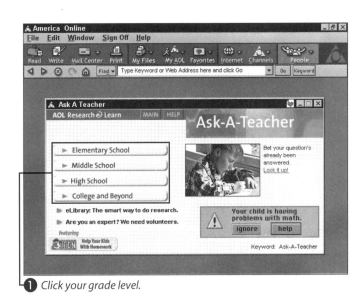

1 Click your grade level.

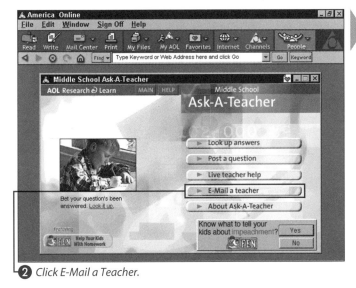

2 Click E-Mail a Teacher.

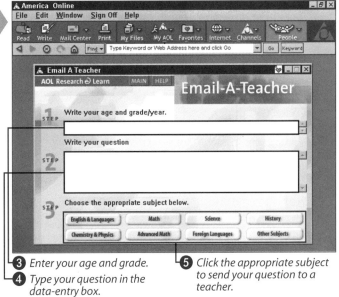

3 Enter your age and grade.

4 Type your question in the data-entry box.

5 Click the appropriate subject to send your question to a teacher.

Enrolling for Online Studies

The previous chapter introduced the idea of online classes for computer topics. Actually, though, America Online offers a wider selection of electronic courses than just computing, programming, and Web page design. From your keyboard, you can continue your education, learn new languages, study history, English, and other subjects — either just for the fun of it or for college credit.

Courses cover both the traditional subjects and those not usually found in college classrooms, such as practical classes on cooking, gardening, parenting, writing, traveling on a budget, and managing your personal finances. Tuition for most of these classes comes in under $50, but you'll find several free course offerings, too. At the time of writing, free courses included the Parent's Advocacy Course, Practical Special Education, New Car Clinic, and my favorite, Home Fishfarming for Profit.

To visit the online campus, click Online Courses on the Research & Learn channel window or use the keyword COURSES. Click the Online Campus button to sign up for not-for-credit courses on academic, professional, and special interest topics. The courses range from 4 to 12 weeks, each featuring live, online lectures (though there are some self-study courses too), a daily message board, e-mail support, and private libraries of research material.

The Course Catalog offers the opportunity to browse the latest offerings. Double-click some titles to see descriptions, instructors' bios and their e-mail addresses, class start dates, and meeting days and times. Registration information is provided with each description. When you find a class that interests you, click the Order Here button under the description and enter your credit card information when prompted. Write an e-mail to the instructor so he or she expects you in class; it may take a day or two for the instructor to get confirmation of your sign-up. You should also receive an e-mail welcoming you to the class and providing information you need to find your classroom and access the course library and message board.

TAKE NOTE

STUDYING FOR COLLEGE CREDIT

You can study for college credit online through the electronic campus of the University of California.

▶ To visit the University of California Extension, use the keyword COURSES to reach the main window and then click the University of California icon. (Or you can go directly to the university with the keyword UCAOL.)

▶ On the resulting window, click the Course Catalog button to see the latest classes available in arts and humanities, business and management, computer science, natural sciences, social sciences, and hazardous materials management.

▶ Also, click the Orientation button for answers to frequently asked questions, a tour of the electronic campus, details on the staff, costs, and program policies.

You can also connect to the University of Phoenix at keyword COURSES.

CROSS-REFERENCE

For more about online courses for computing subjects, see Chapter 11.

FIND IT ONLINE

To get more information about electronic coursework, visit the Online Campus (keyword: ONLINE CAMPUS) and click the Getting Started option.

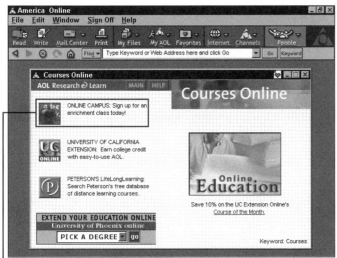

1 Press Ctrl+K, type **COURSES**, press Enter, and click Online Campus on the resulting window.

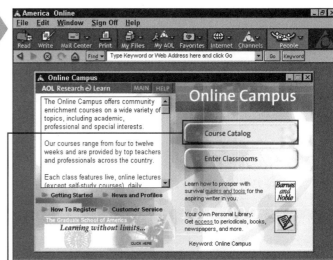

2 Click the Course Catalog button.

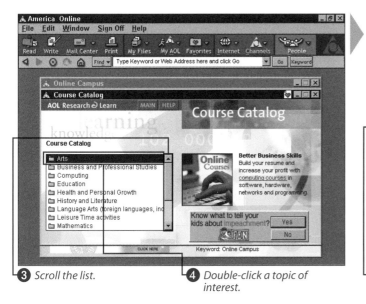

3 Scroll the list.

4 Double-click a topic of interest.

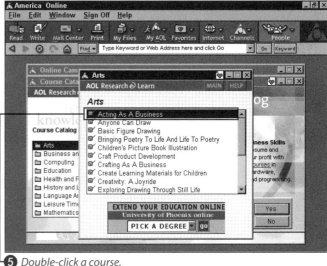

5 Double-click a course.

Using Online Encyclopedias

Encyclopedias used to be a victim of the information age and our fast-paced times. As soon as the publishers got the latest edition in print, the encyclopedia immediately started going out of date. That is why most major encyclopedia publishers have been eager to come to the online world. Here, their works can be more easily updated to stay current with our changing world. In fact, many encyclopedias are updated three or four times a year online.

AOL's Online Encyclopedia Center (keyword: ENCYCLOPEDIAS) has two huge, multi-volume reference works available: *Compton's Encyclopedia* and *Columbia Concise Encyclopedia*. Both are automatically linked from the World Wide Web in special AOL windows.

Compton's Encyclopedia (keyword: COMPTONS) has been providing the computer world with electronic reference for more than a decade now. This is the Web version of the encyclopedia available both in print and on CD-ROM, with more than 34,000 articles and thousands of graphics, photos, and sound files. It also has a Behind the Headlines feature to learn about current events, with entries that fill in background needed to understand what is going on. Also, the Research Assistant offers help for term paper writing, from choosing a topic to citing sources.

Columbia Concise Encyclopedia (keyword: CCE) is a famous one-volume encyclopedia found on many desks these days. It is known for its tightly distilled entries on a wide variety of subjects, from politics and law to history, sports, literature, and science. If you need a quick one- or two-paragraph explanation, this is the encyclopedia for you. Just enter a keyword and let the site list related topics so you can double-click the one you need.

Additional reference works, both on AOL and the Web, are found under the More Encyclopedias button. Among the current offerings are the *Hutchinson Encyclopedia* (for kids), the *Chemistry Encyclopedia*, the *Encyclopedia Mythica*, the *Encyclopedia Smithsonian*, and the *Internet Mental Health Encyclopedia*.

TAKE NOTE

OTHER EDUCATIONAL RESOURCES.

The Research & Learning channel offers several specific departments of reference material:

- ▶ The Arts (keyword: RL ARTS)
- ▶ Consumer & Money Matters (keyword: CONSUMER)
- ▶ Geography & Maps (keyword: GEOGRAPHY)
- ▶ Health (keyword: RL HEALTH)
- ▶ Law & Government (keyword: LAW)
- ▶ Reading & Writing (keyword: READING)
- ▶ Sports & Leisure (keyword: RL SPORTS)

CROSS-REFERENCE

For assistance with online search strategies, see the Appendix.

FIND IT ONLINE

To find even more resources, visit the Research Zone (keyword: RESEARCH ZONE).

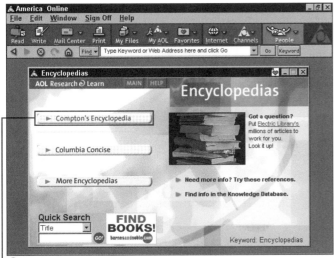

1 Press Ctrl+K, type **ENCYCLOPEDIAS**, press Enter, and select an encyclopedia.

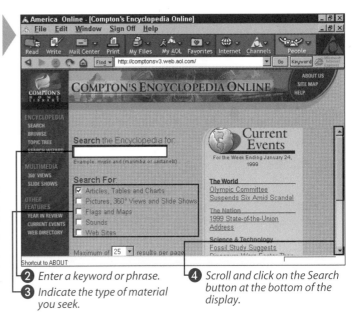

2 Enter a keyword or phrase.

3 Indicate the type of material you seek.

4 Scroll and click on the Search button at the bottom of the display.

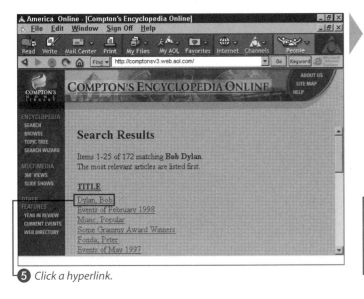

5 Click a hyperlink.

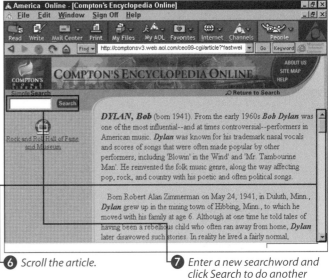

6 Scroll the article.

7 Enter a new searchword and click Search to do another search.

Using Online Dictionaries

Also at your fingertips is a dictionary, a kids' dictionary, a medical reference book and more, all provided by a famous name in the field: Merriam-Webster (keyword: MERRIAM).

Click Search the Collegiate Dictionary (keyword: MW DICTIONARY) to find definitions, spellings, parts of speech, inflected forms of words, etymology, date of the first recorded use of a word in English, examples of usage, derivatives, idioms, synonyms, and usage discussion. If you don't know how to spell the word, just use an asterisk (*) in the data-entry field in place of the letters about which you are unsure.

Click Search the Kids Dictionary (keyword: KIDS DICTIONARY) to search the *Merriam-Webster* for Kids, intended for students in the fourth through sixth grades. It contains more than 33,000 entries, written in language the kids understand. Also available is online help with the search engine and information on how to look up words when you can't spell them.

Click Search the Medical Dictionary (keyword: MEDICAL DICTIONARY) to look through the *Merriam-Webster Online Medical Dictionary*, which provides definitions of more than 35,000 common — and not-so-common — medical terms. Enter all or part of the word to display a list of likely terms.

Additional resources include the invaluable *Merriam-Webster Thesaurus* for looking up related words — use the keyword THESAURUS to reach the database of more than 25,000 English synonyms and antonyms. Or try Merriam-Webster Word Histories for the origin of our language. If you're in a hurry, Word of the Day offers a word and its definition to expand your vocabulary (there's a Word History of the Day, too).

TAKE NOTE

▶ FINDING MORE HELP FOR STUDENTS

Whether you are a student facing learning challenges in the classroom every day or a parent looking ahead to paying for a college education, the Education Resources Center (keyword: EDUCATION) has links to important sites around the system. Don't miss the college preparation section, with practice tests, study ideas, and calendars for juniors and seniors to help schedule college-planning tasks. When it is time to apply for a college, you'll even find tips for how to write an outstanding essay and how to prepare for interviews. Other sections cover financial aid to offset the cost of college, including databases of grants and scholarships.

Also here are support sites for teachers, inviting the exchange of ideas for those teaching kindergarten through twelfth grade. Reports give background on new science experiments, progressing teaching methods, and more.

▶ ELECTRIC LIBRARY

Information junkies feel at home in the Electric Library (keyword: ELP), a subscription-based service that offers unlimited access to millions of documents: articles, transcripts, pictures, and more.

CROSS-REFERENCE
For more about AOL's family-oriented features, see Chapter 16.

FIND IT ONLINE
If you like words, you might like the New York Times' famous crossword (keyword: NYT CROSSWORD).

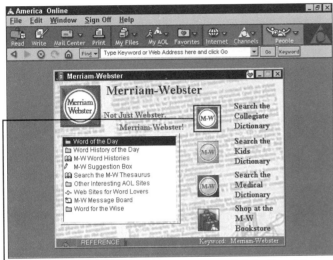

① Press Ctrl+K, type **MERRIAM**, press Enter, and click a Search icon on the resulting window.

② Select either Single Word or Full Text.

③ Type a word or a portion of a word with an asterisk in the data-entry box.

④ Click the Look Up button.

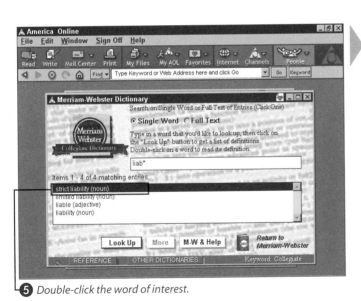

⑤ Double-click the word of interest.

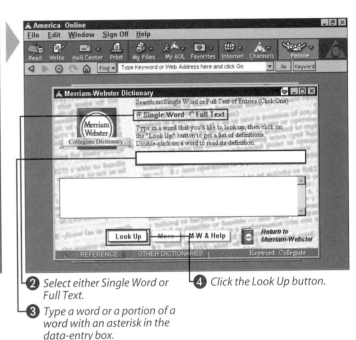

⑥ Use the scroll bar to see the entire text of the entry.

⑦ Click the X (close box) to remove the window.

Finding Directories

esides being a classroom, a library, and a reference desk, America Online must also be the world's largest phonebook. The Research & Learn channel's Phone & Addresses area (keyword: PHONEBOOK) collects the nation's best directories for phone numbers, addresses, maps, and more, many of them on the Web.

A list box at the left of the main window lists references available for searching, including the following:

▶ White and Yellow Pages through a site called Switchboard on the World Wide Web

▶ The AOL Member Directory (as illustrated in Chapter 5)

▶ Directories of associations from around the world

▶ Chamber of Commerce directory

▶ E-mail addresses listed by Switchboard

▶ International Yellow Page index

▶ Directory of toll-free (800) numbers

▶ Zip code decoders

▶ Zipper, a collection of addresses, phone numbers, and e-mail addresses for members of Congress

For a quick way to find people, click the toolbar's People icon and select Internet White Pages from the drop-down menu. This links you to the Internet with options to find phone numbers, e-mail addresses, businesses, newsgroups, and more.

CROSS-REFERENCE

For more on using AOL's White Pages and Yellow Pages, see Chapter 7.

FIND IT ONLINE

To get assistance online with searching, visit Member Services (keyword: HELP) and select the Using Search & Find option.

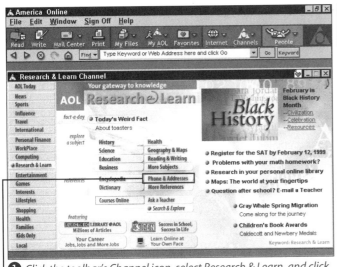

1 Click the toolbar's Channel icon, select Research & Learn, and click Phone & Addresses on the resulting window.

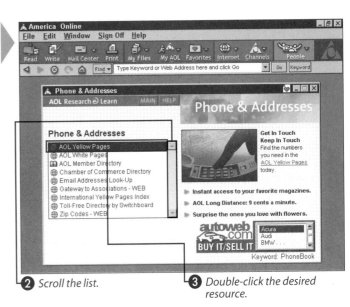

2 Scroll the list.

3 Double-click the desired resource.

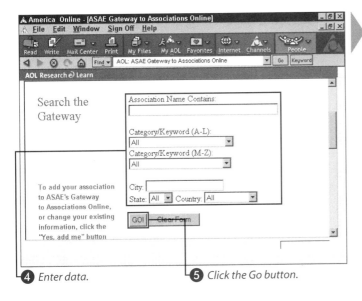

4 Enter data.

5 Click the Go button.

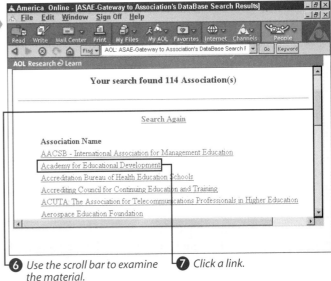

6 Use the scroll bar to examine the material.

7 Click a link.

Personal Workbook

Q&A

1 How can your elementary-school-age child find online help with homework?

_____

_____

_____

2 For older kids, how can you find live tutorial sessions with volunteer teachers online?

_____

_____

_____

3 How can you enroll in an electronic course in, say, English or writing?

_____

_____

4 Where can you find Compton's Encyclopedia online?

_____

_____

_____

5 How can you use the system to research how the federal government works?

_____

_____

6 Suppose you have young children in the house and you want to introduce them to dictionaries. What's a useful online resource to help?

_____

_____

_____

7 Need help preparing for college? Where should you head on AOL?

_____

_____

8 Bonus Question: Uncle Fred is a history buff. Next time he visits, you plop him down in front of America Online and ... what?

_____

_____

ANSWERS: PAGE 343

EXTRA PRACTICE

1 Look over the courses devoted to business topics.

2 Examine the online collection of foreign language dictionaries.

3 Search the Columbia Concise Encyclopedia for information on the Spanish-American War.

4 Find a map of Brazil.

5 Look up synonyms for the word "liaison."

6 Find the names of associations devoted to the fight against heart disease.

REAL-WORLD APPLICATIONS

✔ Educational topics and learning experiences are not limited to the Research & Learning channel, of course. Many of the forums, attracting experts on assorted subjects, also can be quite educational. Click the toolbar's Find button to reach AOL Find, look up the subject of interest, and follow the links to respective forums.

✔ You also can use America Online to create your own real-time study group. Use the People Connection's facilities for private chats and share the name of the chat room only with your fellow students.

✔ If you're a teacher, you might be interested in volunteering for the Homework Help staff. Students can apply too, as "peer tutors" (ages 14 to 18). Use the keyword ASK A TEACHER and choose the schooling level you want to teach.

Visual Quiz

Which window, seen earlier in this chapter, would probably bring you to this area? How could you reach it directly? What would you do here?

_____

_____

_____

_____

_____

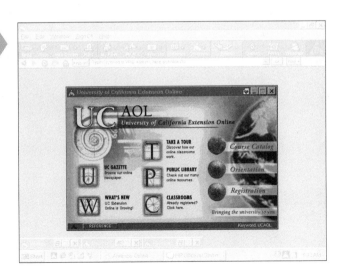

CHAPTER **13**

Finding Fun and Games

I am sure you signed up for America Online solely to use the online dictionary and electronic encyclopedias, to take long-distance learning courses, to be tutored by volunteer teachers, and to use all the other research and educational tools you saw in the previous chapter. Probably you are just being polite now by hanging around for the chapter about features for fun and games. Thank you for humoring me. You won't be disappointed, because here is where you discover that AOL just loves a good time:

▶ Want to know what's hot and what's not in the theaters and on the tube? AOL knows, and shares it all with you online.

▶ Want to meet your favorite authors, read excerpts from the newest books, and discuss plots with fellow book lovers? The online medium is the perfect venue for writers and their fans.

▶ Want to know about the latest in alternative rock, pop, jazz, country, and soul? Crank up the AOL Boom Box and you hear all about the hits right online, plus get a chance to rap with the singers and songwriters.

▶ Want to set up a regular flow of news from the stars? The Celebrity Fix is your ticket to the hottest gossip in town (wherever your town may be).

▶ Or would you rather make your own fun? AOL knows where you can slay a few dragons, play online game shows, command the forces of Order (or of Chaos) for world control, wow 'em in a virtual casino, and hustle 'em in a virtual pool room.

You like to be "in the know" when it comes to your favorite movie stars and directors, singers and musicians, authors and celebrities. We all do. That is why entertainment magazines and celebrity shows dominate the newsstands and the airwaves. Increasingly, these and other major entertainment institutions are realizing they also need to be on America Online to reach the audience they seek.

The Entertainment Channel (keyword: ENTERTAINMENT) is the gathering spot for all kinds of news and background on movies, TV, music, books, and celebrity reports. If it is happening in the limelight, it is happening online.

Checking Out the Movies Page

What's playing? AOL's Entertainment channel knows. Figuring out which movies now showing on the "big screen" are worth your time and money is a big concern for the Entertainment channel. And rather than relying solely on the views of the critics, the channel supplements reviews and commentary with material that helps you make up your mind. The Movies page (keyword: MOVIES) spotlights previews of hit movies, onscreen interviews with stars and directors, photos from the show, and more. They've got it all — critically acclaimed independent films as well as the box office blockbusters.

To read about a certain show, click Movies on the Entertainment Channel main window or use the keyword MOVIES. Current movies are listed in the In Theaters Now section of the window. Click the hyperlinked title of one that interests you for an entire page devoted to that picture, including a photo from the film, a quote from a critic, and a list of related files about the film. Use the scroll bar in the box to the right of the window to examine the list, double-clicking any items you want to explore. The material might include

- Feature stories from assorted magazines and news services
- Movie photos from the software library
- Reviews from assorted publications on AOL and on the World Wide Web

- Video previews and trailers that you can download for offline viewing
- Downloadable movie posters
- Questions and answers with stars and directors from assorted publications
- Interviews with one or more of the movie's principals, including "slide shows" with audio of the questions and answers
- Message boards and chats to discuss the movie

If reading all about the movie makes you want to see it, click the Digital City Movies icon on each movie page for showtimes in your area.

TAKE NOTE

SHORTCUT TO THE STARS

Various star-biz features are linked from this area, including

- E! Online (keyword: E!), with star news and gossip, interviews and features, and reviews of movies (and TV and music).
- *Entertainment Weekly* (keyword: ENTERTAINMENT WEEKLY), the electronic extension of the magazine by the same name.
- MovieLink (keyword: MOVIELINK), the online version of the popular MovieFone interactive telephone movie guide and ticketing service.
- *New York Times* Films (keyword: NYT FILM), with a searchable database of new and old movies, a film guide, and a message board inviting fans to talk about their personal picks and pans.

CROSS-REFERENCE

For more about news and magazines online, see Chapter 8.

FIND IT ONLINE

To get an online overview of the Entertainment Channel and its features, visit the channel's Search & Explore page (keyword: ESEARCH) and click Best of AOL Entertainment.

1 Press Ctrl+K, type **ENTERTAINMENT**, press Enter, and click Movies on the resulting window.

2 Select a movie and click its link.

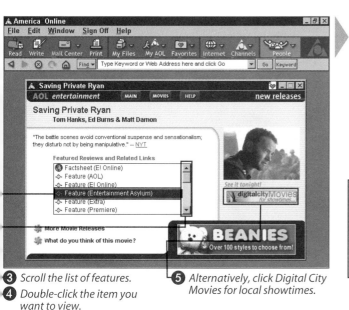

3 Scroll the list of features.

4 Double-click the item you want to view.

5 Alternatively, click Digital City Movies for local showtimes.

6 Click buttons for related material.

7 Click the X (close box) to remove the window.

Taking In Television

Although television has lost viewers to the online world, the online world brings a world of riches to TV fans. *The X-Files, ER,* and *Homicide: Life on the Street* have embraced the interactive world of America Online. AOL's lively TV area not only feeds the flames of fandom, but snags new viewers via the fan community.

Television (keyword: TV) has reviews of new shows, interviews with stars and producers, show listings in major cities, feature stories, and links to the online sites of TV personalities. You also find out what happened when you miss an episode.

A number of major television shows and networks have sites on America Online to communicate with fans and share associated facts, tips, and merchandise:

- ▶ Beverly Hills 90210 (keyword: 90210) offers a fan forum for one of the most popular prime-time soaps in recent years.
- ▶ ER (keyword: ER) serves those who follow the weekly drama set in an emergency room.
- ▶ Frasier (keyword: FRASIER) rehashes the barbs of the weekly comedy.
- ▶ Friends (keyword: FRIENDS) offers a haven for fans of the prime-time 20-something comedy.
- ▶ Late Show Online (keyword: LATE SHOW) goes backstage with Dave Letterman.
- ▶ Melrose Place (keyword: MELROSE) muses about sharp turns in plot.

- ▶ Millennium (keyword: MILLENNIUM) offers a forum for viewers of the spooky, weekly science fiction/fantasy drama.
- ▶ Nick at Nite TV Land (keyword: TV LAND) reminisces about classic TV shows and commercials.
- ▶ Oprah Online (keyword: OPRAH) reigns supreme on everything about Oprah Winfrey.
- ▶ Star Trek Club (keyword: TREK) offers a haven for Trekkers, with news of conventions, episode guides, trivia, and more.
- ▶ X-Files (keyword: X FILES) sorts all the obscure twists and turns in plots and character quirks.

TAKE NOTE

CRITICS GALORE

Critics Inc. (keyword: CRITICS) provides reviews of current and classic films, as well as books, TV shows, compact discs, concerts, and video games. You'll also find message boards for fan banter, contests, databases of trivia and entertainment history, and ratings for alert parents. You also are invited to be the critic and express your own opinions.

LOCAL LISTINGS

You can get local TV listings for much of the United States. Click the TV Quest icon in the Television window (or go to keyword: TV QUEST). You can even create a personalized show planner and print it out. It's like having your own *TV Guide*.

CROSS-REFERENCE

For background about using message boards, see Chapter 6.

FIND IT ONLINE

To chat about your favorite TV shows, visit the TV Community by clicking Chats & Messages on the main Television window (or go to keyword: TV COM).

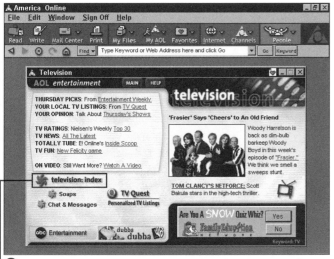

① *Press Ctrl+K, type **TV**, press Enter, and click the Television Index button in the resulting window.*

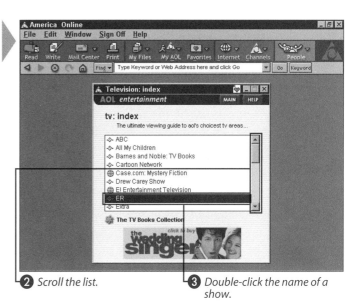

② *Scroll the list.*

③ *Double-click the name of a show.*

④ *Select a feature.*

⑤ *Click the toolbar's Print icon to print the text.*

⑥ *Click the X (close box) to close the window.*

Getting the Latest on Books and Authors

Authors love America Online. And why not? The online medium is a world built upon the written word. It is driven by the same kind of keyboards at which writers make their living. It has hundreds of intimate little chat rooms where the sometimes reclusive artists can hobnob with their public without really coming out of hiding. But most of all, authors love AOL because AOL loves authors. The Books page (keyword: BOOKS) is a celebration of the novels and non-fiction books that are capturing the nation's attention.

AOL's Books features reviews and interviews best-selling authors, agents, and publishers, and also reviews news on the horizon about your favorite writers. There are also live chats with celebrity writers — recent guests have included Amy Tan, Kurt Vonnegut Jr., Robert Fulghum, and Hunter S. Thompson. Hot book excerpts (some produced exclusively for AOL) and book bargains abound.

To reach this ultimate bookshelf, use the keyword BOOKS or click the Books button on the main Entertainment window. Examine the list at the left of the window in the Good Reads section to find currently featured books. Click the hyperlinked name of an author to see details of the book. The resulting window usually provides an overview of the book, a comment or two from critics, perhaps a picture of the cover, and links for reviews, excerpts, and biographical information on the author, as well as links to purchase the book with a credit card.

TAKE NOTE

BOOK MARKS

America Online links to many other book features. Click the Books: Index button on the main Books window for areas such as these:

▶ Barnes and Noble (keyword: BARNES AND NOBLE) is the electronic home of the world's largest bookseller. Online, it offers the same discounts to voracious readers as it does in its stores: 20 percent off paperbacks and 30 percent off hardcovers in stock.

▶ Barron's Booknotes (keyword: BARRONS) are online companions to literary classics. Check out notes on the plot, characters, setting, themes, form, structure, style, point of view, and more. Search the site for titles, authors, and/or categories.

▶ Book Bag (keyword: TBB) is an area intended for teenagers who love books, with reviews of all-time favorites, classics, and contemporary titles.

▶ Book Central (keyword: BC) is a very popular electronic gathering place for bibliophiles and bookworms. Peruse the shelves by author or title, check out the day's features for summaries and reviews, and chat with other book lovers and book authors in the Cafe Booka.

▶ Book Report (keyword: BOOK REPORT) features well-written reviews, recommendations, and discussions of favorite books, along with chat groups, book clubs, and book news from every genre. Unique here, too, is the Works-in-Progress area where professional writers post drafts of new works and invite your feedback.

CROSS-REFERENCE

For more about online shopping, see Chapter 15.

FIND IT ONLINE

To talk about books online, visit the Books Community at keyword: BK COM and select a topic from the scroll box.

1 Press Ctrl+K, type **BOOKS**, press Enter, and select a book title to examine in the resulting window.

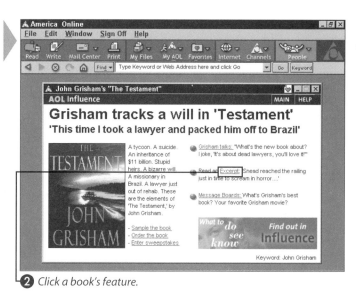

2 Click a book's feature.

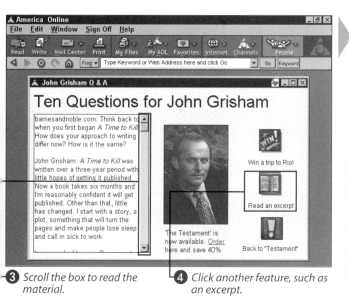

3 Scroll the box to read the material.

4 Click another feature, such as an excerpt.

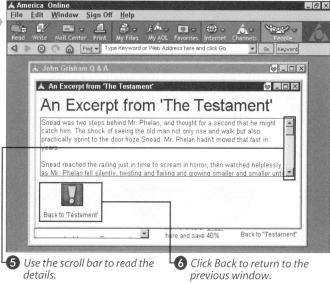

5 Use the scroll bar to read the details.

6 Click Back to return to the previous window.

Tuning Up the Music Machine

If music plays in cyberspace, can you hear it? You can at the Entertainment channel's Music area (keyword: MUSIC), which seeks to bring the music to you — from pop and rock to rap and soul, from The Spice Girls and Puff Daddy to Jewel and Beck, to Kathy Mattea and Merle Haggard. The area invites you to download and listen to new and upcoming releases, get the latest music news, and follow what's hot in music television from MTV to VH1. And, of course, you can buy CDs online from assorted vendors.

Use the keyword MUSIC to reach the area or click the Music button on the Entertainment Channel's main window. From the Releases section on the left of the next window, click the name of an artist of interest to see more details of that recording. In the resulting window, double-click an item in the list box at the right to see or retrieve the feature, which could include sound files for offline playing, text of reviews or feature articles from assorted music magazines, pictures, and other graphics. The data comes from both AOL and the World Wide Web.

TAKE NOTE

PUMP UP THE VOLUME

Click the Music: Index button on the main Music window for links to the following:
- BMG Online (keyword: BMG) provides information on BMG Distribution's current artists from various genres and labels.
- Grateful Dead Forum (keyword: DEAD) offers a haven for Deadheads who keep the spirit alive.
- MTV Online (keyword: MTV) puts the music in television…and online. This is an interactive version, with online video clips, interviews, and news.
- MuchMusic (keyword: MUCHMUSIC) links to Canada's music TV with multimedia slide shows and live chats with musicians.
- Music Boulevard (keyword: MB) sells CDs of all kinds. Search for favorite artists or just browse. You also can see the latest Billboard charts and weekly specials.
- Reprise Records (keyword: REPRISE) provides information on the albums, tours, and lives of its stars, including Eric Clapton, Elvis Costello, and Los Lobos.
- Rolling Stone Online (keyword: ROLLING STONE) offers the electronic extension of the famed music magazine. Rolling Stone brings weekly music news and reviews, photos, and more. The best feature? You can see your face on the cover!

CROSS-REFERENCE

For more about youth-oriented features, see Chapter 16.

FIND IT ONLINE

To get music-specific news, see the Music Axis site (keyword: MUSIC AXIS).

Artists on the Boom Box

▶ Alternative (keyword: ALTERNATIVE) links to alternative rock bands and the Grunge Book.

▶ R&B/Rap (keyword: R&B) houses classic soul and hip-hop sounds.

▶ Classical (keyword: CLASSICAL) offers a forum for people who speak of composers rather than songwriters.

▶ Country (keyword: COUNTRY) hooks you to honky-tonks and hoedowns, and hard-living, hard-playing music.

▶ Jazz (keyword: JAZZ) pays homage to America's first native music.

1 *Press Ctrl+K, type* **MUSIC***, press Enter, and click the name of an artist in the resulting window.*

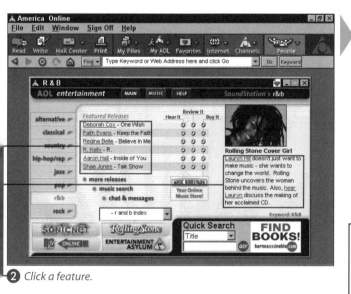

2 *Click a feature.*

3 *Use the scroll bar to see the entire article.*

4 *Select other features.*

5 *Click the X (close box) to remove the display.*

Getting Your Celebrity Fix

Who isn't interested in "the next big thing"? Whether it's movies or books, music or computer games, the fans always want to know what's coming up, and what the stars, authors, singers, and artists are doing with their time right now. Our fascination with these people is what makes them different. It makes them celebrities. On America Online, you can put an entire department to work tracking celebrities for you in all your favorite arenas.

Get your Daily Fix (keyword: DAILY FIX) for the hottest celebrity news on the planet. It knows the comings and goings of movie stars and chart-topping singers, millionaire authors and business moguls, has-beens, wanna-bes and some-day-soons. The Daily Fix has a mission: to see that you hear the ripest gossip before anyone else in your office, on your street, or in your own bedroom. It culls these nuggets from entertainment insiders such as Entertainment Weekly, Extra, and E! Online. New information is summarized and posted online daily, with links to more in-depth stories.

Commit to the Entertainment Asylum

Are you hearing celebrity voices in your head? If you have a thing or two you want to share about the stars, the star-makers, and their shows, lock in to the Entertainment Asylum (keyword: ASYLUM), a site dedicated to listening to you. This is where fans, would-be fans, and former fans sound off, swap jokes, and trade rumors about TV shows, movies, music, books, and celebrities. Check into the special entertainment forums: Comedy Clinic, Action Explosion, Drama Den, SciFiZone, Pulp Shack, Hall of Horrors, and Cult de Sac. Entertainment Asylum provides its inmates with all the online necessities, like live chats with celebrities, reviews on the latest movies, and the hottest gossip from tinseltown.

TAKE NOTE

▶ **THAT'S ENTERTAINMENT**

Entertainment is a big deal online. After all, America Online itself is classified as entertainment in some circles. Here are more entertainment-oriented features you can reach by keyword:

▶ Extra Online (keyword: EXTRA), specializing in entertainment news and reviews. Extra also operates a Soap Opera Central, a Movie & Star Connection, a look behind the scenes with Backstage, and resources for downloading photos of top models and favorite celebrities.

▶ Hollywood Online (keyword: HOLLYWOOD), AOL's old standby, has been serving up entertainment news here since 1993. Look here for entertainment multimedia (video and audio clips), chats, games, contests, and merchandise. They have Hollywood news seven days a week and frequent interaction with stars and legends.

CROSS-REFERENCE

For more about getting daily reports from the news wires, see the discussion of the AOL Today Channel in Chapter 8.

FIND IT ONLINE

Visit the Hollywood Wire (keyword: HOLLYWOOD WIRE) and scroll the list of latest stories.

1 *Press Ctrl+K, type **CELEBRITIES**, press Enter, and click the Entertainment Asylum button in the resulting window.*

2 *Click a feature.*

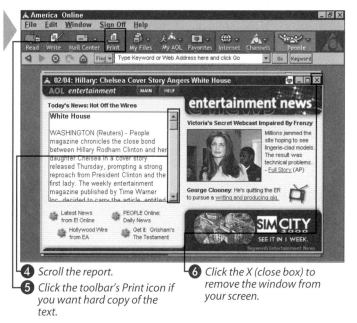

3 *To go elsewhere, type **Entertainment News** in the toolbar's data-entry field and click Go.*

4 *Scroll the report.*

5 *Click the toolbar's Print icon if you want hard copy of the text.*

6 *Click the X (close box) to remove the window from your screen.*

Getting Started with the Games

Computer games have become a subculture. In fact, entire books and movies have started their lives on the other side of a computer screen. But you haven't played computer games until you've played them online. The game parlor on America Online never closes, and its door is open to the world. You just never know who is going to walk in. You think you are the biggest, baddest dragon slayer in this entire quadrant, and then all of a sudden everyone is warning you about a new kid on the block: a Swiss warrior called ThorBane. Naturally, a showdown is inevitable. . . . It is the stuff of online legends.

Actually, AOL games are not limited to such traditional computer fare. Sure, the system has its share of fantasy and adventure, some high-tension space shoot-em-ups, and plenty of war strategy games. However, AOL's game venue also serves those looking for classic games, such as backgammon, bridge, and billiards. And if you are in it for the graphics, you won't be disappointed. AOL's games offer some stunning visuals, along with sounds and animation. Some games even let you "hear" your opponents.

WorldPlay Games

WorldPlay Games (keyword: WORLDPLAY) offers a single game parlor for online competitions, chats, tournaments, and related events. The categories include favorite card games (bridge, cribbage, hearts, poker, and more), puzzle and board games, adventures, and strategy and action games. What's particularly popular? There's a lot to be said for facing down opponents in a paint-smeared arena for a bit of Splatterball. . . .

TAKE NOTE

▶ **GAME BOARDS**

The Games channel takes its fun seriously, offering many more game-related features:
- ▶ Sneak previews of new games in the form of onscreen audio-video slide shows.
- ▶ Links to classified ads and game stores where you can buy computer games for offline play.
- ▶ Games Central (keyword: GAMES CENTRAL) provides connections to game forums (keyword: GAMING).
- ▶ Games Insider (keyword: GAMES INSIDER) offers the very latest on new games, tournaments, reviews, demos, and other activities.

▶ **PAY TO PLAY**

Most of the system's top games, especially those in the WorldPlay, are premium priced. At this writing, the cost is $1.99 an hour in addition to your normal monthly membership and usage charges. Fractions of hours are billed at 3.3 cents a minute. Watch for system notifications of any extra charges, and back out if you don't want to raise the bill.

CROSS-REFERENCE

For more about real-time chats, see Chapter 4.

FIND IT ONLINE

For an online overview of the Games Channel, see its Search & Explore area (keyword: GAMES SEARCH) and click Best of AOL Games.

What Are the Hot Games?

Hot new games are introduced all the time. At this writing, they are:

▶ Casino Blackjack (keyword: ONLINE CASINO) lets you take your chances against real players at the Blackjack and Spanish 21 tables.

▶ Cosrin (keyword: COSRIN) conjures up a fantasy realm where magic exists and monsters roam.

▶ Destructo Discs (keyword: DESTRUCTO DISCS) plays like table shuffleboard, only you can toss a bomb between your opponent's discs!

▶ Multiplayer BattleTech (keyword: MPBT) merges a futuristic setting and weapons with ancient warrior codes.

1 Type **WORLDPLAY** into the toolbar's data-entry field and click Go.

2 Double-click a game.

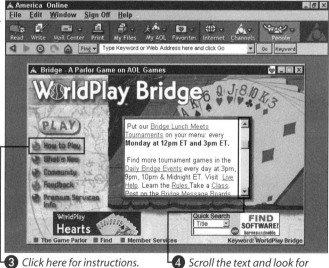

3 Click here for instructions.

4 Scroll the text and look for links, such as those for finding other players.

Finding Non-premium Games

If you want to play more than you want to pay, plenty of games are available at no extra charge. Take a look at what is going on in the Game Shows Online area (keyword: GAME SHOWS).

Top Games

The top game online is Slingo (keyword: SLINGO), where Bingo meets the slot machines. Combining chance and strategy, you compete with up to nine other real people online to fill up your 5 × 5 game card. You can chat with your fellow fingers while you do this, assuming your fingers move that fast. Score points by filling your card along vertical, horizontal, and diagonal lines, getting extra points when gold coins appear and free squares when jokers appear. There's also a new Slingo X-Press version of the game for those who like a faster-paced game.

You can also play various word games from some of the people who brought us TV's *Jeopardy* game show. For instance, Out of Order (keyword: OUT OF ORDER) puts you in competition with up to eight other online players, all trying to unscramble the same words and phrases based on clues and comments from other players. Strike A Match (keyword: STRIKE A MATCH) is a 15-minute, TV-like game show in which you and others try to match words with their common threads and associations.

Trivia junkies have a home in the NTN Studio (keyword: NTN), which brings the popular trivia games often seen in restaurants and bars to AOL. There's no software to download at NTN — just visit, choose a game from one of those featured or from the NTN Trivia games index, and start playing. Now pick the right answer before the time runs out, and you're playing NTN Trivia! Special contests are held at different times of the day (and night), too.

TAKE NOTE

MORE GAMES WITHOUT SURCHARGES

Here are some other games and game-related features of interest, all without any extra charge:

- Antagonist Inc. (keyword: ANT) offers tough reviews for new games, hot downloads, and chats with other gamers.
- BoxerJam Games (keyword: BOXERJAM) offers a non-premium word game from the Jeopardy creators, similar to Strike A Match and Out of Order.
- Brainbuster (keyword: BRAINBUSTER) claims the toughest trivia contests around.
- Heckler's Arcade (keyword: HO) dishes up some twisted games from some strange rangers.
- Parlor Games (keyword: PARLOR) offers chat-based games in the People Connection, from word games to guessing games.
- Rabbitjack's Casino (keyword: RJ CASINO) features regular bingo, full card games, and other diversions.

CROSS-REFERENCE

For information on how to check your billing records, see the Appendix.

FIND IT ONLINE

To talk about games and gaming, visit the Games Community (keyword: GS COMM) and click the Message Boards icon.

1 Press Ctrl+K, type **GAMES**, press Enter, and click the Game Shows Online button on the resulting window.

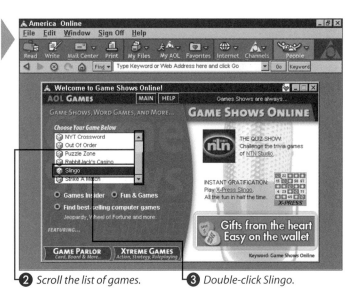

2 Scroll the list of games.

3 Double-click Slingo.

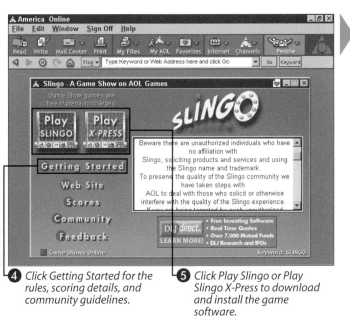

4 Click Getting Started for the rules, scoring details, and community guidelines.

5 Click Play Slingo or Play Slingo X-Press to download and install the game software.

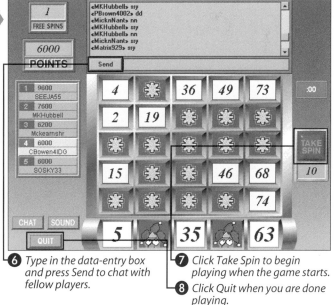

6 Type in the data-entry box and press Send to chat with fellow players.

7 Click Take Spin to begin playing when the game starts.

8 Click Quit when you are done playing.

Personal Workbook

Q&A

1 How can you link to an online version of the popular MovieFone interactive telephone movie guide?

_____

_____

_____

2 Where would you go to find out everything you ever wanted to know about talk show host David Letterman?

_____

_____

_____

3 What is Critics Inc.?

_____

_____

_____

4 It's midnight. The library's closed, and you have a pressing need for the plot summary of _Moby Dick_. Who are you gonna call?

_____

_____

_____

5 Uncle Fred is one of the last great Deadheads. Where can you take him online?

_____

_____

_____

6 What is your daily gossip connection, and how do you reach it by keyword?

_____

_____

_____

7 What is WorldPlay Games?

_____

_____

_____

8 Bonus Question: What are the game shows online?

_____

_____

_____

ANSWERS: PAGE 344

EXTRA PRACTICE

1 Find out what critics are saying about one of the movies currently making the rounds.

2 Get background on one of your favorite TV shows.

3 Look up the latest list of best-selling books.

4 Listen to some music clips online.

5 Look up fresh entertainment news and gossip from *Entertainment Weekly* and *Premiere* magazines.

6 Play a game of Out of Order.

REAL-WORLD APPLICATIONS

✔ Get the latest information on "cultural" events with the Culture Finder. Use the keyword CF to reach this guide to classical music, dance, theater, opera, painting, and more. It features a local events calendar and even games and contests.

✔ The Comic Books (keyword: COMICS) links you to all things animated, from Spider Man to graphic novels.

✔ Visit *Soap Opera Digest* (keyword: SOD) to check out the latest plot twists and talk with other fans.

Visual Quiz

From what you see in this window, how do you know where you are online? How would you reach other windows with similar information? How would you remove this window from your screen?

_____

_____

_____

_____

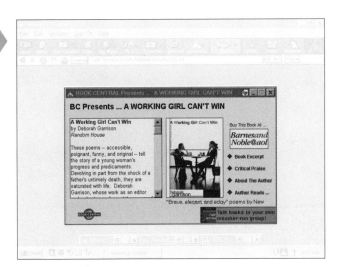

CHAPTER **14**

Exploring Interests and Lifestyles

The term *community* used to refer only to people living in physical proximity to one another. Towns were built within a day's horseback ride of each other. *Neighbors* were defined as people who lived within the sound of each other's axes when firewood was cut. Today, your computer invites you to visit communities that aren't local but global, where the "neighbors" can be people whom you never meet in person but whom you get to know better than the family living in the house next door.

Some things never change, though. Traditionally, communities have been founded on common goals. Fishermen needed to live near the sea. Religious and philosophical societies settled together for fellowship. Individual farmers all saw the same promise in a particularly verdant valley. And today's digital communities are bound by those same old adhesives.

This chapter introduces you to the hundreds of communities that have sprung up on America Online, reached through the Interests and Lifestyles channels. Some are held together by merely a casual interest in the same hobbies.

In others, the electronic residents are bound by mutual needs and shared experiences. Some want no more than to get a good deal on a new car. Others seek no less than love that will change their lives. In this chapter, you learn about

▶ using AOL as a resource for ideas to decorate your room, brighten up the dinner table, take better pictures, get better gas mileage, make peace with yourself, and cherish your loved ones.

▶ exploring AOL for insights into beliefs about religion, ethics, heritage, etiquette, and falling in and out of love.

▶ consulting AOL for help with caring for kids, for parents, for pets, and for yourself.

We all sometimes find ourselves looking for that one reference book that isn't on the shelves. But now help has arrived. AOL's Interests channel (keyword: INTERESTS) is a dig-it-up, jack-it-up, heat-it-up, fix-it-up kind of place where you can get (and give) advice on hobbies, home repairs, photography, cooking, pet care, cars. . . . The list goes on and on.

Visiting the Auto Center

Cars are the common denominator of the modern life. Most of us can use advice on buying a new or used car or truck, caring for this substantial investment, and finding parts and service for repairs. To use AOL for these and other answers, sign on to the system and use the keyword AUTO CENTER or click Auto Center on the Interests channel main window. You can choose from these departments:

▶ Buying (keyword: AUTO BUYING) provides expert advice on your next car purchase, with features on how to get the best price, reports directly from the Internet on current rates for auto loans in your part of the country, and details of *Car and Driver* magazine's latest Buyer's Guide.

▶ Wheels (keyword: WHEELS) reaches the community of car enthusiasts, including links to automotive magazines such as *Car and Driver* and *Road and Track*. Car chat rooms and message boards are here for you to discuss your thoughts about your favorite cars, trucks, motorcycles, or darn near anything with wheels and a motor. This is the place to get and give photos and get the scoop on auto racing, car shows, and conferences. You can even play Auto Racing Trivia here!

▶ Car Care (keyword: CAR CARE) provides information on discounted auto services. Articles here concern which oils, additives, and filters are best, how to save on services and repairs at tens of thousands of centers around the country, and how to get answers from auto experts online. You'll find the hosts of Car Talk — the popular radio program with mechanics Tom and Ray Magliozzi — online to answer your questions, too!

▶ Classifieds (keyword: VEHICLES CLASSIFIEDS) offers deals on vehicles, parts, and services, with a breakdown by domestic, imports, recreational, and commercial vehicles.

TAKE NOTE

IN THE NEIGHBORHOOD

If you're looking for deals on cars and trucks in your neck of the woods, the Local AutoGuide (keyword: LOCAL AUTOGUIDE) lists automotive resources around the United States. You can even get up-to-date traffic reports here.

DRIVING IT HOME

Here are some other features, with keywords, that may be of interest to road warriors and lovers of the automotive life:

▶ *Car and Driver* magazine (keyword: CAR AND DRIVER) offers the electronic link to one of the world's best-known auto magazines, with racing news, reviews, and advice.

▶ *Car Stereo Review* (keyword: CAR STEREO REVIEW) publishes the latest on audio equipment for your vehicle.

CROSS-REFERENCE

For other shopping-related topics, see Chapter 15.

FIND IT ONLINE

To locate the latest additions to the automotive services, visit Find it on AOL (keyword: FIND CENTRAL) and enter **cars** in the query box.

AOL AutoVantage

AOL AutoVantage (AV) provides a variety of car-related services and information, such as:

▶ New car summaries that detail a model's features, the pros and cons of buying the model, specifications, available options, sticker and dealer prices, and road test highlights.

▶ Used car pricing, with the estimated selling and trade-in prices for any car up to 20 years old.

AutoVantage also offers discounts on new car purchases and assistance in locating nearby service centers. The annual fee is $79.95, but watch for special introductory offers. At this writing, the service offered a three-month test drive for $1.

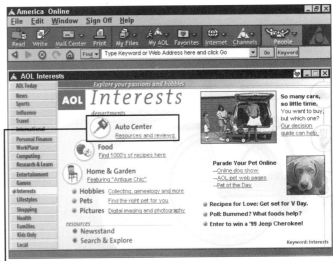

1 Press Ctrl+K, type **INTERESTS**, press Enter, and click Auto Center on the resulting window.

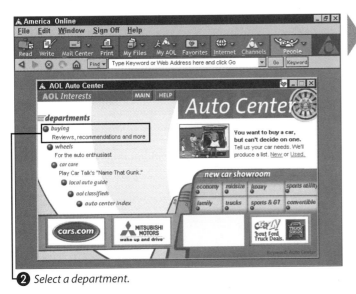

2 Select a department.

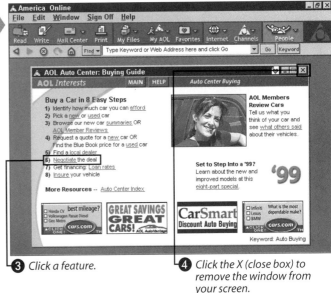

3 Click a feature.

4 Click the X (close box) to remove the window from your screen.

Digging into the Food Pages

People used to question whether cooks would ever use computers. They said no one could type on a keyboard with fingers slippery from butter or dusty from flour. But AOL's Food page (keyword: FOOD) has the cynics eating their words. Whether you are a gourmet or a beginner, this department is a fast, easy resource for recipes, cooking tips, advice on meal planning, table settings, theme dinners, and more, such as news of new cooking products. Following are some of the top links from here:

- Cooking Club (keyword: COOKING CLUB) devotes itself to food and cooking, discussing new ideas in fine dining from across the nation.
- Electronic Gourmet Guide (keyword: EGG) brings chefs, progressive food writers, and the public together for a great recipe database of fast meal plans.
- Global Gourmet (keyword: GG) hosts an international food site with a guide to exotic restaurants and foreign foods you can prepare at home.
- *The New York Times* Food (keyword: NYT FOOD) links you to the Food and Dining sections of *The New York Times*.
- *Woman's Day* (keyword: WD) offers a Cooking section with recipes of the week and tips for the budget cook.

- Food and Drink Network (keyword: FDN) salutes all hedonists, vinophiles, gourmets, and gourmands, inviting them to rally here and talk about food, wine, beer, desserts, even the after-dinner cigars and brandy.
- Meals.com (keyword: MEALS.COM) offers a database of more than 10,000 recipes, free offers, and more from the Meals Online Web site.

TAKE NOTE

TAKING BETTER PHOTOGRAPHS

These are all favorite topics of AOL's Photography forum (keyword: PICTURES). From here, you can find:

- *Popular Photography* Online (keyword: POP PHOTO) publishes the electronic extension of the print magazine, answering technical questions from beginners and old pros.
- Photography Forum (keyword: PHOTOGRAPHY FORUM) answers your picture questions and provides ideas and news for amateurs and professionals alike.
- *Video Magazine* Online (keyword: VIDEO ONLINE) offers users of camcorders and related technology a forum for information.

CROSS-REFERENCE

For more about food and healthy living, see Chapter 16.

FIND IT ONLINE

For information on vegetarian food, use the keyword VEGETARIAN.

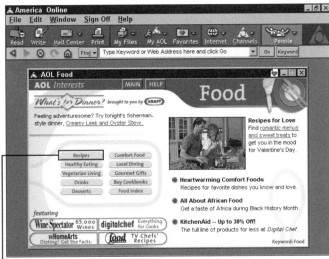

1 Press Ctrl+K, type **FOOD**, press Enter, and select a feature such as Recipes.

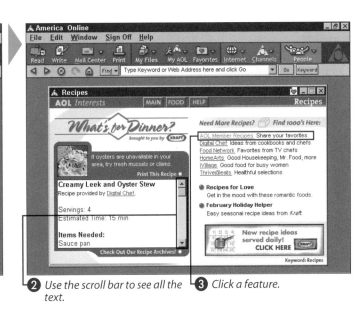

2 Use the scroll bar to see all the text.

3 Click a feature.

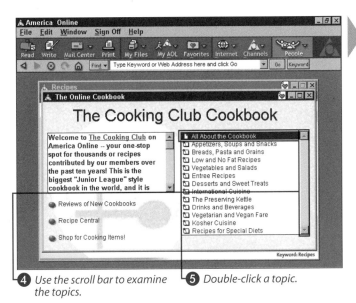

4 Use the scroll bar to examine the topics.

5 Double-click a topic.

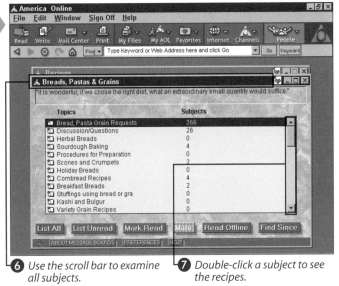

6 Use the scroll bar to examine all subjects.

7 Double-click a subject to see the recipes.

Tending Your Home and Garden

Home improvement jobs are among America's most common weekend pastimes. Of course, not everyone is born with instincts for do-it-yourself projects. If the thought of redoing the kitchen or even just painting the bedroom brings a chill, check out HouseNet (keyword: HOUSENET). HouseNet is the home improvement headquarters for ideas, tips, and techniques. This is where to find plainly written, step-by-step instructions for jobs you can do yourself, from wallpapering to refinishing furniture. Also:

▶ Check out the HouseNet Source Book for contacts with more than 1,000 product manufacturers.
▶ Look through the database for reference books and service associations, searching by type of job, section of the house, or tools and building materials.
▶ Learn formulas for figuring out how much material you need for a job.
▶ Chat with other builders and ask questions of the experts.

Gardening

Gardeners have a reputation for being a solitary set, happy to be left alone with their spades and hoes and a plot of earth to work. Actually, though, gardeners are a gregarious group, eager to share what they have learned from their labors. No wonder, then, that they have taken to online computing in such a big way in the past few years. AOL's Gardening Center (keyword: GARDENING) is the gathering spot for those with a serious green thumb as well as the well-intentioned weekend putterers. The site specializes in tips for lawn care, flower gardening, vegetable gardening, landscaping, and related topics. It also keeps you up to date on major upcoming events in your area and invites you to post questions and answers to its various message boards.

Closely allied with these gardening features are sections of AOL's Home & Garden page (keyword: HOME), which also includes interior and exterior decorating tips and homemaker and crafts projects, the kind of topics Martha Stewart might expound on. In fact, this page covers everything from housecleaning to making over your bathroom. Don't miss this page during the holidays for its extensive gift and entertainment ideas.

> **TAKE NOTE**
>
> ▶ **DO YOUR HOME WORK**
> For home repairs, gardening, decorating, and more:
> ▶ The Garden Spot (keyword: GARDEN) features the weekly Joyful Gardener column.
> ▶ *The New York Times* Gardening section (keyword: NYT GARDENING) features articles with gardening gurus and answers to questions.

CROSS-REFERENCE
For background on using the Internet and the World Wide Web, see Chapter 7.

FIND IT ONLINE
To find home and garden magazines online, use the keyword INTERESTS NEWSSTAND and check the list at the right.

Caring for Pets

Animal lovers have thousands of stories of how their pets' lives have been enhanced by America Online. Someone on the other side of the globe had a suggestion for solving Rover's penchant for, well, roving away from the yard. The Pet Care forum (keyword: PET CARE) brings animal lovers, veterinarians, pet suppliers, and others together for daily, ongoing conversations about dogs, cats, fish, birds, rabbits, reptiles, horses, pigs, and other farm animals — the entire menagerie.

Here's where to brag about your amazingly smart pets, share photos, join a support group for those grieving the loss of a pet, and ask questions of experts.

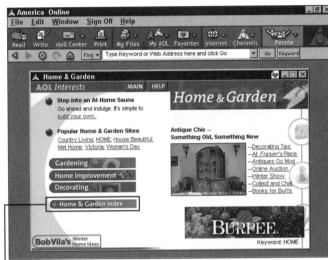

1 *Press Ctrl+K, type **HOME**, press Enter, and click an option such as the Home & Garden Index in the resulting window.*

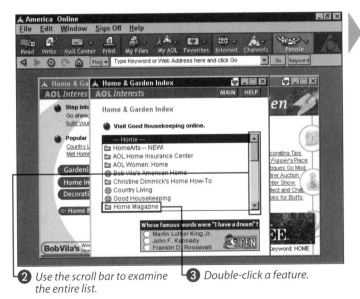

2 *Use the scroll bar to examine the entire list.*

3 *Double-click a feature.*

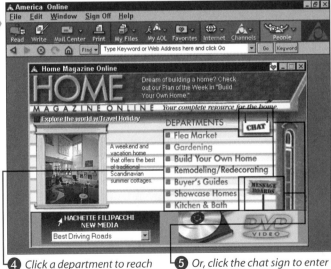

4 *Click a department to reach specific sections, such as gardening, building, and remodeling.*

5 *Or, click the chat sign to enter the chat room, or Message Boards sign to view the message boards.*

Finding the Road to Self-Improvement

What term describes the "essential you"? Parent? Teen? Senior citizen? Soldier? Native American? Are you more of an adjective (political, religious, romantic) or a noun (baby boomer, Catholic, lesbian)? Actually, the more you think about it, the more you realize you are not one word but many, just as you are not a member of a single community but of a number of communities. Some of them intersect, sharing related issues and values. Other communities you belong to may be completely oblivious to each other.

The complexity that is "you" becomes especially apparent as you start exploring the next part of America Online. The Lifestyle channel (keyword: LIFESTYLES) is devoted to such diverse communities. While the Interests channel focuses on the myriad things you do — such as pastimes, habits, and hobbies — Lifestyles is more concerned with all the things you are, from your beliefs and values to your ideals, experiences, and heritage. This is the place to come to talk about your faith; to seek advice for the sticky problems of child-rearing, jobs, school, dating, marriage, and divorce; to set out on a new road seeking love or self-improvement; or just to rediscover the "essential you."

So, you say you know what you need to do — lose weight, exercise more, stop smoking, seek a better job, or talk out the problems in your relationships.

Could you use some help getting motivated and staying on course? A support group may be just what you need. And you have one — or actually, many — online. The Self Improvement forum (keyword: SELF IMPROVEMENT) is dedicated to helping you turn your life around, break bad habits, start good habits, and begin feeling good about yourself.

TAKE NOTE

▶ IMPROVING YOUR OUTLOOK

From the main Self Improvement window, click the link to More Self-Improvement Resources to select a specific group. Here are a few standouts:

▶ Online Psych (keyword: ONLINE PSYCH) offers an enormous reservoir of psychological wisdom, covering topics from disorders, medications, and therapy to support groups, books, reviews, and discussions. From here you can link to hundreds of articles and Web sites, definitions, treatment resources, message boards, and lists. Doctors will also find a professionals' forum. Meanwhile, for fun, check out MindGames on online testing of personality and romantic instincts.

▶ Personal Empowerment Network (keyword: PEN) seeks to remove discrimination and stigmas associated with various mental and physical disabilities and diagnoses, providing a supportive environment for those facing psychological and emotional challenges. Forums here cover issues such as diet, exercise, fitness, parenting and caregiving, relationships, and separation and divorce.

CROSS-REFERENCE
For a refresher on using message boards, see Chapter 6.

FIND IT ONLINE
If you want to see what talk queen Oprah Winfrey has to say about your problems, visit Oprah Online (keyword: OPRAH).

Exploring Interests and Lifestyles

Finding the Road to Self-Improvement

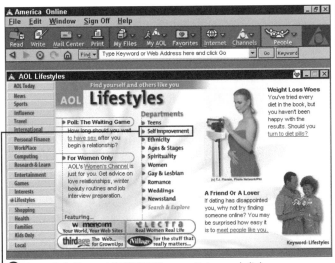

1 Press Ctrl+K, type **LIFESTYLES**, press Enter, and click a department such as Self Improvement from the resulting window.

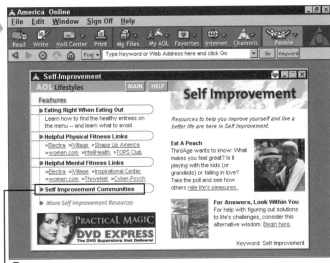

2 Select Self Improvement Communities.

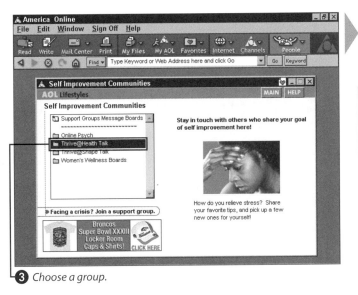

3 Choose a group.

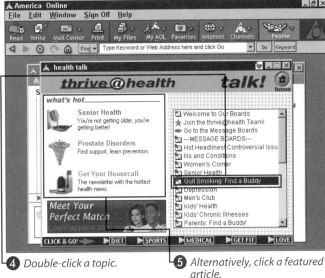

4 Double-click a topic.

5 Alternatively, click a featured article.

Looking for Love Online

Love is always in bloom online, regardless of the season or the time of day. And it really does happen. People fall in love and get married after meeting and dating through the Romance channel (keyword: ROMANCE). In fact, it happens so frequently nowadays, it has stopped being big news.

At the heart of the channel is Love @ AOL (keyword: LOVE AT AOL) with its Photo Personals, a database of online pictures, and profiles of people wanting to meet each other. Besides pictures, the profiles list age, marital status, region, occupations, likes and dislikes, and habits. You can browse the database by region or search for specific characteristics. If you find someone you want to meet, click an icon to send e-mail. Other options let you create, modify, or delete your own personal, with tips on how to get your photo digitized for use online.

Also in Love @ AOL are columns by Dr. Kate, Jaid Barrymore, and NetGirl, the queen of online love advice. Plus, you'll find chat rooms, message boards, party games ("Flirt" and "Score" are virtual dates, as if you needed the practice), daily "lovescopes," and a "love shop" of gifts for your cyber-squeeze.

Reading the Stars

AOL's Horoscope area (keyword: HOROSCOPE) won't let you down with its astrological coverage. Among the offerings is Crystal Ball (keyword: CRYSTAL BALL), the original metaphysical forum on AOL, predicting the future through tarot, runes, astrology, and live readings. Links to other online areas with horoscopes, such as Electra and George, are also available. AOL's News channel even offers your daily horoscope online via the Back Page (keyword: BACK PAGE).

The Astronet area (keyword: ASTRONET) stands out among them all, playing host to many popular metaphysical topics and forums, as well as offering the standard daily horoscopes, live personalized readings, and chats with others. Several well-known astrologers make their home here, including Carole 2000, The Cosmic Muffin, Kramer's Fishing Guide to the Stars, and Mark Lerner's Planet Earth Astrology Online. You can also read your HumorScope, your PassionScope, or your CareerScope. And if you are interested in other forms of fortune-telling, see the message board for those interested in Rune reading, I-Ching, numerology, and related topics.

TAKE NOTE

▶ **OTHER PEOPLE CONNECTIONS**
These channels bring together all kinds of people. For instance:
▶ College Online (keyword: COLLEGE ONLINE) presents a survival guide for current and soon-to-be students.
▶ Cigar Aficionado (keyword: CIGAR AFICIONADO) invites smoking enthusiasts to its electronic extension of the magazine, providing tips, cigar ratings, and a gift shop.

CROSS-REFERENCE
Personals also are in the AOL Classifieds. For more on that, see Chapter 15.

FIND IT ONLINE
Tips for newcomers to the exciting, sometimes intimidating, world of cyber courtship are in the Safety Tips at the Romance channel (keyword: ROMANCE).

1 Press Ctrl+K, type **ROMANCE**, press Enter, and click the Love @ AOL button in the resulting window.

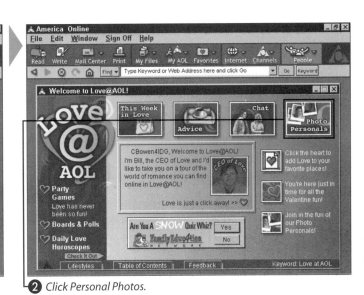

2 Click Personal Photos.

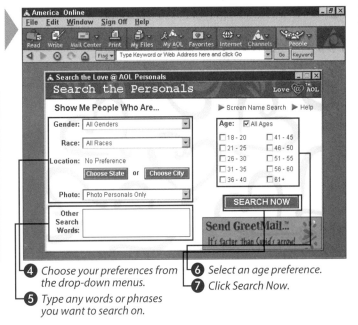

3 Select Search the Personals.

4 Choose your preferences from the drop-down menus.

5 Type any words or phrases you want to search on.

6 Select an age preference.

7 Click Search Now.

Exploring Ethnicity

Some commentators say that reaching racial and ethnic harmony is the most important goal and biggest challenge of the new millennium. America Online has taken a big step toward helping to build the necessary bridges between us by creating the new Ethnicity section (keyword: ETHNICITY).

Besides being a platform for articles and discussions about racial tolerance and understanding, Ethnicity also invites you to explore and celebrate your own heritage and the heritage of others. Linked from here are resources about black cultures around the world, the Jewish community, Asians and Hispanic cultures, and Native Americans, as well as people of European descent, from the clans of Scotland to the survivors of the Holocaust.

▶ American-African interests — from the swapping of family stories to the reporting of breaking news — are supported in Black Voices (keyword: BLACK VOICES) and in NetNoir (keyword: NETNOIR). Both encourage live events with black entrepreneurs and leaders in literature, business, films, music, education, sports, and other activities.

▶ Hispanic Online (keyword: HISPANIC ONLINE) serves Spanish-speaking people around the United States and the world. See its profiles of scientists, athletes, business leaders, and celebrities, and chat about seeing Hispanic treasures on your next vacation or business trip.

▶ Jewish Community (keyword: JEWISH) discusses art, food, and the ever-present traditions. Note that Jews in rural areas without a local synagogue can even use the site's Ask a Rabbi feature to stay connected.

▶ Genealogy Forum (keyword: ROOTS) helps trace roots in all cultures and traditions, even helping you reach beyond America's boundaries for international links.

▶ Tell Us Your Story (keyword: TELL US) devotes itself to recording the stories of American families and especially their immigration to this country. You can submit your own story and then search the database for good reading about the lives of your neighbors' families.

TAKE NOTE

▶ GAY AND LESBIAN COMMUNITIES

▶ PlanetOut (keyword: PLANETOUT) devotes itself to the entire gay culture.

▶ Over the Rainbow (keyword: OVER THE RAINBOW) reports on gay-friendly areas of American and international cities, gay-owned hotels and stores, reviews, and more.

▶ NAMES Project (keyword: NAMES PROJECT) invites members to join the fight against AIDS with the AIDS Memorial Quilt.

CROSS-REFERENCE

For background on using the real-time chat features of AOL, see Chapter 4.

FIND IT ONLINE

For a discussion of racial issues in general, visit the Ethnicity section (keyword: ETHNICITY), click Communities, scroll the list of topics, and select Race Relations.

Research Religions

From Baptist to Buddhist, if you define yourself by your religious beliefs — or are just curious about those who do — put the Religion page (keyword: RELIGION) on your next tour online. It brings together seekers of all kinds. Looking for a lively chat? You can't miss with religion.

Here are some specific links of interest:

▶ Beliefs (keyword: BELIEFS) offers a general guide to the religions, with information about what sets them each apart.

▶ Catholic News Service (keyword: CNS) publishes daily stories and briefs about the Catholic Church.

▶ Christianity Online (keyword: CO) provides music, Web links, Bible references, and chats.

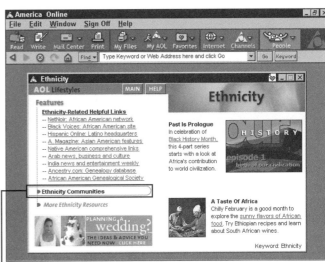

① *Press Ctrl+K, type **ETHNICITY**, press Enter, and click the Ethnicity Communities option on the resulting window.*

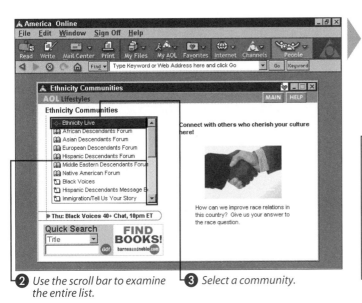

② *Use the scroll bar to examine the entire list.*

③ *Select a community.*

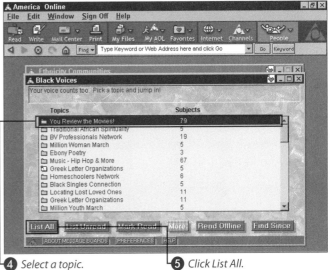

④ *Select a topic.*

⑤ *Click List All.*

Studying Women's Issues

The big Net news of the late 1990s has been the surge in the number of women who now make their home online. AOL's Women area (keyword: WOMEN) brings together diverse areas of interest, from work to computing, from family issues to finance, politics, fashion, and spiritual topics. For some, the Women site is for networking in the older sense of the word, making contacts to aid in the advancement of career and profession, while for others it is a resource for women's health issues, for help with love and relationships, and for family and child-rearing advice.

Departments include the following:

▶ Relationships offers information about affairs of the heart, dating, marriage, separation, divorce, love, and sex, and includes articles, columns, message boards, and answers from experts.

▶ Beauty goes beyond the stereotypes to offer help, information, and advice on fashion, skin care, plastic surgery, product reviews, and most importantly, a positive self-image.

▶ Wellness offers support groups, fitness articles, health resources, martial arts information, details on breast self-exams, and answers to frequently asked questions by kids, teens, and adult women.

▶ Career helps with job decisions, lists of best companies for women, advice from corporate headhunters, business strategies, money management, education opportunities, and advice on starting your own business.

▶ Money offers resources and advice on saving, investing, spending, and managing your money.

▶ Home provides a sanctuary for advice on cooking, gardening, decorating, and even home computing.

TAKE NOTE

▶ **OTHER FEATURES**

▶ Elle (keyword: ELLE) offers information on international style and flair, with coverage of fitness, health, and fashion worlds.

▶ Moms Online (keyword: MOMS ONLINE) houses a community of mothers, where new moms and moms-to-be are always welcome.

▶ Parent Soup (keyword: PARENT SOUP) supports both mom and dad with articles, chat groups, and talks with child experts.

▶ Thrive (keyword: THRIVE) offers a site for healthy living, food, fitness, and sex advice.

▶ Top Model (keyword: TOP MODEL) covers fashion, beauty, and fitness with advice from your favorite models.

▶ Women.com (keyword: WOMEN.COM) offers a complete resource for women connecting to its site on the Web for fashion, business, money, childcare, cooking, family, career, relationships, style, and technology.

CROSS-REFERENCE

For features related to parenting and kids, see Chapter 16.

FIND IT ONLINE

To reach the site devoted to *most* of us, use the keyword BABY BOOMERS.

Finding Your Peer Group

Baby boomers or bobby sockers. Frank Zappa or Frank Sinatra. Vietnam or World War II. The Love Generation. The Beat Generation. Generation X. Generation Y. The Great Depression. The Big Chill. Any of these sound familiar? Ages and Stages (keyword: AGES & STAGES) is a place to find your peers, whether you are a teen or a senior. Message boards and chat rooms abound. Alumni Hall invites college grads, while Military City is the area for active and former servicemen and women and their families. And seniors can check out SeniorNet (keyword: SENIORNET), which covers everything from reminiscing about the past to learning to use the technology of the future.

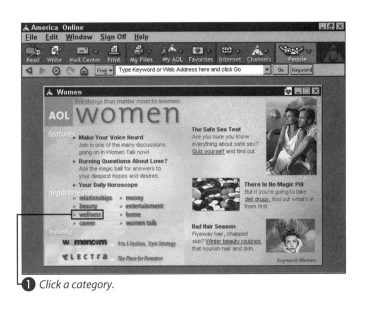

❶ Click a category.

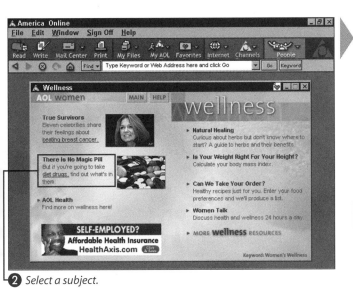

❷ Select a subject.

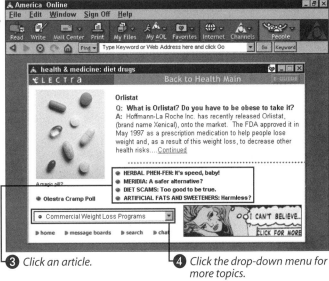

❸ Click an article.

❹ Click the drop-down menu for more topics.

Pursuing Your Hobbies

Have you read through this entire chapter but still haven't found your niche online? Do not despair. You now have all the information you need to explore this multifaceted corner of AOL on your own, searching out the places made just for you.

Using Hobby Central

So, the sun has gone down and you have spent the day painting the bedroom, servicing the car, walking the dog, and generally being responsible. Now, at last, it is time to settle down for some fun with your *real* hobbies, and America Online is ready to join you.

Hobby Central (keyword: HOBBY) is the town square for literally hundreds of recreations, from collecting to crafts, from model-building to star-gazing. Click a topic in the scroll box at the left of the window and follow the links to reach message boards, chat rooms, databases, libraries, and related services.

Topics include antiques, arts, astrology, astronomy, aviation, beanbag collecting, bicycling, bird watching, boating, books and reading, budgeting, collecting, cooking, crafts, dance, do-it-yourself, extreme sports, fishing, gardening, genealogy, historical reenactment, martial arts, motorcycles, musical performance, outdoors, pets, photography, radio communications, scale models, sewing and needlecrafts, and writing.

Using the Channel Guide

Finally, for these channels and other AOL features, you can use AOL's Channel Guide for a quick and easy overview of specific sites and features. It's a great alternative way to explore or just to remind yourself of what you've seen in earlier chapters. To reach it, sign on to AOL, if you are not already there, and use the keyword CHANNEL GUIDE to reach the window. Click a channel listed at the left of the window to see primary features listed in the box at the center of the screen. Now, double-click a feature that looks interesting to go directly to that feature.

TAKE NOTE

USING DEDICATED SEARCH FACILITIES

You can find communities by keywords and phrases using the channel-specific search facilities.

▶ Reach the database of Lifestyles features with the keyword LIFESTYLE SEARCH. For the database of Interests features, use the keyword INTERESTS SEARCH. Databases for other channels are found by visiting the channel directly via its keyword.

▶ Each resulting page has a Search button you can click. You then can enter a keyword or words to find.

CROSS-REFERENCE

For a background on surfing AOL's channels, see Chapter 3.

FIND IT ONLINE

If you don't find your hobby at first glance in Hobby Central, keep scrolling. The last entry in the list is More Hobbies, which you can click for another list.

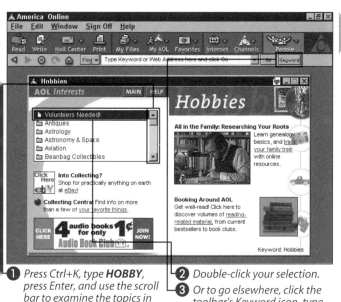

1 Press Ctrl+K, type **HOBBY**, press Enter, and use the scroll bar to examine the topics in the resulting window.

2 Double-click your selection.

3 Or to go elsewhere, click the toolbar's Keyword icon, type **CHANNEL GUIDE**, and press Enter.

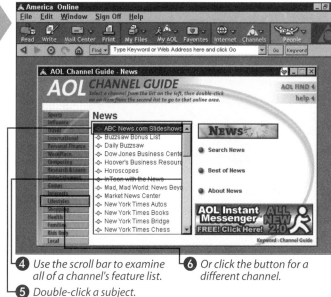

4 Use the scroll bar to examine all of a channel's feature list.

5 Double-click a subject.

6 Or click the button for a different channel.

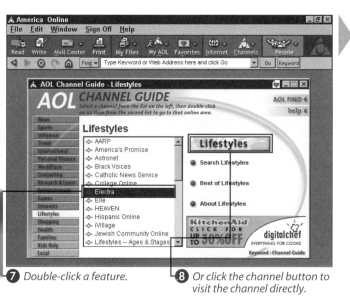

7 Double-click a feature.

8 Or click the channel button to visit the channel directly.

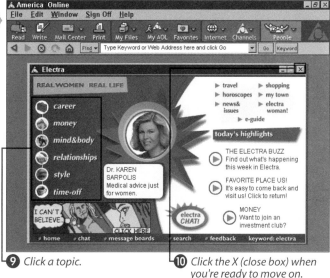

9 Click a topic.

10 Click the X (close box) when you're ready to move on.

Personal Workbook

Q&A

1 Where would you go to chat with those who love to tinker with old Triumphs and other classic sports cars?

_____

_____

_____

2 You want new ideas for next spring's flower garden. Where do you go online?

_____

_____

_____

3 What is Online Psych?

_____

_____

_____

4 What is Love @ AOL?

_____

_____

_____

5 Where would you find people interested in discussing Judaic traditions?

_____

_____

_____

6 What is Moms Online?

_____

_____

_____

7 If you want to research retirement living and related issues, where should you start?

_____

_____

_____

8 Bonus Question: Where would you find resources for bird watching?

_____

_____

ANSWERS: PAGE 344

EXTRA PRACTICE

1. Find a recipe for a chocolate cake.

2. Take dimensions of your bathroom and use HouseNet to determine how much wallpaper you would need to paper its walls.

3. Find a message board devoted to your age group.

4. Look into the Love @ AOL department for profiles of men and women in your state. (No credit if you've already *done* that!)

5. Explore your family heritage in the Genealogy Forum.

6. Find a message board devoted to martial arts.

REAL-WORLD APPLICATIONS

✔ You're moving to a new part of the country and you wonder what weight of motor oil you ought to use in your car in the winter. Check in with folks in the Car Care department (keyword: CAR CARE).

✔ Uncle John is a Civil War buff and he thinks he's stumped you when he asks if there is anything on AOL for him. Surprise! Use the keyword CIVIL WAR to reach the Mason Dixon Room for real-time chats. Also at this site is a Civil War research library and message board.

✔ Do you know someone who is trying to quit smoking or is battling another demon? Many people have found that the online community makes for an ideal support group during such trials. Spread the word about the system's self-improvement sections.

Visual Quiz

Where in this window is the shortcut revealed to reach it more quickly in the future? How would you save this page in your Favorite Places collection?

_____

_____

_____

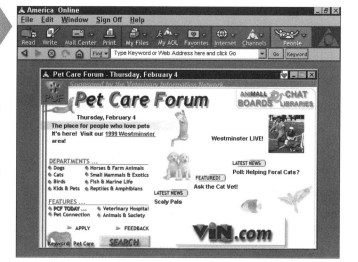

CHAPTER

15

MASTER
THESE
SKILLS

▶ **Finding Products**

▶ **Ordering the Products You Find**

▶ **Visiting the Bargain Basement**

▶ **Surfing the Electronic Classifieds**

▶ **Placing Your Own Classified Ads**

▶ **Setting Automatic Reminders**

Shopping Online

It all started a few years ago when my wife and I needed to cut expenses and discovered just before Christmas that the best solution was literally right at our fingertips: our keyboard. And a powerful shopping magic it is, too. We saved 35 to 40 percent on our gift buying, and without cutting corners. We bought all the presents on our list and even had them delivered directly to us. Not only that, we also saved on time, gasoline, and parking expenses because we did nearly all the shopping without leaving home.

Ironic, isn't it, that the computer technology you may have always thought of as expensive turns out to be the ideal bargain detector? Not only is it convenient and efficient, it is cheaper too. Whether used for Christmas shopping, searching for birthday gifts, or just buying day-to-day essentials such as office supplies and kitchen and household goods, America Online's shopping services make the buying easier, faster — and significantly less expensive.

This chapter has you

▶ shopping in the mall that never closes. It is safe and convenient to boot, with name brand products and big discounts. Just like the malls near home, this one also has special holiday bargains, sales, and promotions. You'll find special interactive features you just won't find in a traditional store.

▶ finding what you want for yourself and for gifts by shopping through categories, from music and videos to computers. Unlike the malls, you can visit all the clothing stores at one time.

▶ noting upcoming birthdays, holidays, anniversaries, and other gift-buying occasions, and letting AOL take the responsibility of reminding you. And the same reminder service can help you keep on top of upcoming meetings and important business dates.

▶ zeroing in on the best bargains of the day, every day, through special areas, directories, and newsletters.

▶ buying and selling through an electronic, global version of America's favorite flea market, the classified ads.

Finding Products

To reach AOL's shopping mall, sign on to the system and use keyword: SHOPPING or click the toolbar's Channels icon and then select Shopping from the drop-down menu. The Shopping channel gives you several ways to find stores and products, enabling you to

- ▶ browse specific categories (Apparel & Accessories; Auto & Travel; Beauty & Jewelry; Books, Music & Video; Computer Hardware; Computer Software; Electronics & Photo; Flowers, Cards & Candy; Gourmet Gifts; Home, Kitchen & Garden; Office Products; Sports & Fitness; and Toys & Collectibles).
- ▶ go directly to specific merchants, shops, and department stores, selecting from an alphabetized list of suppliers.
- ▶ search for stores that carry a specific kind of product or service. AOL has affiliations with scores of top merchants, from Avon to Warner Brothers, from Tower Records and Sharper Image to L.L. Bean, Gap, and Eddie Bauer.
- ▶ get information on daily deals, specials, and collections, such as back-to-school supplies or Christmas gifts.
- ▶ read about the Shopping channel's 100 percent guarantee through their certified merchant program.
- ▶ get help on using the Shopping channel and contacting customer service.

Browsing the Departments

If you have the time to spare, browsing is a fun way to shop online. Begin by going to the main Shopping window by using keyword: SHOPPING. Click one of the categories listed in the upper half of the main window. In the resulting window, AOL displays the stores that carry the items in this category. For instance, for apparel and accessories, AOL might list Gap, Eddie Bauer, AOL Shopper's Advantage, Fossil, Lands' End, One Hanes Place, JC Penney, and J. Crew. At the top of the window is a drop-down menu of other related stores. The center of the window highlights particularly hot items from the merchants, either things of seasonal interest or related to a current event. You can click the graphics to go directly to the products in the stores. Alternatively, you can click a button or a name on the drop-down menu to go directly to the front door of that merchant's online store.

TAKE NOTE

▶ **GO TO THE SOURCE**

Sometimes you may have a specific merchant in mind, and you want to go directly to that store. To find that store, click Store Listings at the bottom of the main Shopping window. The box at the left of the resulting window can be navigated with the scroll bar. Click the name of a merchant to research an online store.

CROSS-REFERENCE

If you're looking specifically for computer products, don't forget the Computing channel's shopping options, discussed in Chapter 11.

FIND IT ONLINE

To see details on AOL's certified merchant program, use keyword: GUARANTEE.

Searching for Stores by Merchandise

At other times, you may have in mind a specific product you are seeking without a particular merchant or department. Click the Search option on the main AOL Shopping Channel (keyword: SHOPPING) window. In the data-entry field at the top of the next window, type a word to describe the product you are seeking. AOL then lists merchants that carry the item. Double-click one of the names to visit the store. Search options also are provided throughout the Shopping channel on key pages. Click the Search button and follow the screen prompts.

1 *Click a category.*

2 *Click the list and select a merchant from the drop-down menu.*

3 *Or click a store button.*

4 *Or click a featured item.*

5 *Or select the Search option.*

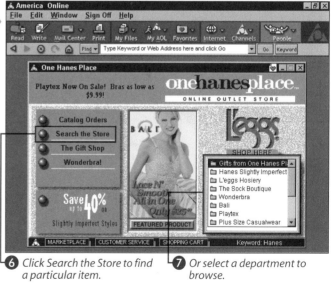

6 *Click Search the Store to find a particular item.*

7 *Or select a department to browse.*

Ordering the Products You Find

Regardless of the way you get to a store — whether it is by browsing the departments, selecting a specific merchant, or searching by product — all goods you find can be purchased with a major credit card and shipped to you. And if it is a gift, it can be sent directly to the intended recipient.

Each store operates a little differently, but all organize goods and services by categories. Many also have search options in their stores so you can type in a word or phrase for a list of related products. After you have chosen a category or item, select a title for more details. If this produces another list of specific products or groups of products, double-click your selection. When the list has been narrowed to a single product, a text box and image are displayed with a description of the item and its price. Buttons at the bottom let you

- ▶ cancel if this is not the product you had in mind. This option closes the window of the current product and returns you to the previous list.
- ▶ click to order the illustrated product. Depending on what you are ordering, the system may need additional answers, such as size, color, options, and add-ons. After you have answered the questions, the item is placed in your electronic "shopping cart" until you are ready to check out and pay up. (Some merchants also offer gift wrapping, gift cards, and

special delivery and query about it at this point.) Now you can select a Checkout option to finish shopping or Return to Shop for more items.

- ▶ review your Shopping Cart/Checkout. This option lets you look up what you have already set aside for purchasing during this session. Options enable you to remove items from the shopping cart if you have changed your mind.

When you finish, you can click a Return to Shopping button to return to your current store. You can now switch to other stores to continue shopping, browse within the same store, and periodically click the Shopping Cart button at the bottom of the window to review contents and remove unwanted items. When you finish shopping, click the Checkout button, and you are prompted for information for billing. Once the order has been successfully placed, you are given a confirmation number for your records.

TAKE NOTE

▶ GETTING SHOPPING SERVICES

Need help? The Shopping Services area (keyword: SHOPPING SERVICES) provides help, tips, and information on ordering from printed catalogs, locating real shopping malls around the country, finding a quick gift, researching products with Consumer Reports magazine (keyword: CONSUMER REPORTS), and more.

CROSS-REFERENCE

For more on money issues, see Chapter 10.

FIND IT ONLINE

To subscribe to the Shopping channel newsletter on the latest news, products, and stores, go to keyword: WEEKLY GOODS.

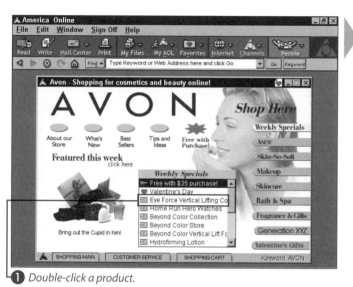

1 Double-click a product.

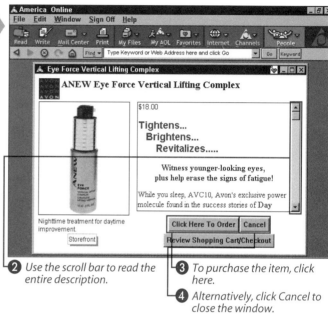

2 Use the scroll bar to read the entire description.

3 To purchase the item, click here.

4 Alternatively, click Cancel to close the window.

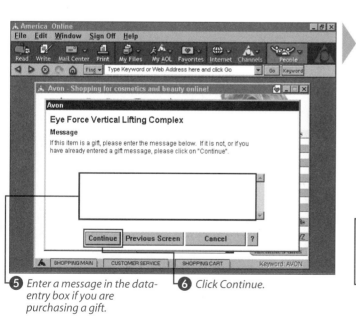

5 Enter a message in the data-entry box if you are purchasing a gift.

6 Click Continue.

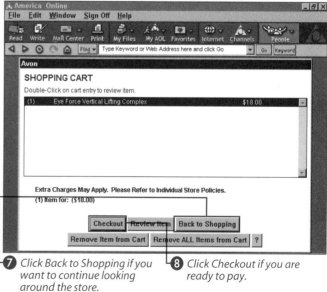

7 Click Back to Shopping if you want to continue looking around the store.

8 Click Checkout if you are ready to pay.

Visiting the Bargain Basement

ot everybody is a super shopper. For some of us — okay, for *me* — there needs to be a big sign saying, "Bargains here!" and "Answers for weary shoppers." AOL saw those of us among the shopping challenged coming . . . .

Hot Savings

The hot savings section (keyword: DEAL OF THE DAY) of the Shopping channel features a Deal of the Day, super values offered by the online merchants. Click the graphics in the center of the window to go directly to the products for descriptions, pictures, and ordering opportunities. You can also use the drop-down menu at the top of the window for a complete list of the day's deals. Buttons here also link you to coupon services, where you can request coupons at no extra charge to use in your offline shopping. And for "deep discounts," shop the Bargain Basement (keyword: BARGAIN BASEMENT) with closeouts, sales, discounts, and specials of all kinds.

Help with Quick Gift Needs

Sometimes it isn't a bargain I need so much as a quick gift idea. A major birthday or anniversary has snuck up on me, and I need a good gift that can be been delivered quickly. Quick Gifts (keyword: QUICK GIFTS) provides a selection of never-fail,

always-appropriate gifts, such as gift baskets, flowers, and gourmet samplers, from selected online merchants. These gifts are always available and can be shipped within 48 hours of your order. Be sure to note the cut-off times posted on each product to determine whether your gift will be shipped today or tomorrow before selecting the shipping method you want.

TAKE NOTE

GETTING CATALOGS

Many mail-order houses now have facilities for online orders through AOL, including Chef's Catalog, Eddie Bauer, Hammacher Schlemmer, L.L. Bean, Hickory Farms, Lands' End, and others. You can type the information from your print catalog right into the online order form. For more on this, use keyword: SHOPPING SERVICES to reach the Shopping Services window and then click the button that reads "Order from Print Catalogs" (or use keyword: ORDER FROM PRINT CATALOGS).

FREE NEWSLETTER

You also can sign up for a subscription to the free e-mail newsletter for bargain hunters. Real Deals covers the latest shopping bargains and discounts. Use keyword: MP DEALS for direct access. The newsletter is delivered to your online mailbox every Tuesday at no extra charge. Just visit the site and click the Subscribe button. If you later decide you don't want it, return to click Unsubscribe.

CROSS-REFERENCE

Many of the links to stores actually connect with sites on the World Wide Web. For more on navigating the Internet, see Chapter 7.

FIND IT ONLINE

To go directly to the AOL Outlet Center for great deals from the AOL Store, go to keyword: AOL OUTLET CENTER.

1 Click the featured item under Deals and Steals.

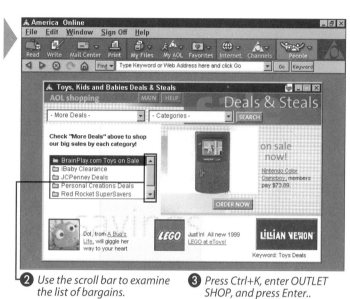

2 Use the scroll bar to examine the list of bargains.

3 Press Ctrl+K, enter OUTLET SHOP, and press Enter..

4 Select a product or promotion.

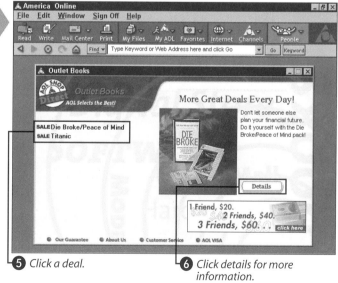

5 Click a deal.

6 Click details for more information.

Surfing the Electronic Classifieds

America's great flea market democracy exists in the classifieds ads of newspapers and magazines, which now have spread to cyberspace. The AOL Classifieds (keyword: CLASSIFIEDS) invite everyone interested in buying, selling, and/or trading just about anything. Looking for cars, computers, houses, a new job, or travel opportunities? Browsing and reading the ads costs you nothing extra. Of course, there are surcharges to post your own ad.

To browse and read the classifieds, sign on to the system if you are not already there and enter the keyword CLASSIFIEDS to reach the main window. Click one of the icons at the center of the display to choose a broad category, and the system lists subcategories in the list box in the lower-left side of the window. Double-click one of the subcategories and further hone the list in the resulting window by clicking the following:

▶ **Region.** Choose from All Regions (the default), West (for Alaska, California, or Hawaii), Northwest (for Idaho, Montana, North Dakota, South Dakota, Oregon, Washington, or Wyoming), Southwest (for Arizona, Colorado, Nevada, New Mexico, Oklahoma, Texas, or Utah), Midwest (for Illinois, Indiana, Iowa, Kansas, Michigan, Minnesota, Missouri, Nebraska, Ohio, or Wisconsin), Mid-Atlantic (for Delaware, Maryland, Virginia, Washington D.C., or West Virginia), Northeast (for Connecticut, Maine, Massachusetts, New Hampshire, New Jersey, New York, Pennsylvania, Rhode Island, or Vermont), Southeast (Alabama, Arkansas, Florida, Georgia, Kentucky, Louisiana, Mississippi, North Carolina, Puerto Rico, South Carolina, or Tennessee), and Outside the U.S. (for Canadian and other international regions).

▶ **Topic.** These, of course, vary from category to category.

To see an ad, use the scroll bar in the box at the left of the window and double-click a title. The ad then appears, along with the screen name of the person who posted it. An option at the bottom invites you to Respond to the Ad. Also, the screen name often is hyperlinked, meaning you can click it to write an e-mail directly to the person posting the ad.

Classified ads are posted on a first-come, first-served basis, so the newest ads are always at the top of the lists.

TAKE NOTE

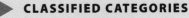

CLASSIFIED CATEGORIES

Here are the departments used in the AOL Classifieds:

▶ General, Employment, Real Estate, Vehicles, Computing, Business, Travel and Personals.

CROSS-REFERENCE

If you are interested in personal ads, also check out the profiles in the Love @ AOL section, discussed in Chapter 14.

FIND IT ONLINE

For more information on how to use the classifieds section, click "Welcome to AOL Classifieds" in the scroll box on the introductory window (keyword: CLASSIFIEDS).

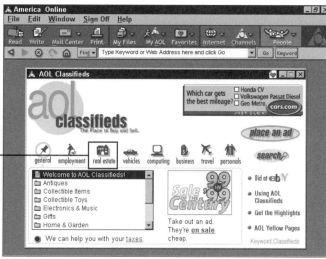

1 Press Ctrl+K, enter **CLASSIFIEDS**, press Enter, and click a category icon in the resulting window.

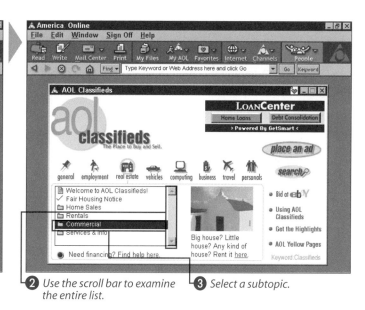

2 Use the scroll bar to examine the entire list.

3 Select a subtopic.

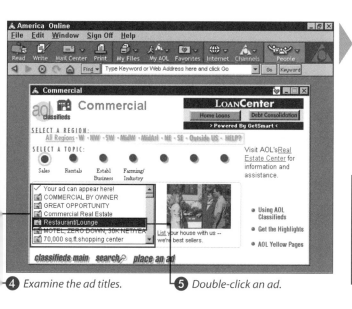

4 Examine the ad titles.

5 Double-click an ad.

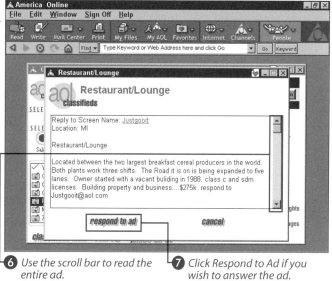

6 Use the scroll bar to read the entire ad.

7 Click Respond to Ad if you wish to answer the ad.

Placing Your Own Classified Ads

If you have something you want to sell — or just tell the world about — you can place your own online classified. Sign on to the system using the screen name under which you want the ad to appear in the "Reply to" e-mail address and use keyword: CLASSIFIEDS to reach the main window. Click the Place an Ad button on the right side of the window. Select the category where you want the ad to be listed, clicking the appropriate category. Fill in the resulting form. Be sure to enter the following:

▶ The headline and body of the ad.

▶ Your personal information (not visible to members unless you also include it in the ad).

▶ The subcategory where the ad should be placed, selected from the drop-down menu. (AOL reserves the right to publish the ad in the sub-category it feels best matches the product or service advertised.)

▶ The two-letter abbreviation for your state in the appropriate box. (Do not enter "US" — the box is reserved either for a two-letter state abbreviation or "XX" to indicate outside the United States.)

▶ The correct Start Date.

▶ Your credit card information.

▶ Click the Send button. If successful, the ad is posted within a few hours of the time you placed the order. Those interested readers respond to you by e-mailing the screen name listed at the top of your ad.

CROSS-REFERENCE

For background on writing online, see Chapter 2.

FIND IT ONLINE

To get information on AOL pricing, use keyword: BILLING.

What Does It Cost to Advertise?

AOL Classifieds can be placed for two weeks, a month, or a year and billed to a major credit card (VISA, MasterCard, Discover, and American Express). Rates vary, depending on the category in which the ad is placed. As of this writing, the rates are as follows:

▶ Employment, Real Estate, and Business ads are $12.95 for two weeks, $19.95 for a month, and $159.95 for a year.

▶ General, Vehicles, and Travel ads are $9.95 for two weeks and $15.95 for a month.

▶ Computing and Personals ads are $6.95 for two weeks and $10.95 for a month.

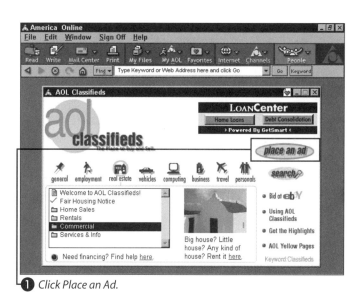

❶ Click Place an Ad.

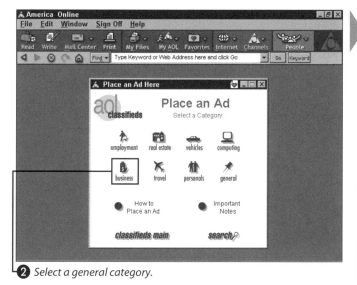

❷ Select a general category.

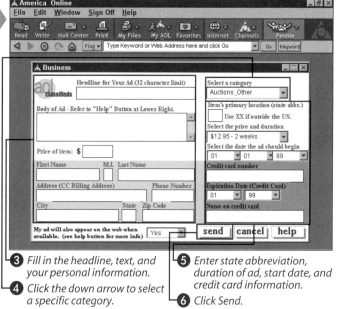

❸ Fill in the headline, text, and your personal information.

❹ Click the down arrow to select a specific category.

❺ Enter state abbreviation, duration of ad, start date, and credit card information.

❻ Click Send.

Setting Automatic Reminders

Now that you are becoming a super cybershopper, word is going to get out. Your mom will be telling her neighbors. Your sister will be using you as a good example to her children. Your friends will expect to hear regular stories of bargains and conveniences brought to you by your computer. And obviously you can never again forget an important gift-giving opportunity. Fortunately for you, America Online is covering your back in the reminder department.

Let the Computer Remind You of Important Dates

What a sweet concept! Electronic reminders of important upcoming dates, automatically e-mailed by AOL to you 14 days in advance so you can get your gift-buying done. And of course, the same computing power can be put to work in aspects of your life. Do you have a big business meeting coming up that would be professionally fatal to miss? Let America Online handle your electronic wake-up call.

To tie a virtual string around your finger, use the keyword REMINDER to reach the main window and click the Create your Reminder button. In the resulting window:

▶ Enter your name and sex.
▶ Indicate whether you want a second reminder four days before the event (recommended).

▶ Click the checkboxes next to the holidays for which you wish to be reminded.
▶ Click Continue.

Now you can add Personal Reminders for birthdays, anniversaries, and other occasions. An on-screen form prompts for the gift recipient's name, the occasion, the date, and whether the event is repeated annually. Optionally, you also can add information about the recipient's age and sex if you'd like the service to provide gift ideas. Click OK and then click Quit.

After a profile is created, the service takes care of sending you gentle reminders through your online mailbox. If you later want to add, delete, or change reminders, just come back to the main window with keyword: REMINDER and click Edit Your Reminder.

TAKE NOTE

REMEMBER THIS SHORTCUT

Besides using keyword: REMINDER, you also can quickly reach your Reminder Profile by clicking the toolbar's My AOL icon and selecting Reminder Service from the drop-down menu.

TODAY NOT TWO WEEKS

If you prefer to receive your reminders on the actual day of an event rather than two weeks in advance, there is a way to do it. Just add 14 days to the actual date of the event when you set up a reminder.

CROSS-REFERENCE

For other ways you can automate America Online, see Chapter 6.

FIND IT ONLINE

To learn more about the Reminder Service, go to keyword: REMINDER and click "How does this AOL service work?"

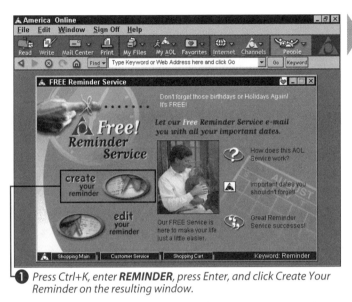

1. Press Ctrl+K, enter **REMINDER**, press Enter, and click Create Your Reminder on the resulting window.

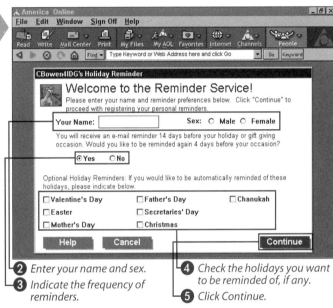

2. Enter your name and sex.

3. Indicate the frequency of reminders.

4. Check the holidays you want to be reminded of, if any.

5. Click Continue.

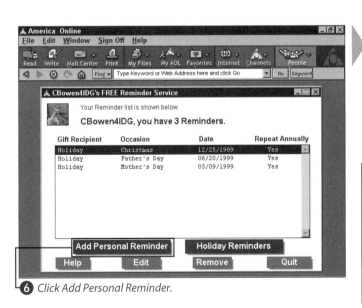

6. Click Add Personal Reminder.

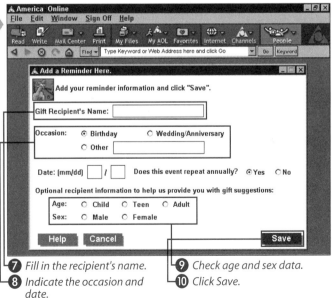

7. Fill in the recipient's name.

8. Indicate the occasion and date.

9. Check age and sex data.

10. Click Save.

311

Personal Workbook

Q&A

1 What is the "shopping cart?"

_____

_____

_____

2 Where can you turn for bargains?

_____

_____

_____

3 What is "Weekly Goods?"

_____

_____

_____

4 If you are looking for a job, where can you find help wanted ads online?

_____

_____

_____

5 How can you sign up for a newsletter about AOL Classifieds?

_____

_____

_____

6 Can you change a classified ad after it has been posted?

_____

_____

7 Where would you find ads for used CD-ROMs and old programs?

_____

_____

_____

8 Bonus Question: Oops — you've forgotten Uncle Fred's birthday. How can you have a gift delivered to him in a hurry?

_____

_____

_____

ANSWERS: PAGE 345

EXTRA PRACTICE

1 Go cybershopping and use the Search option to see what you can find in the way of sweaters.

2 Browse AOL's bookstores.

3 Examine the latest list of all the merchants online.

4 Search the classified ads selling bicycles.

5 Browse the classifieds in the Travel category.

6 Check out the Deal of the Day daily for a three-day period to see the variety of offers.

REAL-WORLD APPLICATIONS

✔ The Reminder Service can be used for other applications besides gift-buying occasions. Got a big meeting coming up? Need to remember to make travel plans for a conference you are attending? Use the Reminder Service as a kind of digital secretary.

✔ AOL's classifieds are global, which is particularly useful if you are relocating and need to find housing in a new part of the country.

✔ Prices online often are lower, but some people don't like to buy anything without first seeing and touching it. So, they make a trip to the mall, check out products, and make notes of brand names and model numbers.

Visual Quiz

How can you arrange to have a message like this automatically appear in your electronic mailbox? How can you change the details of the reminder?

_____

_____

_____

_____

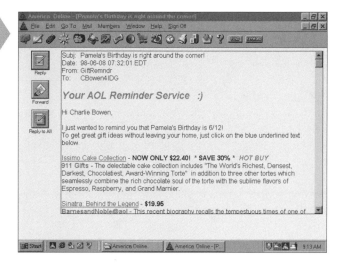

CHAPTER **16**

MASTER
THESE
SKILLS

▶ **Researching Illnesses and Treatments**

▶ **Finding Support Groups**

▶ **Getting Advice from Parenting Experts**

▶ **Protecting Kids**

▶ **Using Parental Controls**

▶ **Using the Kids Online Channel**

▶ **Finding Digital Cities**

Finding Family Interests

Family is defined in many ways. The spectrum reaches from the traditional mom-pop-2.3-kids-dog-named-Spot families to the extended see-you-next-Christmas families to households of unrelated people who have decided to face the future as unconventional families. Despite the diversity, though, all families share some basic concerns:

▶ Fighting sickness
▶ Keeping the peace
▶ Teaching the children
▶ Growing together

The last four of America Online's channels provide tools and connections for happier families. The Health channel (keyword: HEALTH) has wellness information for kids and men and women of all ages, from medical reference books to the news of breakthroughs in treatments and cures. The Families channel (keyword: FAMILIES) has advice on parenting, advice about protecting kids online, and ideas for enriching family life. The Kids Only channel (keyword: KIDS ONLY) is a kid-safe section of the system for electronic clubhouses, games, news, and more. The Local channel (keyword: LOCAL) has links to useful resources literally all across the nation, in hundreds of "digital cities."

In other words, with this chapter you are

▶ tracking the latest health and fitness news for you and your loved ones, of all ages. This is like having a medical news service right at your elbow.
▶ using medical reference materials to become a better-informed patient during your next doctor's office visit.
▶ getting help from experts on tricky questions of parenting, from discipline to nutrition.
▶ learning how to keep your children safe online through Parental Controls.
▶ exploring the special kids-only clubhouse where children from around the world can meet, play, and learn.
▶ visiting local communities around the country.

Researching Illnesses and Treatments

The Health channel is a one-stop resource for today's health news, a health tip of the day, and features on pain relief, depression, sports injuries, and various medical conditions from cancer treatments to asthma and diabetes. Central to the Health channel is its extensive database of more than 150 different medical conditions and treatments, a kind of online medical library you can browse or search by keyword for facts, resources, and support groups.

The Health channel is reached with keyword: HEALTH or by clicking the toolbar's Channels icon and selecting Health from the drop-down menu. Click the Illnesses & Treatments button on the AOL Health window (or use keyword: ILLNESSES to go there directly). In the resulting window, use the list box in the lower left to select from one of the general topics, among them Addictions; Allergies and Respiratory Disorders; Alternative and Complementary Medicine; Bones, Joints and Muscles; Brain and Nervous System; Cancer; Dental and Oral Health; Diabetes, Thyroid and Endocrine Disorders; Digestive Disorders; Disabilities; Ear, Nose and Throat; Eyes and Vision; Heart and Blood Disorders; Infectious and Contagious Diseases; Kidney and Urinary Tract Disorders; Mental Health; Pain Relief; Reproduction and Sexual Health; and Skin, Hair and Nails.

If you know your specific topic but aren't sure where to find it, try clicking the hyperlink "Alphabetically" to look for your topic from 26 lettered folders displayed on a subsequent window. You can also enter a word or phrase in the data-entry field in the upper left of the window and click the Search button.

From a subgroup of topics presented on the next window, double-click a selection, continuing with subsequent screens until you reach the list of features, including explanations of symptoms and treatments, medical glossaries, and links to related sites on the World Wide Web. Groups and message boards where you can interact with others interested in the condition are also listed.

TAKE NOTE

A VIRTUAL APPLE A DAY

There are many more related medical features online to explore:

▶ The AOL Medical Reference (keyword: MEDICAL REFERENCE) are in-depth databases of health news and research.

▶ Health News (keyword: HEALTH NEWS) has breaking medical news from sources such as *The New York Times* and the Associated Press.

▶ Fitness, good nutrition, positive attitude, and basic precautions all play a part in keeping you healthy.

CROSS-REFERENCE
To search for more breaking health stories, use the news resources illustrated in Chapter 8.

FIND IT ONLINE
To find out about getting health-related newsletters, use keyword: TO YOUR HEALTH.

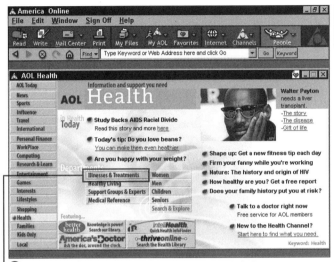

1 Press Ctrl+K, type **HEALTH**, press Enter, and click Illnesses & Treatments in the resulting window.

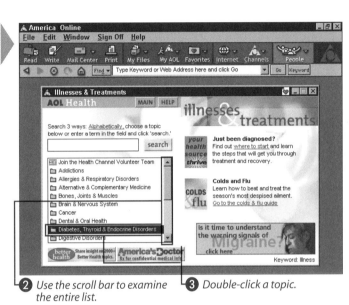

2 Use the scroll bar to examine the entire list.

3 Double-click a topic.

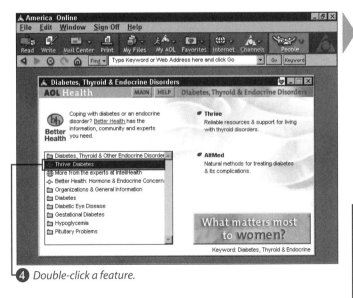

4 Double-click a feature.

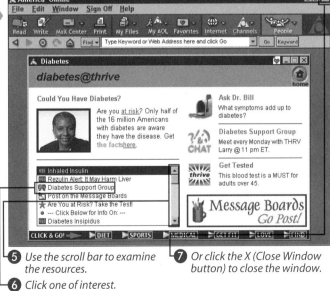

5 Use the scroll bar to examine the resources.

6 Click one of interest.

7 Or click the X (Close Window button) to close the window.

Finding Support Groups

The Health channel links directly to support groups relating to all kinds of illnesses, bringing victims and their families together with experts and others familiar with the condition. Use keyword: HEATH SUPPORT to reach to reach scores of message boards and chat rooms where you can exchange advice and experiences.

Support groups cover topics as diverse as stress, dating, family violence, and depression. Also on the site are advice columns from medical professionals and links to AOL and Web pages by physicians, nutritionists, pediatricians, and family counselors.

Health Ideas for Each of Us

AOL also breaks down medical data by age and by gender.

▶ Women's Health (keyword: WOMEN'S HEALTH) covers matters such as mammograms, pap smears, and breast self-examinations. Also here are reports on women and smoking and how to improve coronary health. Message boards invite women to share experiences from motherhood to menopause, to get and give support for eating disorders, fertility problems, and Toxic Shock Syndrome.

▶ Men's Health (keyword: MEN'S HEALTH) focuses on topics as diverse as baldness and sexual issues to prostate cancer. It has the latest information on heart attacks, stroke, and cancer, and tips on how to beat cholesterol and starting (and sticking to) a heart-healthy diet and exercise program.

▶ Children's Health (keyword: CHILDREN'S HEALTH) looks at parenting issues, vaccinations, exercise, and diet. There is advice on how to assess your child's health and what to do when kids get sick. Information resources cover newborns, toddlers, and preschoolers as well as older children.

▶ Seniors' Health (keyword: SENIORS' HEALTH) shows you how to reduce the risk of illness in later years and how to cope with existing health problems. Special attention is paid to age-related problems such as osteoporosis, arthritis, and Alzheimer's disease. Tips are provided for exercise that lowers blood pressure, lessens bone loss, and strengthens the heart and lungs.

TAKE NOTE

▶ **MORE HEALTH SITES**

Here are other sites you can reach by keyword:
▶ Addictions (keyword: ADDICTION)
▶ Emotional Well-Being (keyword: STRESS MANAGEMENT)
▶ Relationships & Sexuality (keyword: RELATIONSHIPS)

CROSS-REFERENCE

Fitness also is a topic of the Sports channel. See Chapter 8 for information about getting and keeping in shape.

FIND IT ONLINE

For online information about relieving stress and pain, use keyword: PAIN RELIEF.

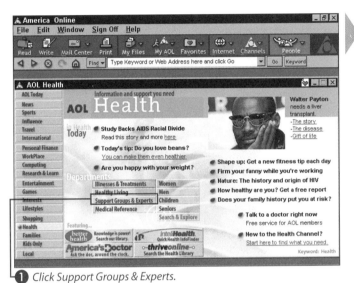

1 Click Support Groups & Experts.

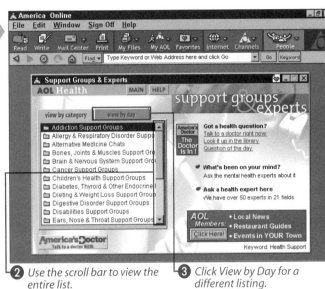

2 Use the scroll bar to view the entire list.

3 Click View by Day for a different listing.

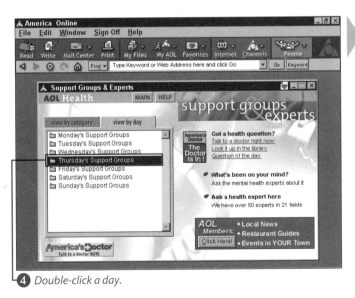

4 Double-click a day.

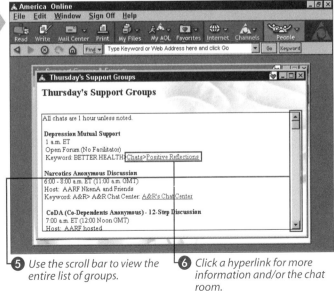

5 Use the scroll bar to view the entire list of groups.

6 Click a hyperlink for more information and/or the chat room.

Getting Advice from Parenting Experts

The Families channel (keyword: FAMILIES) has a little something for everyone, from advice on parenting, whether the children are newborns or teenagers, to planning family vacations to tracing your family tree. Some of the links from here go to features you have already visited, such as online banking (Chapter 10), entertainment reviews (Chapter 13), and online shopping (Chapter 15). Other features, such as resources for online safety, are unique to this venue.

No one is more of an expert on your kids than you, of course, but even experts need some advice sometimes. The Parenting department (keyword: PARENTING) is your primary connection to the professionals. Come here for tips, ranging from how to determine if your teenager is smoking to what to do to make your child's birthday party especially memorable. The site also solicits your thoughts and ideas, with polls on daycare and whether advertising should be permitted in schools, sharing the results with you.

More Parenting Resources links:

▶ Parent Soup (keyword: PARENT SOUP) offers information from serious advice from child psychologists to comic relief through shared stories of others in the same boat. More than 500 related groups are accessible from here. Use the site's Parenting Resource Library for tips on all kinds of issues. Child-rearing experts visit the message boards to field questions on pediatrics, breastfeeding, child dentistry, discipline, and more. Also here is an online store for toys, books, tapes, and baby supplies.

▶ Moms Online (keyword: MOMS ONLINE) provides a daily break for those in motherhood mode, whether it is serious advice you need from a peer or just someone to blow off steam with. A particular hit here is *The Daily Alexander,* a newsletter following the trials and tribulations of one mother's journey.

▶ The Babies center (keyword: BABIES) focuses on newborns and parents-to-be, answering frequently asked questions about health, finances, baby products, and preserving those precious memories. It also discusses single parents, problem births, and adoptions.

▶ Electra's Solution Center: Children (keyword: ELECTRA) links to resources for child care guides, contacts, polls, and networks.

TAKE NOTE

▶ WELLNESS 2000

Try these sites for health:
▶ Alternative Medicine (keyword: ALTERNATIVE MEDICINE) discusses alternatives to traditional care.
▶ Ask the Experts (keyword: MEDICAL EXPERTS) fields assorted questions for doctors.
▶ Wellness and Disease Prevention (keyword: WELLNESS) provides news and developments.

CROSS-REFERENCE

For more on women's issues and related subjects, see Chapter 14.

FIND IT ONLINE

For health information on reproduction and related issues, including conception and pregnancy, use keyword: REPRODUCTION.

Naming a Newborn

Need help choosing a name for your newborn? America Online can give you a hand. Parents Soup offers the A to Z Baby Name Finder (keyword: BABY NAME).

The feature provides information on the origins and meanings of more than 14,000 names. They also can generate names based on gender, religion, ethnicity, and even number of syllables. And you can scroll through an updated ranking of the latest top 50 boys' and girls' names as well as the site's favorites, such as Victoria, Renee, Kristen, Kai, and Alexis.

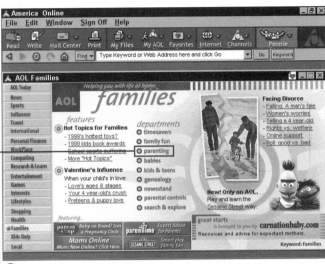

1 Press Ctrl+K, enter **FAMILIES**, press Enter, and click the "Parenting" link on the resulting window.

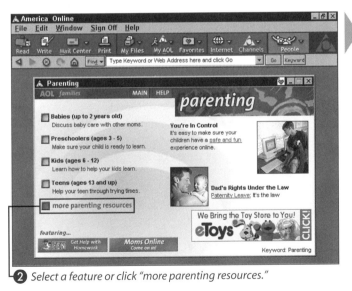

2 Select a feature or click "more parenting resources."

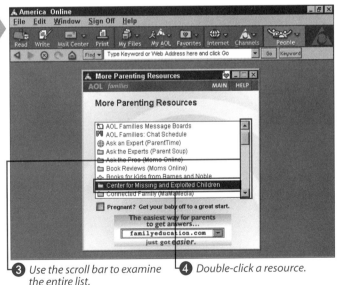

3 Use the scroll bar to examine the entire list.

4 Double-click a resource.

Protecting Kids

Looking for quality movies, books, and software for your young children? The Family Fun section (keyword: FAMILY FUN) has tips, as well as ideas for family vacations and stay-at-home activities you can do together. The site has literally hundreds of casual recommendations for entertainment, travel, baby supplies, good books, and kid-safe computer programs.

Of course, a big issue nowadays for families is not what to see online but what not to see. Some features — particularly many of those reachable through the Internet — are inappropriate for children and young teens. The Kids and Teens department (keyword: KIDS AND TEENS) has tips on how parents can safeguard the household's youngest Net surfers.

More Family-Friendly Sites Available

Here are some other family-oriented resources you can visit directly by keyword:

▶ Family Life (keyword: FAMILY LIFE) provides stories on the challenges and joys of parenthood.

▶ Family Computing (keyword: FAMILY COMPUTING) publishes the electronic extension of the computer magazine by the same name, with reviews, games, and educational products.

▶ Family Travel Network (keyword: FAMILY TRAVEL NETWORK) offers tips on traveling with kids, good family deals, and ideas of vacation spots.

▶ Family Newsstand (keyword: FAMILIES NEWS-STAND) provides articles from popular parent and kid magazines and deals on subscriptions.

▶ Scouting Forum (keyword: SCOUTING) focuses on boy and girl scouting activities, with material for parents and children.

Still can't find it? Try searching for yourself. Use keyword: FAMILIES SEARCH to reach the search center and then click the Search button and enter a keyword in the resulting window.

TAKE NOTE

▶ **ADDITIONAL HEALTH SITES OF INTEREST**

Here are more health sites of interest to your family:

▶ Allergies and Asthma (keyword: ALLERGIES) provides information on treatment and news.
▶ Bones, Joints and Muscles (keyword: BONES) offers news on arthritis, back ailments, chronic pain, and muscle and joint disorders.
▶ Brain and Nervous System (keyword: BRAIN) discusses neurological disorders.
▶ Cancer (keyword: CANCER) covers diagnosis to chemotherapy.

CROSS-REFERENCE

For more on movies, TV, and other entertainment, see Chapter 13.

FIND IT ONLINE

To get an overview of the Families channel, go to its Search & Explore page (keyword: FAMILIES SEARCH) and click Best of Families.

Make More Time with Timesavers

At the heart of many family problems is time — or the lack of time — for things to do together. AOL even has a department to help with this sticky problem. Family Timesavers (keyword: FAMILY TIME-SAVERS) links to tools and tips for cutting the time devoted to chores and to getting the most out of the time you have with the family. Link directly to facilities for online banking, online shopping, and electronically efficient vacation planning. Looking for a new car? Save that car lot-surfing time by researching online. There are even links to budget calculators, house-finders, movie reviews, and school aids.

1 Click Family Fun.

2 Click a hyperlink.

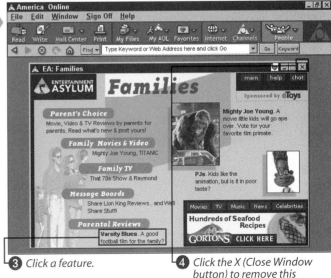

3 Click a feature.

4 Click the X (Close Window button) to remove this window from your screen

Using Parental Controls

Essential to the protection of children online is the use of AOL's Parental Control options, which enable parents to designate any of four different levels of access to AOL and the Internet for each child's screen name, depending on ages and maturity.

▶ Kids Only designation is a good choice if your household has children under 12. This restricts access to the Kids Only channel. An account limited to Kids cannot send or receive Instant Messages, the private communication described in Chapter 4, nor can it enter member-created chat rooms or use premium services. Also the mailbox for this account can receive and send only text-based e-mail, so letters with files attached with embedded pictures cannot be received.

▶ Young Teens designation is recommended for children 13 to 15 years old. This setting enables the children to visit some chat rooms, but not member-created or private chats. It also blocks them from Web sites and Internet newsgroups that are considered inappropriate for young people.

▶ Mature Teens is the suggested setting for youths ages 16 and 17. It enables access to all AOL areas, including all chat rooms, but continues restriction to Web sites appropriate for the age group.

▶ 18+ is the designation that provides unrestricted access to all features of the Internet and AOL.

To get started, sign on the system and use keyword: PARENTAL CONTROLS to reach the main window. (Alternatively, you can click the toolbar's My AOL icon and select Parental Controls from the drop-down menu.) Click the Set Parental Controls Now button at the bottom of the window to review current settings. Review the current designation for each screen name under this account and click the appropriate check boxes to make any changes.

Continued

TAKE NOTE

▶ SAFE COMPUTING FOR CHILDREN

In addition to the Parental Controls features described here, it is wise for parents to create a separate screen name for each child who uses the account. To do that, sign on with the master account screen name, then use keyword: SCREEN NAMES and follow prompts on the screen to create a new screen name as described in Chapter 5. The system asks for an age designation for the account, using the four categories described in the next section. Consider also storing the password for each child's screen name online and not sharing the password with the child. This is the best way to prevent your children from revealing the password to others online.

CROSS-REFERENCE

For other ways to automate and regulate your usage of AOL, see Chapter 6.

FIND IT ONLINE

AOL also maintains a message board to discuss Parental Controls. Go to keyword: PARENTAL CONTROLS and scroll to the bottom of the message in the center.

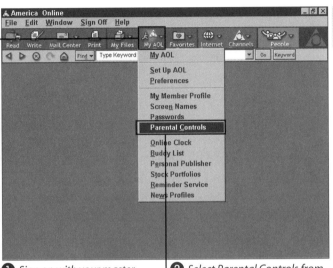

① Sign on with your master screen name and click the toolbar's My AOL icon.

② Select Parental Controls from the drop-down menu.

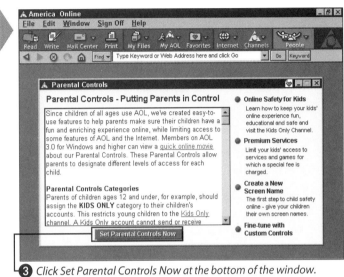

③ Click Set Parental Controls Now at the bottom of the window.

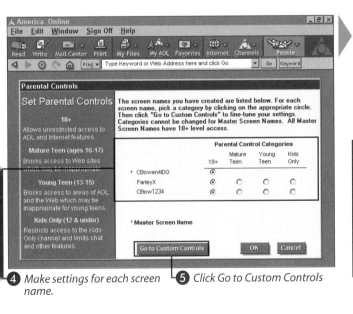

④ Make settings for each screen name.

⑤ Click Go to Custom Controls

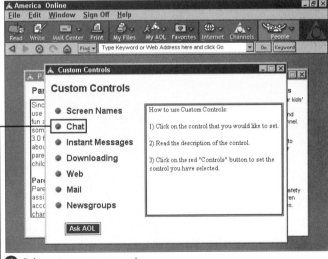

⑥ Select an area to customize.

Using Parental Controls

Continued

Customizing the Settings

Sometimes you need more control than the Parental Controls category settings provide. To take control and customize specific settings, begin with the Go to Custom Controls button on the Parental Controls window. Now click the feature you want to set, read the resulting description, then click the red Control button at the bottom of the screen and make choices about each of your screen names. The categories are as follows:

▶ **Chat.** You have four possible settings. You can block access to all conference rooms through AOL, all member-created chats (leaving featured, hosted chat rooms available), all the AOL People Connection chats (most are geared toward older audiences), and/or all hyperlinks that are sent in AOL chat rooms that access to the World Wide Web.

▶ **Instant Messages.** The option here is either to activate or deactivate these electronically "whispered" messages. If you deactivate IMs for a screen name, the child cannot receive any unsolicited messages.

▶ **Downloading.** Two options can be set here. You can block the downloading of software from any AOL software library. The user of that screen name also cannot view file descriptions. The second option enables the master account holder to block a screen name's access to FTP

(File Transfer Protocol) sites — that is, software libraries — on the Internet.

▶ **Web.** This specifies how much, if any, access to the World Wide Web the child has. For instance, Access Only Kid Approved Sites restricts access to sites deemed appropriate for children ages 6 to 12 by Microsystems Inc., a company that regularly monitors Web sites. Access Only Teen Approved Sites restricts access to Web pages Microsystems finds appropriate for ages 12 to 16.

▶ **Mail.** This links to the same e-mail preferences described at the end of Chapter 5, regulating what mail can come to the mailbox of this screen name. Options range from blocking all mail to blocking just mail from the Internet to restricting receipt to designated people.

▶ **Newsgroups** (that is, message boards on the Internet, as described in Chapter 7). Here you can block messages in a variety of ways, including the receipt of graphics and sounds.

TAKE NOTE

▶ **LIMITING ACCESS TO PREMIUM SITES**

Parental Controls also can regulate a child's access to Premium Services. To block a screen name from extra-cost features, use keyword: PARENTAL CONTROLS to reach the main window and click the Premium Services button. Click the checkbox beside the screen name to be blocked and click OK.

CROSS-REFERENCE

For more on using the World Wide Web, newsgroups, and other Internet features, see Chapter 7.

FIND IT ONLINE

If you have a question about using Parental Controls, click the Ask AOL button at the bottom of any window in the customizing section.

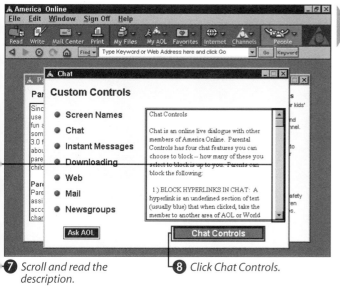

7 Scroll and read the description.

8 Click Chat Controls.

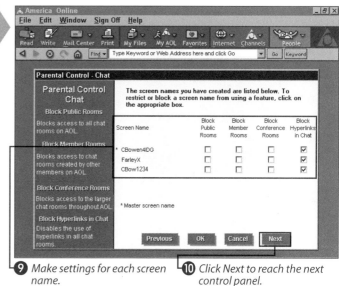

9 Make settings for each screen name.

10 Click Next to reach the next control panel.

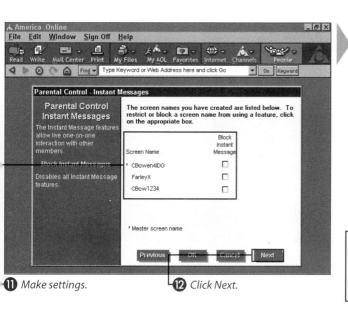

11 Make settings.

12 Click Next.

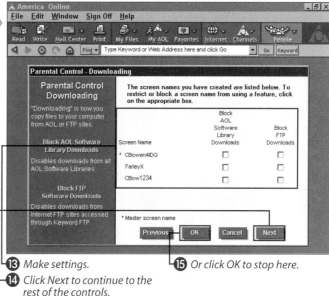

13 Make settings.

14 Click Next to continue to the rest of the controls.

15 Or click OK to stop here.

Using the Kids Online Channel

Remember the clubhouse you built as a kid? It admitted dogs, cats, spiders, praying mantises, even little sisters and little brothers, but not grown-ups! The electronic version of this sanctuary is the Kids Only channel (keyword: KIDS ONLY), devoted to games and talk, homework help and comic books, sports and show business, and surfing the Web. The site also invites kids to find pen pals, to display their artwork, stories, and poems, to join special online clubs, to subscribe to online newsletters, and more. The channel has these departments:

- ▶ Games (keyword: KO GAMES) offers a selection of online recreations for kids of all ages, from foretelling the future with a crystal ball and fortune cookies to sports trivia games and a "name that tune" competition.
- ▶ Create (keyword: KO CREATE) invites you to draw or color in the channel's arts and crafts department. It includes the Extremely Tall Tales section, with chat room and message boards where kids talk about their writing.
- ▶ Clubs (keyword: KO CLUBS) houses kid-oriented message boards and chat rooms devoted to computing, animals and pets, sports, music, games collecting, and the like.
- ▶ Shows and Stars (keyword: KO SS) spotlights the showbiz section, with links to the Cartoon Network, Nickelodeon, and more.

- ▶ Sports (keyword: KO SPORTS) makes a homerun with kid-oriented connections to information on baseball, basketball, football, and other sports, their stars, and tips for playing better and safer.
- ▶ Homework Help (keyword: KO HH) links to the Ask a Teacher service described in Chapter 12, along with connections to the online dictionary, encyclopedias, and message boards.
- ▶ Chat (keyword: KO CHAT) offers kid-specific chat rooms, including scheduled and featured chats each day of the week.
- ▶ Web (keyword: KO WEB) provides a simplified browser for kids not used to surfing the World Wide Web. It opens with a Kids Online AOL NetFind to locate features.

TAKE NOTE

▶ KIDDING AROUND

There are yet more sites just for kids:
- ▶ Kidzine (keyword: KIDZINE), from ABC television, offers an imaginative site with games, puzzles, contests, and cartoons.
- ▶ Kids Hall of Fame (keyword: KO FAME) covers kids doing cool things around AOL.
- ▶ Kids Speak Out (keyword: KO SPEAK) features surveys and sounding boards for kids.
- ▶ Kids News (keyword: KO NEWS) offers the headlines of interest to youngsters.
- ▶ Highlights for Children (keyword: HIGHLIGHTS) publishes the electronic extension of the famous kids' magazine.

CROSS-REFERENCE
For more about games, see Chapter 13.

FIND IT ONLINE
For more about protecting kids (and yourself) online, visit Member Services (keyword: HELP) and select the Online Safety & Security topic.

Safety Tips for Children

▶ Never give your password to anyone, even relatives or your best friends.

▶ Don't tell anyone online your home address, your telephone number, or any other personal information.

▶ If someone says something to you that makes you feel unsafe or threatened, call for help with keyword: KO HELP.

▶ Never say you will meet someone in person you first met online without asking a parent.

▶ Always tell a parent about any bad language you saw online.

▶ Do not accept things from strangers, including e-mail, files, Web addresses, or pictures.

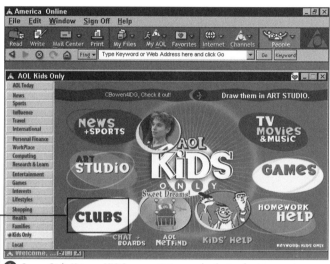

① Press Ctrl+K, type **KIDS**, press Enter, and select a feature such as Clubs on the resulting window.

② Click a category or select one from the drop-down menu.

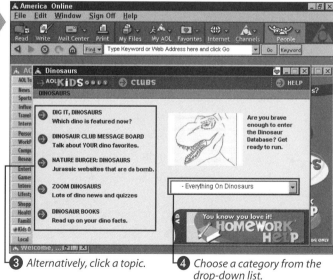

③ Alternatively, click a topic.

④ Choose a category from the drop-down list.

Finding Digital Cities

America Online's Local channel (keyword: LOCAL) has created community-specific resources in dozens of major cities across the nation and abroad. If you are a new resident in one of these cities, planning to move to or visit one, or you just want to follow the goings-on in cities where your friends and family live or your business is headquartered, use the Local channel to get an overview. Go directly to the ten most popular features using these keywords:

- ► Local News (keyword: LOCAL NEWS) invites you to click a city from a list and get business news, sports, weather, and headlines from that community.
- ► WebGuide (keyword: WEBGUIDE) offers a directory to Web-based community information. Select a city and then, in the resulting window, click the hyperlinked sections for the lowdown on everything from entertainment to finance.
- ► Local Traffic (keyword: LOCAL TRAFFIC) gives you traffic reports from Washington to L.A., including road reports, weather problems, and maps.
- ► Personals (keyword: LOCAL PERSONALS) offers a search tool for finding personal classifieds by city.
- ► Local Movies (keyword: LOCAL MOVIES) gives a local theater list, show times, and member-supplied reviews.

- ► Local Restaurants (keyword: LOCAL DINING) provides a search facility for finding local eateries by cuisine, price, and location.
- ► TV schedules (keyword: TV NAVIGATOR) gives you local television listings on the city you select.
- ► AutoGuide (keyword: LOCAL AUTOS) reports deals on cars and trucks, auto services, and the like in the selected city.
- ► Real Estate (keyword: LOCAL REAL ESTATE) covers the communities' real estate markets and offers local listings.
- ► Directory (keyword: LOCAL DIRECTORY) has white pages and yellow page listings for the selected communities. To search for a person, enter their name.

TAKE NOTE

AMONG THE CITIES

New cities are coming online all the time. View the map on the main window to see if your city is represented, or click City Index for a full list. Among the cities listed are those in these regions:
- ► **Northeast:** Albany, Boston, Buffalo, Harrisburg, Hartford, New Haven, New York
- ► **Northwest:** Salt Lake City, Seattle, Portland
- ► **Midwest:** Cincinnati, Chicago, Cleveland
- ► **Mid-Atlantic:** Baltimore, Hampton Roads
- ► **Southeast:** Atlanta, Charlotte, Ft. Lauderdale
- ► **Southwest:** Albuquerque, Austin, Dallas-Ft. Worth
- ► **West:** Los Angeles, Sacramento, San Diego

CROSS-REFERENCE

For information on using AOL's global white pages and yellow pages to find phone numbers anywhere in the country, see Chapter 7.

FIND IT ONLINE

To get an overview of the Local channel, visit its Search & Explore page (keyword: LOCAL SEARCH) and click About Digital City.

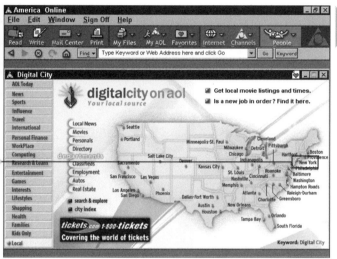

① Press Ctrl+K, type **LOCAL**, press Enter, and click a city.

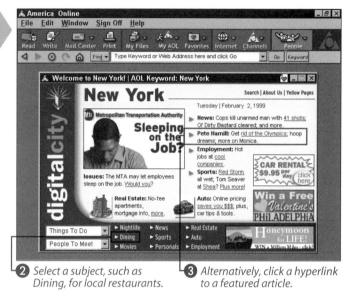

② Select a subject, such as Dining, for local restaurants.

③ Alternatively, click a hyperlink to a featured article.

④ Click here for reviews.

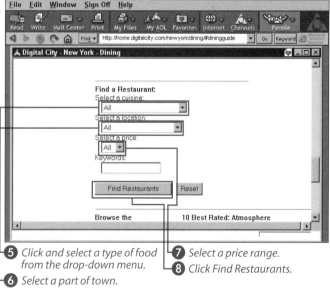

⑤ Click and select a type of food from the drop-down menu.

⑥ Select a part of town.

⑦ Select a price range.

⑧ Click Find Restaurants.

Personal Workbook

Q&A

1 How would you find experts online who could talk to you about heart disease?

_____

_____

_____

2 What is Parent Soup?

_____

_____

_____

3 Where can you get ideas for family vacations?

_____

_____

_____

4 What is the AOL resource for magazine articles about parenting?

_____

_____

_____

5 What are the four access levels offered in the Parental Controls feature?

_____

_____

_____

6 Where can you find games designed for children?

_____

_____

_____

7 What's the Kids Hall of Fame?

_____

_____

_____

8 Bonus Question: How can you find what's playing in the theaters right now in Philadelphia?

_____

_____

_____

ANSWERS: PAGE 345

EXTRA PRACTICE

1. Find resources that cover dieting and weight loss.

2. Locate online material on mental health issues like depression and anxiety.

3. Find sites intended for new moms and dads.

4. Look up currently released movies to see which seemed to be best suited for small children.

5. Pick a cartoon character like Scooby-Doo, Freakazoid, Jonny Quest, Pinky and the Brain, or Wonder Woman and use the Kids Only Channel to get background.

6. Find out what the traffic situation is in Los Angeles.

REAL-WORLD APPLICATIONS

✔ Adoptees are using the Families channel as a support group when on a quest for their birth parents. The Adoption Forum (keyword: ADOPTION) covers issues related to adoptees, adoptive parents, and birth relatives.

✔ Interested in the homeschooling of children? The Home Schooling Forum (keyword: HOMESCHOOLING) is a parents' resource for practical data on homeschooling alternatives.

✔ So you're writing your novel but stuck for a name for your latest character? Let AOL shove that writer's block with the Baby Name Finder (keyword: BABY NAME). Somewhere in those 14,000 files is bound to be the name you're looking for!

Visual Quiz

How would you reach this window? Of which channel is it a part? What would you or some other member of your family do here?

_____

_____

_____

_____

_____

Appendix A:
Personal Workbook
Answers

Chapter 1

see page 4

1 **What is the maximum number of letters and numbers allowed in an AOL password?**

A: Up to eight letters, numbers, and symbols are allowed in an AOL password.

2 **For billing, are there other options besides a major credit card for payment?**

A: Yes, besides a major credit card, you also can choose to pay by direct withdraw from your checking account. Note, though, that AOL currently charges $5.00 a month as a handling fee for this electronic funds transfer.

3 **How many screen names can be created with each America Online account?**

A: Up to five screen names can be created per account.

4 **What is the significance of the master account screen name?**

A: The master name, created when the account is opened, controls creation of all subsequent screen names for that account. It cannot be deleted without deleting the entire account.

5 **Where is the "control panel" for on your AOL software?**

A: The Preferences area of the software controls most functions of the AOL software. Reach it through the Preferences option under the toolbar's My AOL icon.

6 **It's a good, clever idea to have *password* as your password, right? Okay, if not, why not?**

A: No, no, no! Never use *password* as your password. That trick never works. It's even been used in movies and novels.

7 **How can you find a weather forecast for your area?**

A: Weather is one of the icons available on the AOL Welcome screen. To reach it, sign on and click the Your Weather icon on the resulting display.

8 **Bonus Question: How do you abort a call to the network after you've launched the sign-on procedure but before the connection is made?**

A: To abort a logon, just click the Cancel button that appears at the bottom of the display while the data call is being made.

Appendix A: Personal Workbook Answers

Chapter 2

see page 24

1 **How can you tell when a letter in your mailbox was sent to you?**

A: The date that a letter mailed to you appears in the subject line displayed in the New Mail folder of your mailbox. Also, the date (along with the time) appears in the header of the letter itself when you open it.

2 **What are at least two ways to print a letter that's on your screen?**

A: To print an e-mail currently on your screen, either (a) click the Print icon on the toolbar, (b) select File from the menu bar and, from the resulting drop-down menu, click Print, or (c) use Ctrl+P, the keyboard short (that is, hold down the Ctrl key and press the letter P).

3 **What is the default for the number of days AOL keeps your previously read letters as "old mail," and how do you change that number?**

A: AOL routinely keeps previously read letters for three days, making them accessible in your mailbox's Old Mail folder. You can change this number of days to any number between one and seven by using the Mail Preferences options.

4 **What are at least two ways to reach your online mailbox window?**

A: To reach your mailbox, you can (a) click the You Have Mail icon on the Welcome screen, (b) select the Read icon on the toolbar, (c) click the toolbar's Mail Center icon to drop down a menu of options that include Read Mail, or (d) hold down the Ctrl key and press the letter R.

5 **How do you address a letter to more than one recipient?**

A: To address e-mail to multiple recipients, in the Send To: field, separate the screen names with commas, such as *CBowen, KatCastner, DavePey, JoeDobbs*.

6 **How do you send e-mail to non-AOL members through the Internet?**

A: To send mail to someone via the Internet, in the Send To: field of the message display, enter the Internet address, such as `cebowen@ramlink.net` or `charlesbowen@compuserve.com`.

7 **How do you compose a letter to another AOL member containing different colors of type?**

A: Select the block of text you wish to make another color, click the Text Color button above the data entry field and, from a pallet of 64 colors, choose the color you want.

8 **Bonus Question: How can you check the spelling of a letter before sending it?**

A: Compose your letter as usual, position the cursor at the beginning of the text, and click the last icon below the Subject: line (the one with "ABC" and a check mark in it).

Chapter 3

see page 48

1 **What are at least two ways to enter a keyword?**

A: You enter a keyword by (a) clicking the toolbar's Keyword button, (b) clicking into the toolbar's data-entry field, or (c) pressing Ctrl+K.

2 **What does the History Trail feature do?**

A: The History Trail, accessible on the toolbar, keeps a list of all the recent sites you have visited recently, enabling you to quickly return to any of them with a click of the mouse.

Appendix A: Personal Workbook Answers

③ **Which channel would you visit if you were interested in learning how to cook dishes from other countries?**

A: International channel (keyword: INTERNATIONAL) has data on cultures and statistics on countries of the world, including global recipes.

④ **How do you save a page as a Favorite Place?**

A: To save a page on your Favorite Place site, just click the heart-shaped icon that appears in the upper-right side of the display's title bar.

⑤ **What do you do to return to one of your Favorite Places?**

A: To return to a Favorite Place, click the toolbar's Favorites icon and select Favorite Places from the subsequent drop-down menu. In the resulting menu, click the site you want to visit and press the Enter key.

⑥ **What is the fastest way to go back to the page you were viewing just before the current one?**

A: The toolbar's Previous button (the arrow that points to the left) can be clicked to go back to the screen you were viewing before you made your last selection.

⑦ **What are at least two ways to get to the AOL's Find Central to search for keywords?**

A: To reach AOL's Find Central, either (a) use keyword: FIND CENTRAL, (b) click the Find button on the toolbar, or (c) click the Find option on the Channels screen.

⑧ **Bonus Question: What is the keyword for the AOL's list of keywords?**

A: The keyword for the Keyword List is KEYWORD. You wonder where they come up with this stuff....

Chapter 4

see page 74

① **List at least two ways to reach the People Connection feature.**

A: You can reach People Connection by either (a) * entering keyword: PEOPLE, (b) clicking the People Connection icon at the bottom of the left column in the Welcome display, or (c) clicking the People icon on the toolbar and select People Connection from the drop-down menu.

② **What are the three types of AOL chats?**

A: The three types of AOL chats are featured chats, which are public and moderated by AOL volunteer hosts; member chats, rooms opened and hosted by your fellow AOL members; and private chats, member-created chats that are by invitation only.

③ **Name at least three ways to reach an AOL chat room.**

A: To reach an AOL chat room, check on the People Connection's Find a Chat option and then either browse the categories and chats, search by keyword, or examine the list of scheduled chats. Alternatively, you can click the Chat Now option on the People Connection, which will select a random chat room for you.

④ **How do you hide the text from a particular member in a chat room?**

A: Scroll the list of screen names of chatters in the chat room, and double-click the name of the one you want to silence. In the resulting display, check the Ignore Member box.

⑤ **How do you find a member's profile information in a chat room?**

A: Examine the list of chatters in the room, and double-click the name of the one you want profiled. In the resulting display, click the Get Profile button.

Appendix A: Personal Workbook Answers

6 What steps do you follow to create your own public chat room?

A: To start a chat room of your own, click the Start Your Own Chat button on the Find a Chat screen or click the toolbar's People icon and select Start You Own Chat from the drop-down menu.

7 How do you send an Instant Message?

A: To send an Instant Message, either click the toolbar's People icon and select Instant Message from the drop-down menu or use the Ctrl+I keyword shortcut (hold down the Ctrl key and press the letter I).

8 Bonus Question: What is the purpose of the Buddy List feature and how do you set it up?

A: The Buddy List enables you to watch for acquaintances to arrive on the system. To set it up, either enter keyword: BUDDY or click toolbar's My AOL icon and select Buddy List from the drop-down menu.

Chapter 5

see page 96

1 How can you use incoming e-mail to add names to your Address Book?

A: To add names to your Address Book, open the letter as usual and click the Add Address icon that appears among those on the right side of the display.

2 What do you do to add pictures to entries in your Address Book?

A: To add pictures to your Address Book, select an existing entry and click the Edit icon (or use the New Person icon to create a new entry). Click the Picture tab at the top of the display and then click the Select Picture option.

3 How do you use your Address Book to automatically address a letter you are sending?

A: To use the Address Book to address an e-mail, click the toolbar's Write icon and in the Write Mail display, click the Address Book icon at the right. Then choose a name from the Name/Address display and click the Send To button.

4 What procedure do you follow to create a group of related addresses in your Address Book?

A: To create a group of related addresses in your Address Book, click the New Group icon. In the Group Name: field, type in the name you want to assign this group, such as Friends, Relatives, Chess Club. In the Addresses field, enter the screen names and/or Internet addresses of the people you want included in this mailing list, separating each name with a comma.

5 How do you reach your Personal Filing Cabinet from the toolbar?

A: To reach your Personal Filing Cabinet, click the toolbar's My Files icon and select Personal Filing Cabinet from the down-down menu.

6 What are the three main parts of your Personal Filing Cabinet?

A: There are three main folders in the filing cabinet. Mail, message boards, and Download Manager.

7 How can you automatically save all incoming mail in your Personal Filing Cabinet?

A: To automatically save all incoming mail in your filing cabinet, select Preferences from the My AOL icon, click the Mail option, and put a checkmark beside Retain all mail I send in my Personal Filing Cabinet.

Appendix A: Personal Workbook Answers

8 Bonus Question: How can you use the Log Manager to make a transcript of a chat session?

A: To activate the Log Manager, click the toolbar's My Files icon and select Log Manager. Then in the Chat Log section of the dialog box, click the Open Log button.

Chapter 6

see page 118

1 What are the three levels of a message board?

A: The three distinct parts of forum message boards are topics or the board's broad categories, subjects or the groups of messages that are posted within each topic and posts, that is, the individual messages that make up each subject group.

2 How do you reply to a message on a message board?

A: To respond publicly to a message on a forum board, just click the Reply button and write your text.

3 How do you customize AOL message boards?

A: To customize AOL forums, press the Preferences button at the bottom of any message or list of topics or subjects and fill in the resulting on-screen form.

4 What special AOL feature is called into play by the Download Later option button?

A: Using the Download Later option in forum libraries allows you then to use the AOL software's Download Manager to manage more than one download in a session and oversee the entire process from a single window.

5 How can you interrupt a download in progress?

A: If a download is taking longer than you anticipated, click the Finish Later button.

6 What option do you select if you want to contribute a file to a forum's library?

A: To contribute a file to a forum's library, click the Upload button in the library and fill in the on-screen form.

7 How do you set up the Automatic AOL feature?

A: To set up the Automatic AOL feature, click the toolbar's My AOL icon and select Preferences from the drop-down menu. Then click Auto AOL, and on the resulting screen, select the tasks for automating.

8 Bonus Question: How do you read offline the messages retrieved for you by Automatic AOL?

A: To read the messages retrieved by Automatic AOL, go to your Personal Filing Cabinet and double-click the notes you want to see.

Chapter 7

see page 144

1 Name two ways to reach the Internet Connection.

A: To reach the Internet Connection, use keyword: INTERNET, or click the toolbar's Internet icon and select Internet Connection from the drop-down menu.

2 How is AOL's main Web page (www.aol.com) similar to windows on AOL itself?

A: Aol.com is divided into categories (Travel, Entertainment, Sports, Personal Finance, etc.) that mirror AOL's own channels, seen in Chapter 3.

3 What does HTML mean?

A: HTML stands for *Hypertext Markup Language*, the technical name of the universally used language of the Web to create those hyperlinked pages.

④ What is an URL?

A: An URL (*Uniform Resource Locator*) is the unique address assigned to a page on the World Wide Web, the equivalent of a keyword assigned to an AOL page.

⑤ Name at least three ways to reach AOL's NetFind search engine.

A: To reach NetFind, use keyword: NETFIND, click the Go to AOL NetFind button on the Internet Connection display, and then click the toolbar's Find icon and select Find it on the Web. Then click the toolbar's Internet icon and choose AOL NetFind from the menu (or enter the Web address `www.aol.com/netfind` in the keyword box).

⑥ How can you use AOL to find electronic mail addresses on the Internet?

A: To find Internet electronic mail addresses, visit the AOL NetFind feature (keyword: NETFIND) and click the E-mail Finder link.

⑦ Where do you go on AOL to find links to Internet newsgroups?

A: To find Internet newsgroups, visit the Newsgroup Center (keyword: NEWSGROUPS) and click the Add Newsgroups icon.

⑧ Bonus Question: What add-on software program can you obtain to publish your own pages on the Web?

A: To create your own Web pages, download AOL's Personal Publisher software (keyword: PERSONAL PUBLISHER).

Chapter 8

see page 170

❶ Where is your first stop online for celebrity gossip?

A: The Influence channel (keyword: INFLUENCE) is the system's center for gossip and personality profiles, columns on the media, money, and more.

❷ How do you go about searching for a story from the day's news?

A: To search the News channel's database, enter keyword: NEWSSEARCH. On the resulting display, click the Search icon and then enter a word or words that describe the story for which you are looking and press the Enter key.

❸ Where can you find weather forecasts for the nation?

A: To get the latest weather outlook, visit the system's online weather center (keyword: WEATHER) where you can search by city, state, telephone area code, or zip code.

❹ How can you reach the electronic extension of major magazines online?

A: To reach major magazines, visit the Newsstand with keyword: MAGAZINE and view the scrollable list of current titles.

❺ Where's the best place to find the hour's top sports news?

A: For news from the athletics world, visit the Sports channel (keyword: SPORTS) and then click the Top Stories icon. Or for the direct route, use keyword: SPORTSNEWS.

❻ Where do other sports fans gather and talk about their favorite fields, courts, rinks, rings, and tracks?

A: To chat it up with other online sports fans, visit The Grandstand (keyword: GRANDSTAND).

Appendix A: Personal Workbook Answers

7 How do you find latest trends and raves in dining, drinking, lodging, and design?

A: Sounds like a job for The Good Life (keyword: THE GOOD LIFE) which reports on the best in travel, style, design, entertaining, and dining.

8 Bonus Question: How can you assign America Online to be your personal editor, automatically gathering news for you?

A: To automate AOL's news resources, having stories of interest automatically delivered to your e-mail mailbox, use the News Profile feature (keyword: NEWS PROFILE).

Chapter 9

see page 192

1 How can you use the Travel channel to find the bargains on travel and vacation packages?

A: To find the latest vacation deals, check the Travel Bargains department (keyword: TRAVEL BARGAINS), which specializes in information on low-cost airfares, inexpensive car rental, and budget lodging.

2 What if you're focusing specifically on airfares? How can you find the latest, lowest costs?

A: To find the lowest airfares of the day, check out Farefinder (keyword: AIRFARE FINDER).

3 Suppose you're going camping in a new area. What's an AOL site that can help you plan?

A: Outdoor Adventure Online (keyword: OUTDOOR) can help with planning outdoor adventures, with tips on lodging and products for campers and hikers.

4 So, you're getting married! If you still have time for a little online research, which AOL service is especially designed for honeymooners?

A: The Knot (keyword: KNOT) can help for planning wedding trips, with advice from experts and other couples about the most romantic destinations.

5 If you're planning a ski getaway, where can you go online for tips and travel hints?

A: Check out the Ski Zone (keyword: SKI ZONE) for vacation deals and news of ski conditions.

6 Where can you go to speak and read French online?

A: French is among some 15 different languages spoken in real time at The Bistro (keyword: BISTRO).

7 If you are a globe-trotter (or a global wanna-be), where can you get a quick hit of international travel news?

A: For world travellers, the first stops ought to be International Travel (keyword: INTERNATIONAL TRAVEL) and International News (keyword: INTL NEWS).

8 Bonus Question: How can you use America Online to find a electronic pen pal in Spain?

A: To find pen pals around the world, use keyword: SPECIAL DELIVERY.

Chapter 10

see page 210

1 For what purpose is Hoover's Business Reports used?

A: Hoover's Business Reports (keyword: HOOVERS), profiles of some 2,500 companies, with basic statistics on 10,000 more.

APPENDIX A: PERSONAL WORKBOOK ANSWERS

② Who or what is The Motley Fool?

A: The Motley Fool (keyword: FOOL) is AOL's own lively, irreverent publication about investing, a gold mine for beginners.

③ How many stock portfolios can be created for each screen name?

A: Up to 20 portfolios can be created for each screen name (and each can hold up to 100 stocks).

④ Where can you find a graph that charts one of your stock's recent performance?

A: To get graphs, select a stock in your portfolio, click the Details icon, and then select the time span, from the past month to the past three years.

⑤ A friend tells you about a hot stock. How can you quickly check its historical performance?

A: The Historical StockQuotes and Charts (keyword: HISTORICAL QUOTES) database covers stock and mutual fund performance. You can create your own charts or download data in a format of your choice.

⑥ You want to get into investing, but you need some pointers for starting. Where can you turn for the basics?

A: Investing Basics (keyword: INVESTING BASICS) is an online reference shelf for beginners for how to avoid foolish mistakes.

⑦ Where can you can look for an online forum that serves veterinarians?

A: Visit the WorkPlace channel (keyword: WORKPLACE), click the Professional Forums icon and scroll the resulting list of professionals online.

⑧ Bonus Question: Where can you find online help with writing a resume for a job?

A: Finding a Job (keyword: FINDAJOB), helps with resume writing, interviewing, job listings and more.

Chapter 11

see page 228

① Where can you find the schedule of online computing classes?

A: To find online computing classes, use keyword: ONLINECLASSROOM and, at the resulting site, click the Class Schedule button to see what is coming up today and over the next few weeks.

② How do you save a transcript of a class you missed to disk?

A: To find and save a class transcript, use keyword: ONLINECLASSROOM and click Class Transcripts button. When you've found the transcript you want and have it on your screen, click File on the menu bar and Save from the drop-down menu.

③ What do you do to find an online list of computer-related message boards?

A: To locate computer-related message boards, check into the Chat & Messages screen (keyword: COMPUTING CHAT).

④ How can you locate tips to assist you in helping your mom learn to use her Macintosh computer?

A: To find hints of all kinds, use keyword: COMPUTING TIPS and then select Mac Tips, PC Tips, or AOL Tips from the next screen.

⑤ What is Youth Tech?

A: Youth Tech (keyword: YT) is a feature for computer-using teenagers, designed by and for teens, with games, contests, and surveys.

Appendix A: Personal Workbook Answers

6 You're in the market for a new computer and you want to check reviews of some of the newest systems. Where do you go computer shopping online?

A: The Buyer's Guide (keyword: BUYERSGUIDE) has reviews from leading computer magazines on new computers and all kinds of peripherals, including the latest modems and printers.

7 What is the Daily Download?

A: The Daily Download (keyword: DAILY DOWNLOAD) spotlights a different program each day, either freeware, shareware, or brand-new commercial software.

8 Bonus Question: How would you go about learning whether the manufacturer of your modem has an area on AOL?

A: To determine if a computer or peripheral maker is represented online, use the Company Lookup. Use keyword: COMPANIES to reach the database.

Chapter 12

see page 244

1 How can your elementary school-age child find online help with homework?

A: To reach the Homework Helper, use keyword: KO HH. In the resulting screen, click the Ask a Teacher button.

2 For older kids, how can you find live tutorial sessions with volunteer teachers online?

A: To get live help with school work, use keyword: ASK A TEACHER and click either the Middle School, High School button, or the College and Beyond button. On the subsequent screen, click the Seek Live Teacher Help option.

3 How can you enroll in an electronic course in, say, English or writing?

A: To take electronic courses online, use keyword: COURSES to reach the introductory display, click the Online Campus icon and review the catalog of classes currently offered.

4 Where can you find Compton's Encyclopedia online?

A: To find Grolier's and other electronic encyclopedias online, use keyword: ENCYCLOPEDIAS and click the name of the reference work you want to use.

5 How can you use the system to research how the federal government works?

A: The Law & Government (keyword: LAW), with legal self-help, federal law details, and cultural data from the CIA World Factbook.

6 Suppose you have young children in the house and you want to introduce them to dictionaries. What's a useful online resource to help?

A: The Kids Dictionary (keyword: KIDS DICTIONARY) is intended for students in the fourth to sixth grades. It contains more than 33,000 entries, written in language the kids will understand.

7 Need help preparing for college? Where should you head on AOL?

A: The Education Resources Center (keyword: EDUCATION) has a college preparation section, with practice tests, study ideas, and calendars for juniors and seniors to help schedule college-planning tasks.

8 Bonus Question: Uncle Fred is a history buff. Next time he visits, you plop him down in front of America Online and ... what?

A: Take Uncle Fred to the history section (keyword: HISTORY), which offers museums, folk stories, links to other cultures, highlights of the U.S., and world events.

Appendix A: Personal Workbook Answers

Chapter 13

see page 260

❶ How can you link to an online version of the popular MovieFone interactive telephone movie guide?

A: MovieLink (keyword: MOVIELINK) is the online version of the MovieFone film guide and ticketing service.

❷ Where would you go to find out everything you ever wanted to know about talk show host David Letterman?

A: *The Late Show* Online site (keyword: LATE SHOW) is your link for the Top Ten archives, Late Night history interactive games, and everything about David Letterman and his friends.

❸ What is Critics Inc.?

A: Critics Inc. (keyword: CRITICS) offers reviews of current and classic films (as well as books, TV shows, compact disc, concerts, and video games), as well as message boards for your own commentary.

❹ It's midnight. The library's closed and you have a pressing need for the plot summary of *Moby Dick*. Who you gonna call?

A: Barron's Booknotes (keyword: BARRONS) are online companions to literary classics.

❺ Uncle Fred is one of the last great Deadheads. Where can you take him online?

A: Grateful Dead Forum (keyword: DEAD) keeps Jerry's music and spirit alive.

❻ What is your daily gossip connection and how do you reach it by keyword?

A: The Daily Fix (keyword: DAILY FIX) is your connection for regular celebrity news.

❼ What is WorldPlay Games?

A: WorldPlay Games (keyword: WORLDPLAY) offers a single game parlor for premium online competitions, chats, tournaments, and related events.

❽ Bonus Question: What are the game shows online?

A: The Game Shows Online area (keyword: GAME SHOWS) feature games that you can play for no extra cost.

Chapter 14

see page 278

❶ Where would you go to chat with those who love to tinker with old Triumphs and other classic sports cars?

A: The Wheels section (keyword: WHEELS) of the Auto Center is the community of car enthusiasts, including links to message boards arranged in alphabetical order by car types.

❷ You want new ideas for next spring's flower garden. Where do you go online?

A: The Gardening Center (keyword: GARDENING) specializes in tips for lawn care, flower gardening, vegetable gardening, landscaping, and related topics.

❸ What is Online Psych?

A: Online Psych (keyword: ONLINE PSYCH) covers assorted psychological topics from disorders, medications, and therapy to support groups, books, reviews, and discussions.

❹ What is Love @ AOL?

A: Love @ AOL (keyword: LOVE AT AOL) is a database of online pictures and profiles of people wanting to meet each other. Profiles list age, martial status, region, occupations, likes and dislikes, and habits.

Appendix A: Personal Workbook Answers

⑤ Where would you find people interested in discussing Judaic traditions?

A: The Jewish Community (keyword: JEWISH) discusses art, food, and traditions.

⑥ What is Moms Online?

A: Moms Online (keyword: MOMS ONLINE) is a community of mothers where new moms and moms-to-be are always welcome.

⑦ If you want to research retirement living and related issues, where should you start?

A: SeniorNet (keyword: SENIORNET) and AARP (keyword: AARP) both cover assorted issues related to retirement.

⑧ Bonus Question: Where would you find resources for bird watching?

A: For birdwatching (and scores of other hobbies and pastimes), check into Hobby Central (keyword: HOBBY).

Chapter 15

see page 298

❶ What is the "shopping cart?"

A: As you order merchandise from online retailers, you read descriptions and click to place them in your electronic "shopping cart," until you are ready to finish. Now you can select a Checkout option to pay for the material in your shopping cart.

❷ Where can you turn for bargains?

A: The best sources of regular online bargains is the system's Deal of the Day feature (keyword: DEAL OF THE DAY).

❸ What is "Weekly Goods?"

A: Weekly Goods (keyword: WEEKLY GOODS) is a free e-mail newsletter that covers the electronic stores and hot deals.

❹ If you are looking for a job, where can you find help wanted ads online?

A: Job openings are posted in the AOL Classifieds (keyword: CLASSIFIEDS) in the Employment category.

❺ How can you sign up for a newsletter about AOL Classifieds?

A: To sign up for the Highlights newsletter, which has classified tips, events, and specials, use keyword: CLASSIFIEDS HIGHLIGHTS.

❻ Can you change a classified ad after it has been posted?

A: No, you can't change an ad after it is posted, but AOL can delete one before its expiration date. Send e-mail to the screen name *CustSvcPR* and include the Document ID found at the bottom of your online ad.

❼ Where would you find ads for used CD-ROMs and old programs?

A: To find deals on old computers, peripherals, and software, see the Classifieds' Computing category.

❽ Bonus Question: Oops — you've forgotten Uncle Fred's birthday. How can you have a gift delivered to him in a hurry?

A: For super-fast gift delivery, visit the system's Quick Gifts (keyword: QUICK GIFTS) department, which promises a selection of never-fail, always-appropriate gifts.

Chapter 16

see page 314

❶ How would you find experts online who could talk to you about heart disease?

A: To find health authorities online, visit the Health channel (keyword: HEALTH) and click Support Groups & Experts option.

APPENDIX A: PERSONAL WORKBOOK ANSWERS

2 **What is Parent Soup?**

A: Parent Soup (keyword: PARENT SOUP) offers all kinds of parenting information, with more than 500 topic groups accessible.

3 **Where can you get ideas for family vacations?**

A: For family-oriented vacation ideas, see the Family Travel Network (keyword: FAMILY TRAVEL NETWORK).

4 **What is the AOL resource for magazine articles about parenting?**

A: Family Newsstand (keyword: FAMILY NEWSSTAND) has articles from popular parent and kid magazines and deals on subscriptions.

5 **What are the four access levels offered in the Parental Controls feature?**

A: Parental Control offers these four levels of access: Kids Only, Young Teens, Mature Teens, and 18+.

6 **Where can you find games designed for children?**

A: The Kids Only channel is Games department (keyword: KO GAMES) offers a selection of online recreations.

7 **What's the Kids Hall of Fame?**

A: Kids Hall of Fame (keyword: KO FAME) is all about kids doing cool things around the system. You can nominate someone great online. Click the How It Works button for details and then click the Artists, Leaders, and Writers buttons to see some of the recent selections.

8 **Bonus Question: How can you find what's playing in the theaters right now in Philadelphia?**

A: Check out the Digital Cities channel (keyword: DIGITAL CITY) to find movie listings around the country.

Appendix B:
Shortcuts and Keywords

Keyboard Shortcuts

These were the most frequently used keyword shortcuts:

ACTION	KEY(S)
Add top window to Favorites	Ctrl++
Cancel an action	Escape
Cascade Windows	Shift+F5
Copy a block of text	Ctrl+C
Cut a block of text	Ctrl+X
Find text in current Window	Ctrl+F
Get member profile	Ctrl+G
Log off the system	Alt+F4
Move to previous button	Shift+Tab
Move to next button	Tab
Open a new text file	Ctrl+N
Open an existing file	Ctrl+O
Open Keyword window	Ctrl+K
Locate a member online	Ctrl+L
Open Compose Mail window	Ctrl+M
Paste	Ctrl+V
Print a file	Ctrl+P
Read new mail	Ctrl+R
Save a file	Ctrl+S
Scroll up a page	Page Up
Scroll down a page	Page Down
Select (block) all text	Ctrl+A
Send an instant message	Ctrl+I
Spell check text	Ctrl+=
Tile Windows	Shift+F4
Undo editing changes	Ctrl+Z

You don't need to press the keys in a keyboard shortcut at precisely the same time. Instead, press Shift or Control, and then hold it down while you press the other key in the combination.

Also, you can create your own keyboard shortcuts. Click the Favorites icon on the toolbar. Point to My Shortcuts and click Edit Shortcuts from the menu that appears. In the Shortcut Title field, enter a name for the shortcut. In the Keyword/Internet Address field, enter the keyword or Web address you want to associate with the shortcut and click Save Changes.

Useful, Important, and Curious Keywords

Here are just some of the thousands of keywords in use on America Online to help you continue exploring on your own.

Help and Account Management

Access numbers, AOL local (ACCESS) A database that enables you to search for telephone numbers with which you can log on to America Online (just the ticket if you are planning to move or to log on from the road with the laptop.) The database can search all numbers or just the 9600 baud numbers. It also provides news of new access numbers and has features for reporting problems, tips for the modeming traveler, and so on.

Appendix B: Shortcuts and Keywords

America Online Product Center (AOL PRODUCTS) Provides online ordering for various products, from tee-shirts with the company emblem to books and manuals and related merchandise.

Billing (BILLING) Enables you to modify the name and address you have set up for your online account and your billing information, to see the current month's billing summary, to request detailed billing information, and/or to cancel your account.

Buddy List (BUDDY) Lets you create and maintain your Buddy List for finding friends and acquaintances online.

Canceling AOL Membership (CANCEL) Also can be handled online in the Members' Online Support (HELP), by selecting Accounts & Billing, and then selecting the Cancel Your Account option.

Clock (CLOCK) Lets you keep track of your time spent online. The feature also can be selected from the AOL software's Go To menu.

Credit Requests (CREDIT) Enables you to file a request form for credit on your bill because of a bad download, slow system, billing error, or other problem.

Directory of Services (DIROFSERVICES, DIRECTORY, or SERVICES) A searchable database of information on all services on America Online, providing for each entry the service name and description, keywords and search words (when applicable), and the menu path to access the service.

Help Desk (HELP) Takes you to the AOL customer service department for answers, tips, and advice on scores of different problems in connecting and using AOL.

International Access (INTERNATIONAL ACCESS) Provides details of how to access AOL outside the United States.

Keyword List (KEYWORD LIST) Provides a downloadable list of keywords in use throughout the system.

Member Directory (MEMBER or DIRECTORY) Enables you to find out about your fellow members and to search for people that share your interests. You can search the directory by the member's full profile, which contains personal information (screen name, real name, and location), occupation, hobbies and interests, and more.

NetFind (AOL NETFIND) Lets you search for sites of interest on the Internet's World Wide Web.

Parental Controls (PARENTAL CONTROLS) Give parents the ability to control access of subaccount names to various features such as chat, instant messages, and conference rooms.

Password, How to change, (PASSWORD) Go to Members' Online Support (HELP or SUPPORT) and select the Account & Billing options.

Price Plans (PRICING) Lists America Online's assorted pricing plans.

Profile, Creating and editing online, (PROFILE) Provides other members with a quick biography of you that can be viewed in the Member Directory (DIRECTORY).

Reminder (REMINDER) A service that enables you to have AOL automatically remind you of upcoming important dates.

Screen names, Creating (SCREEN NAMES) Takes you to the area where you can create additional screen name sand associated passwords. You may have up to five screen names.

Suggestions to AOL (SUGGESTIONS) Can be made by electronic mail. A Suggestion Box option is provided in every department of America Online for your use if you have ideas or feedback about any aspect of that department.

Terms of Service (TOS) The rules for use of America Online can be viewed online. Any changes in the terms are indicated by a change in the date on the menu of the section.

Upgrading the Software (UPGRADE) Gives you access to downloadable files for the latest upgrades for the AOL software.

Web Page, Creating (MY HOME PAGE) Provides help on creating your own home page on the World Wide Web using Personal Publisher.

What's Hot (HOT) Gives you a heads-up on what's stirring on the system.

What's New (NEW) Provides reports on the newest features to be brought online.

New and Old Favorites

Academic Assistance Center (HOMEWORK, TUTORING, or RESEARCH) A service for students needing aid with concepts they are learning, help with their homework, or for those who want to hone skills that have become rusty. It is a resource for finding teachers dedicated to helping students achieve their academic goals. A popular area is the Homework Help section, designed to provide general assistance in several different areas. You can use a "Teacher Pager" option to try to call someone to help you.

Afterwards Coffeehouse and Cafe (AFTERWARDS or ARTS) Late of New York City, now America Online's place to be for real-time discussion of the arts, music, and literature.

American Association of Retired Persons (AARP) Associated with the famed nonprofit, nonpartisan organization dedicated to helping older Americans, a group with more than 33 million members.

AOL Live (AOL LIVE) One of America Online's largest areas, AOL Live is a gathering place for live events and hobnobbing with visiting celebrities. Calendars of upcoming events and transcripts of previous appearances are also available.

Auditoriums (CENTERSTAGE, AUDITORIUM, or SHOWS) Online chat rooms designed for especially large groups of real-time talkers and listeners (up to 300 at a time). Structured events — such as speeches, panel discussions, roundtables, and so on — are scheduled in auditoriums.

AutoVantage Online (AUTO) Provides a variety of car-related information, such as new car summaries that detail a model's features, the pros and cons of buying the model, specifications, available options, sticker and dealer prices, and road test highlights. Also available are used car pricing and summaries.

Aviation and pilots (FLY) The Aviation Forum is the gathering place for amateur and professional fliers. The feature includes message boards devoted to club news and information, general aviation, commercial aviation, military aviation, and aircraft maintenance.

Baby Boomers Club (BABY BOOMERS) A meeting place for those born in the baby boom years, generally identified as the years between 1946 and 1969. Visitors discuss common interests, historical events, and styles that have affected and shaped their lives.

Barnes & Noble (BARNES) The online site for the famed national bookseller, with options for looking up titles and placing orders.

Bed & Breakfast U.S.A. (BED & BREAKFAST) From the same people who provide the printed version of "Bed & Breakfast U.S.A.," which has its roots in a 16-page publication in 1975.

Appendix B: Shortcuts and Keywords

Bicycle Network (BIKENET or BICYCLE) Provides communications for all kinds of bicyclists, including recreational cyclists, mountain bikers, tourists, advocates, commuters, racers, and others.

Book Central (BOOK CENTRAL) A place to talk about your love of the printed word.

Book Reviews and Bestseller Lists (BOOKS) Provided in the Books and Writing section.

Business data (BUSINESS) Provided in a variety of services, from company analysis and commentary.

Buzzsaw (BUZZSAW) An AOL original, a daily satire and humor site in which writer Bill Shein takes on the wilds of Washington.

Capital Connection (CAPITAL) Provides various political information services as well as discussion areas. Among the offerings are congressional names, addresses, phone numbers, and fax numbers. Also active are features related to current elections and campaigns nationally and locally.

Car and Driver Online (DRIVING or CAR AND DRIVER) The electronic extension of the famed automotive magazine, providing comprehensive vehicle tests to every car, pickup truck, van, and sport-utility vehicle that is marketed for consumer use in America.

Cartoon Network (CARTOON NETWORK) Online link to television's first all-animation network and home to some famous toon stars, including the Flintstones, Tom & Jerry, Bugs Bunny, Popeye, The Jetsons, Jonny Quest, Yogi Bear, Droopy Dog, and more.

Child Safety Online (CHILD SAFETY) Provides information on safe Web surfing for children and families.

Classified ads (CLASSIFIEDS) Can be read and posted online. The bulletin board invites everyone interested in buying, selling and/or trading.

College Board (COLLEGE, CB, or COLLEGE BOARD) A 90-year-old national, nonprofit association of more than 2,500 institutions and schools, systems, and associations and agencies serving both higher and secondary education.

Commerce Business Daily (CBD) Produced by the U.S. Department of Commerce and the Government Printing Office, Commerce Business Daily is a daily synopsis of available government contracts for products and services for federal agencies that exceed $25,000 in value. The publication lists notices of proposed government procurement actions, contract awards, sales of government property, and other procurement information.

Company Profiles-Hoover's Handbook (COMPANY PROFILE) Created and is managed by The Reference Press, Inc., of Austin, Texas, this site includes profiles of more than 900 of the larger, more influential and faster-growing public and private companies in the U.S. and the world.

Computer Viruses (VIRUS) Details of the latest computer virus warnings and what you can do about them.

Computing (COMPUTING) A major America Online department, linking to scores of computer specific forums, including features relating to applications, development, DOS, Apple Macintosh, Windows, games, graphics and animation, hardware, multimedia, music and sound, OS/2, personal digital assistants, telecommunications and networking, users groups, and more.

Consumer Reports (CONSUMER REPORTS) Provided by the publishers of the famed monthly magazine of the same name, provides product reviews, ratings, and advice, as well as summaries of CR's tests and evaluations.

Contests (CONTESTS) Gives the details of opportunities for winning money and prizes online.

Cooking Club (COOKING CLUB) Devoted to food and cooking, it discusses new ideas in fine dining from across the nation. The service's Cookbook offers recipes for everything from appetizers to desserts, even providing tips for wines to accompany each course.

Critics Choice (CRITICS) Cincinnati-based syndicate specializing in reviewing entertainment. Its features are syndicated to newspapers, as well as audiotext systems.

Cycle World (CYCLE WORLD) Produced by the print magazine of the same name to serve online motorcycle enthusiasts. Each month, two weeks after the printed *CW* goes on the newsstand, a substantial portion of the issue — including tests, evaluations, news stories, columns, most features, and race coverage — go online.

Decision Point Stock Market Timing and Charts Forum (DECISION) Offers technical analysis and advice on using market timing models and stock analysis techniques that Swenlin has developed over 12 years of research.

Dictionaries (DICTIONARY) Links you to several different keyword-searchable dictionaries.

Digital Cities (DIGITAL CITY) Lists the assorted U.S. and international cities that have created online connections.

Disney Adventures (DISNEY) A magazine for kids, ages 7–14, that covers science, sports, entertainment, comics and puzzles, and more.

Education, teachers, and students (EDUCATION) Topics in a wide range of America Online features, from services to help children with homework and to study for tests to college preparation and parent and teacher networks.

Entertainment (ENTERTAINMENT) Features are available throughout the system.

Ethics and Religion Forum (RELIGIONS) Explores all the religious and ethical issues. Among the forum's message boards are those devoted to ethics and debate Christianity, Islam, Judaism, New Age and philosophy, paganism, other religions.

File Search (FILE SEARCH) Find downloadable free and shareware programs of all kinds anywhere on AOL.

Flight Simulation Resource Center (FLIGHT) A source of hints, files and information on various flight simulation programs. The medium of exchange here is tips traded with other die-hard flight fans and aircraft files uploaded to the software library for others to try.

Flying Magazine (FLYING MAGAZINE or FLYING MAG) Written by pilots for pilots, or for those who want to become pilots; has been around in print for more than half a century.

Gadget Guru Electronics Forum (ELECTRONICS) Devoted to discussed of all types of consumer electronics equipment, from bread machines to tools and gardening equipment.

Gallery (GALLERY) A forum operated for the sharing of computer images in GIF (Graphic Image Format) form.

Game forums Discuss all aspects of computer and non-computer gaming. Central to all these activities are the Online Gaming Forums (OGF or GAMING), which provides bulletin boards, news facilities, libraries, chat areas, and more for all forms of gaming.

Genealogy Club (ROOTS or GENEALOGY) A place to exchange knowledge and experiences while providing any needed guidance in the research of ancestry.

Grandstand (GRANDSTAND) A place for sports fans to, as the founders say, "talk, write, and at times, yell about the latest happenings on and off the field, court, rink, ring, and track."

Appendix B: Shortcuts and Keywords

Ham Radio Club (HAM RADIO) The gathering place for amateur radio operators who have earned the license as well as those who like to listen to stories from the airwaves.

Hollywood Online (HOLLYWOOD) Features sneak previews of new motion pictures. You can download pictures of your favorite stars from the "Pictures and Sounds" library, read about the cast and production notes in "Movie Notes," and talk about the movies on the "Movie Talk" message board.

Hoover's Business Resources (HOOVER) Provides business information created and maintained by The Reference Press, Inc., of Austin, Texas, including detailed company profiles on the largest U.S. and international companies, company profiles of emerging companies and capsule profiles on more than 7,300 public and private U.S. companies.

Horoscopes (HOROSCOPES) Gives you your daily zodiac shot. Just click your sign from the resulting menu and reading the good word.

Internet Connections (INTERNET) Takes you to the intersection of AOL's assorted Internet services, including the World Wide Web, newsgroups, mailing lists, and more.

Investors' Network (INVESTORS) A forum dedicated to helping you make educated investment decisions. Its "Investing Today Message Board" invites members to discuss the market and a wide range of investment strategies with other private investors online.

Israel Interactive (ISRAEL INTERACTIVE) Based in Israel, Israel Interactive offers interviews with Jewish newsmakers, features on life in that country, and message boards.

Kaplan Online (KAPLAN or TEST PREP) Provides information and suggestions about various college entrance exams.

Kids Only Online (KOOL or KIDS) An America Online department for youngsters from age 6 to 13 or so, featuring message board for topics of all kinds and a library with programs and articles of interest to the young.

Knowledge Base search system (KNOWLEDGE BASE) Microsoft lets you to search all the documents on Microsoft products from tens of thousands of articles. To find an article, select the "Search the Knowledge Base" option, and, when prompted, enter a word, phrase, or a combination of words about your desired topic.

Komputer Clinic (KOMANDO) Kim Komando's forum for finding computer solutions for various problems.

LaPub (LAPUB) An electronic corner bar that loves a good time. Check the main menu for current information on all the nightly action.

Military City Online (MCO) An information resource for service people and their families on military posts. The feature, a division of the Army Times Publishing Co., provides news and information concerning military jobs and careers, benefits, and fellow service members and their families.

Morningstar Mutual Funds (MORNINGSTAR, MUTUAL FUNDS, or FUNDS) An independent, privately owned company that focuses exclusively on helping investors make investment decisions.

Motley Fool, The (FOOL) Hosted by David Gardner (MotleyFool) and Tom Gardner (TomGardner), this area is the electronic reincarnation of an alternative financial publication of the same name that used to appear in print, described by its editors as a "literary-cum-investment rag."

National Education Association (NEA or PUBLIC) Provides a public forum in which users can find a variety of information and interactive opportunities.

National Geographic (NGS or NATIONAL GEO-GRAPHIC) The electronic version of the famed travel/geography publication. It also provides material from *National Geographic Traveler* and *World* magazines, as well as a variety of news stories and press releases.

National Public Radio Outreach (NPR, RADIO, or TOTN) Presents education outreach materials to educators and the general public alike. Materials include teachers' guides, newsletters, and brochures that support particular NPR programs.

National Space Society (NSS or SPACE) A nonprofit, publicly supported organization promoting space research, exploration, development, and habitat.

netmarket (NM) Formerly known as Shoppers Advantage, netmarket is sometimes called the Comp-U-Store gateway. It is the first of the online shopping services, now boasting more than 3 million members.

Newsgroups, Internet, (NEWSGROUPS) Can be visited through the Internet Center (INTERNET). You can select newsgroups from a number of categories to place in your own private Newsgroup list, and you can add/subtract from this list as your interests expand or focus.

The New York Times News and features are the basis for the new @times interactive service (TIMES). @times has as its centerpiece *The New York Times'* entertainment guide, which offers a wide range of reviews, articles, and information on cultural, arts, and leisure activities in the New York area.

Nightly Business Report (NBR) An online extension of the TV broadcast of the same name, providing business, financial, and economic news every week night.

People Connection (CHAT, PEOPLE CONNECTION, or TALK) Includes many rooms for people to chat in real time about various topics. You also can start a new room for any topic of your choosing, and have other members join you for discussion.

Personal Finance (FINANCE) The intersection for all the system's business and financial features.

Popular Photography magazine (PHOTOS) Provides tips on taking pictures and buying photo equipment and to interact with other photographers.

Post Office (POST OFFICE) Links to the system's electronic mail features, including options to Read New Mail, Compose Mail, Check Mail You've Already Read, Check Mail You've Sent, Edit Address Book, Fax/Paper Mail, and Internet Mail.

Real Estate Online (REAL ESTATE) Helps people buy, sell, rent, finance, and invest in real estate. The resource also invites discussion and debate of issues and sharing of information on real estate topics.

Reference Desk (REFERENCE) A central department for the system's major reference features, including AOL's assorted directories, its electronic magazines and newspapers, databases, the Compton's Encyclopedia, and so on.

Role-Playing Game Forum (RPG) Supporting imaginative activities ranging from sword fights and arcane mystic tomes to piloting your starship to distant galaxies.

Romance channel (DATING or ROMANCE) An online dating service designed to link people of common interests who are interested in cultivating additional interests.

Scholastic Network/Scholastic Forum (SCHOLASTIC) A network for teachers and students, providing access to well-known authors, journalists, scientists, educators, and other experts.

Scientific American (SCIAM) Provides access to editorial content, interactive discussions, and additional information for the science, technology, and business community.

Scuba Club (SCUBA) Intended for divers of all experience levels as well as diver wanna-bes. Topics include general diving, dive instruction, dive medicine, as well as various specialty dives like wreck, cavern, and cave diving, and still and video photography.

SeniorNet (SENIOR) A nonprofit organization for older adults interested in using computers. SeniorNet members are 55 or older and have an interest in learning about and with computers.

Smithsonian Online (SMITHSONIAN) Backed by the famed national museum complex in Washington, D.C., provides online displays based on many of the museums' exhibits.

Sports (SPORTS) An America Online department linking various features about viewing and participating in and assorted sports and recreational activities.

Star Trek Club (STAR TREK) The online gathering place for fans of Trek culture, from the '60s TV series, to the current *Next Generation* series, to the movies and books.

State Department Travel Advisories (TRAVEL ADVISORIES) Details about conditions of risk abroad that might affect travelers are offered by the U.S. State Department's consular information program.

Stereo Review (STEREO REVIEW) The electronic extension of the famed monthly about home audio and a/v equipment and recordings, attracting readers from beginners to experienced audiophiles.

StockLink (STOCK) Helps you keep track of prices on stocks listed on the various exchanges such as NYSE and NASDAQ (with a 15- to 20-minute delay), maintain an updated portfolio, and more.

Student Access Online (STUDENT) Sponsored by test-prep company Princeton Review, provides resources for college students to expand graduate school and career options and get in touch with other students nationwide.

Study Skills Service (STUDY) Contains lessons on how to study, brochures for parents on how to help their children learn, study skills sessions and message board interaction, a study skills survey, course content outlines, information from the U.S. Department of Education, and more.

Tax Forum (TAX FORUM) Fields various tax-related questions on the message board. Also, you can download helpful tax files from the software library, as well as spreadsheet templates and other items for simplifying record-keeping.

Television topics Discusses in the TV Viewers Online (TELEVISION) feature, which enables you to find your favorite network, channel, or show and discuss with like-minded folks.

Travel (TRAVEL) An America Online department linking online travel and vacation features.

Washington Week in Review Online (WWIR) An electronic extension of public television's longest running public affairs program.

Weather (WEATHER) Provides weather news, U.S. and foreign city forecasts, tropical storm and hurricane advisories, and a weather discussion board. Color weather maps are also available for downloading.

White House Forum (WHITE HOUSE) Provides press statements from the White House's Office of Media Affairs and discussions with other visitors about presidential issues.

Worth Online (WORTH) An electronic version of *Worth* financial magazine. You can read or download current and past stories from the magazine's monthly issues.

Writers Club (WRITERS) Covers and discusses all aspects of the writing business, with messages boards on fiction, nonfiction, poetry, and more.

Appendix C:
Helpful Tips

Getting Help Online and Offline

Help is all around you if you know where to look. Here are some of the best resources, offline and online for finding help with additional AOL questions.

Finding Answers Offline

Answers to your questions may already be in your computer, and you don't even have to sign on to the system to find them. Use the Offline Help system by clicking the Help option on the menu bar and select Offline Help from the drop-down menu. Select one of the three tabs at the top of the display, either:

▶ Contents, to see help by broad categories, such as signing on, using e-mail and other AOL features, managing and securing your account and screen names and troubleshooting. To the left of each topic is a book icon. Double-click the icon to see what topics are listed under that category. Then to see a topic, double-click its title. Also, you can close a book by double-clicking its icon.

▶ Index, which provides a data-entry field and an alphabetical list of topics. Type a topic, such as *chat rooms*, in the data field and press Enter to see the system scroll the list to that topic. Click the index entry you want to see and click the Display button at the bottom of the screen. (Alternatively, if you don't want to enter a topic in the data field, you can use a scroll bar at the right of the screen to scroll the alphabetized list of index entries.)

▶ Find, to search for topics by keywords or phrases.

In a data-entry field at the top of the screen, enter the words you want to find, such as **personal filing cabinet.** Topics containing the words are listed at the bottom of the screen; highlight one of interest and click the Display button at the bottom of the screen to view it. (Also, an Options button lets you specify whether to look for all or just some of the words in your search strategy and other variables.)

Going Online for More Help

You have other opportunities online. The Member Services department has the latest information on connecting and navigating the system, finding people, places, and things, using e-mail and the World Wide Web, and related topics. Reach the page by signing on to the system and either using keyword: HELP or clicking the Help option on the menu bar and selecting Member Services Online Help from the drop-down menu. The online help department provides assorted ways to locate the answers you are seeking.

The easiest way to find help, if you have time to browse, is to scan lists of topics to zero in on the specific area you need. Alternatively, you can search the database by clicking the Find It Now button at the bottom of the Member Services (keyword: HELP) display. In the data-entry field at the top of the resulting screen, type words or phrases related to your question.

APPENDIX C: HELPFUL TIPS

Getting Help from Fellow Members

Members Helping Members (keyword: MHM) is a service built around an active message board that lets you communicate with others who may have faced and solved the problem that is worrying you. The board is filled with tips for navigating AOL. Also online is a collection of answers to top AOL questions, from keywords to billing. Also, when you have become an old pro at AOL-dom, you can even volunteer to join the ranks of online helpers; the application is online at this site.

Speaking Online and Writing E-Mail for Help

Volunteers on the Members Helping Members team also operates a live help room to field general questions about AOL and its features, open seven days a week from 9 a.m. to 2:45 a.m. Eastern Time. Visit Member Services (HELP) and click any of the topics listed at the left of the screen. In the resulting display, click the Ask the Staff button, which lists among the resulting articles one entitled "More Ways to Get Help." This text file includes important hyperlinks. If you want to

- write an e-mail question to the staff, click the hyperlink on the highlighted word "e-mail" in the paragraph numbered "2." You are taken to a screen where you indicate the type of question (general, technical, Internet, billing, and so on). You then are prompted to type the question and click a Send button to post it. Expect an answer in your online mailbox from a technical representative.
- speak to someone live, click the hyperlink on the highlighted word "online" in the paragraph numbered "3."

Getting Help by Telephone

If all else fails, you can always phone. The America Online technical staff maintains several telephone numbers for assistance:

- For general questions and problems, call 1-888-265-8006.

- For screen name or password problems, call 1-888-265-8004.
- For billing questions, call 1-888-265-8003.
- For questions about access numbers, call 1-888-265-8005.

You also can reach America Online by fax at 1-801-622-7969. Be sure to include your full name, address, phone number, and AOL master screen name.

Checking on Accounting and Billing

Questions relating to rates, charges, and billing have their own section of the system. The Accounts & Billing department (keyword: BILLING) also has facilities for displaying details on your own bill, summary of charges, billing address, and related data. Use the scroll box at the right of the display to find folders and specific articles on billing issues and questions, such as the details of the latest rate structure, various billing methods, and how to change from one to another and how to correct billing errors. Of particular note here are

- links for changing your billing information (keyword: CHANGE) in case you have moved, married, or changed your phone number.
- the Frequently Asked Questions folder which has details on various discount offers and, at the bottom of the list, a link to talk live to a billing representative online in a live help room.

Need the details of your AOL bill? Visit the Accounts and Billing screen (Figure 17-9) with keyword: BILLING and select an option at the left of the screen to

- change your billing name or address.
- change your billing method or payment plan.
- display your current bill summary, including your next billing date, the current account balance, the free minutes remaining on the account, the credited minutes remaining, other credits, and last month's bill.

▶ display your detailed bill for the current or previous month, with specifics on the dates and times online for each screen name and the charges.

▶ display you billing terms.

Canceling an Account Must be Done by Phone or Mail

If you decide to cancel your America Online account for any reason, deliver notice to the AOL customer service department by one of the following methods:

▶ Phone, with a call to 1-800-827-6364
▶ U.S. Mail, with a letter to America Online, P.O. Box 1559, Ogden, UT 84401
▶ Fax, to 1-801-622-7969

With either letter or fax, be sure to include your full name, address, phone number, and AOL master screen name. This information verifies you as the contact person for the account. You will receive notation of the termination by U.S. mail within in about ten days and you will be billed for service through the end of the current billing month.

If you cancel an account within the last 72 hours of your billing month, you may be erroneously charged an additional monthly fee for the next billing month. If you have a problem with this or any other bill matters, contact the customer service department.

Staying Abreast of What's New

Several key resources keep you up to date on what is new and what is coming to the channels of AOL:

▶ What's New on AOL (keyword: NEW) features the Hot 5 list with the newest, most valuable sites to date. Many are seasonal — tax help in the spring, gift suggestions at Christmas, and so on — others are just in the New and Cool Department. Also click the Latest icon for a quick list of areas that are new to the system.

▶ The Pulse of AOL (keyword: PULSE OF AOL) is a status report on AOL systems information. Want to know when the system will be down for routine maintenance? It's in the briefing. So are details on new access and upgraded access numbers around the country, listed state by state, reports on the latest high-speed connections, and more.

▶ Chairman/CEO Steve Case, who founded America Online in 1985, offers a monthly "Community Update" online, along with previous months' reports. Use the keyword: STEVE CASE to reach the main page. Each month's report includes news of new features and improvements and tips on what is on the horizon. Also click the This Month's Highlights icon to see AOL areas that have been recommended by the AOL staff. And click Steve's Favorite Places for a personal list of hits on AOL and the Web.

Finally, on the third floor of America Online's headquarters in Virginia, they call her "Prairie Dog," but her real name is Meg Booker and to most of AOL's grateful online community, she is known simply as Meg the AOL Insider. The Seattle, Washington, native is the official AOL tipster and advisor. Her tips and suggestions, news, and AOL observations are regular daily reading for thousands. Check out the daily tips and AOL news and backlog of earlier reports with keyword: AOL INSIDER.

Making Suggestions and Getting Perks

Got ideas for new features? Use the keyword SUGGESTION to reach the suggestion box. Double-click the general area in which you wish to contribute a thought. The system opens a screen and invites you to use the space for your suggestion or question. Click the Send button at the bottom of the display to post it. You should receive a reply by e-mail within 24 hours, though it may take a bit longer if the system is experiencing unusually high demand.

And membership has its privileges. America Online has a much-touted Members Perks program that offers all kinds of discounts and savings on travel, magazines, long-distance phone plans, and all kinds of products. To get a rundown on the latest offers, sign on to the system and then either click the toolbar's Perks icon or use the keyword PERKS to reach the main display. The major offers are promoted with graphics and icons in the center panels. You also can click a More AOL Member Perks link in the lower left of the screen to get the latest complete list. Among the major perks are

- AOL Rewards (keyword: AOL REWARDS), which enable you to reduce your monthly fee and/or buy merchandise with points earned by taking part in online surveys or buying specific products or services.
- The AOL Visa Card (keyword: AOL VISA), for special rates for AOL members and Reward Points to be used for discounted service and products.
- Sign on a Friend (keyword: FRIEND), which enables you to earn a $20 credit when a friend you recommend becomes a member.
- Deal of the Day (keyword: DEAL OF THE DAY), with discounts of assorted projects.
- Business Perks (keyword: BUSINESS PERKS), for benefits to businesses and professionals online.

Search Strategies for AOL Databases

America Online operates powerful databases of features, screen names, Web sites, and more. They all work from AOL Find Central (keyword: FIND CENTRAL), all using the same search engine strategies. Here are the basics on how the Find feature works, plus some more advanced techniques.

Simple Searches

Type a topic word of interest in the data-entry field, and click the Find button. The results will display in the lower window.

- For more precise results, use more than one topic word at a time and select Specific to find areas containing all of your words.
- For an expanded search, use more than one word and use Broad. It will find areas containing any of your words.

Note: Unlike search engines you may have used on the Internet's World Wide Web, results at the top of the list are not necessarily more on-target than the others.

It is smart to phrase it by typing in multiple words or a phrase rather than a single word to increase your chances of finding useful results. Be as descriptive as possible. For instance, enter *Macintosh business software* rather than simply *Macintosh software*. Also, target your searches by using *NOT* to limit your results to articles containing only the words you want. For example, if you want topics about history but aren't interested in American history, search for *history not American*.

Also:

- Capitalization doesn't matter. AOL databases see *lincoln*, *Lincoln*, *LINCOLN*, and *lInCOlN* as the same.
- Don't bother with minor words, including articles (*a*, *an*, and *the*), prepositions (*on*, *between*, *under*, and so on), and conjunctions (*but*). (*AND* and *OR* are recognized as connectors, described later.)
- Suffixes are ignored. The words *compute*, *computes*, *computed*, and *computing* are treated the same. However, this does not apply to compound words. So while a search for *race* will find *racing*, it will not find *racetrack*, *racecar*, or *raceway*.
- AOL databases do not ignore prefixes, so a search for *employment* would not uncover *unemployment*.

Advanced Searches with *AND*, *OR*, and *NOT*

For more elaborate searches, use logical connectors — *AND*, *OR*, and *NOT* — to link multiple search words and phrases.

- *AND* is automatic, so you do not need to use *AND* to link search words together. Use multiple search terms simply by typing in each word separated by a space.

▶ As an alternative for *OR* searching, you can type in more than one word, and select Broad. The search returns areas that match each of the words in your search.

▶ Use the word *NOT* to narrow your search. For example, typing *LINCOLN NOT GETTYSBURG* finds all articles that mention Lincoln except those that also mention Gettysburg. You also can use *NOT* more than once in a search, such as *music NOT classical NOT jazz*.

Also, use the special character *?* (question mark) to represent any single character. So, *star?* will find *stare*, *stark*, *stars*, and *start*. You can also use *?* if you aren't sure of a word's spelling, as in *advis?r* or *station?ry*. Meanwhile, the asterisk (*) represents any number of characters in a search (including none). For example, searching for *ear** will find areas about ears, earaches, earphones, earrings, earth, and earthquakes.

In addition, the tilde (~) allows you to perform a "fuzzy logic" search. This works like a spelling checker on a word processor. Every character after the ~ in your topic word is considered to possibly be wrong or misplaced, thereby ensuring that valid search results are not ignored because of a minor error. For example, typing *~content* will search for topic words *constant*, *contact*, and *contents*. (Of course, fuzzy searches are less precise.) Note that all characters before the ~ are treated as normal letters. For example, whereas *con~tent* would still find *constant*, *contact*, and *contents*, *cont~ent* would not look for *constant*.

When No Results Are Found

If your search generated no results, recheck your spelling. The search engine doesn't spell-check. Also:

▶ Are you looking for an AOL subscriber? Try the Member Directory, located in Find People.

▶ It is possible that you have chosen a topic that is too specific. Try broadening your search. For example, if you are looking for information on *sponge cake* but that phrase turns up nothing, you might try *cake* or *dessert* as a topic word.

▶ If you are using multiple words, select the Broad button.

When You Get Too Many Results

If your search produces too many results to be useful:

▶ Browse quickly through the results; perhaps the ideal destination is among those listed and easily identified.

▶ Be more specific. Also, make sure that you have the Specific button selected.

▶ Add words to narrow your search.

▶ Use the word *NOT* to eliminate certain results. For example, *music NOT rock* will find areas related to, for example, classical music and jazz, but not rock music.

▶ If you still can't narrow down what you are looking for, look quickly through some of the areas you have found. You might come up with ideas on how to refine your search.

Index

A

Index

Continued

Index

Index

G

INDEX

Graphics Arts and CAD Forum, 238
Graphics Arts Forum, 238
Graphics preferences, 20–21
Grateful Dead Forum, 268
guest sign-on, Personal Filing Cabinet, 102

HTML, 147
Hutchinson Encyclopedia, 252
hyperlinks, 50, 146
    adding to e-mail, 64
hypertext links, 52

header, e-mail, 26
Health channel
    about, 315
    illnesses and treatment, 316–317
    support groups, 318–319
HEALTH keyword, 65–66, 315
HEALTH NEWS keyword, 316
HEALTH SUPPORT keyword, 318
heart disease, 66
Help Desk
Help Desk, Computing for Beginners, 120–121
HELP DESK keyword, 120–121
HIGHLIGHTS keyword, 328
HIGHMARK keyword, 218
HISPANIC ONLINE keyword, 290
HISTORY keyword, 256
History Trail, 54–55, 66, 174
    clearing out old, 54
HO keyword, 274
HOBBY keyword, 294–295
HOLLYWOOD keyword, 270
Hollywood news, 62
home and garden, Interest channel, 284–285
HOME keyword, 284
home repairs, 64
homework help, 246–247
Honeymoon Travel, 198
HOROSCOPE keyword, 288
hosts, for chats, 76
hotels, 58–59, 204–205
HOUSENET keyword, 284

Ignore option, chat, 82–83
illnesses, 66
illnesses and treatment, Health channel, 316–317
ILLNESSES keyword, 316
income-planning strategies, 58
Index, Offline Help system, 357
Influence channel, 58, 184–185
INFLUENCE keyword, 58, 184–185
INFLUENCE SEARCH keyword, 184
INNER CIRCLE keyword, 184
INSIDE FLYER keyword, 196
installing AOL software, 5–7
Instant Messages, 87
    Buddy List, 90–91
    Internet, 86
    logging, 109
    Web site, 86
Intelligent Concept Extraction, 150
Interest channel
    about, 279
    auto center, 280–281
    food, 282–283
    home and garden, 284–285
INTERESTS keyword, 64, 279
International channel, 58–59, 206–207
    about, 193
    atlas, 206
INTERNATIONAL keyword, 58–59
INTERNATIONAL TRAV keyword, 206

Continued

Index

Continued

Index

Index

INDEX

INDEX

Workplace channel, 222–223
WORKPLACE keyword, 60–61, 222
WORLDPLAY keyword, 272–273
Write icon, e-mail, 32–33
Write Mail window, 32
writing and sending letters, e-mail, 34–35
WWW preferences, 20–21

X FILES keyword, 264

Yahoo!, 150
Yellow Pages, AOL, 154–155
You Have Mail icon, 27
Youth Tech, 234
YT keyword, 234

Z

ZIP files, 128, 132